EXPLORING JUDAISM

SOUTH FLORIDA STUDIES IN THE HISTORY OF JUDAISM

Edited by
Jacob Neusner
Alan J. Avery-Peck, Bruce D. Chilton, Darrell J. Fasching,
William Scott Green, James F. Strange

Number 210

EXPLORING JUDAISM
The Collected Essays of David Kraemer

edited by
David Kraemer

EXPLORING JUDAISM
The Collected Essays of David Kraemer

edited by

David Kraemer

Scholars Press
Atlanta, Georgia

EXPLORING JUDAISM
The Collected Essays of David Kraemer
edited by
David Kraemer

Copyright ©1999 by the University of South Florida

All rights reserved. No part of this work may be reproduced or transmitted in any form or by any means, electronic or mechanical, including photocopying and recording, or by means of any information storage or retrieval system, except as may be expressly permitted by the 1976 Copyright Act or in writing from the University of South Florida.

Publication of this book was made possible by a grant from the Tisch Family Foundation, New York City. The University of South Florida acknowledges with thanks this important support for its scholarly projects.

Library of Congress Cataloging-in-Publication Data

Kraemer, David Charles.
    Exploring Judaism : the collected essays of David Kraemer / edited by David Kraemer.
        p. cm. — (South Florida studies in the history of Judaism ; no. 210)
    Includes bibliographical references.
    ISBN 0-7885-0623-4 (cloth : alk. paper)
        1. Talmud—Criticism, interpretation, etc. 2. Judaism. I. Title.
    II. South Florida studies in the history of Judaism ; 210.

BM500.2.K75 1999
296—dc21   99-055951

04 03 02 01 00 99   5 4 3 2 1

Printed in the United States of America
on acid-free paper

Table of Contents

Preface and Acknowledgments vii

Part One
THE QUESTION OF METHOD

1. On the Reliability of Attributions in the Babylonian Talmud 3

2. Rabbinic Sources for Historical Study 21

Part Two
STUDIES IN THE HISTORY OF JUDAISM

3. Images of Childhood and Adolescence in Talmudic Literature 35

4. Child and Family Life in Judaism 51

5. On the Relationship of the Books of Ezra and Nehemiah 63

6. Local Conditions for a Developing Rabbinic Tradition 83

7. Scriptural Interpretation in the Mishnah 95

8. The Formation of Rabbinic Canon: Authority and Boundaries 103

9. Judaic Doctrines of Evil and Suffering 125

10. Prozbul and Rabbinic Power 137

Part Three
LITERARY STUDIES

11. The Beginnings of the Preservation of Argumentation in Amoraic
    Babylonia 149

12. Scripture Commentary in the Babylonian Talmud: Primary or
    Secondary Phenomenon? 161

13. Rhetoric of Failed Refutation in the Bavli 177

14. New Meaning in Ancient Talmudic Texts: A Time Poem..................193

15. Composition and Meaning in the Bavli...207

Part Four
APPLIED SCHOLARSHIP

Introduction..231

16. A Developmental Perspective on the Laws of Niddah........................233

17. The Scientific Study of Talmud...245

18. Critical Readings and Religious Insight: New Readings in the Bavli..257

19. Jewish Ethics and Abortion..267

20. Dramatizing the Torah..277

21. When God is "Wrong"..283

22. Disputes that Unite...289

23. The Spirit of the Rabbinic Sabbath..295

24. Jewish Death Practices: A Commentary on the Relationship of Humans and the Natural World... 305

Bibliography... 317

PREFACE AND ACKNOWLEDGMENTS

It has been both exciting and sobering to collect my earlier articles and essays for republication in this volume. It has been exciting because I have had the opportunity to review my writings and examine the development of my approaches and opinions. It has been sobering for precisely the same reasons.

This extended reconsideration of my scholarly project has caused me to be aware of how profoundly my ideas have changed. I began my studies as a student of Professor David Weiss Halivni, now of Columbia University. Under his influence, I concentrated early on a higher criticism (=source criticism) of the literature of the rabbis, particularly the Bavli. The question I was taught to ask was primarily "how did this text get to be the way it is?" and the key to answering this question was to divide the purported sources of the text one from the other and consider them chronologically. This was a history of the traditions behind the received text, and once certain questions were answered, there was nothing much left to do.

Of course, such a "blind alley" is intolerable for a young scholar (at least it was for this young scholar). A scholarly career cannot (or should not) be limited to refining details under the umbrella of an otherwise finished theory. So I went out "to discover the world" and, under the influence of a number of significant scholars and approaches, my interests turned in other directions. From source criticism I turned to literary and rhetorical criticisms, and from a focus on text and tradition I turned to a focus on religious belief and practice. Particularly influential in this turn was Professor Jacob Neusner, whose critique of the "naive" historiography of many rabbinics scholars I could not dismiss. But equally as influential were scholars such as Martin Jaffee, who taught me the importance of scholarship in oral cultures, and others who worked in the sociology of religion and anthropology. In my most recent work, I have been most influenced by those who work in ritual and material culture; in this connection, I am particularly grateful for the lessons I have learned from Vanessa Ochs.

I want to thank Professor Jacob Neusner for inviting me to publish this volume in his Studies in the History of Judaism series. I have learned over the years that most journal publications have a relatively limited "shelf-life." Books, on the other hand, call out from the library shelf, inviting even the casual reader to "dip in" from time to time. My hope is that the republication of many of my earlier pieces in this volume will allow a new generation of students to

viii   Exploring Judaism: The Collected Essays of David Kraemer

consider my contribution to the study of rabbinic Judaism.

I must add a word to explain my choices for what to include in this volume. First, I have not included any reviews. Second, I have not included articles that were already effectively reproduced in earlier books (that is, articles that were rewritten as chapters in one of my books). Only if any article contains material that is, before this, unique to the journal publication is it reproduced here. Finally, I have included (in part IV, "Applied Scholarship") only those "popular" articles that illustrate the application of my scholarly method to matters of more general concern. This is not, in other words, a collection of all of my articles and essays to this point. For those who are interested in my full ouvre, I append a comprehensive personal bibliography at the end of this volume.

The sources of the essays included in this volume are as follows:

Chapter One: *Hebrew Union College Annual*, v. 60 (1989): 175–190.

Chapter Two: *Judaism in Late Antiquity*, v. 3, *Issues and Debates*, ed. by J. Neusner and Alan J. Avery-Peck (Leiden: E.J. Brill, 1998), pp. 201–212.

Chapter Three: *The Jewish Family: Metaphor and Memory*, ed. by David Kraemer (New York: Oxford U. Press, 1989), pp. 65–80.

Chapter Four: *Religious Dimensions of Child and Family Life*, ed. by Harold Coward and Philip Cook (Victoria: University of Victoria, 1996), pp. 113–121.

Chapter Five: *Journal for the Study of the Old Testament*, v. 59 (1993): 303–321.

Chapters Six and Seven: *Hebrew Bible/Old Testament: The History of its Interpretation*, v. 1, ed. by Magne Sæbø (Gottingen: Vandenhoeck and Ruprecht, 1996), pp. 270–284.

Chapter Eight: *Journal of Biblical Literature*, v. 110, n. 4 (Winter, 1991): 613–630.

Chapter Nine: *The Millennial Encyclopaedia of Judaism, The Religion*, ed. by W. S. Green, et. al., forthcoming.

Chapter Ten: *S'vara: A Journal of Philosophy, Law, and Judaism*, v. 2, n. 2 (1991): 66–70.

Chapter Eleven: *New Perspectives on Ancient Judaism*, v. 4, *The Literature of Early Rabbinic Judaism: Issues in Talmudic Redaction and Interpretation* (Studies in Judaism, Lanham: University Press of America, 1989), pp. 37–46.

Chapter Twelve: *AJS Review*, v. 14, n. 1 (Spring, 1989): 1–15.

Chapter Thirteen: *Shofar*, v. 10, n. 2 (Winter, 1992): 73–85.

Chapter Fourteen: *Proceedings of the Rabbinical Assembly* (1987): 215–225.

Chapter Fifteen: *Prooftexts*, v. 8, n. 3 (September, 1988): 271–291.

Chapter Sixteen: *Conservative Judaism*, v. 38, n. 3 (Spring, 1986): 26–33.

Chapter Seventeen: *Judaism*, v. 36, n. 4 (Fall, 1987): 471–478.

Chapter Eighteen: *Conservative Judaism*, v. 42, n. 3 (Spring, 1990): 48–53.

Chapter Nineteen: *Tikkun*, v. 8, n. 1 (January–February, 1993): 55–8.

Chapter Twenty: *Sh'ma: A Journal of Jewish Responsibility*, 24/463 (December 10, 1993): 1–3.

Chapter Twenty-One: *Sh'ma: A Journal of Jewish Responsibility*, 26/499 (October 13, 1995): 1–3.

Chapter Twenty-Two: *Sh'ma: A Journal of Jewish Responsibility*, 28/543 (December 12, 1997): 1–3.

Chapter Twenty-Three: *Conservative Judaism*, v. 49, n. 4 (Summer, 1997): 42–9.

Chapter Twenty-Four: Originally presented as a paper at the Center for the Study of World Religions, Harvard University, February, 1998; to appear in *Judaism and the Natural World*, ed. by Moshe Sokol, "Religions of the World and Ecology" (Cambridge, Mass.: Harvard University Center for the Study of World Religions, forthcoming).

I am grateful to all of the above publishers who have granted their permission to reprint these essays.

Part I

The Question of Method

INTRODUCTION TO CHAPTER ONE

This essay is my first major piece speaking to directly to a question of methodology. In it, I respond to the critiques of Jacob Neusner and W.S. Green concerning the "gullible" methods of others as they work with rabbinic sources. My conclusions suggest a kind of compromise: the cautions of Neusner and Green are well taken, but their conclusion is too extreme. That, in any case, was my opinion a decade ago.

At the time I wrote this essay, I had long been the student of David Weiss Halivni and was much influenced by his work. Halivni had, at that time, staked out an interesting position for himself. His work was based on the recognition that the oral traditions of the rabbis underwent significant transformations in the course of their transmission. But he asserted that he could, through careful comparison of rabbinic sources and informed speculation, often recover the "original" forms of rabbinic teachings. Thus, while his work was not as "gullible" as that of many others, it did offer a key to writing histories of rabbinic teachings—and histories based upon those teachings (Halivni was not interested in writing "history" as such).

As a consequence of this influence, I, along with many others, was disturbed by the conclusions suggested in the work of Neusner and Green. It seemed so iconoclastic (which indeed it was!)—even nihilistic. Still, in view of the indubitable correctness of many of their insights, I had to take this methodological critique seriously. At the same time, I believed that, in the evidence I had compiled for my Ph.D. dissertation (which at the time of this essay also came to form the foundation of my work in *The Mind of the Talmud*), I had discovered a key to answering some of their objections. There is a sort of evidence, I argued, that avoids the pitfalls of the history writing which Neusner and Green dismiss.

My argument for this possibility is presented below. Interestingly, many who want to write rabbinic histories have called upon this essay to support their claims: Isaiah Gafni refers to it often in his presentations, and Michael Chernick included this piece in his *Essential Papers on the Talmud* (NYU Press, 1994). Nevertheless, I am no longer sure that I stand by the conclusions of this essay. In the next piece in this section, written nearly a decade later, I call upon other scholarship to question even the present conservative claims. I invite the reader to consider these pieces together and judge for him- or herself which position seems more reasonable.

Chapter One

On the Reliability of Attributions in the Babylonian Talmud

Historical scholarship of classical Babylonian Jewry has credulously assumed the accuracy of attributions in its primary source of evidence—the Babylonian Talmud. Jacob Neusner has properly criticized such methodological complacency, and consequently has insisted that we have access only to the Judaism attested in the final document. But Neusner himself has suggested a variety of tests by which attributed traditions could be verified, and despite his assumption that, given the nature of the evidence, such tests have nothing to yield, two of the tests will, in fact, serve to verify traditions recorded in the Bavli. First, because the Yerushalmi and the Bavli may be spoken of as being "external" to (that is, independent of) one another, commonly attested traditions may be assumed to have emerged from the circle of disciples of the sage or sages with whom they are associated. Second, because traditions of different generations of sages in the Bavli are distinguished by characteristic and "superficial" literary features, these traditions may be assumed to have taken their present form within a relatively brief period after the generation to which they are attributed. Thus, histories, though not biographies, based upon this material may indeed be written.

The composition of histories of the Jews in third-to-fifth century C.E. Babylonia depends upon the reliability of attributions in the Babylonian Talmud. This document, virtually the only significant source of information on the Jews of that period and place, claims to record traditions that were authored by rabbinic sages who flourished in those centuries. If these claims can be accepted, then we have some record of the views expressed in those Jewish communities, generation by generation. If, on the other hand, the Bavli's claims for the authorship of individual traditions cannot be accepted, we will be forced to admit that those centuries are essentially invisible to us, and that the only picture we may truly have is that recorded in the document at its completion, that is, in the fifth-to-sixth century.

Despite the obviously crucial nature of this determination, those whose work depends upon the reliability of such attributions have merely assumed that they are generally accurate, without articulating the defensibility of that assumption. The only ones to have diverged meaningfully from this methodological complacency are Jacob Neusner and his students, who rightly criticize this approach as being overly naive and uncritical.[1] The question they ask is this: why, just because a document asks us to believe that a certain authority made a certain statement at a certain time, should we grant that it is so? The Bible claims to record the words of Abraham. Would we admit that such reports are historically accurate? The Zohar wants us to believe that it contains the words of the second-century sage, R. Shimon b. Yoḥai and his circle. Would we on that basis represent its ideologies as really second-century phenomena?[2]

Having articulated this critique, Neusner and those who follow him have been forced to accept the consequences: detailed histories of the centuries in question are now illegitimate. The admission of this condition is explicit. In the introduction to the third printing of his *A History of the Jews in Babylonia* (reprint Chico, California, 1984), Neusner makes clear that the methodological assumptions on the basis of which he composed that history must now be recognized as fatally flawed. He writes, both simply and to the point: "By the criteria laid out in the preceding sections, the book has some merits, but not many.... The twin-pillars of fundamentalism stand firm and tall here (p. xxx)." In several other books which trace the development of certain central rabbinic concepts, we similarly see the consequences of Neusner's methodological skepticism.[3] In those works, he claims that we may only know of the existence of a concept at the final stage of the development of a document in which it is attested. No matter that the same idea might be attributed to a sage of the third century (or even earlier); if it appears for the first time in the Bavli, then we can only verify its currency in the sixth century, not before (the issue is "verification," not assumption).

Let me illustrate the historiographic difference this methodological assumption will make. Speaking of the relation between the written and oral Torah, the Yerushalmi (Hagigah 1:7, 76d) records the following traditions:

> R. Zeira in the name of R. Eleazar: "Though I write for him the great things [translate here: 'most'] of my Torah ... (Hos. 8:12)." And is most of the Torah written? [Surely not!] Rather, more abundant are those things that are derived from the written [Torah] than those derived from the oral... R. Yoḥanan and R. Yudan b. R. Shimon—One said: If you have kept that which is oral and have kept that which is

written, I shall make a covenant with you, but if not, I will not make a covenant with you ...

Neusner notes that the myth of the dual-Torah (written and oral) is nowhere fully articulated prior to the Yerushalmi, as this text testifies.[4] According to his approach, therefore, we should conclude that the myth was only fully conceptualized in rabbinic circles by ca. C.E. 400, that is, the closing of the Yerushalmi. If he were to lend credence to the attestations, on the other hand, then the same myth would be evidenced by ca. 250.

What is at stake here is more than a mere difference of ca. 150 years. If the myth of the dual-Torah may only be pinned down to the end of the fourth century, then it is the experience of Judaism under early Christian Rome within which we must seek its roots. Moreover, as an apologia for rabbinic tradition, we will have to see it as a relatively late development. If, on the other hand, the myth is to be associated with R. Yoḥanan, R. Eleazar, and their circle, then we will have linked this same apologia with sages who stood in close relation to the Mishnah and its author. In that case, the response will be understood as being more or less from the same period, and the historical context will be that of the pagan Roman Empire. But how, short of uncritical credulity, can we go beyond the final redaction of a given rabbinic text? In what way could we judge that attributions give us access to the generations they claim to represent?

Neusner suggests the following reasonable tests by which attributions could be affirmed:[5]

1. A tradition may be cited in a source "entirely external to the rabbinic tradition."

By "external," I believe what is intended is a text that could not be dependent upon the rabbinic text that we seek to verify, or which itself could not be the source of that same text. If the texts could be dependent, we would have gained nothing. If it was "external" to any such dependence, on the other hand, then we would have gained a great deal. Such an external citation would of course demonstrate that the rabbinic document was not merely inventing the tradition for its own purposes. Neusner contends that no such external sources are available to us.

2. "The final date of compiling a collection in which a story (or here, tradition—D.K.) first occurs commonly supplies the final date for the present form of all the materials in that collection...."

This is the skeptical view which, as we saw above, Neusner presently employs. For purposes of the present discussion, therefore, it adds nothing.

3. Internal evidence may help us to confirm an earlier dating. If later traditions are clearly dependent upon earlier traditions, then the earlier traditions may be considered to be verified.

This approach, potentially, is of immense value in the dating of Yerushalmi and, in particular, Bavli traditions, because of the frequency with which this phenomenon is found in those documents. However, though Neusner was willing to use this test in his work on the Mishnah,[6] he has been unwilling to apply it in work on the Bavli and Yerushalmi. Why so? Apparently, if one is willing to take the skeptical approach to the extreme, then no attributed tradition may be taken to verify any other attributed tradition. Since there is no reason to give credence to any such tradition, the whole corpus becomes subject to the same doubt.

4. Though not included explicitly in his list, Neusner (still, in *The Pharisees*) clearly goes on to consider what "reason" will dictate. It may be that such a criterion is rendered meaningless in a confrontation with extreme skepticism, but in combination with other verifications it may, nonetheless, have a place.

5. Finally, Neusner adds the following test[7]: "If... we knew that there was a characteristic mode of formulating ideas, always particular to one authority or school, and never utilized by some other authority or school, we should have a solid, because superficial, criterion for sorting out valid from invalid attributions (my emphasis—D.K.)." This, we will see, is a test that holds immense promise.

Test #2 (the final composition of a text) will, as we said, not be useful in considering the possible verification of Amoraic attributions, because it already grants that such verifications are impossible. Tests #3 and #4 also are of little use as primary verifications because they might easily be criticized as being overly credulous. We will return to them, therefore, only in combination with other, more certain tests. Tests #1 and #5, on the other hand, do provide a key to verifying attributions, and if evidence of the sort that they describe is available, then we will be able to retreat from the position that critical skepticism has now demanded we occupy.

In seeking a source that is "external" enough to be of some benefit, it is not necessary, as we have already implied, that such a source be external to the rabbinic tradition as a whole. It is only necessary that the source be demonstrably independent of the text in question. If, for example, both the Bavli and the Yerushalmi quote a Mishnah, we have discovered nothing that we did not know previously. Both documents are obviously dependent upon the Mishnah, and so the fact that they both quote a Mishnah adds nothing. If, on the other hand, both these documents quote a common Amoraic source, and if we could demonstrate that the Bavli was not dependent upon the Yerushalmi (as the Yerushalmi, having come to closure one to two centuries before,[8] was obviously not dependent on the Bavli), then we will have shown each document to be "external" to the other, and to be available as a source for verification of a mutually preserved tradition.

That "externality" (independence) is an accurate description of the relationship of the Bavli and Yerushalmi is a virtually undisputed conclusion in contemporary scholarship.[9] Neusner himself makes this argument persuasively and at length in his *The Bavli and Its Sources: The Question of Tradition in the Case of Tractate Sukkah*.[10] There he demonstrates that, while the Bavli and Yerushalmi might have shared common sources—the Mishnah, Tosefta, and some brief Amoraic traditions— "The Bavli and the Yerushalmi assuredly stand autonomous from one another." (p. 50). The expository programs of each are entirely independent, and all evidence indicates that the latter document, the Bavli, was in no way dependent upon the former. Even if the Yerushalmi were available to the authors of the Bavli—and, aside from chronology, there is no evidence that it was[11]—the fact that shared Amoraic traditions almost never correspond exactly points to the fact that the framers of the Bavli were independent of the Yerushalmi in all respects, even with respect to common Palestinian traditions.

This being the case, we may rightly speak of these documents as sources for the verification of commonly recorded Amoraic traditions. Since they did not derive these traditions from one another, they must have drawn them from a common third source, that being the circle of the sage to which the common tradition is attributed.[12] Because early communication between the Palestinian and Babylonian communities is widely attested, whereas significant later communication is, as we saw, denied by available evidence, it is only a source such as this (the circle of the sage) that may reasonably be claimed to have supplied the tradition to both independent documents.

To see what sort of conclusions this verification test would yield, I examined all traditions attributed to R. Yohanan in the Bavli, tractate Shabbat, and compared these traditions to the record of the Yerushalmi. Of a total of 113 such traditions, I found that 75 have no parallel whatsoever in the Yerushalmi. Nine record the same opinion in the name of a different authority, while three record the same attribution dealing with the same issue but with a different legal ruling. Twenty-six are, to one degree or another, closely parallel, and in these instances it is generally impossible to imagine that the independent documents could have shaped these traditions without a common source. An example of such a parallel follows:

Yerushalmi Berakhot 1:5 (3b)

R. Yohanan in the name of R. Shimon b. Yohai: [people] such as ourselves who are involved in the study of Torah, even to recite the Shema we do not interrupt (our activity, i.e., our study).

R. Yohanan said about himself: [People] such as ourselves who are not [properly] engaged in the study of Torah, even for Prayer we interrupt.

Bavli Shabbat 11a

> R. Yoḥanan said: they taught it only with respect to [people] like R. Shimon b. Yoḥai and his colleagues, for Torah [study] is their livelihood, but [people] like ourselves, we interrupt for reciting the Shema and for Prayer.

To be sure, there are important differences between these two versions. But the parallels are also unmistakable, and it is inconceivable that these two traditions are totally independent of one another. Rather, both the similarities and differences are what might reasonably be expected of an original oral tradition which came to be repeated and deliberated upon in what later became two independent traditions. There is little doubt, therefore, that this Bavli tradition, as a text that derives in basic content from the circle of R. Yoḥanan, may be considered to be *verified*.

The same may be suggested, though with less confidence, for traditions that record different legal rulings or that are attributed to different, though commonly associated sages (e.g., Yoḥanan, Eleazar, R. Shimon b. Laqish). Particularly in the former instances, mistakes of this sort are typical of independently preserved oral traditions. The Mishnah itself is not infrequently preserved with such differences by the Bavli and Yerushalmi.[13] Of course, mere superficial parallels should be disregarded, but where similarities reasonably require a common source, even when differences are significant, the source for a tradition (if only in essence) should be sought in the circle of the sage or sages to whom it is attributed.

But what is the meaning of the whole sample in which less than 25% may be verified with confidence? We may note, to begin with, that the literary record of the Bavli is more comprehensive than that of the Yerushalmi, even with regard to prominent Palestinian sages. Parts of that "more comprehensive record" might be the product of artificial attributions, that is, invented traditions that were later attributed to R. Yoḥanan. But just because there is no Yerushalmi parallel does not mean that this is necessarily the case. Even unparalleled traditions might in fact derive from the circle of R. Yoḥanan; we simply have no evidence for this. Caution would, in any case, bid that we not grant any presumptive reliability to such traditions; other confirming evidence would be necessary before this presumption could be made.

Of course, it is not only the traditions of R. Yoḥanan that find expression in both Talmuds. Prominent early Amoraic sages of each major rabbinic community are represented in the document of the other. The same tests and reservations may, therefore, be extended to a good number of Amoraic traditions. Granted, we may still speak with confidence regarding only a relatively small minority of all Amoraic traditions. We have, nevertheless, begun to establish a foothold in the process of historical verification.

The second verification test that will yield positive results is that which seeks a mode of formulating ideas that characterizes one group of sages but not another (#5 above). Such a test may be deemed reliable because it uncovers patterns that are not essential to the subject at hand—they are "superficial." Of course, to isolate such patterns one must begin by presuming that the attributions are "accurate." It is only by examining together all traditions attributed to a certain sage or group of sages (united, for example, by presumed chronological proximity) that one may ascertain whether such patterns exist in the first place. If, after presuming accuracy, one discovers no patterns, then it is necessary to conclude that the attributions have not been verified. However, if one uncovers such patterns of formulating ideas, it is safe to assume that they are not the product of an artificial, final formulation. Precisely because such patterns are, at first glance, hidden, it is extremely unlikely that they could have been imposed on a broad scale by some later hand. The system for identifying traditions (that is, the attributions) in which such patterns are embedded may, therefore, be understood to convey a reasonably reliable confirmation.

Moreover, this test does not require that these "characteristic mode[s] of formulating ideas" be "always particular to one authority or school and never utilized by some other authority or school." To the contrary, such exclusivity is suspect precisely because it might easily be identified by a reader. Furthermore, it is those patterns that cannot be so identified, and which cannot, therefore, be thought to be the product of artifice, that are more reliable sources of verification. It is for this reason that this test should seek "patterns," that is, broad but significant differences that distinguish one group from another. If such patterns are discovered, then a "presumptive reliability" will have been established. Unlike the test examined above, this will not actually "verify" individual traditions. But attributions as a whole will no longer require the same skepticism. Again, as we will see, the circle of the sage under discussion will emerge as the most reasonable source for the particular Amoraic traditions.

With respect to these traditions in the Bavli, at least, such patterns may be shown to exist. In earlier research (which I supplement here), I examined the stylistic characteristics of Amoraic traditions in detail.[14] I discovered that, while there are only occasional features that characterize the traditions of one Amora in particular,[15] there are patterns that quite clearly characterize the traditions of a generation of Amoraim as a whole. These patterns are, as I pointed out, particularly persuasive in the present context, because there is no room for suspicion that they were imposed by a later author to create a unique individual characterization. Unless we were to consider the possibility that the whole literature of the Bavli is the product of a cunning, intentional deception, these patterns must be considered significant evidence in support of the attributional record of the document as a whole.

What follows is only a review of the most salient characterizing features that I have identified. These features are true of the traditions of the most prolific sages of each generation (Rav and Samuel; R. Yoḥanan and Resh Laqish; R. Judah and R. Huna; R. Sheshet, R. Ḥisda, R. Naḥman, R. Joseph and Rabba; Abbaye and Rava) and so may be said to be representative of the generation as a whole.

The earliest Amoraic generations barely diverged from the stylistic model of the Mishnah. The traditions of Rav and Samuel are overwhelmingly brief,[16] and these statements more often prescribe halakha (like the Mishnah itself) than suggest interpretation. They are also, like the Mishnah, overwhelmingly in rabbinic Hebrew[17] (the predominance of Hebrew over Aramaic in Rav's traditions is 4.56:1, and in those of Samuel 4.88:1). The same tendencies are apparent in the next generation with the production of R. Judah and R. Huna,[18] and, with minor exceptions, also with that of the early Palestinian Amoraim, R. Yoḥanan (whose traditions prefer Hebrew over Aramaic by a ratio of 5.78:1) and Resh Laqish[19] (according to the record of the Bavli).[20]

In contrast, the argumentation of the first two Amoraic generations is extremely limited. Most cases are short and simple, extending for only one or two steps. Overwhelmingly, it was the brief, formulated conclusions that were preserved in these generations, and not the debates that produced them.

The stylistic development exhibited in traditions of the third Amoraic generation is substantial. The preference for Hebrew expression in this generation is either substantially reduced (in the traditions of Rabba, Hebrew is preferred by a ratio of 1.22:1) or altogether eliminated (the traditions of R. Joseph prefer Aramaic over Hebrew by a ratio of 1.54:1). There is still a preference for brief formulation, but the predominance of such traditions over argumentation is now significantly diminished.[21] In fact, for the later sages of this generation, the record of their argumentational production equals that of their briefer traditions. Moreover, the brief traditions of this period exhibit a self-consciousness and a rhetorical edge not witnessed before. Self-justification is not uncommon.[22] Reasoning, and not only the conclusion that results from it, is now a common subject of expression. The tone of many statements shifts from simple exposition of earlier traditions to a clear indication that what is being said is in *response* to what preceded. Clearly, the earlier preferred models are being supplemented and displaced.

Furthermore, all manners of argumentation are more commonly represented in this generation. This includes objections from tannaitic sources, objections from logic alone (which appear in great number for the first time in this generation), and simple dialogues. It also includes occasional argumentational texts of great length and sophistication. The profile of traditions from this (the third) Amoraic generation characterizes it as one of great creativity and innovation.

This is even more the case in the next generation, that of Abbaye and Rava. Statistically speaking, the trends witnessed earlier come to fruition at this time.[23] Aramaic is preferred above Hebrew in the traditions of both Abbaye (1.79:1) and Rava (1.18:1). Though on a one-to-one basis brief traditions maintain a large plurality over argumentational texts, if one considers the sheer literary bulk of each, argumentation for the first time approaches brief formulations in quantity.[24] Moreover, the majority of brief traditions is now explanatory, confirming a trend evidenced in the previous generation, in which prescriptive traditions dominated earlier on, whereas explanatory comments were more common at a later stage. Also, like the immediately preceding record, self-consciousness in expression is widespread,[25] and even argumentation has finally taken its place as the object for detailed comment.

Most noteworthy is the quantity of argumentation attributed to sages of this generation. The number of argumentational traditions in the names of Abbaye and Rava far exceeds that of any other generation. This quantitative growth is evident, moreover, for exchanges of all lengths, including those that persist for many steps.[26]

We have shown, then, that the traditions of each Amoraic generation are characterized by a certain literary pattern, and that the patterns serve to distinguish one generation from another (or one productive period from another) in significant ways. Because these patterns differ, and because they are "superficial" to specific subjects of deliberation, these data may be said to offer "verification" of the presumptive reliability of attributed Amoraic traditions.

This verification is supported by application of the first test discussed above (the "externality" of the Bavli and Yerushalmi with relation to one another) to the language statistic (Hebrew/Aramaic) of R. Yohanan. (We apply this test to his traditions because his is the only name recorded in such significant numbers in both the Bavli and the Yerushalmi.) As we indicated above, the traditions of R. Yohanan, according to the record of the Bavli, prefer Hebrew over Aramaic by a ratio of 5.78:1. According to the Yerushalmi's record, the ratio is 4.6:1. While there is clearly a slight discrepancy in these numbers (a discrepancy which could, in any case, be explained by a number of factors, including the precise body of traditions selected for preservation, the stereotyped expectation in Babylonia that R. Yohanan, a Palestinian, would be more likely to express himself in Hebrew, and so forth), what is more significant is the fact that both documents record an overwhelming preference for Hebrew expression. Such a preference is not replicated in the Bavli except in the case of the earliest Amoraim. Independently, therefore, both the Bavli and the Yerushalmi attest to the same picture of R. Yoḥanan's traditions, and this, in turn, supports the reliability of the language statistic as a whole. By the criteria established in the test discussed most recently, this and other such factors would already have provided verification of the traditions as a whole. This independent support suggests that such a conclusion is not in error.

The nature of the verification, however, may only extend as far as the evidence will allow. How, precisely, should this "presumptive reliability" be defined?

The patterns that have been discerned characterize, as we said, only one generation from another, but not individuals. This suggests that conventions of formulation and preservation were shared by the sages of each generation (or by the redactors of the traditions of that generation who, nevertheless, redacted those traditions not long after they had originally been formulated), mostly eliminating uniqueness in expression as it might relate to individual personalities. This being so, traditions attributed to the sages of a given generation may be presumed to accurately reflect a view held in that generation, but not necessarily by that individual. What might have been unique to an individual was blurred by convention, but generations as a whole preserved their distinct personalities.

Even given this limitation, we have gone a significant distance beyond the paralysis with which we began. Based upon this latter test, we may presume that Bavli traditions record views that reflect the age in which they are claimed to have been formulated. Unless our task is to compose biographies, therefore, we have gained a useful tool. Histories of ideas may, in fact, be written, and developments between one generation and the next may be duly noted.

In combination with the earlier test, presumptions of reliability may be defined even more precisely. If a Bavli tradition is closely paralleled in the Yerushalmi, then we must assume that the tradition in question originated in the circle of the sage to whom it is attributed. Again, this does not confirm that the sage actually expressed the recorded opinion, let alone the words themselves. But it does confirm that his immediate circle believed he did. So, again, if it is history that we want to write, the data may be confidently employed. It is only biography to which we have little access.

Building upon these two tests, the other tests now take on some significance. To begin with, because traditions may now be said to be grounded in given generations, those later traditions that clearly depend upon prior traditions may be understood to strengthen their presumptive reliability. This is particularly true where these traditions exhibit the patterns by which their generation is characterized. In addition, building upon the foundation laid by this variety of mutually reinforcing tests, there is also now a place to ask whether it is reasonable to imagine "that the whole literature is pseudepigraphic in an extreme sense."[27] Given the fact that differences between the generations are not flattened, and the fact, admitted by all, that the Bavli and Yerushalmi clearly depended upon earlier traditions in their compositions, it seems impossible to support such a conclusion. To the contrary, evidence supports a view that traditions were formulated in relative chronological proximity with the sages to whom they are attributed,[28] and the final document (the Bavli and, most likely, the Yerushalmi) did not, for the most part, eliminate the uniqueness of the sources that it employed.

There are some who would want to claim that verifications can be made even more specific. Lieberman understands[29] that the *baraita* at B. Eruv. 54b, describing Moses' repetition of oral traditions to the priests and the elders, encapsulates the process by which rabbinic traditions were "published." Since the process begins with a single authority figure, it is tempting to claim that later rabbinic attributions were accurate to this extent as well. But the relation of the legend to purported later models is too transparent to accept uncritically. All we know from this text is that the rabbis claimed to publish traditions in a manner similar to Moses, lending authority and credence to the rabbinic procedures. However, just as we would reject a literal reading of the text as it applies to Moses, so too must we be dubious about its implied claims. The author of this text has too much to gain by convincing us.

In a similar way, Halivni believes that the gemara at B. Eruvin 32b alludes to the process by which Amoraic traditions were published.[30] There, after a lengthy deliberation, several sages ask R. Nahman whether a given conclusion has been "fixed as *gemara*?" After an affirmative answer, the conclusion is repeated as a brief "apodictic" tradition in typical Amoraic form. In other words, after debating different sides of an issue, a given authority would see to it that the conclusion of the debate was formulated as a brief, easily repeated tradition. Again, if we take this text at its word (as interpreted by Halivni), we will be tempted to connect traditions with the authority to whom they are attributed.

But there are two difficulties with such a step. First, we would have to grant that this particular interpretation is the correct one. Given our distance from the source, and the alternative interpretations that have been proposed,[31] we must at least admit that the matter is not settled. Second, even if Halivni's reading of this text is the most convincing,[32] this does not mean that what is "reported" here is representative of the whole. If this were the precise process by which Amoraic traditions were published, then why is this the only example of such a report? If, on the other hand, this text was meant to act as a general illustration of the Amoraic process of publication, then why was it not more explicit? In either instance, enough questions remain to make this an inadequate foundation upon which to build a structure.

Single cases of any kind are insufficient evidence upon which to build. A far more extensive kind of evidence would be necessary before presumptive reliability could be granted to individual attributions. Unfortunately, I do not see that such evidence is available. We are at present unable, therefore, to go beyond the general circle of the sage to which a tradition is attributed. Thus, as we noted above, biography remains off-limits to historians of classical rabbinic society.[33] On the other hand, other matters of history, dependent though they might be on the dates supplied by rabbinic attributions, may legitimately (though cautiously) be pursued.

Given these conclusions, let us return to our original illustration to see how the history we now write will be altered. As we noted then, because the myth of the dual Torah is fully conceptualized in rabbinic literature for the first time only in the Yerushalmi, Neusner assumes that it originated at about the time of the closure of that document (ca. 400). But compare, now, the related Bavli version (Gittin 60b):

> R. Eleazar said: The majority of the Torah is in writing and the minority oral, as it says, "Though I write for him the great things [= "most"] of my Torah, they are reckoned a strange thing (Hos. 8:12)."
> ...
> R. Yohanan said: The Holy One, blessed be He, made a covenant with Israel only on account of the things preserved orally, as it says…

The relation of the traditions in the two versions is striking and unmistakable. In both instances the name of R. Yohanan is associated with the opinion that claims that God's covenant with Israel was in some way dependent upon the oral Torah. In both instances R. Eleazar is connected with an opinion that emphasizes the primacy of written Torah, if only as the source for derivation. The biblical text quoted in both versions is the same as well.

Based upon the verification tests reviewed earlier, we may be confident that these opinions originated in the circles of the sages to whom they are attributed. This being so, we may affirm that the myth of the dual Torah originated by at least the middle of the third century in the Palestine of pagan Rome. The sages in whose circle these views were current were early Amoraim, and R. Yohanan had in his youth even been—or so the Talmud reports—a student of R. Judah Ha-Nasi. It was, of course, this same Judah whose Mishnah they revered and—if this myth is to serve as evidence—whose legitimacy they self-consciously sought to defend.[34] The rabbinic sages did not wait for nearly two centuries to recognize that the Mishnah required some kind of explicit mythical empowerment. On the contrary, these sages saw fit to articulate an explicit empowering myth for the Mishnah at a relatively early stage. It was, moreover, a myth of incomparable power—one that would become the single most prevalent Torah-myth in rabbinic Judaism for all centuries to follow.[35]

Notes

1. Several of Neusner's many statements of this critique are spoken of below. To these should be added, in particular, William Scott Green, "What's in a Name? The Problematic of Talmudic 'Biography'," in W.S. Green (ed.), *Approaches to Ancient Judaism: Theory and Practice* (Missoula, 1978).
2. Neusner has expressed this critique on numerous occasions, including in the introduction to the third edition of his *History of the Jews in Babylonia*. His most extensive statement of this view is to be found in *Reading and Believing: Ancient Judaism and Contemporary Gullibility* (Atlanta, 1986).
3. See *Messiah in Context: Israel's History and Destiny in Formative Judaism* (Philadelphia, 1984) and *Torah: From Scroll to Symbol in Formative Judaism* (Philadelphia, 1985).
4. *Torah: From Scroll to Symbol in Formative Judaism*, pp. 75–77.
5. See *The Pharisees, Rabbinic Perspectives*, pp. 233–235.
6. See e.g., *Eliezer ben Hyrcanus: The Tradition and the Man* (Leiden, 1973), v. 11, pp. 63–169, and *The Mishnah Before 70* (Atlanta, 1987).
7. See *Judaism in Society*, p. 31.
8. The Yerushalmi is generally assumed to have come to a close ca. 400 C.E. Present debate about the Bavli puts its closure somewhere between 427 and 600.
9. See J.N. Epstein, *M'vo'ot l'sifrut ha-amoraim* (Jerusalem, 1962), pp. 290–2, and Y. Greenwald, *Ha-ra'u m'sadrei ha-bavli et ha-yerushalmi?* (New York, 1954), pp. 56–70.
10. Atlanta, 1987.
11. See now Martin Jaffee, "The Babylonian Appropriation of the Talmud Yerushalmi: Redactional Studies in the Horayot Tractates," in *New Perspectives on Ancient Judaism*, vol. 4, *The Literature of Early Rabbinic Judaism: Issues in Talmudic Redaction and Interpretation*, ed. by Alan J. Avery-Peck (Lanham, 1989), pp. 3-27. Jaffee notes certain redactional similarities between Yerushalmi and Bavli tractate Horayot, and suggests that the latter document has been influenced by the former in its redactional choices. He admits that any influence is limited to redaction alone (see p. 6, n. 9). Even if Jaffee is correct, the fact that the authors of the Bavli did not amend their Palestinian traditions on the basis of the Yerushalmi record only strengthens the conclusion that they possessed their own earlier, independent tradition to which they were willing to give priority. This will therefore not affect our conclusion.
12. (I have now come to doubt the correctness of this assertion, other equally plausible explanations being available. See the next essay, along with its introduction, for a refinement of the conclusions suggested here.)
13. See M. Schachter, *Ha-Mishnah b'Bavli u-viYerushalmi* (Jerusalem, 1959).
14. David Kraemer, *Stylistic Characteristics of Amoraic Literature* [hereafter, SCAL] (Ph.D. dissertation, Jewish Theological Seminary, 1984).
15. SCAL, p. 87 and n. 11.
16. SCAL, pp. 49–53, 57.
17. My study of the language of expression of Amoraic traditions was conducted subsequent to my SCAL research, and so the specifics are included below. I did not examine the traditions of all sages who had earlier been the subject of study, but only of a smaller representative sample (as the presence or absence of statistics below will reveal). To arrive at these figures, I first examined all "brief" traditions attributed to Rav and Abbaye. Discovering that the ratio does not vary significantly over the whole sample, I restricted my examination, in the case of other sages, to smaller parts of their corpus, but in no case did I examine less than half of all "brief" traditions attributed to a given sage. Furthermore, I did

not examine "argumentational" traditions. My sense, though, is that such traditions would tend, more than brief traditions, to prefer Aramaic (the opposite is certainly not the case). Since earlier Amoraim are associated with relatively little argumentation, this omission will not affect their ratios significantly. For later Amoraim, on the other hand, this will mean that their preference for Aramaic should be slightly increased.

18. SCAL, pp. 62–4.
19. SCAL, pp. 69–70, 72.
20. A preliminary review of the frequency and scope of argumentation in the Yerushalmi supports the same conclusion. In the Yerushalmi, *Seder Zeraim* and tractates Shabbat, Eruvin, and Pesahim, I counted only forty argumentational sequences that persisted for three steps or more (most were four steps, a few extended to up to a dozen). This is the total number of such sequences, involving the participation of any sage. This is a relatively small number, of course, and there are clearly a far larger number of brief traditions attributed to the same sages. I have not examined those traditions to determine whether they prefer halakha or interpretation. See also below on the testimony of the linguistic record in traditions attributed to R. Yohanan, as it supports the general reliability of the Bavli's record of Palestinian Amoraic traditions.
21. SCAL., p. 80f.
22. SCAL., p. 81f.
23. SCAL, p. 109f.
24. In SCAL, I counted 1366 argumentational sequences that involved Abbaye and Rava, and 2125 brief (apodictic) traditions in their names. If one includes brief traditions that are followed by a single response in this number (what I called one-step argumentation) then the total number of apodictic traditions attributed to these sages is 2318. However, if each responsive step of an argumentational sequence is counted (being that each such step is more or less equivalent in length to an apodictic statement), then the number of argumentational statements attributed to these sages is ca. 1800 and the total number of steps in the argumentation in which these sages participate is at least 2821. (I say "at least" because I grouped all sequences of five steps or more into a single category, and for purposes of this counting I considered each to be only five steps, though some were considerably longer.)
25. SCAL, p. 110.
26. SCAL, p. 132.
27. Neusner, *The Pharisees*, p. 235.
28. Though, to be sure, they were often "re-formulated" in the course of transmission, as Halivni has demonstrated extensively in his *Meqorot umesorot*. As a general observation, it is necessary to caution that even with the presumed reliability that I have demonstrated, what we have at best is still a working presumption. All traditions must still be subjected to the variety of critical tests that Halivni and others have employed.
29. *Hellenism in Jewish Palestine* (New York, 1950), pp. 83–99.
30. *Meqorot umesorot* (Jerusalem, 1982), pp. 91–95.
31. See Albeck, *Mavo la-talmudim* (Tel-Aviv, 1969), pp. 576–7.
32. This reading is supported, indirectly, by J. Kaplan in *The Redaction of the Talmud* (New York, 1933), p. 196.
33. That is, in this we continue to agree with the conclusions of Neusner and Green; see above, n. 1.
34. This observation is found abundantly in Neusner's works on the Mishnah. In connection with R. Yohanan and his relationship to the Mishnah, see also D. Halivni, "The Reception Accorded to Rabbi Judah's Mishnah," in E.P. Sanders (ed.), *Jewish and Christian Self-Definition* (Philadelphia, 1981), p. 209.

35. My thanks to Burt Visotsky, Shaye Cohen, and Ruth Fagen for their kind suggestions in the preparation of this article.

INTRODUCTION TO CHAPTER TWO

This essay represents my more mature position concerning the possibility of using rabbinic sources for the composition of histories of Jews in Late Antiquity. In this piece, I attempt to show why, in my estimation, most conventional histories that would depend upon this "evidence" are ill-advised. The kinds of conclusions we might like to draw are beyond our grasp. In other words, I conclude, with Neusner, that the best we can do, for the most part, is read the received documents in the order of their composition—and little more.

Unfortunately, the debate concerning "doing history" with rabbinic sources has not been a sober one, and there has been frequent misrepresentation of the views of the "other" party to the debate. This tenor has contributed to the formation of a dichotomized field and, as is so often the case when discussions become debates, the parties engaged in the debate have failed to appreciate what the issues truly are. Let me explain.

Those who have argued that rabbinic documents can be used to write conventional histories, including Richard Kalmin, Isaiah Gafni, and many others, have asked why the rabbis would "invent" teachings and traditions and attribute them falsely to this or that Talmudic sage. Why, in other words, would the rabbis *lie*? And, if they would not lie, then why should we dismiss the value of rabbinic traditions for doing history? Should we not assume that there is at least a "historical kernel" in many of the traditions we have preserved?

These are good questions—though not ones without answers. Still, for present purposes, let us grant that the rabbis would not "lie" about who said what—that they genuinely believed the veracity of each and every teaching they repeated. We are still obliged to ask whether well-meaning people might unwittingly participate in a process that inevitably distorts "original" teachings to such an extent that they finally preserve no historical evidence we can confidently rely upon.

In the essay that follows, I draw upon the primary scholarship of others to argue that, in the case of the rabbis whose compositions we seek to mine for historical evidence, the condition just described is in fact present. The rabbis taught in a primarily oral setting. This does not mean that they did not also preserve teachings in writing (they did), only that the oral mode dominated (for an excellent exposition of the relationship between oral teaching and writing in such a setting, see Susan Niditch's *Oral World and Written Word* [Louisville, Kentucky: 1996]). Recent scholarship has shown that oral preservation and transmission inevitably changes the material at hand. For material preserved and transmitted over the course of many generations—as in the case of traditions preserved in most of rabbinic literature—these changes will make it impossible to access an "original" teaching with confidence. These is not to say that we may not preserve an early version of a given tradition. It is simply to recognize that, given the technologies of preservation and transmission which the rabbis depended upon, we can rarely know whether we have such an early version or not. (On rare occasion, external evidence might allow us to verify an early dating with some greater confidence).

So, when we say we cannot do conventional histories, we are casting no aspersions on the ethics of the rabbis. We are simply being mindful of processes over which they had no control. And, when we recognize this reality, we will be forced to admit that we can do very little of the sort of detailed "generation-by-generation" work that has characterized much rabbinic history writing in this century. What we can do, instead, is the sort of histories of Judaism represented by much of Neusner's later work, or by my *Responses to Suffering in Classical Rabbinic Literature*. Yes, we can do history, but of a very different sort than that to which we are accustomed.

(A more recent and complete statement of my methodological conclusions may be found in the first chapter of my *The Meanings of Death in Rabbinic Judaism* [Routledge, 1999].)

Chapter Two

Rabbinic Sources For Historical Study

Scholars, mostly Jewish but also non-Jewish, have been using Rabbinic sources for historical study for well over a century. These studies—one "History of the Jews in the Talmudic Period" or another—have been, almost without exception, what Jacob Neusner terms "gullible." They have assumed, in other words, that the rabbinic record can, more or less, be taken at its word and that, once one has determined the "original version" of a teaching and discounted obviously fabulous material, one may accept that teaching as historically reliable.

By this stage in the development of Judaic scholarship, the folly of these earlier habits is broadly recognized. Neusner and others have pointed to a variety of crucial and even fatal flaws in the approach described above, and there is hardly a scholar writing today about the history of Jews in Late Antiquity who doesn't at least pay lip service (though often no more than lip service!) to the much repeated critique. But even the critical questions that have been articulated—Can we believe rabbinic attributions for purposes of dating a tradition? Why should we believe what any given tradition reports? and so forth—do not capture the full scope of the problem of using such records for writing history. In the following pages, I will describe the obstacles that would have to be overcome before we could be sure that a rabbinic record contained historically reliable evidence. I will conclude that these obstacles are effectively insurmountable and that most sorts of political, social or religious histories cannot be constructed on the basis of rabbinic testimony.

Let us begin with the nature of rabbinic teachings themselves. Rabbinic tradition claims of itself that it was an oral tradition, passed from master to disciple by word of mouth. If we accept this claim,[1] then we shall have to ask about the reliability of transmission in oral cultures. Those who have studied oral cultures notice a great degree of fluidity and change in the repetition of traditions. This is true even of recitations of the same person from one repetition to the next, even when the speaker claims that he has repeated the tradition or story in a form that is identical—word for word—with the previous recitation. Walter Ong reports that even in oral societies where verbatim repetition is a goal, success is quite limited.[2] Where training (memorization) begins early and traditions are chanted or sung, success is greater, but even such repeaters "make changes... of which they are unaware."[3] The most successful instances of verbatim repetition are found in the context of ritual performance, but even here changes are regular. The many differences in formulation in the prayers and blessings of Jewish liturgy will attest to this reality.

If rabbinic teachings were originally transmitted orally, then the many variations in traditions from one record to another are evidence of the reality just described. It is in the nature of an oral tradition that teachings change from one recitation to the next, mostly unnoticed. If we could capture and compare snapshots of these recitations, as we often can in the rabbinic case, we would be able to demonstrate the ubiquity of such changes, large and small. Compare any chapter of the Tosefta with the record of related baraitot in the Yerushalmi and the Bavli and you will have no question of the consequences of oral transmission. Compare the attributions and details of "the same" teaching in different rabbinic documents or in different contexts in the same document and you will be unable to avoid the same conclusion. It is unnecessary to demonstrate or "prove" this claim; examples are found literally on every page of the classical rabbinic corpus.

The unsensed changes that typify all oral traditions are often a function of the habits, assumptions, beliefs and prejudices of the context in which any given tradition is repeated. Again, examples in the rabbinic corpus are abundant. I offer just one example: When we compare the responses of R. Yohanan and his colleagues to suffering as recorded in the Bavli (Berakhot 5a) to those preserved in Song of Songs Rabbah (2, 35), we find that in the former version sufferings are rejected ("[I want] neither them nor their reward!") whereas in the latter, acceptance in recommended ("Don't say this but, rather, say 'The trustworthy God!'"). These and other differences in the respective formulation of the traditions are significant, and they conform completely to approaches to suffering which widely and unmistakably typify the respective traditions (the Babylonian and the Palestinian rabbinic).[4] The rabbinic repeaters may not have been aware of the changes they were introducing into their teachings, but change them they did, under the inexorable pressures of the settings in which they were living.

The next problem with the rabbinic evidence, as we preserve it, lies in the simple fact that teachings which were originally given oral expression, by and before living, authoritative masters of the tradition, are now (more or less) "frozen" in writing. Oral and written expressions differ in significant ways, and if "the medium is the message" then the reduction of oral rabbinic teachings to the written form will have changed them radically. I cannot improve on Martin Jaffee's articulation of the consequences of this step:

> ...the passage of a literary work from exclusively oral to written/oral transmission is profoundly transformative. What was once present as direct address and shaped inevitably to suit the needs of the moment as these took shape in the interaction of speaker and audience is now deprived of the fluid form which constitutes its social reality. A tradition, once reformulated and changed with each performance, is now stabilized and objectified in a form which exerts a powerful control over future performances or readings. What was formerly "authored" at each recitation must now be reproduced "as it is written."[5]

To this description, Walter Ong adds several important observations. "Written words," he writes, "are isolated from the fuller context in which spoken words come into being." What difference does this make? "Spoken words are always modifications of a total situation which is more than verbal... In oral speech, a word must have one or another intonation or tone of voice—lively, excited, quiet, incensed, resigned, or whatever." Context, tone, audience, and the like all affect the meaning of a communication. Written communication, in contrast, will always "lack a verifiable context." When words are written, removing the eyes, the brow, the hand movement, the tone of voice, then the force of the words will be thrown into doubt, their meaning subject to differing interpretation. As Ong points out, one need only consider the hours an actor spends determining how best to utter the written words of a script (and the drastically different interpretations of how to utter and perform the same words) to appreciate how radically a transformation of medium affects the message.[6]

The writing of originally oral teachings shifts context in more than one way. In whatever document rabbinic traditions find their written home, the choice of a precise context for quotation is rarely that of the "original" speaker or later repeater. It is, instead, ultimately the decision of the "author" or "redactor" of the document. This fact is particularly evident in the Bavli, where traditions are constantly quoted in "new" contexts—interpretations of texts from *Toharot* find themselves in discussions of teachings from *Nashim*, statements that "originally" pertained to one Mishnah are quoted over and over again in connection with others, and so forth. If we admit that all meaning is contextual (and I, following many others, insist that this is true) then the choice of a context for written record transforms earlier meanings perhaps significantly. And once a teaching has found a written home, its earlier oral context—and therefore meaning—can never be fully recovered.

Of course, written records, too, are subject to the manipulations of copying and transmission. Only mechanical printing can reproduce a text with (almost) complete accuracy. Manual copying is, by its nature, fraught with problems and imperfections. Eyes skip, hands slip, short-term memories fail. One sees on the page what one has been prejudiced to see, and one copies the version of one's memory, not the version on the page. Moreover, rabbinic teachers and copyists often doubted the accuracy of the written word before them. They didn't understand a particular step or conceived a different interpretation. If the interpretation demanded a different reading, they often did not hesitate to change the reading in front of them. Naturally, what they found in front of them was already transformed by earlier interpretations, so they could find precedent for the steps they were now taking. And why not? In the end it would be impossible to recover the "original" version in any case.

So, to use the evidence of a rabbinic text for history, one would have to correct for errors and changes and recover the "original" written record. One would then have to correct for changes in context and meaning that accompanied the reduction of the evidence to writing; one would have to reconstruct the pre-written oral version. One would then have to correct for all of the (often) many changes that transformed the evidence from the time of its first articulation to its last oral repetition. If one could recover that "original," one could then commence with the act of interpretation.

It is safe to say that such a recovery is virtually impossible. This is not to say it could never be done. It is only to admit that one could never be sure when one had actually captured the "original" teaching, if there ever was an original to begin with. (It is equally possible that a teacher articulated a teaching with slight modifications from one repetition to the next, in which case we cannot speak of an original). It is for these reasons that the method demonstrated by Halivni's *Meqorot Umesorot* is perceived as so subjective and has been followed by so few. Halivni is properly sensitive to the storms of oral transmission. But he imagines that he has the information he would need to reconstruct the original, and it is here that his confidence does not persuade others. Oral studies suggest that we do not have the information we would need to know when any given reconstruction has hit the mark. We cannot rely on such reconstructions, therefore, even if, on unknown occasions, they are correct.

Where does this analysis leave us? Are there other approaches or other kinds of information that might lead us to conclusions about which we could be more confident?

Students of the rabbinic period have long recognized the potential contributions of archeology to our understanding of the world in which the rabbis lived and taught. Some have even argued that the archaeological record might be used to confirm or challenge the reliability of the rabbinic evidence. In a balanced discussion of the potential contributions of archaeology to rabbinic history, Eric Meyers enumerates the following: First, he observes, archeology can help "set the lives and teachings of men in their true contexts," adding, crucially, that it can "tell us a great deal about the impact [or lack of impact! –DK] of men on their fellow men."[7] This is undoubtedly correct, and it is clearly necessary to reconstruct as much as we can of the historical setting before we can interpret the teachings of any given period. Next, Meyers observes, archaeology can supplement the ancient record, or bring greater clarity to obscure texts. It can also offer correctives to the textual record, contradicting, as it sometimes does, the written tradition.

But it is precisely the contradictions that render this whole direction so problematic. When the picture suggested by the material record contradicts the picture of the rabbinic literary record—as is not infrequently the case—then it is the rabbinic record we must call into question. In such circumstances, the rabbis may be speaking for a small elite, or they may be speaking theoretically, but they are surely not preserving history. From such examples, we learn to doubt the rabbinic evidence. But from cases in which the material remains support the rabbinic record we do not learn to trust that same record, for we could not have known whether or not to rely on the rabbis' testimony without the material proof. In reality, it is archaeological inquiry which genuinely serves as the foundation for history, for even the mute testimony of material remains obviously reflects *some* reality. The rabbinic record, in contrast, may well reflect the reality of the mind and have no direct connection to any lived reality. At best, the rabbinic texts can be relied upon to contribute only slight details.

Perhaps the most important potential contribution of archeology, as Meyers understands it, is to help date rabbinic texts—a matter of central concern in this discussion. To illustrate this possibility, Meyers observes that the practice of ossilegium—secondary burial—discussed in detail in the minor tractate *Semahot*, is shown by archaeology to have been common in the first four centuries of the common era, but not later. This fact, he argues, disproves the common opinion which sees this minor tractate, as other minor tractates, as a geonic work, and broadly supports the earlier dating proposed by Zlotnick. The problems with this suggestion are, however, manifold. To begin with, the tractate claims for itself a tannaitic origin, that is, second century and not later. But the archaeological remains at best give us a *terminus ante quem* of the mid-fourth century—hardly a proof of the text's claims for itself! Furthermore, this entire method presupposes that rabbinic writers have no particular motivation to anachronize or idealize (=preserve earlier authoritative teachings as valid for all times). But the same method, applied to Maimonides' *Mishneh Torah*, would demand a dating of the early first century for that work (How else to explain the extensive treatment of the laws of the Temple in a language resembling one used in the first century?). Archeological evidence dates the attested practices, not the literary record which might, even many centuries later, preserve descriptions of the same practice.

But if it is risky using archaeological evidence to date documents, perhaps we can be more secure using it to date isolated traditions, as the example just considered seems to suggest. Indeed, in recent research I have come upon an example which strikes me as just such a case. In the largest of the burial caves at Beth Shearim (cave 20), archaeologists have found more than one-hundred and fifty burials in large stone sarcophagi. A striking feature of these sarcophagi— mentioned in reports but barely commented upon—is their lids: all are covered by immense stone lids with gabled "roofs" and blunt, uncarved "acroteria" at each of the four corners. These acroteria resemble nothing so much as the "horns" of ancient altars, Jewish and pagan, found by archaeologists in Israel. What makes this resemblance so interesting is a teaching first found in the Tosefta, dated by many scholars to the mid-to-late third century, which declares "anyone who is buried in the Land of Israel is as though buried under the altar" (Tos. A.Z. 4:3). Is this resemblance of design and teaching a mere coincidence, or does this Tosefta shed light on the mute burial phenomenon and the phenomenon provide a date for this teaching of the Tosefta?

The major problem with seeing here more than mere coincidence is the fact that the altars which the lids most resemble date to centuries long before the burials at Beth Shearim. It is obviously unlikely that the community of Jews associated with Beth Shearim were familiar with the ancient form. It is not impossible, of course, that these Jews uncannily captured the form of the ancient altar by means of interpretation of the scriptural commandment describing altars, but this conclusion, too, would require a leap of faith. It is far more likely that, like their pagan neighbors, these Jews sought to borrow architectural forms that characterized Hellenistic and Roman Temples. But, far from disproving the relationship speculated above, this very borrowing suggestively supports it. With all of the acculturation of Jews residing in the Roman Empire during this period, it is still noteworthy that they would employ pagan symbolism in their burials. If the gabled roofs with acroteria symbolically communicate "Temple," we have to assume that, to Jewish eyes, this Temple was the Jewish Temple. In other words, in the absence of a visual witness to the Jerusalem Temple, destroyed several generations before these burials, these Jews would have envisioned their Temple according to models with which they were familiar in their environment. Therefore, burying their deceased beneath these powerful "Temple" symbols, they may well have been expressing their belief that, here in the most important Jewish burial ground in Palestine, they were in effect burying them beneath the altar.

I am, as I said, tempted by this interpretation, but it remains, in the end, only an interpretation. Possibly the rabbinic text has contributed to our understanding of the burial practice at Beth Shearim, but only possibly. And this lack of clear conclusion should serve as a cautionary tale to those who would use these bodies of evidence to illumine one another. Undoubtedly, there are occasions when this approach genuinely provides us a window to ancient realities. But the temptation to over-interpret or make assumptions too quickly is ever present. Just because a rabbinic text *might* explain a material discovery doesn't mean we should assume it does. We must press ourselves to consider alternatives, because they, too, may provide the correct explanation.

In an earlier article, "On the Reliability of Attributions in the Babylonian Talmud,"[8] I examined at length the question articulated in the title, a question central to the present deliberation. I argued at that time that there are two methods available for verifying attributions with at least moderate confidence. In retrospect, it seems to me that even those relatively moderate claims are probably too ambitious.

In discussions of the problems of verifying attributions (in the Bavli and, by extension, in other rabbinic documents), Neusner observed that if a tradition were cited in a source "entirely external to rabbinic tradition" this could be considered valid verification of that source and its attribution.[9] I then suggested that it is unnecessary that the source be entirely external to the tradition; what is necessary is that the source be independent of the traditions being evaluated.[10] Thus, if we agree with the common scholarly opinion that the Bavli, as a completed document, is independent of the final Yerushalmi—that it does not know the earlier completed document and therefore cannot borrow from it or otherwise be dependent on it—then parallel teachings which appear in both documents can be considered "verified" and we may rely upon them to do traditions history. By "verification," I argued, we must mean that the parallel teachings in fact derive from the "circle" of the named sage.

But there are two problems: first, even if this conclusion is accepted, we have in fact gained relatively little and, second, it now seems to me likely that I went beyond what the evidence would allow. In my analysis of traditions attributed to R. Yohanan in the Bavli, tractate Shabbat, I found that only 38 of 113 have any parallel in the Yerushalmi. Of those 38, 9 give the same opinion in the name of a different authority and 3 give different rulings. Only 26 are closely parallel—less than a quarter of the sample. Three-quarters of the sample, in other words, admit to no verification whatsoever. If this sample is representative,[11] a large majority of attributed rabbinic teachings may not be used for purposes of writing history.

It seems to me now that I probably went too far in arguing that such verification brings us back to "the circle" of the identified teacher. All we really know, based upon this sort of evidence, is that two different rabbinic documents (say, the Bavli and the Yerushalmi) preserve traditions which derive from a common source. This source might be the circle of the named sage, but it could just as easily be the circle of a later repeater, separated by generations from the "original" teacher. We can be sure that there was once a common tradition; we can be sure that the tradition split and came to be recorded in different documents. When this split occurred and how far removed it was from the first articulation of the teaching we can never know.

A second method for verifying attributions which may be defensible is described by Neusner in the following words: "If... we knew that there was a characteristic mode of formulating ideas, always particular to one authority or school, and never utilized by some other authority or school, we should have a solid, because superficial, criterion for sorting out valid from invalid attributions."[12] It seems to me that Neusner errs in insisting that the "modes of formulation" be unique to one party and never be utilized by another; such purity could easily be the product of stereotyped, artificial formulation. But the rest of Neusner's proposal captures an important truth. If we could discover some superficial criterion of formulation which is not rhetorically obvious, and therefore could not be the result of artifice, then we will have a means of verifying that certain teachings indeed were formulated at one time and not another.

In earlier research,[13] I discovered that amoraic teachings in the Bavli are in fact characterized by such stylistic criteria, criteria which change from one period to another and allow us, therefore, to identify certain modes of formulation with different periods. In one period brief teachings of law predominate, in a later period interpretive elaborations or argumentational exchanges become much more common. I see no way to explain such characteristics—detectible only through a detailed accounting of large numbers of traditions attributed to teachers of a given period—as fiction. I argued then, therefore—and continue to believe now—that a sort of traditions history, yielding a history of religious ideas, can be constructed on the foundation of these many teachings.[14]

But, even after such painstaking analysis, the value of this evidence for history remains quite limited. What we may verify by such an approach is the relative dating of large numbers of attributed teachings. Nothing in this method will allow us to verify a particular teaching, no matter how characteristic its form. We may therefore interpret the meaning of the form of teachings characteristic to a given period, to the extent that form has meaning, but we may never know whether Rabbi so-and-so said this or that, nor whether he did this or that. In *The Mind of the Talmud*,[15] I offered the sort of history (a history of religious ideas) that I think such evidence justifies.[16] I see no way of going beyond what I did there.

Where does this leave us? As Neusner has repeatedly argued, the only dating we may be relatively sure of is the date of the final formulation of a document. (I say "relatively" because there is ample room to debate the date of redaction of all classical rabbinic documents except the Mishnah.) We may say with confidence that teachings preserved in the Mishnah represent the canonical rabbinic tradition of the late second-to-early third century. Teachings preserved in the Yerushalmi represent the canonical rabbinic tradition in Palestine in the mid-fifth century. Many of the preserved traditions may have originated at an earlier time, but we can never be sure when this is so, nor can we ascertain how later repetitions of a tradition relate to earlier ones. We only know for sure how it was received in the final, redactional stage. So we may analyze and interpret the canonical record of the Yerushalmi and Genesis and Leviticus Rabbah and compare that record to the earlier record of the Mishnah. In his writings, Neusner has shown the value of such an approach (even if we may dispute his particular interpretations). Such a history of religious ideas we may indeed write.

We may also, in at least some cases, do a history of large bodies of traditions and interpret their literary forms. I am confident that the Bavli will allow such an approach; the work has yet to be done to ascertain whether other rabbinic documents preserve the same sort of evidence.

But beyond this, the literary records of the rabbis allow very little. We may seek to write religious and social histories of the Jews in Late Antiquity, but, on the basis of the literature, we may never be sure of precise datings. So, for example, b. Shabbat 151b–152a reveals much about attitudes toward aging among rabbis in Babylonia in late antiquity. But from what period precisely? Did attitudes change from one period to the next? Do attitudes reflect social realities? How do rabbinic attitudes compare with those of other Jews? Such questions, unfortunately, can never be answered with confidence, at least not on the basis of the talmudic record.

To say more, we have to turn to other kinds of evidence, that is, to extra-rabbinic sources and archaeological remains. These too will have to be read with a skeptical eye, ever-aware of the limits of any evidence and the difficulty of any interpretation. But from these sources, we may actually learn something about the world in which the rabbis lived. Moreover, given the nature of the evidence (the archeological record can usually be dated with some confidence; most non-rabbinic documents do not present the same difficulties of dating as the rabbinic composites), we may be more precise in dating what we discover.

As I said at the beginning of this essay, the obstacles are immense, mostly insurmountable. Rabbinic sources for historical study? Barely.

Notes

1. Even if we do not accept the "Oral Torah" claim in its extreme form, admitting instead, with Lieberman and others, that rabbinic sages and their disciples sometimes kept personal written notes, we still have to assume a basically oral context. Because of the difficultly of producing books and widespread illiteracy (education was not necessarily synonymous with actual reading), memorization and oral repetition were the most common forms of "textuality" in the ancient world. Thus, even if canonical texts were sometimes written—even if they were first composed in writing—their authoritative versions (plural) were surely those spoken by recognized authorities.
2. Walter J. Ong, *Orality and Literacy: The Technologizing of the Word* (London and New York: Methuen, 1982), pp. 62.
3. Ibid., p. 63.
4. See my lengthy discussion in *Responses to Suffering in Classical Rabbinic Literature* (New York: Oxford U. Press, 1995).
5. Martin S. Jaffee, "How Much 'Orality' in Oral Torah? New Perspectives on the Composition and Transmission of Early Rabbinic Tradition," *Shofar* v. 10, n. 2 (Winter, 1992): 66. Reuven Firestone offers a magnificent case study of an oral tradition and its written records in *Journeys in Holy Lands: The Evolution of the Abraham-Ishmael Legends in Islamic Exegesis* (Albany: SUNY Press, 1990). See particularly pp. 15–8 and 153–5.
6. Ong, pp. 101–2.
7. "The Use of Archaeology in Understanding Rabbinic Materials," in *Texts and Responses: Studies Presented to Nahum N. Glatzer...* (Leiden: E.J. Brill, 1975), p. 31.
8. HUCA 60 (1989): 175–190. Reprinted in *Essential Papers on the Talmud*, ed. by Michael Chernick (New York: NYU Press, 1994), pp. 276–292. This article appears as chapter one of the present volume.
9. See *The Pharisees: Rabbinic Perspectives* (Hoboken, N.J.: Ktav, 1973), p. 233.
10. "On the Reliability...," *HUCA*, p. 179.
11. It seems to me that, if anything, this sample probably overstates the frequency of possible "verifications" by this method. To test this method, I chose to focus on traditions attributed to R. Yohanan, one of the most frequently mentioned sages in both the Yerushalmi and Bavli. Other important sages, such as Abbaye and Rava, are frequent spokesmen in one Talmud (the Bavli) but not the other. The thousands of teachings attributed to these sages, among many others, cannot, therefore, be verified in this way.
12. *Judaism in Society* (Chicago: University of Chicago Press, 1983), p. 31.
13. *Stylistic Characteristics of Amoraic Literature*, Ph.D. dissertation, Jewish Theological Seminary of America, 1984.
14. For a fuller discussion of this approach, see "On the Reliability...," pp. 183–7.
15. New York: Oxford U. Press, 1990.
16. One may surely disagree with my particular interpretation of the literary phenomena. Here I am arguing only on behalf of the method.

Part II

Studies in the History of Judaism

INTRODUCTION TO CHAPTER THREE

This piece, one of my earliest, was originally presented as a paper at a conference on the history of the Jewish family held at the Jewish Theological Seminary. It is, in retrospect, an interesting illustration of how to do history "right" according to an earlier paradigm. According to the paradigm that will define my later historical work, it is a flawed beginning.

On the one hand, I ask many of the "right" questions here. I am sensitive to the problems with using such materials to write history, social or otherwise. I begin by defining the nature of rabbinic testimonies and distinguishing between rabbinic imaginations and lived realities. I do not find myself tempted to equate childhood in rabbinic teachings with childhood in the "real world." I am mindful of the rhetoric and prejudices of rabbinic texts as an ethical literature. This must be read, therefore, as an essay on rabbinic attitudes toward children and childhood in antiquity.

On the other hand, though I notice some differences between this rabbinic teaching and that, I do not properly distinguish between rabbinic documents and the contexts in which they originated. This work is topically organized, ignoring completely the chronology of the production of the teachings. I might insist that I do not detect any important differences in attitude between the teachings of one document and another, but the truth is that I did not look for such differences, so this conclusion may be predicted by my approach. If I were now to do a detailed study, I would begin by examining testimonies in their documentary context, document by document. Who knows what conclusions might emerge from such an approach?

All of this being said, in view of the nature of societies in antiquity, I think it more likely that we would find differences of attitude between urban and rural communities or wealthy and impoverished classes than between one relatively homogenous document and another. It would be difficult if not impossible to recover such different attitudes from the sorts of document the rabbis produced. Therefore, whatever the flaws with the method, it seems to me that the conclusions suggested here are likely to be accurate.

Chapter Three

Images of Childhood and Adolescence in Talmudic Literature

The study of the image of children in the literature of the Talmud is an awkward task. When we speak of the study of children, we are interested primarily in the questions posed by psychology and sociology, such as those relating to children's emotional and sexual development, their place in society, and so forth. But psychology and sociology are both modern disciplines, and if the questions that they frame are applied to pre-modern subjects, we are likely to be faced with a great deal of frustration. Where the evidence provided by the ancients is tactile, as in art, dress, or toys, for example, we may simply view the subjects through new lenses. But where the evidence is restricted to the literary record, as is overwhelmingly the case for the society of the rabbis, it is not the whims of history that have determined what has survived, but the minds of people. Under these circumstances the first question we must ask ourselves is why those individuals preserved what they did. They were the ones, after all, who framed the questions that the literature sought to address. Unfortunately, if those questions do not accord with the ones that we are now interested in asking, there is not much that can be done; our new lenses simply cannot view what is not there to see. What we are left to do, then, is to adjust for the prejudices of the ancient authors and to hope that we might, through very careful examination, see what they perhaps did not intend us to see at all.

Of course, this latter problem is precisely the one with which we are faced when we ask modern questions concerning children in the Talmud and related literature. The vocabulary and questions of this literature are those of

Reprinted from *The Jewish Family: Metaphor and Memory*, ed. by David Kraemer. Copyright (c) 1989 by Jewish Theological Seminary of America. Used by Permission of Oxford University Press, Inc.

"Torah," that is, the terms of the literature are overwhelmingly legal, and even when this is not the case, the exclusive intent is to instruct. If children's games or dress or nature are not the concern of the law, then the literature of the Talmud is unlikely to preserve any observation relating to these things. Yes, this literature contains hundreds of references to "minors," but minors are not children. Minors are a legal category—that category of people (in this case, usually Jewish people) who are exempt from observing commandments and who cannot be held responsible for their actions. In contrast to minors are "adults," again a legally significant category. Adults, according to this usage, are individuals obligated to perform the commandments and legally responsible for their actions. The children whom we are concerned with, however, are those who cry and play and grow and develop. About these children we would like to know a great deal. How were they treated by adults, for example? Did adult society during the time of the Talmud recognize a distinct quality in childhood, or were children merely little, not yet legally responsible adults? More important, did ancient Jewish society recognize childhood to be a developmental continuum or did children merely become adults in one fell swoop, say, at age thirteen? These children are the concern of modern scholarly disciplines but these were not generally the children with whom the rabbis were concerned. Their children, as we said, were the children who had to be trained in Torah but were not yet ready to accept its obligations. When asking about that other species of children, then, we have woefully little to work with.

It is for this reason that there is so little modern literature that asks these questions of the traditional literature. I have been able to discover only one book—*The Jewish Child,* by W. M. Feldman (1918)—that speaks of the traditional Jewish attitude toward children at any length.[1] And even there, I might add, the author was forced to pad the book with chapters on such matters as mathematics in the Talmud, presumably because children learned math in school. Despite this, I will make the perhaps foolish attempt to ask the new questions. These questions are primarily those framed in Philippe Ariès's *Centuries of Childhood* (New York, 1962) or in the general psychological literature. I have already alluded to some of them. Ariès points out, for example, that in pre-modern Europe childhood was not recognized as a distinct stage, with its own unique traits. In terms of their dress and games, children were merely little adults. Was the same true in ancient rabbinic society? Relatedly, Ariès comments that formal education usually began relatively late and that when it did begin, there was no difference, for example, between the education of a ten- and a fifteen-year-old. Again, there was no recognition of a developmental continuum. Development is central, of course, to the psychological under-standing of children. Did the rabbis recognize such development? Were they sensitive to the cognitive and sexual development of children? Central, too, to the psychological description of childhood are certain crucial periods of sexuality. Did the rabbis admit such periods of childhood sexual development, and did they recognize childhood sexuality at all? It may be impossible, of course, to offer definitive answers to these questions based on the evidence of the talmudic literature, but we will discover that very definite directions can be suggested.

Before attempting to examine the evidence, however, I must first define what I mean by *childhood*. If I were defining this inquiry as a talmudist, I might be tempted to conclude childhood at age thirteen. At that time, after all, the child becomes a bar mitzvah, commonly understood to be "a man." But were I to do this, I would be defining the scope of my questioning by the ancient answers. Here I would fall into the very trap that I warned against previously. Instead, for purposes of questioning, I will consider childhood anything that comes before adulthood, and I will only consider someone an adult who has attained the age of marriage and family responsibility. It is at this point that people generally establish their own homes, and it is only then that they can be spoken of as being adults in an adult society. This definition is useful for two reasons. First, it enables us to consider the full developmental continuum if there is one. Second, it offers us the opportunity to see whether or not the talmudic literature admitted an adolescence—a period crucial to the discussions of psychology. In this way, I hope, we can ask the questions that we define and not those defined by the rabbis.

As is to be expected, rabbinic literature has very little to say about childhood beyond the legal definition. The one general evaluation of childhood as a period speaks of it as a "garland of roses," apparently a reference to its ease and comfort because it is contrasted in the same context with the "thorns of old age" (b. Shabbat 152a). Elsewhere children are spoken of as being frivolous and irresponsible. They are thought to be easily tempted by gifts and money, for example (b. B.B. 156a), and there is a general desire to restrict their involvement in monetary transactions though exceptions are made in certain circumstances (see b. Gittin 59a). In another context, children are compared to the evil inclination and to women; that is, they are to be "pushed away with the left hand and drawn close with the right" (b. Sanhedrin 107b). Presumably this ambiguous tension is due to their lack of seriousness, a bad influence for responsible adults (see Rashi, ad loc.).

This latter comment necessitates a consideration of the sexuality of children. The parallel between children, on the one hand, and "the evil inclination" (i.e., the sexual urge) and women, on the other, is surely more than coincidental. The rabbis were apparently aware of the sexuality of children, at least in later childhood. R. Nachman b. Isaac reports that a decree had been issued declaring that non-Jewish children should be considered ritually impure to a severe degree. The purpose of this decree was to help ensure that Jewish children would not engage in sexual experimentation with non-Jews. At what age, it is asked, does this decree take effect? R. Judah the Prince is reported as concluding that for a boy it begins at age nine, and Ravina (or R. Johanan) adds that for a girl it begins at age three, each of these being the age at which sexual intercourse is considered to be legally significant (b. A.Z. 36b–37a, b. Shabbat 17b). Elsewhere the Mishnah comments that a man may sleep naked in the same bed as his daughter until she grows up (either age nine or twelve, according to two views in the Gemara), seemingly oblivious of the sexual awareness of a young girl. But R. Ḥisda limits the permission granted by this Mishnah to a girl who is not embarrassed to stand naked in front of her father. If she is conscious of her sexuality, however, then the leniency of the Mishnah cannot be granted (Kiddushin, Mishnah 4:12 and Gemara 81b). Sexuality is a recognized part of talmudic childhood, then, if only in limited scope. The age at which it becomes emotionally significant is undefined; we know only the age of legally significant sexuality. Still, we know that a girl might become sexually aware prior to age nine, according to the view of R. Ḥisda, and this is certainly long before actual sexual maturity.

Important, too, is the tone of these expressions concerning the sexuality of children. In none of these instances is their sexuality spoken of as being evil or tempting. Concern is expressed for the daughter's sensitivities, not for the father's temptation. Separation from non-Jewish children is declared on the basis of homosexual coupling—a transgression of which idolators are frequently accused—and not for fear of sex as such. Even in the first instance, where children are spoken of in the same breath as the evil inclination, it is not clear that this is the reason children are to be avoided. Rashi makes the not untenable suggestion that the concern is merely for frivolity. But even if sex is the concern, the fear of it is not decisive. We must recognize, after all, that while pushing away with the left hand, we are to draw the child close with the right. The right hand, we must recall, was always considered to be the stronger of the two.

Moreover, this evaluation of a neutral attitude toward sexuality is confirmed by another tradition that speaks of childhood. At b. Sanhedrin 110b the following question is posed: "At what point does a child [begin to merit] enter[ing] into the world to come?" A number of suggestions are offered, ranging from conception to the beginning of speech to birth in between. But nowhere is there thought of a child's sin; nowhere is there original sin. Sexuality, though present, need not be atoned for. Only on reaching legal majority can a person be held liable for the misuse of his or her sexuality.

Naturally, the most effort is expended in rabbinic literature discussing the education of children.[2] Avot (5:21)[3] reports that five is the appropriate age to begin training in Scripture, and ten the age for the study of Mishnah. In somewhat different fashion, Rav reports that general education began at age six or seven (b. B.B. 21a). Regardless of the actual age, it should be noted that children were often spoken of as "reciting their verses" (see, e.g., b. Hagigah 15a and parallels). This, apparently, was what children were commonly found to be doing.

Talmudic literature also reflects extreme sensitivity to informal education and to the pedagogical necessities of the education of children. R. Isaac reports a directive to parents to educate their children with patience and sensitivity (b. Ketubot 40a). Similarly, Rav declares that discipline should not be harsh (b. B.B. 21a). With respect to the way children learn, R. Zeira warns that a person should not promise to give a child something and then fail to do so because this will teach the child, too, to be a liar (b. Sukkah 46b). Above all, education should begin early, and repetition and example are its very foundations (b. Sukkah 42a).

Perhaps the most crucial feature of these texts that relate to education is their clear awareness of childhood as a developmental period. Learning at first begins informally, and it requires a special sensitivity. When a child begins speaking, he is encouraged to begin slowly the cognitive task of childhood—memorization of Scripture. This task admits the limitations of the child's intellect—at age five (or six or seven) he begins merely to memorize; understanding will come later. Gradual development is assumed throughout, not uniformity and not immobility. Furthermore, the recognition of this process is not limited to education. It extends from intellectual development to sexuality and from a child's earliest years to his more advanced. Permit me to illustrate.

Midrash Kohelet Rabbah 1 (2) records a lengthy description of the stages of human development, a description that we will have occasion to refer to again later. With respect to a child's earliest years, the midrash[4] describes that "at a year old [a child] is like a king seated in a canopied litter, fondled and kissed by all. At two and three he is like a pig, sticking his hands in the gutters." This is, of course, a child whom we would all recognize. At the other end of the spectrum, the Mishnah itself speaks of the couple of years before puberty as a period of significantly improved intellectual comprehension and, therefore, recognizes that oaths taken at this time are at least potentially valid (m. Niddah 5:6). In the same connection, this is also the time when a child is to begin fasting on Yom Kippur (m. Yoma 8:4).

If, on the basis of these sources, we were now to draw a map of childhood, it would look something like this: At one, a child is a king, that is, spoiled and the center of attention; at two and three, he is dirty by virtue of play; at five through seven, he begins his elementary education; at the same point he is considered to be intelligent enough to sell chattels (though this legal concession was only to ensure that he would be able to purchase food if necessary; see b. Gittin 5a). Before age nine the child might become aware of his or her sexuality; at nine, sex for a male becomes a legally significant event; at ten, eleven, or twelve, the child will experience significant cognitive development—and the girl probably before the boy; and finally, at approximately age twelve or thirteen, the girl and then the boy will arrive at puberty. Though we might have focused on different details of some of these stages, still it is the general picture that is significant, not the details. Childhood, we see here, quite clearly, is considered in rabbinic literature to be a period of evolution. It is a process of development that begins in the earliest years and apparently never ceases. Quite unlike the world that Ariès describes, the child in talmudic society was not described merely in adult terms or as the negation of adulthood. Rather, the child demands special sensitivities and considerations, and these change as the child approaches closer and closer to adulthood.

Sexual adulthood, these texts report, is expected to come at around the twelfth or the thirteenth year. Is that the end of childhood, in the rabbinic mind, or is it something else? Is there any recognition of development beyond the bar mitzvah?

What, then, does age thirteen represent, and what does it mean to be a *gadol,* an adult? It has commonly been assumed that at thirteen a child becomes an adult in the literal sense of the word. For this reason the book by Feldman, mentioned earlier, concludes its deliberations at this age. Thereafter a person is an adult and so should not be spoken of in a book on children. This wisdom must be challenged, however, for the evidence does not support this view.

But first it is necessary to say a few words on the nature of boundaries in talmudic literature. The Mishnah and that literature that follows in its path are literally casuistic. This means that, with rare exception, general rules are not stated, but rather specific cases are formed to illustrate those rules. There is no need, however, for such cases ever to have occurred. *Casuistic,* in this context, also does not mean case law; and, in fact, to illustrate certain general rules, it was necessary to formulate cases that could probably never occur.[5] Mishnah should not be considered case evidence, therefore, but conceptual expression. This, of course, affects our whole understanding of the literature.

When stating boundaries, then—as legal systems frequently must do—this literature will have to compose cases that embody the boundaries. Cases are often chosen, therefore, not because they are common, but precisely because they are uncommon! They illustrate not the case that falls at the center of the bell curve but the far less common one that falls at its edge—that is, the one that defines the limit. Consequently, when the Mishnah speaks of a three-year-old girl as having sex, this is not because such a thing happened frequently, or even that it happened at all (though, unfortunately, it may have), but simply because that is where the system defines the boundary for legally-significant sex for a female.

The same must be understood to be the case with respect to the "age thirteen" boundary. Why thirteen was chosen as the boundary is obviously connected with puberty. For some reason the rabbis believed that this was the point that legal responsibility should begin. But this did not mean, as the common wisdom suggests, that they considered thirteen-year-olds to be adults. At most it means that they were viewed as being at the edge of adulthood for certain purposes. But there is far more to consider before we can understand what this means.

The Bible, of course, knows nothing of age thirteen as a boundary. There the age of significant transition is twenty (see, e.g., Exod. 30:14). This was the age at which the census began and the age at which an individual was obligated to participate in military formations (see Num. 1:18 ff.). Though not widely recognized, twenty was also an extremely significant age for the rabbis, a fact that is crucial to our question, When does a child become an adult?

First, to adduce the evidence.[6] The opinion of R. Huna, Rava, and the Tanna of the School of R. Ishmael is well known: If one passes age twenty without taking a wife, he is tantamount to being a sinner (b. Kiddushin 29b). Whether twenty was the last point at which a man should marry, as suggested here, or whether it was merely the point to begin seriously seeking a mate, as we shall consider later on the basis of other sources, it is clear that twenty represents a significant transition with respect to marriage. The same point, perhaps surprisingly, may be crucial to a woman. R. Hisda observes that if a woman marries by age twenty, then her fertility will be long-lived. If she marries after this point, however, her fertility will diminish accordingly (b. B.B. 119b). The same age is crucial in ritual areas. A baraita at Hullin 24b suggests in the name of Rabbi [Judah the Patriarch] that one should not be appointed *shaliah tsibbur* (representative of the congregation in prayer) or perform the priestly blessing unless he is twenty (cf. y. Sukkah chap. 3, end, and Soferim 14:13, Higger, p. 267). According to a prevalent opinion, twenty is the age at which a person may legally begin selling property he inherited from his deceased father (b. B.B. 155b–156a). It is also the age at which the law generally despairs of one developing signs of sexual maturity (b. Yevamot 80a).

Neither is twenty ignored by the longer lists that evaluate the stages of human development. Avot 5:21 considers twenty the age "to pursue." Whether this is the age to begin earning a living, as some commentaries suggest, or the age to begin army service, or even the age of divine accountability, is unimportant. What is important is that twenty is again a point of significant transition. Incidentally, the suggestion that twenty is an age with divine significance is based on a midrash at b. Shabbat 89b, where it is made clear that, though thirteen may be the age for human accountability, for the court in heaven responsibility begins at age twenty. The list at Kohelet Rabba 1 (2) also notices age twenty, saying that at that point a man "is like a neighing horse, adorning himself and seeking a wife." Significantly, in this latter list twenty appears in a far more select grouping, and it is chosen even in the absence of any mention of age thirteen. We will return to this point later.

Undisputably, then, twenty is a significant age according to a wide selection of rabbinic texts. Why is it significant? The answer seems to be connected to marriage. Several of the texts allude to marriage very strongly, and sometimes even when no such allusion is obvious, the connection to marriage is still the likely one.[7] Kiddushin believes twenty to be the last point at which a man should marry. Avot supports this connection as well, saying that eighteen is the age for huppah and twenty the age for pursuit.

However, the possibility must be considered that twenty was not the last point for marriage, but perhaps the age at which finding a mate should be taken that much more seriously. Midrash Lekach Tov (to Kohelet 1:2) speaks of the "pursuit" of age twenty as the pursuit of a wife. This midrash is parallel to the one from Kohelet Rabba, already quoted, where twenty is the age when a man begins seeking a wife "like a neighing horse." This is the age when urgency begins, not ends. Even in the text at b. Kiddushin 29b–30a, where age twenty for marriage is stated so forcefully, the several years after that seem not yet to be considered full adulthood. There Rava claims that a man has some opportunity for ethical persuasion of his son because he still has some control over him until age twenty-two or, according to another version, until age twenty-four. These ages are supported by an earlier rabbinic text quoted in that context in which the extent of the meaning of the word youth is debated, and again the two possible end-points that are considered are twenty-two or twenty-four.

It is perhaps not difficult to understand the apparent contradiction between these texts. Avot and the context in b. Kiddushin, which speaks of twenty as the very latest one should marry are both speaking as teachers of religious ethics. This, we know, is the general intent of Avot. In b. Kiddushin, too, this is quite clear—the immediate argument there ends with R. Hisda's praise of himself for having married at age sixteen and his addition that fourteen would have been even better, having afforded him the opportunity to spit in the eye of Satan. The point, obviously, is that early marriage will ensure that one avoids sexual temptation. This is an ethical teaching though, not a statement of reality. Though these texts might be stating the ideal, the others mentioned earlier are probably recording what was true in actuality. The rabbis may have felt it to be best that a man should marry by age twenty. However, those texts that merely observe the way things are likely to happen apparently believe that marriage might wait several years after that.[8]

At approximately age twenty, then, Jewish men married, began to have families, and began to make a living on their own. This was also the point that they could expect to have achieved full physical maturity. In the fullest sense, then, this is the first point at which they can be spoken of as being fully adults. If they were adults only at age twenty, then what were they in the teenage years? Are those the years of an adolescence, in any sense, or are they merely years of undefined transition?[9]

The best-known statement regarding adolescence is perhaps the tradition in Avot (5:21) that "fifteen [is the appropriate age] for Talmud." "Talmud," in Mishnaic parlance, meant sophisticated deliberation and questioning, and so this should be understood as an evaluation of the intellectual development of adolescents; that is, at fifteen they are able to handle, for the first time, the subtleties of sophisticated reasoning.[10] This is not the only text, however, that connects education to the middle teens. At B.B. 21a, Rav repeats a legend concerning the founding of public education in Israel. Most curiously, we are told that the first unsuccessful attempt at doing so involved the gathering of sixteen- and seventeen-year-olds (!) for primary education. The obvious question here is, why, in constructing such a legend, should its authors have chosen this age for demonstrating the way things should not be done? The failure of this attempt is connected with the rebelliousness of children at this age; that is, if you are going to wait until this point to begin education, there is no way you are going to succeed, considering the natural "independent spirit" of teenagers. This text is particularly instructive in two ways: first, the middle teens are not considered inappropriate for education as such.[11] In fact, in the mind of the legendary educational pioneer, this is a natural and necessary point to speak of education. Surely, if teenagers were already involved in marriage and making a living, this thought would be absurd. Rather, the teens are appropriate for education so long as that is not the time education first begins. Second, the text recognizes the independent, rebellious spirit of teenagers and admits that if they have not been socialized earlier, this point is entirely too late. Furthermore, the text later speaks of the beneficial effects of peer pressure, and though the immediate reference is to younger children, connecting peer pressure to unsuccessful educational attempts makes it clear that the same advice would apply to rebellious teenagers. Undoubtedly, this description of the adolescent is one that we all recognize.

In that the sources recognize these years as a time for continuing education, it is not surprising to find that they comment on the form that education should take. R. Isaac reports a decree of the rabbinical academy at Usha which says that stricter and more emphatic discipline is required after age twelve (b. Ketubot 50a and see Rashi). The same text to which we referred at b. Kiddushin 30a speaks of the later teen years as the appropriate time for a certain moral education because the parent still has some influence over the child. This latter point is crucial for what it again suggests, that is, that even older teenagers are not yet independent of their parents. If the development of a full sense of autonomy is one of the central tasks of adolescence, as these texts readily admit (in the references to seeking marriage), then the fact that it has not yet been successfully accomplished supports our suspicion that this is, in fact, an adolescence.

In this connection, the rabbis were fully cognizant of the fact that responsibility for one's own property and family helped to define adulthood and that adolescents, therefore, could not be considered fully adults. That responsibility for children was a crucial factor is demonstrated by the statement of R. Yohanan at b. Yevamot 47a. This is one of several occasions on which the rabbis of the Gemara have a hard time accepting the literal meaning of *katan* (minor) or *gadol* (adult). In this particular text, R. Yohanan claims that an adult without children is termed a minor. Because adolescents were not yet married and, therefore, did not yet have children, his definition is certain to include at least the teenage years. At another point (b. B.M. 12a–b) R. Yohanan says that a "minor" is a legal adult who is still dependent on his parents. Here adulthood is understood to require material independence, and as teenagers were still dependent on their parents, these years cannot yet be considered adulthood. The Gemara at b. Ketubot 18a supports this evaluation by reporting that, with respect to his father's things, an "adult" is still called a minor.

Further information concerning these years can be discovered by referring again to the texts that speak of age twenty and by asking what they thought the case was before that age was reached. Of course, the traditions that connected twenty to marriage knew teenagers to be single. Those who considered a twenty-year-old man to be "full-bearded" (the texts on ritual performance) knew that, prior to this, a boy might still be developing physically. Finally, the tradition that limited property sale, when possible, to a child aged twenty, obviously thought that prior to this a child could not be considered able to handle such sales responsibly. There, in fact, the text says explicitly that teens are likely to be seduced by the offer of money and do not understand, therefore, the responsibility that they are undertaking.

In sum, rabbinic teenagers bear certain very distinct features in common with our own. In practical terms, they are still maturing physically. They are of independent spirit but often irresponsible. In a literal sense, they are generally still dependent on their parents. Their intellects, though now first capable of adult sophistication, are not yet fully accomplished. This is reflected in the importance of advanced education but is complicated by the recognized adolescent propensity for rebelliousness. They are not only subject to peer pressure, but they are also believed still to be subject to parental influence. This latter influence, however, is tenuous, and there is a recognition both that the time to apply it is limited and that certain modes of discipline are necessary for it to be effective.

There is little doubt, then, that rabbinic society recognized an adolescence and that full adulthood was a stage beyond this. It was a period about which we know very little, to be sure, but what we do know supports a picture that has many features in common with modern adolescence. In terms of independence or lack thereof, in terms of intellectual development, in terms of increased but unfulfilled sexuality—in all of these ways, at least, teens in rabbinic society were very much like our own teens. There can be no question, of course, that there were also significant differences, but to establish the differences was never the challenge. Our task, rather, was to determine whether or not there was a recognized developmental stage between puberty and adulthood. What we have discovered is that there was.

Should any question remain concerning this conclusion, more complete reference to the midrash from Kohelet Rabba should help to dispel it. The text there reads as follows:

> R. Samuel b. Isaac taught in the name of R. Samuel b. Elazar: The seven "vanities" mentioned in Kohelet correspond to the seven worlds that a man beholds. At age one he is like a king, seated in a litter while all hug and kiss him. At two and three he is like a pig, sticking his hands in the gutters. At ten he skips like a kid. At twenty he is like a neighing horse, adorning himself and seeking a wife. Having married, he is like an ass [that is, a beast of burden]. When he has had children he becomes brazen like a dog, in order to bring in bread and food...

Clearly, when choosing seven crucial periods of human development, the author of this tradition had to be quite selective. It is instructive, then, that, in making his choice, he saw ten and twenty as crucial points and ignored thirteen. The same is not the case in our other list, at Avot 5:21. We probably would have expected the choice in Avot, and we should be equally surprised at the selection of Kohelet Rabba. By what criterion did he make this selection?

The list in Kohelet Rabba seems to be determined by one's mundane condition, not by the sublime. At one, a baby is dependent and spoiled. A young child is playful but dirty. At ten, a child is energetic and even wild. He wanders off on his own, in his grown-up play, running where his heart desires. The next crucial change comes when he marries and beings to support the responsibilities of a family. How is this? During his teen years he continues to play, and continues to avoid responsibilities. Puberty may bring increased sexual awareness, but in rabbinic society there was no way to act on it. Therefore the irresponsibility of the early teens continued to marriage. Since in rabbinic times the many ritual functions that are now connected with bar mitzvah were not yet associated with it—fringes and *tefillin* were donned earlier, and serving as *shaliah tsibbur* should ideally have waited to much later (as we saw, age twenty)—thirteen was not as momentous, in an obvious way, as it has now become. For them, rather, the teens were understood as a unit, and only with the approach of marriage did an individual once again experience radical change.[12]

What we have discovered, then, is that the childhood known to the rabbis was a developmental continuum. Children were not merely little adults but individuals with their own preferences and capabilities. When young, they played and became dirty. Somewhat later, they began their education, but an education that was carefully attuned to each cognitive stage. Sexual awareness was admitted during childhood though such awareness, of course, became more acute at puberty. At that time, too, tremendous strides were known to have been taken in cognition.

Furthermore, adulthood did not begin at puberty. As we have seen, there was a transition between child and adult, a transition that we can properly term adolescence. This was a period of both sophistication and irresponsibility and also one generally without sexual fulfillment. Adulthood proper began with marriage and family, usually around age twenty.

All this is not to say that rabbinic childhood was identical to ours. But, like our society, theirs also knew of a developmental spectrum from infancy to adulthood, and each stage was viewed in accordance with its capabilities and limitations. This is rather unlike the pre-modern Europe described by Ariès, and our conclusions, therefore, should serve as a caution to those who blithely distinguish between the modern world and what preceded it; development is not linear. The ancient world was equally as diverse as the modern.

NOTES

1. Solomon Schechter wrote an article entitled "The Child in Jewish Literature," which appeared in the *Jewish Quarterly Review* (original series) 2 (1890),1–24. Schechter combines legal and non-legal sources in an undiscerning way and includes texts and ceremonies from all periods of Jewish history. Nonetheless, his work is a valuable introduction to this subject, and he adds several important sources to those I cite later.

2. Of course, the rabbis were often generally concerned with males and not females. This is true in their discussions of children as well. Much of the evidence is limited, therefore, to male children, and it would be foolish to use "nonsexist" language in this context. Here *nonsexist* would simply be non-correct.

3. Avot 5:21 is a later addition to the Mishnah and not part of the original Mishnaic tractate; See J. N. Epstein, *Mavo lenusach ha-mishnah* (Jerusalem, 1948), p. 978. It is, therefore, incorrect to attribute this tradition to Judah b. Tema, whose name precedes it. For convenience I will merely refer to it as Avot.

4. It is impossible to know even the assumed author of this tradition; the several parallels (Yalkut Shimoni and Midrash Lekach Tov, both on the same verse from Kohelet) are inconsistent in their attribution.

5. For example, a Baraita quoted at b. Niddah 54a teaches that "if a woman bleeds one day and does not bleed one day [in repeating fashion] then she may have sex on the eighth day and its eve, and then four days out of the eleven… if she bleeds two days and then does not bleed two days, then she may have sex on the eighth day and the twelfth and the sixteenth and the twentieth… if she bleeds three days…" and so on—all the way up to eight days of bleeding and eight days not. Obviously, this text is not considering cases that actually occurred. It is not the least bit concerned whether such combinations are possible. Rather, it is attempting to demonstrate the full implications of the cycle of a woman's seven-day period followed by the eleven-day intervening period. This is a theoretical text, not a case study, and it shares this feature with almost all texts of the same genre.

6. Louis Ginzberg supports our evaluation of twenty as being the age of majority; see his book *An Unknown Jewish Sect* (New York, 1976), pp. 45–46. With respect to punishment in the heavenly court, for which we cite b. Shabbat 89b (see later), Ginzberg adds y. Bikkurim II, 64c and y. Sanhedrin XI, 30b. He also makes reference to Jubilees (49:17) and Karaite sources in support of the importance of age twenty. I believe that Ginzberg's conclusion that twenty is a vestige of some "old halakha" does not accurately represent the full picture. I argue later that twenty is a contemporary fact in rabbinic society and that though thirteen may be the halakhic definition of majority, it is a definition that needs to be understood in limited terms. Twenty is an important point of transition of far more than vestigial interest.

7. As in the texts that limit the performance of communal ritual duties to age twenty. In order to be a proper representative of the community it was thought best that a man have the responsibility and accompanying sobriety of a wife and family. The reason may simply be, however, that at that point one had the appearance of maturity owing to a full beard.

8. The parallel of classical Greece is informative in this regard, and may support our conclusion. In Athens, the normal age for a man to marry was thirty, for a woman it ranged from sixteen to nineteen, though because of concern for virginity some girls may have married at fourteen. Plato speaks of twenty-five to thirty-five as the age at which men should marry. Notably, the statement that women should marry very early seems to have been a moral instruction owing to "the Greeks' fanatical emphasis on premarital virginity." The

evidence does not support that it was universally upheld, however. Plutarch states that the recommended age is too young and says that Spartan girls waited until they were somewhat older. In addition, the record of Greek visual art seems to admit that girls were not married as early as the literature would have liked. Of course, rabbinic society was also "fanatical" for virginity, and so the same dichotomy of ideal and reality is not unexpected. For the Greek materials, see W. K. Lacey, *The Family in Classical Greece* (Ithaca, N.Y., 1968), pp. 106–7, 162, 179, and illus. 35.

9. I am preceded in asking this question by Norman Linzer of the Wurzweiler School of Social Work. See his book *The Jewish Family, Authority and Tradition in Modern Perspective* (New York, 1984), pp. 119–54. His reference to the psychological material is quite extensive, and for this connection I direct the reader to his work. His examination of the rabbinic sources, on the other hand, is far less complete than that found here.

10. Of course, this corresponds precisely to the observations of modern cognitive sciences. Adolescence is known to be the first point at which a person is able to construct contrary-to-fact propositions; see D. Elkind, *Children and Adolescents* (New York, 1974), pp. 102–3. It is also the first time that an individual is able to subordinate "the real to the realm of the possible and... link... all possibilities to one another by necessary implications..."; see P. N. Johnson-Laird and P. C. Wason, eds., *Thinking: Readings in Cognitive Science* (New York, 1977), p. 159. Perhaps no better description for the process of *talmud* could be found!

11. Education during this period is supported by the Greeks as well. According to the Gortyn Code, boys aged twelve to sixteen were known as "youths," and it was during this period that they learned writing, basic laws, and "certain forms of music." School scenes on Greek pottery also suggest that this age was a time when youths were educated. See Lacey, *The Family, p.* 211, and illus. 32–33.

12. Though I have attempted to avoid legal definitions, comparison with Roman law and its identification of developmental stages is instructive. In Roman law, puberty was assumed to occur at twelve for a female and fourteen for a male. Before this one was an *impubes,* and only beginning at this point did one become a minor. Legal minority then lasted until age twenty-five. See Adolf Berger, "impubes," in the *Encyclopedic Dictionary of Roman Law* (Philadelphia, 1953), p. 495. Boaz Cohen adds that, before age seven, one was considered an *infans* under Roman law; Cohen also points out that occasional exceptions to the age of majority were found, with a lower limit of age eighteen. See B. Cohen, *Jewish and Roman Law* (New York, 1966), II, Hebrew section, 1–9. These parallels establish that puberty was not identical with adulthood in the classical world and that a variety of developmental stages between early childhood and the early twenties was recognized.

INTRODUCTION TO CHAPTER FOUR

In 1994, I was invited to participate in a conference organized by the Centre for Studies in Religion and Society at the University of Victoria. The conference, celebrating the UN Convention on the Rights of the Child, was dedicated to the theme "Stronger Children—Stronger Families," and a volume entitled *Religious Dimensions of Child and Family Life* was the immediate product of that conference. The following paper on "Child and Family in Judaism" is one of several dedicated to "Child and Family in such-and-such religious tradition" included in that volume.

My interest in this topic began with my work preparing *The Jewish Family: Metaphor and Memory*. As I said in my introduction to the previous essay, my own contribution to that book, on "the child" in rabbinic literature, proceeds according to conventional methods of doing history. The present essay, though more recent, offers no refinement on that earlier work. Instead, I here bring together representative scholarship of others, some taken from my edited volume and some drawn from elsewhere, to paint a broad picture of the Jewish family through history.

The simple point of this essay, which seems to me unimpeachable as a general observation, is that Jewish families have always reflected profoundly the mores and customs of their host cultures. Or, to put it in rhetorically more provocative terms, Abraham's "Jewish" family looked more like the family of his non-Jewish neighbor, Maimonides' more like the family of his non-Jewish neighbor, and mine more like my non-Jewish neighbor, than each of our Jewish families looks like the other. On the basis of this simple historical observation, I draw certain conclusions concerning "family values" in Judaism through the centuries.

Chapter Four

Children and Family Life in Jewish Tradition

The story of the Jewish People begins with a family. According to the biblical account, this family, the family of Abraham and Sarah, would have only two children, and only one of these would be the carrier of God's covenantal promise. But the small size of this family would make little difference, for, by virtue of this story of origin, the nature of this people's identity was already and forever established—the offspring of Abraham, through Isaac and then Jacob, were a family, collectively designated "the children of Israel (=Jacob)."

These "children of Israel" could never forget the centrality of family and children to their collective mission. The story of Abraham and his God is first and foremost a story about the miraculous generation of children. For years, Abram and Sarai lived together without children. God promised Abram a covenant through his children and miraculously brought him a child, Ishmael, in his old age. But this child would not carry the covenant into the next generation. Instead, Sarah (now so renamed) would bear the promised child—long after menopause, following a full life of barrenness. But this new child, Isaac, was destined to lie on the sacrificial altar, threatening the covenant and the future people with the possibility of "still-birth." Barrenness and fruitfulness, survival of children or their extinction—these were the paired symbols on which the people's identity was founded.

The relationship between this people who imagined themselves a family and the individual families which constituted this people would be a complex one. To begin with, if "family" was to be the operative metaphor for this people's identity, then "family" needed to be conceived as extended and flexible. No people-as-family could be "nuclear" in any sense of the word; to accom-modate the shifting size and nature of a people's population, the "family" which gave it definition needed to be as adaptable as the people it defined.

Indeed, this is precisely what Jewish history would confirm.[1] As in other cultures, when biblical culture spoke of "family," it meant a group larger than we mean—what we would call a clan. The Bible does speak of "the father's household," meaning something like our "family," but this institution is hardly central to biblical definitions of the desired society. The Bible's family is extended, a people within a people.

The Bible's family is also various and flexible. Of biblical families we know, some have few children, some have many. Some are characterized by monogamy, some by multiple wives, and some by a combination of wives and "handmaidens." In some cases, Israelite men marry Israelite women, in others they marry foreigners. Pre-exilic families are different from post-exilic families, and no final definition of the preferred family and its qualities is ever suggested. Biblical families were as other families around them, at least as far as we can tell. As would be true through all of history, "Jewish" families of the Bible looked far more like those of their neighbors than like Jewish families in other places and ages.

But this flexibility, this lack of precise definition, in no way diminished the centrality of the family in Jewish self-conceptions nor the centrality of children as the building-blocks of the family. However it looked, and however large it might be, the family was the basic unit of this people who was a family—and would always be.

In part, the centrality of the family in Judaism was a consequence of what Jewish tradition took to be the Torah's first command: "Be fruitful and multiply" (Genesis 1:28). Understood not as a blessing but, as we said, a command, Jewish men (at least) saw themselves fulfilling a religious obligation when they had sex with their wives and produced children. With children, alone, could the world be filled. Through children, alone, could the teachings of the family of Abraham be passed on.

The obligation to assure this "passing on" was unmistakably codified in the Torah's teachings—particularly in Deuteronomy—and reference to the duty to "teach one's children" came to be recited by Jewish men (at least) every evening and morning. The fundamental words of Jewish faith ("Hear, O Israel...") were the first words of Torah a Jewish child would learn (=memorize), and this would soon be followed by his adoption of other practices, required by the same biblical paragraph (Deuteronomy 6:4–9), which reminded a Jew of his identity (again, we are forced to admit, these practices were restricted to males). At a very young age, he would begin to wear the ritual fringes on the corners of his garments. As soon as he could maintain his personal cleanliness, he would wear the leather straps (*tefillin*) around his arm and head (for these practices, see Bavli Sukkah 42a).

Unmistakably, then, children were central to the Torah's concerns and the (extended) family to its system of values. But we should be careful before drawing too much from these observations. Many of the biblical narratives which portray families and their activities simply convey the reality which the authors view in the world around them. There is no evidence that they consciously prefer this reality to another; they simply seem to know little of other possible realities. In the same fashion, the legal portions which require the training of one's children are primarily concerned with the transmission of the tradition. *Obviously* children are required for such transmission to take place, but these laws say nothing about the value of children as such. Nor do they tell us how many children we should have, what other obligations we might have to them, and so forth. On the other side, the Torah is similarly terse and ambiguous concerning a child's obligations to his or her parents. True, the Torah does demand that children honor and fear their parents, but never, in the Bible at least, is such honor and fear defined.

Perhaps for lack of earlier definition, it fell to the rabbis of the late first century and beyond to begin "codifying" the family and expressing values which had earlier gone unexpressed or had not been held at all. These rabbis required, for example, that a man have at least two children (Mishnah Yevamot 6:6). They defined "honor" as basic physical and material support, and "fear" as conducting oneself according to standards of strict hierarchy—not to sit in your father's regular seat, nor stand in his regular place, nor contradict him, nor (even) support his opinion (He is your father! Why should he require *your* support?) (see Talmud Bavli, tractate Qiddushin 31b).

They required a man to take a wife, and they spoke of marriage in the most enthusiastic terms. According to rabbinic teachings, a man who takes a wife finds peace, blessing, protection and more (see Bavli Yevamot 62b). A man who remains without a wife is not a man. But, despite their sometimes hyperbolic praise of marriage, these and similar traditions should not be construed as praising the unique and special relationship between a husband and a single, special wife. Ancient Jewish tradition, biblical and rabbinic, always accepted polygyny.

In fact, it is here, in the relationship of husband and wife, where we might most easily see the distance between contemporary "family values" and traditional Jewish values relating to the family. A single, brief reference will make the point. The Talmud relates that

> Rav, when he went to Dardashir, would declare: "Who will be mine for the day?" And R. Nachman, when he went to Shekhunzib, would declare: "Who will be mine for the day?" (Bavli Yevamot 37b)

What we see here is reference to the ancient Jewish equivalent of the *muta*, or "pleasure," marriage of Islam, an institution known also in ancient Persia—the world where these rabbis lived. These short-term marriages were generally contracted when a man traveled away from home. The agreement involved the exchange of a small sum of money, but no further commitment. Children who might result from the marriage were apparently not the father's responsibility. What distinguished this institution from prostitution was merely the way it was designated (it was contracted as a "marriage"); from the modern perspective, there is surely little difference between the two.

Whatever our objections to such "marriages," there is no legal reason for them to have been prohibited. In a polygynous society, a man's possessing (not an inappropriate term) one wife did not prevent him from taking another—for whatever period of time. But, beyond the legality of such a practice, what is notable for our purpose is what the reality of such relationships reveals concerning ancient Jewish values of wife and family. Clearly, if a man took a second or third wife, this was not understood to diminish the dignity (the "image-of-God"-ness) of his first wife. Neither were the rabbis concerned that the temporary marriage might do the same to the women with whom a man entered into such a relationship. A woman's "personhood" was obviously not of concern here. If anything, a man's pleasure was the highest priority.

Nor were such attitudes and values restricted to the ancient Babylonian Jewish world (though the actual institution of temporary, short-term marriages may have been). The documents discovered in the Cairo Geniza, a repository of religious documents of the North African Jewish community from approximately the ninth to the twelfth century, show that polygyny was far more common in those centuries than has been recognized. Moreover, many men apparently took "handmaidens" for their pleasure, whom they would support and, on some occasions, even set up in apartments. Typically, these "hand-maidens" would be kept in nearby cities where men did their business. Their wives and children stayed behind in what might be described as their "official" homes.[2]

I must emphasize: the point of mentioning these details is not to recover the blemishes of earlier Jewish societies. It is simply to illustrate what Jewish family values were, and what these values sometimes permitted or led to. I think it is safe to say that these are not values which would be approved by most modern societies. They surely would not be approved by contemporary Jewish societies—religious or non-religious. Nor have they been approved by European Jewish societies, at least, for centuries. But—and this is the crucial point—they are *not* contrary to what might be called "Torah-values," and the fact that they are no longer approved has more to do with the influences of the host-cultures in which Jews have made their homes than with any natural Jewish moral intuition (more on this later).

Much the same may be said regarding Jewish family values which relate to children. In the earliest rabbinic record available to us, the Mishnah declares:

> A father is not obligated to feed his daughter... Just as sons do not inherit until after the death of their father, so too daughters are not fed until the death of their father. (Mishnah Ketubot 4:6)

Elsewhere, the Talmud expands this ruling to apply to sons as well. In its words: "A man is not obligated to feed his sons and daughters when they are minors."

Before seeking to make sense of these laws, it should quickly be added that the Talmud immediately restricts their extent. First of all, the absence of a parent's obligation is said to apply to minors but not to "small minors," defined as children up to their sixth birthday. Before that time there *is* an obligation. Only subsequently does the law refuse to require a parent's (or, to be more precise, a father's) support. Moreover, though there may be no *bona fide* obligation after this age, the Talmud insists that there is a strong moral duty (it is a *mitzvah*). The Talmud even reports that the community and its leaders were willing to bring the full weight of community pressure to "encourage" unwilling parents to support their children. Finally, though there may be no actual obligation, wealthier parents may be forced to support their children as an act of "tzedakah" (charity). Since tzedakah is a tax in the traditional Jewish community, enforceable by law, this meant that the community authorities could, in limited circumstances, force parents to support their children when the "official" law no longer required it (for all of above, see Bavli Ketubot 49a–b).

Not denying the fact that subsequent authorities took steps to improve the situation, we still cannot hide from the fact that the law concerning support of children was, from its foundation, nothing less than objectionable. We might perhaps explain this problematic statute by suggesting that the ancients valued individual children less than we do. We know, for example, that the Romans practiced exposure of infants; at least Jewish law did not condone such heinous acts. But falling back upon comparative judgments or reference to historical context does little to save the substance of the law for contemporary sensibilities. And, I would argue, this is precisely the point. When we consider laws such as these—and the values they express—we are forced to admit that traditional religious values simply are not the same as contemporary values, in matters of family as in many other matters. We are perhaps not surprised by this recognition (how could it be otherwise), but we may, nevertheless, be troubled by it. We bring different experiences, perspectives, and sensibilities; con-sequently, our system of values is often different from that of our ancestors. These differences have to be reckoned with. It will not be possible merely to apply traditional family values to the contemporary context. Before any such application is possible, an act of creative "translation" will be necessary.

Translation will be necessary for another reason as well. As we noted near the beginning of this chapter, when we speak of "family," we mean something different that Jews of old: we, for the most part, mean the nuclear family, Jews in the traditional world meant the extended family. But this is hardly the only important difference. In the pre-modern world, families were units of production, in the modern world they are units of consumption (children no longer produce in most families; instead, the require significant expense). In the pre-modern world, infant and child mortality rates were shockingly high. So, too, were rates of the death of mothers in childbirth. By contrast, we may assume that our children will survive us, and medical science has guaranteed that the vast majority of women will survive even difficult childbirths. Again, our experiences are different, our perspectives are different. Inevitably, our family values are different as well.

In light of what we have just said, it will come as no surprise that the United Nations Convention on the Rights of the Child and traditional Jewish values pertaining to the family are often in tension. A few selected examples will suffice to illustrate this tension. Article 29 of the Convention directs that a child's education "shall be directed to... The preparation of the child for responsible life in a free society, in the spirit of... equality of the sexes" (paragraph d). By comparison, Jewish tradition certainly does not assume that the sexes should be equal, either in families or in society. According to the halakha (=Jewish law), certain labors had to be performed by a wife for her husband (certain kinds of handiwork and household service), and he had specified responsibilities toward her (food, clothing, conjugal relations)(for these regulations, see Mishnah Ketubot chapters 4 and 5). The responsibilities, while theoretically correlative, hardly appear to have been equal. Moreover, Jewish men (including husbands) were obligated to study Torah, in the broadest sense of that term. Jewish women (including wives), on the other hand, were prohibited by some from studying Torah, while others gave permission for women to study only Written, but never Oral Torah (=rabbinic literature, including the Mishnah, the Talmud, and other rabbinic works). Again, the roles of the sexes hardly appear to have been equal. One could argue, I suppose, that the sexes, though assuming different roles and positions, were "equal" (indeed, precisely this claim has been made by many spokespeople for Orthodox Jewry in recent years). But this would require our accepting the possibility of a "separate but equal" reality—a position which has fallen into disrepute (rightly, in my mind) in recent years. Unmistakably, the spirit of this paragraph of the convention is informed by modern, primarily Western values. It could even be said that traditional Jewish family law was constructed so as to assure that such values (the equality of the sexes?!) could never find a foothold in reality.

To provide another example of the same sort of tension: Articles 12–14 of the Convention speak of a child's right to freedom of thought, conscience, opinion, and expression. The traditional Jewish view concerning the possibility of such a right will readily be appreciated if we consider the common legal categorization of children. In Jewish legal writings (beginning with the Mishnah), minors are typically categorized in two combinations. In the first, minors are put in the company of deaf-dumb individuals and imbeciles, and in the second, minors are joined with women and slaves. What minors, deaf-dumb individuals, and imbeciles have in common is the presumption that they have limited intellectual and moral capabilities. Their responsibilities and rights are reasonably limited on account of these limitations and, until they emerge from these categories, their legal status will remain limited. It would be absurd, from the traditional perspective, to guarantee the freedom of thought, conscience, and expression of such persons. On the contrary, by virtue of their "handicaps," it only makes sense to limit such freedoms.

The latter combined category suggests similar conclusions. What women, slaves, and minors clearly have in common in Jewish law is the fact that their religious obligations and, therefore, their rights are severely circumscribed (again, so much for the equality of the sexes). These limitations will certainly not lead us to expect the *protection* of their rights of expression. On the contrary, it is reasonable to suppose that such a notion, as it might pertain to these categories of persons, would be deemed ridiculous in the traditional setting. Indeed, if we take this argument one step further, it is probable that any right to freedom of thought and expression for the population at large (as opposed to, say, for the rabbinic elite) is foreign to traditional Jewish thinking (as, I would imagine, it is to most traditional systems). Again, we should notice that the UN Convention is informed by modern values and conceptions, values which, though perhaps supported by most of us, are foreign to the traditional Jewish religious system.

Needless to say, there are also many elements of the Convention which traditional Jewish teachings would quickly support. The obligation to respect the rights and duties of parents and members of the extended family are important traditional values, as is the obligation to respect local custom. The protection of the right of the child "to preserve his or her identity, including nationality, name and family relations" (article 8) also constitutes a protection of traditional values, Jewish and non-Jewish. These articles are important, but they demand less of our attention. What requires our notice and deliberation is the point made immediately above—the fact that, in many of its elements, the Convention represents the codification of *modern* values, values which will often be in tension or outright conflict with traditional Jewish teachings. One way to address this tension is to call it to our attention and to leave it at that.

Indeed, if we assume that there are singular Jewish family values, specified in a universally accepted and unchanging canon, then there will be nothing we *can* do with this tension other than notice it. This will be the perspective of some contemporary Orthodox Jews, and it is a perspective which cannot be ignored.

But there is an alternative response to the noted tension. Earlier, I made the argument Jewish families have always changed through time. Often, these various family structures have expressed what were, at those times, traditional Jewish family values—whatever the precise shape of the given family. What I did not sufficiently emphasize is the degree to which Jewish families were influenced by the surrounding culture, to the point that its values were sometimes assimilated as "Jewish" values, values that are now every bit as traditional as values which find their origin in the Torah.

Let me offer one example. We saw above that traditional Jewish societies were once polygynous (allowing a man to have multiple wives). Others, however, were monogamous. If we examine carefully the history of these phenomena, we discover that monogamy came to be supported by Jewish authorities only when they came under the sway of Christian culture. In Christian settings, Jews, with their neighbors, insisted that a man should take only one wife, supporting that insistence by reference to a story which was now interpreted as preferring this model—the story of Adam and Eve. Outside of the Christian context, Jews never made this argument.[3] When under Christian control, Jews nearly always did.

In the European setting, at least, monogamy became a traditional *Jewish* value, though it appears clear that the value originated in Christianity. Does this origin make the value less worthy? Does it mean that religious Jews should not support it? Surely not. Does the fact that monogamy originated outside of Judaism make it less traditional? After all these centuries, again, surely not.

Jewish culture was always extremely adaptable. When it saw what it understood to be superior values, even when these values were not native Jewish values, it absorbed them and Judaized them. In this manner, Jewish tradition was, over the centuries, immensely enriched.

In my view, this history should provide a model for the response of Jews today to a document like the UN Convention on the Rights of the Child. There are many values expressed in that convention, from freedom of expression to the equality of the sexes, which are modern values. However, they are values which emerge from a profound wisdom, and they have much to offer the value system of traditional Judaism. At this point in time, perhaps, they remain in tension with that same Judaism. But if Jewish societies today respond as they have so often in the past, then values now in tension will soon appear fully traditional. When that comes to pass, then traditional Judaism will have been considerably enriched. The UN Convention is, in the noted respects, a noble source of future "Torah."

Notes

1. What follows illustrates the present point briefly. For more documentation, see Shaye J. D. Cohen, ed., *The Jewish Family in Antiquity* (Atlanta: Scholars Press, 1993), David Kraemer, ed., *The Jewish Family: Metaphor and Memory* (New York: Oxford U. Press, 1988), and Steven M. Cohen and Paula Hyman, eds., *The Jewish Family: Myths and Reality* (New York and London: Holmes and Meier, 1986).
2. The evidence for the claims of this paragraph can be found in Mordechai A. Friedman, *ribbui nashim beyisrael* (*Jewish Polygyny in the Middle Ages: New Documents from the Cairo Geniza*) (Jerusalem: The Bialik Institute and Tel-Aviv U., 1986).
3. See Isaiah Gafni, "The Institution of Marriage in Rabbinic Times," in Kraemer, *The Jewish Family*, pp. 21–5.

INTRODUCTION TO CHAPTER FIVE

This article represents an extension of critical methods I learned to employ in my study of rabbinic texts to a different genre of literature. This specific work emerged as I was reading *Ezra* and *Nehemiah* with students in a class on the History of Jews and Judaism in Antiquity. The class was divided into two sections: one on the "history" (=primarily political history) of Jews in this period and the other on the "texts" that represented the beliefs of Jews during the same period (=intellectual history). To prepare for the "history" sessions pertaining to the period of return from the Babylonian exile, I depended upon the well-known histories of the Jews in this age. These, I found, typically read *Ezra* and *Nehemiah* in combination, essentially accepting their testimony as reliable evidence for the history of the period. The first couple of times I taught this course, I did the same. But, at the same time, as I read the books of *Ezra* and *Nehemiah* to examine their ideological rhetoric, I began to see significant differences in the beliefs and prejudices of the different books—differences that militate against a recombination of their respective "historical" testimonies (in the fashion of the historians). In fact, as I began to realize the scope of their differences, I came to realize that a history based upon these literary sources may be altogether impossible to write—at least not with any confidence.

This article presents the detailed argument for the vastly different authorship—and authorial ideology—of these two biblical books. I am pleased to say that the case I make here has generated significant responses (though, sadly, too many people continue to write histories of this period, employing these books as sources, without any awareness of the problems of such an enterprise); the article was even chosen for inclusion in a Sheffield Reader of important essays taken from the first ten years of *The Journal for the Study of the Old Testament*. The methodological cautions which inform my work on rabbinic literary sources are appropriate for the study of any literature that might serve as a historical source. The following case serves as ample illustration of both the method and the dangers of neglecting it.

Chapter Five

On The Relationship of the Books of Ezra and Nehemiah

Modern study of the book(s) of Ezra and Nehemiah[1] has been dominated by a powerful historicist bent. Being primarily interested in the history of the period for which these documents are the primary witnesses, scholars of the books have sought to recover the correct chronological order of the events that they presumably record. On account of this prejudice, such scholars have assumed that the Ezra-Nehemiah narrative is seriously confused. Attempts to restore the "original" order have resulted in various rearrangements of the narrative and documentary materials. For these purposes, the materials at hand, whether considered to be contained in one or two books, have been read as a single historical account.[2]

A necessary corrective to this approach is offered by Brevard S. Childs. He writes,

> In my judgment, the usual critical move which disregards the present form of the tradition and seeks to reconstruct a more historical sequence on the basis of literary and historical criteria runs the risk of failing to understand the theological concerns which are reflected through the canonical process. It seems obvious that an accurate historical report of the Persian period according to the canons of modern historical writing is not being offered, but that the biblical material has been shaped and transmitted toward another end.[3]

Childs then goes on, all too briefly, to describe his sense of the ideological agendas of this canonical book.[4] In doing so, he makes eminently clear that considerations other than those of the historian give shape to the final literary documents. Following Childs's lead, Tamara Cohn Eskenazi undertakes the only full-length literary study of the canonical book of Ezra-Nehemiah, exhibiting a fine literary sense in her close reading of the text and showing the important contributions that this previously neglected methodological perspective can make.[5]

Eskenazi's method is one that I fully endorse. The caution that we are dealing here with literary formulations and not with self-conscious historical records is one that cannot be repeated too often. Naturally, the recognition of this condition has consequences regarding the way these materials may be approached—highlighting their rhetoric and ideological prejudices and diminishing their value as historical sources. All of this is amply accounted for in Eskenazi's study. But I am of a different mind from Eskenazi in one crucial matter, and this difference leads me to conclusions that diverge significantly from hers or, for that matter, from any yet proposed.

I am speaking of Eskenazi's choice to read Ezra-Nehemiah as a single book rather than as two distinct works. Her reason for doing so is well understood. The ancient canonical traditions (before Origen) apparently all consider Ezra and Nehemiah to be one book. Thus, a canonical approach, following Childs, bids that they be considered together.

But this choice is, in my opinion, an ill-advised one. To begin with, the fact that the ancient believing community received these works as a single book is far from probative when considering their original status as literature. The community may have read them together, at a point subsequent to their formulation, for various reasons, including reasons that approximate those of the modern historians (they were concerned, after all, with these works as a record of holy history). From their canonical status, we learn nothing about the literary condition of these works at their inception.

Moreover, reading Ezra and Nehemiah as one forces Eskenazi to make a jump that I think cannot ultimately be supported. In order to claim a unity for the agendas of the two books, Eskenazi argues that the first major segment of Nehemiah is about the expansion of the "house of God"—obviously a major concern in Ezra—to include the city of Jerusalem as a whole.[6] But, unlike in Ezra, where the centrality of the "house of God" is explicit and pervasive, the house is nowhere mentioned explicitly in the relevant sections of Nehemiah. In fact, on each occasion where Eskenazi notes the house of God in Nehemiah, the explicit text speaks of the city and its walls, giving no hint that these are to be judged as anything other than that. The strongest support of Eskenazi's claim is the expression of opposition by the Temple's opponents, in their correspondence with Artaxerxes, in terms of the city and its walls (Ezra 4.7–24). But the context in which this correspondence is quoted denies the equation that Eskenazi wants to make, speaking of "the House of God which is in Jerusalem" (see, e.g., 5.2 and 6.5, my emphasis), not of the House of God which is Jerusalem. Furthermore, the voice of the letter is that of the opponents—the story's antagonists—so their usage is hardly determinant in the mind of the reader. What is more important, as I see it, is the purpose for which the quoted document is appropriated, and that is clearly the Temple. For the author of Ezra, in fact, the Temple is the center of concern. This same centrality does not extend to Nehemiah.

On the other side, there are many reasons to assume, prima facie, that these are distinct works. Most of these have been noted before, and there is no reason to review them all here. Just to mention a few of the most important factors:

> 1. the book of Nehemiah, in the middle of the canonical whole, bears an introduction that clearly marks what follows as an independent composition.[7]
> 2. the repetition of the identical list in Ezra 2 and Nehemiah 7 is no problem if the two books are distinct.
> 3. Similarly, the fact that the discussion of Ezra's activities is dropped between the end of Ezra and Nehemiah 8 is more easily accounted for if these are two works.
> 4. Important stylistic differences also distinguish the two.[8]
> 5. Not to be underestimated, as well, is the power of the opinion held by some, at least by the time of Origen, that these are two books and not one. Whatever the antiquity of such an opinion, its wisdom has to be weighed seriously.
> 6. Most importantly, as I will demonstrate in detail below, the two works, when considered independently, exhibit important ideological differences that make it extremely difficult to read them as a single unit.[9]

This last point is, I think, the most important reason for undertaking the sort of reading proposed here. M.A. Thronveit articulates the justification for such an approach this way:

> The safest course would be to take seriously the a priori assumption of separate authorship and investigate both works individually from a theological point of view, leaving the question of authorship open until the intent and message of both are better understood.[10]

Thronveit arrives at this position after reviewing the many attempts—ultimately inconclusive, in his judgment—to determine the relationship of the authorships of these works and Chronicles based upon linguistic criteria. His conclusion is that the most promising means of answering the question of authorship is to begin by reading the works independently.

Reading the works as just described, with the overall methodological emphases otherwise recommended by Eskenazi, I conclude that the relationship of the books of Ezra and Nehemiah is, in a general sense, analogous to that of I and II Maccabees; that is to say, they report an overlapping but not identical historical period, but from significantly different ideological perspectives. The book of Ezra is a priestly book; its concerns are the Temple, the priesthood and levites, and purity—that is, the cult. The book of Nehemiah, in contrast, is a lay book, sometimes exhibiting antagonism to priestly concerns and supporting, instead, what might be called scribal values.[11] After justifying these claims, following, I will remark upon their consequences for Ezra-Nehemiah scholarship.

My analysis of the books and their respective ideologies begins by reviewing the overall structure of each book, asking how structure carries with it the ideological preferences of its author. Next, I compare and contrast the respective treatments of the figure of Ezra in each book, with a mind to the same concerns. Third, I analyze the treatment of common motifs in the two books, seeing how these treatments support the ideologies previously identified. Finally, I examine the place of Torah in each of these books, showing how variant assumptions regarding the place of Torah in the restoration community reflect the very same biases indicated in the other materials. I will show that, in each of these areas, the different perspectives described above are powerfully confirmed.

Structure and Theme[12]

Ezra devotes its first six chapters to the rebuilding of the Temple. Chapter 1 records the decree of Cyrus confirming the right of the Jews to return to Judea to restore their sanctuary. Chapter 2 is a lengthy list of those returning; the context establishes that the purpose of their return is to rebuild the Temple (v. 68). Chapter 3 records the successful rebuilding of the altar for the purpose of offering sacrifices, the celebration of the Sukkot holiday (marked by the offering of sacrifices), and the celebration of the laying of the foundation of the House of God. Chapters 4 and 5 narrate the opposition of the local population to the rebuilding effort and the reconfirmation of the right of the community of Jewish returnees to do so. Chapter 6 speaks of the support of the Temple project out of the royal treasuries, the completion of the rebuilding, and the celebration of its rededication— accompanied by sacrifices, the purification of Priests and Levites (alone), and the bringing of sacrifice in celebration of the Passover.

Chapter 7 introduces us to Ezra, ascribing to him several roles and purposes. But the bulk of the chapter, the letter of Artaxerxes to Ezra, speaks of the Temple, its sacrifices and its supplies. Ezra himself characterizes the purpose of the king, expressed in the letter, as being "to beautify the house of the LORD which is in Jerusalem" (v. 27). Chapter 8 first lists the leaders of those going up with Ezra. It then speaks of the recruitment of Levites and Temple servants and of other preparations for going up to the Temple. It ends by describing the first acts undertaken by the returnees upon their arrival—the weighing out of gold and vessels for use in the House of God and the bringing of sacrifices. Finally, chapters 9 and 10 recount the events surrounding the intermarriage crisis; the language of the account is strongly priestly (see below on intermarriage).

Overall, it may be seen, the thematic structure of the book of Ezra is built upon priestly concerns. To be sure, certain small details diverge from this single-mindedness, but they are, when weighed against the whole, entirely insignificant. The Temple and its cult, and the purity of those who serve and worship there, constitute virtually the full range of interests to which the author of this book devotes himself.

The book of Nehemiah poses a striking contrast. Chapters 1–7 describe the rebuilding of the city, of its walls, and of the community that dwells within them, all under the direction of Nehemiah. Chapter 1 shows Nehemiah inquiring into the well-being of the inhabitants of Jerusalem. Concern is expressed for the disrepair of the walls and gates of the city. Nehemiah laments the condition that is reported to him, accounting it as a product of the disobedience of the people. His language is marked strongly by Deuteronomic expression.[13] In chapter 2, the king empowers Nehemiah to return and oversee repair of the city. Local inhabitants are said to oppose the city's repair. So, by night and in secret, Nehemiah surveys the city's walls and gates. Further acts of opposition are then mentioned. Chapters 3 and 4 describe the repair effort. Notably, upon being rebuilt, the *gates* are sanctified by the High Priest. There follows, in chapter 3, a long list of the assignments of various groups of builders. Priests, Levites and Israelites undertake various assignments, building side by side. The chapters go on by describing further opposition and the establishment by Nehemiah of guards to assure that the repair effort will not be interrupted. Chapter 5 diverges from the foregoing themes, speaking of Nehemiah's enforcement of various aspects of the Torah's social legislation, including the return of lands and the release of debts. Chapter 6 returns directly to the concerns of earlier chapters. Chapter 7, finally, repeats the list of Ezra 2, but with a very different purpose (see below).

In ch. 8, we are again introduced to Ezra. Crucially, the account is now in the third person. Central to Ezra's activities in this chapter is the reading of the Torah scroll in public. The Sukkot holiday is celebrated with the construction of booths—no sacrifice is mentioned. Chapter 9 begins with the separation of Israelites from foreigners. In response to the offense, the people read Torah, confess their sins and prostrate themselves. Following, the people gather to bless God, recounting the history of Israel as a preliminary to the re-establishment of the covenant. This history includes the giving of Torah to Moses at Mt. Sinai *for the first time in any such biblical historical review;* the Temple is ignored completely. Chapter 10 tells of the covenanting, listing the parties to that covenant. It then refers to renewed efforts to observe various laws of the Torah, including the Sabbath and the offering of various agricultural gifts to the priests.

Chapter 11 returns us to the project for repopulating Jerusalem— the building of city and community go hand in hand and continue to be central. A lengthy list of "chiefs of the province" who dwelt at Jerusalem follows. Chapter 12 continues with a list of Priests and Levites who "went up with Zerubbabel." No precise purpose is described for this "going up," but, since the chapter continues by describing the celebration of the dedication of the wall of Jerusalem, it is clear that all activities have been directed toward this end. Chapter 13, the final chapter, describes various offenses against Torah by the people and efforts to ameliorate this condition. Notably, Nehemiah discovers various offenses by the High Priest and expels him from the Temple (vv. 4–9).

This book is not so single-minded as is the book of Ezra. Because of its apparent variety, it may be simplest to characterize its concerns by means of negation—unlike Ezra, the book of Nehemiah is not significantly concerned with the Temple and the cult. The first major section of the book is concerned with the viability of the city and the community. The Temple goes virtually unmentioned here—the two minor references (2.8 and 6.10) are entirely by-the-way[14]—and this despite the fact that the Temple itself is apparently not in good repair (see 3.34, "will they sacrifice?").[15] A similar omission has been noted in the ritual history rehearsed in ch. 9, and here, as elsewhere in the latter part of Nehemiah, the center stage is now occupied by Torah. If the book of Ezra is a priestly book, Nehemiah represents the wedding of the concerns of the governor and the (non-priestly) scribe. Furthermore, as will be spelled out later, this wedding is forged with not a little antipathy toward the priest and his competitive centrality.

The Figure of Ezra

The present apparently confused state of the so-called Ezra memoir is the primary reason that scholars have sought to rearrange the material in these books. But at the root of this alleged confusion is a factor that has been largely ignored by students of these books: the accounts of Ezra in the book of Ezra and in Nehemiah differ radically in their pictures of Ezra and his purported activities. These differences align precisely with the ideological divergence already identified.

In the book of Ezra, we are first introduced to Ezra with a lengthy and detailed pedigree (7.1–5). Though Ezra is characterized as both a priest and a scribe, it is his priestly connections that are important— he is descended from Aaron (v. 5), the original High Priest, from Zadoq (v. 2), the traditional high-priestly line from the time of David, and from Seraiah (v. 1), the last of the High Priests at the time of the destruction. No more illustrious sequence of connections could be imagined! Furthermore, though Ezra is described also as a scribe whose purpose is to teach God's law (v. 10), such an activity is never undertaken by Ezra in the narrative of this book.[16] In fact, when we first hear Ezra's own voice (7.27)—inescapably establishing our impression of who he is and what his concerns are—he praises the king for seeing fit to "beautify the House of the Lord" and praises God for choosing him to stand at the head of that task. Ezra devotes himself, in the book of Ezra, to the Temple and the cult.

It is the matter of the intermarriages and the reaction to them, consuming the last two chapters of the book, that requires the most detailed attention in the present context. The ninth chapter begins with Ezra's report of his introduction to the offense, spoken of in these words: "the holy seed has become intermingled with the peoples of the land; and it is the officers and prefects who have taken the lead in this trespass" (v. 2, NJPS translation). The language is the language of the priesthood; trespass *(ma'al) is* a technical term for committing offense with respect to holy things.[17] What is objectionable is that the holy seed (a term with precedent only at Isa. 6.13)[18] is being intermingled with unholy seed. Notably, Deuteronomy's prohibition of intermarriage with the surrounding nations (7.3–4) is supported by no such justification; there the concern is the attraction of idolatry, as befits the apparent context of the Deuteronomic legislation.[19] So the concern voiced here is a new one and may be understood to represent the unique and particular prejudice of the present author.

The chapter continues in the same vein. Ezra responds in horror and remorse to what he has learned. He initiates acts of mourning and repentance; the timing of these acts is correlated with the times of sacrifices (vv. 4–5). His prayer describes the sin of the people—the reason for their earlier exile—in general terms, but the context sets the sin clearly as the profanation of holy seed. The land that they have come into and in which they have sinned is described as a land of *"nidda"*—a term otherwise found only in priestly contexts.

Chapter 10 continues with the response to the intermarriages. The leaders, with Ezra, undertake a covenant to separate from the foreign women. In the course of the narrative, Ezra's name is given either without qualification (10.1, 5) or with emphasis on his priestly identification (10.10, 16); his actions continue to illustrate his priestly concerns, and the language brought to relate his activities remains priestly as well; "trespass" is ameliorated through "separation," each word being repeated several times (see vv. 2, 6, 8, 10, 11 and 16).

So, in the book of Ezra, Ezra is a well-connected priest whose exclusive concern is the strengthening and purification of the cult. His primary activity involves the elimination of intermarriages, an offense that is newly and uniquely described in priestly terms. As befits the emphasis of the book as a whole, Ezra is a man of the priesthood.

Now consider the Ezra of Nehemiah. The portrait of this Ezra, related exclusively in the third person, is restricted primarily to ch. 8 (after this, Ezra recedes from prominence and is nowhere central to the narrative). Again, in the course of the narrative, we discover that Ezra is both a scribe and a priest, but—in contrast with the picture in Ezra—in Nehemiah, Ezra acts everywhere as a scribe and nowhere as a priest. Here, Ezra the scribe, introduced with no pedigree, devotes himself to the reading of Torah in public and the instruction of the people. With the leaders of the people and the Priests and Levites, Ezra does not bring sacrifices but studies Torah (vv. 13–18). Learning about the Sukkot holiday, they respond by constructing booths; nowhere is sacrifice mentioned, and this despite the fact that, in the Priestly law, Sukkot is the holiday that is accompanied by the most sacrifices (by far—see Num. 29.12–38). Rather, instead of offering sacrifices day by day, they celebrate by reading Torah day by day (Neh. 8.18). Supporting the thrust of what is recounted here is the weight of the appositives that accompany Ezra's name: on only one occasion (8.2) is Ezra described simply as a priest; on two occasions (8.9 and 12.26) Ezra is both a priest and a scribe; in all other instances, five in all (8.1, 4, 5, 13; 12.37), Ezra is spoken of as being a scribe alone. In sum, the narrative exposition and the linguistic signals combine to make a single, unmistakable point.

Thus, the Ezra remembered in Ezra is not the Ezra known in Nehemiah. In Ezra, Ezra is a priest, a man concerned with the cult and its purity, while in Nehemiah he is a scribe, a man of the book, who is entirely unconcerned with the Temple or sacrifices. These are two different Ezras, the one bearing little relationship to the other. The disparate portraits do, however, bear powerful relationship with the ideological bents of the books in which they appear.

Motifs

The differences in these books in the treatment of various common motifs or details align precisely with the prejudices that we have identified. I analyze these variant treatments in no particular order.

Crying
On several occasions in these books the people, or some segment of the people, are moved to tears. This occurs twice in Ezra, first when the elders who remember the first Temple see its paltry replacement (3.12), and second in

response to the recognition of the intermarriage offense (10.1), which, as we have seen, is a priestly concern in this context. In Nehemiah (8.9), they cry following the public reading of the Torah, apparently for fear of not having fulfilled its precepts.

People cry in each book over the primary ideological concern of the book, as identified above.

Sukkot

Sukkot is observed in both books. In Ezra (3.4) it is a holiday of sacrifices; booths are not even mentioned. In Nehemiah it is a holiday of booths and of the reading of Torah; sacrifices are not even mentioned in this connection.

Opposition

Both books report that elements of the local population opposed the efforts of the returning community. In Ezra (chs. 4–5), this opposition is directed exclusively against the effort to rebuild the Temple; in Nehemiah (2.10–20; 3.33–38; 4; 6) it is directed against the effort to rebuild the wall and gates of the city.

Sources

The centrality of various kinds of sources (lists, letters, documents), particularly in Ezra but also in Nehemiah, has often been noted. What has not been noted is the different purposes to which these sources are put. A few examples will suffice to illustrate this difference.

I have already alluded to the different purpose for the quotation of the much-discussed list of returnees at Ezra 2 and Nehemiah 7. The list in Ezra is introduced simply by identifying those included as the ones who returned. But it is followed by speaking of those who came to the House of the LORD in Jerusalem and volunteered to support the rebuilding project (vv. 68–69); the return leads to rebuilding. In contrast, in Nehemiah the list is framed in such a way as to make clear that return leads to rebuilding and repopulation of the city (see 7.4–5 and 69–71, where "the work" for which donations are made is, given the context, clearly the rebuilding and repopulation effort). Note that even the Priests, along with the Levites and others, make donations—they give of their uniquely priestly wealth. Obviously, then, the donations are not directed to the priesthood itself.

In Ezra, other sources similarly address the priestly concerns. Thus, the list at the end of ch. 1 is a list of the vessels of the House of the Lord. The correspondence preserved in chs. 4–5 concerns the right of the returnees to rebuild the Temple. Cyrus's decree, at the beginning of ch. 6, affirms that right and describes the dimensions of the House to be built (!). And so forth.

The contrast in Nehemiah is unmistakable. The list in ch. 3 records those who together built the walls and gates of the city. The list in ch. 7, as we have seen, is also directed toward rebuilding and repopulation. The covenantal history, in ch. 9, is concerned with Torah and its observance—the Temple is completely ignored. The list at the beginning of ch. 10 records those who affirm this very same covenant. The list in ch. 11 reflects the concern for repopulating the city. Again, whatever the sources that might have been available to the authors of these two books, they employ these sources consistently to serve their different purposes.

Intermarriage

We have already seen that the objection to intermarriage in Ezra is framed in terms of priestly definitions. In Nehemiah, the matter is somewhat more complex, but the characteristic differences do again emerge.

We first read of the separation from foreigners in Nehemiah at the beginning of ch. 9. We are not told what motivates the separation, but it is notable, at least, that "the seed" that separates here is not "the holy seed," as in Ezra, but simply "the seed of Israel" (v. 2). (In Nehemiah it is the city that is holy rather than the seed; see 11.1.) When we return to discussion of the separation, at 10.29–31, the motivation is added: they separate "to the Torah of God... to walk in the Torah of God which was given by the hand of Moses, the servant of God...." Unlike in Ezra, where the separation is only "from," as an act to eliminate the pollution of the holy seed, here the separation has a positive purpose—to unite with the Torah of God. Notably, this affirmative motivation has neither a parallel in Ezra nor a precedent in Deuteronomy, where the concern is separation from idol worship (conceived and expressed as a negation).

The final mention of separation from foreigners in Nehemiah (13.13) makes explicit reference to Deut. 23.4–5. What is crucial here is that, aside from the fact that the concern is not priestly—it rests on historical causes—the motivation to separate is described as emerging from a reading of Torah. Again, Torah is central. The scribe has superseded the priest.

Covenant

Covenants are undertaken in both Ezra (10.2–8) and Nehemiah (chs. 9–10).[20] In Ezra, the covenant has but one purpose—to purify the seed of Israel by expelling the foreign women and their offspring (10.3).[21] In Nehemiah, by contrast, the covenant is conceived far more generally. The blessing that introduces the covenant places the giving of Torah and its observance at the center of its history. At the same time, the only major element of Israelite history that is conspicuously absent from the blessing is the building of the Temple of Solomon.

Sin and Punishment

Both books offer explanations of recent travails of Israel, typically understanding them as punishments for sin. Both books articulate this ideology in general terms (Ezra 9.6–7; Neh. 1.6–7; 9.26, 28–29, 34) and then propose specific trans-gressions that are understood to lie at the root of the attendant punishment. In Ezra, the specification focuses on the intermarriage and that alone. This is evident in the shift from the general to the specific in 9.10–12 and 9.14. By contrast, the only specification in Nehemiah (13.18) offers Sabbath transgression as the sin at the root of recent disasters. But the general description in ch. 1 (v. 7) lists several categories of laws that have been transgressed (*misvot, huqqim, mishpatim*), suggesting that, whatever the specifics may be, they extend well beyond any individual transgression or category of transgressions. Furthermore, it is clear that sin is conceived in Deuteronomic terms (see 1.6–9; 9.28). In Nehemiah, neither the language nor the conception is priestly.

Priests, Governors and Scribes

Though there are priests, governors, and scribes in both books, they have different functions in each. In Ezra, not only priests but also governors and scribes (Ezra) serve priestly purposes (the rebuilding of the Temple, the offering of sacrifice, the elimination of intermarriages in terms described above). In contrast, in Nehemiah, priests serve the purposes of the governor (the rebuilding of the city and reconstitution of the community) and the scribe (reading and teaching the Torah in public; see below).

Torah

The centrality of Torah to the Ezra traditions has been widely discussed. What has not been recognized is (1.) the fact that this centrality is true only in the book of Nehemiah, and (2.) that the visions of Torah in Ezra and Nehemiah differ radically with one another. The difference parallels, and perhaps lies at the foundation of, the characteristic ideological differences that we have earlier identified.

In Ezra, the Torah document—when referred to explicitly—acts exclusively as justification of priestly laws and then only by assertion. There is no evidence, anywhere in this book, that the Torah is actually read in public, let alone studied, and there is no indication, at places where explicit reference is made to a written law, that that law is constituted of anything but priestly matters. So, at 3.2, they build the altar and offer sacrifices on it "as written in the Torah of Moses." In v. 4 of the same chapter, the Sukkot festival is celebrated "as written," but what is written is, apparently, only the obligation to bring sacrifices. Later on, the Priests and Levites are appointed to their proper place in the divine worship "according to the writing of the book of Moses" (6.18). This is the sum total of explicit references to a written Torah in the book of Ezra.

Now, consider the place of the book of the Torah in Nehemiah. Here the Torah is something that is read aloud in public (ch. 8). The text goes to extraordinary lengths to emphasize the public nature of the reading—mention of the presence of "the whole people" (*kol ha‘am*) is repeated no fewer than nine times (vv. 3, 5, 6, 9, 12, 13; this construction does not appear in Ezra). In fact, in Nehemiah, such reading of Torah is the public ritual; it has replaced sacrifices almost entirely. Its replacement of sacrifice is likewise evident at the beginning of ch. 9 where the reading of Torah constitutes part of the ceremony of atonement for having married foreigners (v. 3). No more do sacrifices effect atonement; confession, prostration and the reading of Torah do.

Furthermore, the Torah is not merely read here—it is interpreted and explained (8.8). Such reading and interpreting of the Torah leads to discovery: by reading the Torah, the people discover that they are to celebrate Sukkot by constructing booths (8.14–17; crucially, they discover nothing here about sacrifices). They also discover that they are to separate themselves from foreign women (13.1). Torah, in this book, is an open, public document that is meant to be read and learned, discovered and observed.[22] To be sure, the Torah is sometimes alluded to, as justification, in the manner of Ezra (see Neh. 10.35 and 37). But this is not the approach that predominates. Rather, it is a public, variegated Torah (its laws are both priestly and nonpriestly) that characterizes Nehemiah—precisely the sort that would come to characterize the scribal office in later Israel; perhaps what we see here is the first hint of such a development.

The difference between priestly and scribal law requires further elaboration. In the ancient world, priesthoods were guardians of sacred traditions. The traditions that they guarded were, in particular, the secrets of the cult and the performance of its rituals. Such knowledge enabled the priests to conduct their art correctly. Of course, it was this priestly art for which the people depended on the priests—it was the source of priestly power. The sacred knowledge, standing at the foundation of their power, was jealously guarded by the priests.[23]

In consideration of this relation between priesthoods and their laws, the image of Torah we find in Ezra—with its priestly inclinations—is fully to be expected. Again, in Ezra, the Torah is a book that describes the laws of the sacrificial cult. It is guarded, not publicized, and it is alluded to only as authoritative justification of laws that pertain to the priest. This Torah is revealed only to the extent that the priests require. If it supports their center of power, well and good. Otherwise, there is no need to share its content.[24]

The scribe, in contrast, has no essential investment in jealously protecting the law. On the contrary, his craft is devoted to the copying and promulgation of the law. This may well explain why scribes in Israel would later (at least) conclude that sacred power resides in the book itself and with those who devote themselves to it. Of course, this power is not restricted to a priesthood; thus, neither should the law be. In Nehemiah, we see this ideology in its nascent form—the Torah is brought out into the open and made central to the new ritual. It is available to all and there is no limit on what one might discover therein, beyond the actual substance of the document itself. And, given the alternatives made available through interpretation—clearly a part of the scribal project as described here—even this may not be a limit.[25]

Opposition to the Centrality of the Priesthood in Nehemiah

Another element of the different views of Torah in the books at hand needs to be emphasized. I am speaking of the fact that, if the sacred law, properly guarded, is at the source of priestly power, then the scribal approach to Torah, which seeks to disseminate it and render it public, undermines this source of priestly power. This is but one of several pieces of evidence in Nehemiah of its opposition to the centrality of the priesthood.

The most obvious evidence for the book of Nehemiah's undermining of priestly centrality is its almost complete neglect of the Temple and sacrifice, as we have noted in detail above. Related to this is the obvious displacement of sacrifice or Temple with Torah, in a way that may be understood as "granting sanctity to the Torah, not to the Temple".[26] This displacement of sanctity, noted by Eskenazi, typifies much of the approach in Nehemiah.

Eskenazi touches on several of these displacements. In connection with Neh. 3.1, she notes the fact that the gates of the city are being sanctified—an act that one would more expect in connection with the House of God.[27] Of course, such sanctification, directed at a nonpriestly property, undermines the centrality of the Temple as such. The same is true in connection with the purification of all the people at Neh. 12.30 (and cf. Ezra 6.20). On this matter, Eskenazi comments, "The purification of all the people... demonstrates that they are brought into the same ritual status as priests and Levites...This amplifies the point made by the Israelite pedigrees: the sanctity of the people, not merely of clergy, matters."[28] In just this way does the author effectively undermine the centrality of the priesthood.

To these points we may add the following: In ch. 3, the Priests, Levites and Israelites are described as engaging in the construction of the city, side by side. Thus does the author claim that this construction is what is truly important, so important that even the Priests and Levites must serve this end. Moreover, he shows that, for what really matters, the Priests and Levites are in no way superior to the Israelites as a whole. Particularly striking in its statement of this same opposition to the priesthood is the recounting of the cultic abuses of the High Priest, at 13.4–9, and of Nehemiah's actual expulsion of the High Priest from his chamber in the Temple. Morton Smith comments on this event:

> By all traditions of ancient religion the high priest was the final authority on cult law, especially on purity law, and above all on purity law as it applied to his own temple. Yet here is Nehemiah, not a priest at all... not only declaring unclean and forbidden what the high priest has declared clean and permitted, but also overriding the high priest's ruling and cleansing the Temple of the pollution which he said the high priest has introduced into it.[29]

More explicit opposition to the priesthood, and undermining of its authority, could hardly be imagined. The same scenario repeats itself at the end of this last chapter, where it is Nehemiah the layman who purifies the priests of their pollution from foreigners. What, from the priestly perspective, could be more humiliating?

Conclusions

We have seen that Ezra is a book that speaks for a priestly authorship. It believes that post-exilic sacred history leads to the rebuilding of the Temple and the rehabilitation of the cult. Sin, in its view, is the pollution of the cult, and atonement, therefore, can only be achieved by the removal of that pollution. As is to be expected, the Priests are its main actors, and its great hero, Ezra, is the Priest who accomplishes the necessary purification.

The book of Nehemiah contends that the realm of the sacred far exceeds the limits of the cult. Not only is the Temple holy; so too is the city as a whole. Not only is the priesthood holy, but so too is Israel at large. Since the city and the laity are central to this authorship's conception of the sacred, sacred history, in this book, leads to rebuilding of the city; the Temple, though possibly in disrepair, is ignored. And, as the city replaces the Temple, so the Torah replaces sacrifices and scribes replace priests. In this context, sin is an offense against the Torah, more generally conceived, and the hero, again Ezra, is the one who teaches Torah and thus brings the people back to its observance. By the same token, Nehemiah, the other great hero, is the one who assures the viability of the community as a whole, who oversees the covenanting that is centered on Torah, and who takes control of the priesthood that has itself polluted the sacred precincts.

The fact that these characterizations do not account for all of the details of these books should not be taken as a challenge to their basic soundness. Theoretically, these documents could have been composed either by authors who witnessed the same events or by authors who had access to a common record. There can be no surprise, therefore, that their accounts sometimes overlap. Presumably, Ezra was both a priest and a scribe; foreign women were expelled by the community; the Temple did operate and sacrifices were offered there. But what is more important is the undeniable differences in the use of these materials that resulted from the divergent ideologies of the authors. They did not fully censor out what did not support their individual pictures. They did, however, shape it with a stamp that was so powerful as to leave their prejudices in little doubt.

These conclusions have important consequences for those who would want to employ these books as evidence for the period that they purportedly describe. Generally speaking, Ezra and Nehemiah are two competing, perhaps even contradictory (but not complementary) accounts of the same history. For the most part, therefore, they constitute poor sources for traditional histories. They are prejudiced, ideologically motivated witnesses—hardly the sort whose testimony a critical historian should gullibly repeat. Only where their overlap is significant, such as in those few areas listed in the previous paragraph, is there room for greater confidence. But these areas are few, and there is very little, therefore, that can be said without hesitation.

Still, there is undoubtedly in these books an ideological history to be told. Recorded in them we see the beginnings of a debate that would, in fact, have major consequences in the history of Judaism for the next five hundred years. The question that these authors are debating is that of the locus of the sacred. Is religious power in Israel to be found in the priesthood and the cult or in the Book and those who disseminate it? For the next many hundreds of years the view represented by the author of the book of Ezra would predominate, at least among the parties who had recognized political power. But the alternative supported by the author of the book of Nehemiah would never disappear and, over the long term, it was this view—the vision of the lay teacher of Torah—that would emerge triumphant.[30]

Notes

1. On the question of whether these are one or two books, see below.
2. An excellent review of the approach described herein—itself an example of this approach—is H.H. Rowley's essay on Ezra and Nehemiah in *Ignace Goldziher Memorial Volume* (pt. 1; Budapest, 1948), pp. 117–49, repr. in Rowley, *The Servant of the Lord, and Other Essays on the Old Testament* (London: Lutterworth Press, 1952), pp. 135–68.
3. B.S. Childs, *Introduction to the Old Testament as Scripture* (Philadelphia: Fortress Press, 1979), p. 635.
4. Following the tradition of the Hebrew canon, Childs treats the books as one.
5. T.C. Eskenazi, *In an Age of Prose: A Literary Approach to Ezra-Nehemiah* (SBLMS, 36; Atlanta: Scholars Press, 1988).
6. See *Age of Prose*, p. 2 and pp. 53–57.
7. See Talmon, "Ezra and Nehemiah (Books and Men)," IDBSup, p. 318.
8. Ezra includes narrative and documents in both Hebrew and Aramaic; Nehemiah restricts itself exclusively to Hebrew. Ezra's memoir in Ezra is primarily a first-person account; his activity in Nehemiah is witnessed and recounted in the third person.
9. I find A. Kapelrud's argument for the unity of the "Ezra-narrative" on the basis of linguistic criteria to be unconvincing. First, he assumes the unity a priori; thus, he is likely to find common post-exilic usages as evidence of unity. Second, Kapelrud admits that Neh. 8 is distinct from the Ezra materials in many important ways; see his review in *The Question of Authorship in the Ezra-Narrative: A Lexical Investigation* (Skrifter utgitt av det Norske Videnkaps-Akademi i Oslo. II. Hist.-Filos. Klasse, 1944, no. 1; Oslo: J. Dybwad, 1944), p. 93. Given the differences, the choice between unity and independence based upon this evidence alone is highly arbitrary. For a good illustration of the difficulty of using lexical characteristics to determine authorship, see S. Japhet, "The Supposed Common Authorship of Chronicles and Ezra-Nehemiah Investigated Anew," *VT* 18 (1968), pp. 330–71.
10. M.A. Thronveit, "Linguistic Analysis and the Question of Authorship in Chronicles, Ezra and Nehemiah," VT 32 (1982).
11. I use the term "scribe" perhaps anachronistically. Various functions are attributed to scribes in ancient Israel (pre- and post-exilic) as well as in neighboring societies; see J.M. Myers's discussion, *Ezra-Nehemiah* (AB, 14; New York: Doubleday, 1965), pp. 60–61, and the excellent brief essay by A. Demsky, *EncJud* XIV, cols. 1041-43. My argument, following, is that the accounts of Ezra's responsibilities as a scribe may not reliably be used as evidence for this period because they are in tension with one another. When I speak of "scribal" ideals below, I anticipate the scribe of the late Second Temple period.
12. A more detailed outline may be found in Myers, *Ezra-Nehemiah,* pp. xxxviii–xli. For a comprehensive analysis of the structure of the books, see Eskenazi, *Age of Prose,* pp. 37–126.
13. See, e.g., vv. 5 (Deut. 10.17) and 9 (Deut. 30.4 and 19.29).
14. The former reference is omitted by the *LXX.*
15. Caution is necessary, however, in making this suggestion because of textual uncertainties. See J. Blenkinsopp, *Ezra-Nehemiah: A Commentary* (OTL; Philadelphia: Westminster Press, 1988), p. 243.
16. Ezra is described as a scribe twice in this chapter (vv. 6 and 11). In v. 6, his skill as a scribe is praised but we have no information defining the scribal task. Verse 11 somehow associates Ezra's scribal function with the laws of YHWH, but again, what that association might be is not spelled out. In v. 10, Ezra is praised for preparing himself "to investigate the teaching [Torah] of YHWH, to observe and to teach ordinances and judgments in Israel" (my

translation). Though the fact that Ezra is a scribe is not mentioned in this verse, the context strongly intimates that these activities are a function of Ezra's scribal commitments. Nevertheless, as mentioned, Ezra never undertakes to investigate or teach scripture in this book. We are left with the impression that the descriptions are somehow formulaic; they have no immediate association to reality.

17. The term is used especially in Leviticus, Numbers, Ezekiel and Chronicles—that is, in documents that speak from a priestly perspective.

18. Itself a late gloss. See Blenkinsopp, *Ezra-Nehemiah*, p. 176.

19. The description of the people as "holy" in Deut. 7.6 is not to be equated with the notion of holiness expressed here. There, holiness means to separate from idol worship; "holy to the Lord" means "separated [from idolatry] to the Lord." Here, in Ezra, the holiness of the seed is an essential, priestly holiness, residing in the seed by its very nature.

20. The term used in Neh. 10 is not b^erit but ^amana. There is no question that the two terms are synonymous, as suggested by the verb, *krt*, used for undertaking such a commitment—this is the common biblical term for entering a covenant; see Gen. 15.18; 21.27, 32; 26.28; etc.

21. I understand the statement, "and do according to the teaching [torah]," to qualify what is specified earlier in the verse; that is to say, "doing the Torah" is here equated with expelling the foreign wives and children.

22. A similar characterization is employed by Eskenazi, *Age of Prose*, p. 191. She does not, however, distinguish between the Torah ("book," "text") seen in Ezra and that in Nehemiah.

23. See E.O. James, *The Nature and Function of Priesthood* (New York: Barnes & Noble, 1955), pp. 208, 223–24; and L. Sabourin, SJ, *Priesthood: A Comparative Study* (Leiden: Brill, 1973), p. 6.

24. It may be wondered whether there is anything beyond priestly law (including laws of particular interest to the priests outside of P) in the Torah book of Ezra. Perhaps the debate that lies at the heart of the many differences that I have outlined is the very identity of the "Torah of Moses," with the author of Ezra supporting a circumscribed, priestly identity and the author of Nehemiah arguing for a much broader Torah—essentially the document that we know. In any case, it seems to me to be more productive to explore the identity of the Torah as explicitly referred to—in Ezra and independently in Nehemiah—than to try to divine the identity of the Torah that may or may not lay at the foundation of individual laws as described in these later books. This latter approach is hopelessly mired in confusion and imprecision. An excellent review of the problem may be found in C. Houtman, "Ezra and the Law: Observations on the Supposed Relation between Ezra and the Pentateuch," in A.S. Van der Woude (ed.), *Remembering the Way...* (OTS, 21; Leiden: Brill, 1981), pp. 91–115.

25. See M. Fishbane, *Biblical Interpretation in Ancient Israel* (Oxford: Clarendon Press, 1985), pp. 110–11.

26. Eskenazi, *Age of Prose*, p. 106.

27. Eskenazi, *Age of Prose*, p. 84.

28. Eskenazi, Age of Prose, p. 117-18.

29. *Palestinian Parties and Politics That Shaped the Old Testament* (London: SCM Press, 1987; New York: Columbia University Press, 1st edn, 1971), p. 101.

30. I am grateful to S. Garfinkel and, especially, to T. Eskenazi for their generous critiques and comments which helped me to refine many points in my argument.

INTRODUCTION TO CHAPTER SIX

This essay and the next were both written for a collection on the history of biblical interpretation, *Hebrew Bible/Old Testament: The History of Its Interpretation*, edited by Magne Sæbø. In fact, only this first piece is a "history" in the proper sense. But since its subject is the history of rabbinic bible interpretation, the following essay, discussing bible interpretation in the Mishnah, forms the next "chapter" of the history begun here.

This chapter begins by exploring the relationship of the early rabbis with parties and social groupings of the late Second Temple period. In this discussion, I depend primarily upon the scholarship of others, but specific conclusions are my own. In these pages, the reader will find my judgments concerning the continuity or innovation of rabbinic Judaism with respect to the Judaisms that came before. In the latter part of the essay, I explore the question of whether there were significant precedents for rabbinic methods of reading scripture, in late Second Temple Judaism or elsewhere. My conclusion is agnostic, inclining toward negative. Crucially, unlike many who have addressed this question before, I refuse simply to assume that rabbinic methods and readings are the same as Pharisaic methods and readings. I seek bona fide precedents—examples that do not emerge from retroactive attributions—and do not find them (with small exceptions, to be noted). Thus, the next chapter, speaking of the earliest documented rabbinic readings, represents a new chapter in Jewish readings of scripture.

My approach in these chapters represents, I believe, a reasonable approximation of a current consensus on how such histories must be written. Having said that, I have no doubt that scholars who want to find continuity instead of disjuncture will find flaws in both my individual judgments and my conclusions.

Chapter Six

Local Conditions for a Developing Rabbinic Tradition

Bibliography: S. J. D. COHEN, "The Significance of Yavneh: Pharisees, Rabbis, and the End of Jewish Sectarianism," *HUCA* 55 (1984) 36–42; D. DAUBE, "Rabbinic Methods of Interpretation and Hellenistic Rhetoric," *HUCA* 22 (1949) 239–264; R. EISENMAN/M. WISE (eds.), *The Dead Sea Scrolls Uncovered* (Shaftesbury, Dorset and Rockport, MA: Element, 1992); H. FISCHEL, "Studies in Cynicism and the Ancient Near East: The Transformation of a Chria," *Religions in Antiquity* (ed. J. Neusner), *NumenSup* 14 (Leiden: E.J. Brill, 1968); idem, "Stories and History: Observations on Greco-Roman Rhetoric and Pharisaism," *American Oriental Society Middle West Branch Semi-Centennial Volume* (ed. D. Sinor), *Oriental Series* 3 (1969); D. GOODBLATT, "The Place of the Pharisees in First Century Judaism: The State of the Debate," *JJS* 20, n. 1 (June 1989) 12–30; M. GOODMAN, *The Ruling Class of Judaea: The Origins of the Jewish Revolt Against Rome A.D. 66–70* (Cambridge, England: Cambridge U. Press, 1987); D. HALIVNI, *Midrash, Mishnah and Gemara: The Jewish Predilection for Justified Law* (Cambridge, MA: Harvard U. Press, 1986); idem, *Peshat and Derash: Plain and Applied Meaning in Rabbinic Exegesis* (New York: Oxford U. Press, 1991); S. LIEBERMAN, *Hellenism in Jewish Palestine* (New York: Jewish Theological Seminary, ²1962); J. NEUSNER, *Reading and Believing: Ancient Judaism and Contemporary Gullibility* (Atlanta: Scholars Press, 1986); idem, *Judaism: The Evidence of the Mishnah* (Chicago: U. of Chicago Press, 1981); A. SALDARINI, *Pharisees, Scribes and Sadducees in Palestinian Society* (Wilmington, Delaware: Michael Glazier, 1988), pp. 128–132.

The history of Rabbinic Judaism proper begins following the war with Rome and the destruction of the Temple in CE 70. But there are important continuities between Rabbinic Judaism and pre-destruction Judaisms, and attention to these continuities allows for a fuller appreciation of the unique developments of this latter Judaism, including its characteristic methods of reading scripture.

The centuries before the first Jewish war with Rome were complex and difficult. The Hasmonean dynasty, though originating as a small group of anti-Hellenistic pietists, quickly adopted Hellenistic ways. The Hasmoneans' claim on the High Priesthood—without descent from the traditional High Priestly family—and on the royal throne—without descent from the House of David—engendered not a little opposition, contributing to the overall religious turmoil which characterized this period. The political leadership of Judea shifted from the Hasmonean kings to the Romans, to Herod and his son, then back to the Romans. Jewish leadership was, at best, imperfectly established, enjoying only limited support and subject always to competing claims. Even the narrow evidence of the Qumran scrolls shows that the Hasmoneans were blessed by some and cursed by others.[1] The High Priests, recognized leaders of the Jews for much of the Second Temple period, were, from the reign of Herod onward, virtual unknowns, making it improbable that they could claim the genuine allegiance of many. Yet it is likely that the traditional authority which accrued to the High Priest served to enhance the standing of even these insignificant figures. The Pharisees may or may not have been the most popular religious party (depending upon how one reads Josephus' report),[2] but even if, now and then, they could claim this distinction, their access to official corridors of power was at best only occasional. In light of this turmoil and confusion, it is no wonder that these centuries witnessed the birth of a deeply divided Judaism.

With all of this complexity, one thing seems clear: there were no rabbis, in the common sense of that word, before the destruction of the second Jerusalem Temple. No non-rabbinic document dating from the first century mentions the rabbis. Gamaliel and Shimeon ben Gamliel are referred to in Acts (5:34) and Josephus (*War*, 4.3.9 [159]), but both are known merely as leading Pharisees. The rabbis later identification of these individuals as patriarchs of the rabbinic movement may thus be understood as a rhetoric of traditional authority—"we are descended from them and we should therefore be accorded the same respect and authority." Aside from these two well-known Pharisees, no rabbinic figure who would have lived during these decades is ever spoken of; astoundingly, the great "Hillel the Elder" goes entirely unnoticed by Josephus though, if the rabbinic record were to be believed, Hillel should have been the most important religious leader of the Herodian age.[3] The title "rabbi" is found already in the Gospel of Mark, but there it is a mere honorific term, not the appellation given to the member of an elite group of individuals ordained to serve in a particular capacity. This vast silence where there should not be allows for only two reasonable interpretations—either there were no bona fide rabbis during this period or they were as yet so insignificant as to escape contemporary notice. Given the weight of the evidence, the emerging consensus among scholars prefers the first interpretation.

But none of this is to say that rabbinic Judaism was a complete novelty on the Judean landscape. On the contrary, in an ancient, traditional society such as that of Judea, it would be unthinkable for a group of pious individuals such as the rabbis to offer a model of correct religious practice without promising significant continuities with well-known forms. In fact, reference to evidence from the centuries leading to the birth of rabbinic Judaism shows that, whatever the innovations the rabbis might have offered, there are also strong roots for their religion in late second Temple society. Unfortunately, in the matter which concerns us here—rabbinic methods of interpreting scripture—the evidence for such roots is lacking.

The rabbis' own claim of important Pharisees as their own, coupled with significant parallels between positions attributed to the Pharisees (by Josephus or the authors of the Gospels) and opinions recorded explicitly in rabbinic documents, make the argument for meaningful continuities between the Pharisees and the rabbis irrefutable. Thus, there is no doubt that the rabbis aspired to enjoy the reputation for expertise in the law which is ascribed to the Pharisees in both Josephus and the Gospels. Naturally, they also sought the same respect and popularity which accompanied such a reputation in Jewish society. The Pharisees' support of a "tradition of the elders," described by Josephus, also obviously characterized the religion of the rabbis (see the beginning of tractate Abot), and there can be no doubt that the rabbis sought to build on the legitimacy of such a tradition in the Pharisaic context to support their own extra-biblical teachings. At the same time, the rabbis never explicitly identify themselves with the Pharisees, and there is no evidence that the Pharisees, as a distinct group, survived the defeat to Rome. The Pharisees thus contributed significantly to the emerging rabbinic tradition, but it would be incorrect to say that the rabbis were merely a post-destruction outgrowth of the earlier Pharisees.[4]

Neusner identifies in the Mishnah, the earliest of the rabbinic documents to come to completion, the legacy of both priests and scribes.[5] The priestly legacy may be found in the many detailed tractates which devote themselves to laws of sacrifice, purity and the Temple. Indeed, a greater proportion of the Mishnah's laws are devoted to concerns of the priesthood than to those of any other group. But the rabbis obviously could not have hoped literally to replace the priests; without a Temple, the religion of the priests was now defunct. Nor should the rabbis' appropriation of priestly concerns be understood as a mere claim for continuity with earlier, pre-destruction Judaism. As *Yoma* chapter 1 and other similar texts make clear, the rabbinic authors held the priests as such in some contempt and claimed to be more expert in even the priestly law. It is the elders (= the rabbis) who direct the High Priest in his service, and he who serves them. Thus it is once again expertise in the law which is offered to support the rabbis' authority, and attention to priestly concerns may be under-stood to represent their claim to command all of Judaism as articulated in the Torah of Moses. Or, to put it in other words, if the priests no longer have an arena in which to perform, this should be the cause of relatively little concern; the elders were more central to Judaism than the priests, and their arena—the Torah—remains intact.

Concerning second Temple scribes whose legacy presumably informed the composition of emerging rabbinic Judaism little may be said. Scribes were individuals who enjoyed an uncommon technical training. Their skill demanded neither elevated birth nor particular beliefs.[6] Nevertheless, their intimate involvement with scrolls of the law meant that some scribes acquired mastery of that law. As a consequence, they were much respected in the community at large, and the rabbis undoubtedly hoped to enjoy the same respect. Moreover, the Gospel narratives commonly speak of scribes found in the company of Pharisees, and the rabbis would comfortably have identified with such an association and its symbolism. Thus, though the rabbis were not, as a group, scribes, the Mishnah's scribal qualities may be understood to represent their claim for continuity with the scribal tradition and values.

The rabbis were also undoubtedly related to individuals referred to by Luke (7:30 and elsewhere) merely as "lawyers" (νομικοὶ), meaning experts in the law of the Torah. Again, these individuals do not comprise a coherent and identifiable group in pre-destruction society, but mention of such a recognized expertise makes it clear that honor accrued to those who were masters of the Torah. The rabbis' overriding concern with matters of law shows them as lawyers in much the same sense as those spoken of by Luke. But, again, this is only one of several qualities which informed the composition rabbinic religion, a piece in a much more complex whole.

The rabbis' religion represents an original synthesis of these earlier forms, a synthesis also characterized by genuine innovations. Why did this newly defined system emerge at the time that it did, and why with these particular emphases and not others?

As far as the chronology of this development is concerned, the defeats to Rome, both in the war of the destruction and the Bar Kokhba war, were the most significant factors. Had the Temple not been destroyed and Bar Kokhba, the messianic "Prince of Israel," not been defeated, it is likely that second-Temple Judaism, in the multiple expressions described above, would have continued for some time. But mere note of these events is not enough. Without considering the ways in which they irrevocably transformed second Temple society, we will be unable to grasp fully the complex of factors which contributed to the emergence of early Rabbinic Judaism.

M. Goodman, in his *The Ruling Class of Judaea*,[7] argues that Judean society in the first half of the first century had no popularly recognized ruling class. Not long before, Herod had destroyed all viable competitors for leadership in Judea and, following his death, his house stood thoroughly discredited. As mentioned, Herod had himself assured the weakness of the high priesthood, and the Romans subsequently did nothing to restore what status had been lost. There were, during this period, no independent wealthy families of note, and besides—so Goodman argues[8]—little power accrued to individuals in Judean society by virtue of wealth alone. Whatever the merit of Goodman's precise reconstruction, one thing is clear: no earlier ruling class survived the war of the destruction unscathed. The destruction of the Temple meant that the priesthood, weakened as it was, was now entirely without a base of power. Wealthy landowners, if they escaped the actual brutalities of war, found their properties confiscated. There was no king, no council, no legislative body to provide direction in the years following the defeat.[9] Nor, as far as we can tell, did any religious party survive the defeat intact. There was thus a (near) complete vacuum of leadership in the period immediately following the destruction, and it was in the space of this vacuum that the rabbis and their Judaism began to form.

But the picture is still incomplete. There was one sort of religious expression which remained dynamic during these centuries and emerged with particular force in the aftermath of the destruction, that is, apocalyptic prophecy, which found particular eloquence in the post-destruction apocalypses of Baruch and Ezra.[10] These pseudonymous prophecies imagine that the current age—the age following the defeat to "Babylon" and the destruction of the Temple (purportedly the first, but really the second)—heralds the imminent coming of the Messiah. Only with the immediate expectation of the redeemed world could the horrors of the recent war be tolerated. These contemporary expressions reflected a need felt by at least significant portions of the late-first century Jewish populace, and it is this same need which finally came to the fore in the revolt led by the messianic hopeful, Bar Kokhba. Perhaps, then, the most significant religious leadership following the first Roman war was the radical prophetic leadership—those who hoped to restore the Temple, the Priesthood, and the Jewish king.

The rabbis, as we saw, advanced a distinct alternative to this vision. Borrowing the Pharisees' zealousness for the law, their concern for purity and their "tradition of the elders;" the lawyers' Torah-expertise, the scribes' technical competence, and the priests' pivotal religious position, the rabbis' suppressed concern for the end-time and turned their attention to Torah, now in a new, larger sense. It is likely that the rabbis' way spoke to few Jews in the decades between the wars, and had the revolt of the second century succeeded, the rabbis may well have passed into oblivion. But there was defeat, and the ensuing vacuum was even more complete than it had been. The rabbis sober synthesis now had the chance to offer direction when other Judaisms could not.

Having identified the roots of emergent Rabbinic Judaism, we now confront an insurmountable problem. While we may go some distance in reconstructing the ideologies of the Pharisees and priests, and we may describe the social positions of all the groups discussed above with some relative confidence, we are at a loss to say anything about their approaches to reading scripture. Unfortunately, despite the wealth of the documentary record which remains to us from this period, we do not have a single work that may be assigned to any of these groups (including the priests and Pharisees!) with confidence, nor do contemporary witnesses describe their methods of reading or interpretation. Josephus, of course, attributes an extra-scriptural, ancestral tradition to the Pharisees (*Antiquities* 13.10.6 [297–298]), but what characterizes this tradition is precisely that it is *extra*-scriptural; whatever connection it might have had with the biblical text, through interpretation or otherwise, is seemingly denied. Josephus also writes that the Pharisees have a reputation for being the most accurate interpreters of the law, but he gives no hint concerning the methods by which this accuracy was presumably achieved. And the Pharisees are the best-documented of the groups which concern us here! Thus, unless we were to retroject rabbinic methods into the Pharisaic context—an unfortunately all too common scholarly practice which depends upon a complete and fatal circularity—we are forced to say that, whatever the traditions of reading of the rabbis' more direct predecessors may have been, we have no means of recovering them. Thus, we have no way of saying what methods of scriptural interpretation the rabbis may have learned from any of these pre-destruction groups.

If we look to those pre-destruction documents which do reveal characteristic means of reading earlier, authoritative scripture, we also confront an absence of compelling precedents. The most common means of "reading" earlier scripture in the centuries between the Maccabees and the Mishnah was either to build upon and "read into" earlier biblical stories, creating thereby new "biblical" texts (e.g. Jubilees, Enoch) or to write new narratives in accepted biblical forms, generally attributing such narratives to earlier biblical heroes (Judith and I Maccabees are examples of the first sort, the apocalypses of Baruch and Ezra examples of the latter). Neither of these models was employed by the rabbis, who insisted upon a clear distinction between canonical Hebrew Scripture and their own traditions (though this distinction was gradually muddied as the rabbis came to call their own teachings "Torah"). Neither does the *pesher* literature, discovered at Qumran, offer a precedent for rabbinic readings. The simple "quote of scripture—this refers to..." form of these documents is almost never paralleled in classical rabbinic works, and the methods which characterize rabbinic interpretation find no hint of a parallel in these same Qumran compositions. Even the controversial 4QMMT document, which shows affinity with early rabbinic concerns, offers us little in this context. MMT is a polemical epistle; whatever means might have been used to derive the laws for which it argues are not so much as hinted at in its lines.

D. Halivni argues that the Temple Scroll records a brief scriptural interpretation which is identical with that of the rabbis, *ad locum*, and therefore evidence of the greater antiquity of their method.[11] But the Temple Scroll and parallel rabbinic midrash merely declare (using similar but not identical language) that, in order for the law requiring a rapist/seducer to marry the victimized woman to be in force, they must otherwise be fit to marry one another. On the basis of the evidence which Halivni offers, all we may know with confidence is that this was a commonly accepted law in late Second Temple Judaism and that the term used to express the law, a particular form of the older Hebrew root ר-א-ה (a form unprecedented in biblical literature) had already entered literary usage by the time of the composition of the Temple Scroll. Otherwise, all we see in this law of the Temple Scroll is a legal assertion which may or may not have been based upon a particular method of reading.

Halivni's work also offers another possible key to recovering more ancient precedents for rabbinic methods of reading scripture. In the same context as the case just discussed, Halivni discusses three simple midrashim, recorded in the Mishnah, which he argues must have originated long before the destruction of the Temple. His argument is based, in each case, upon the realia assumed in the precise details of each midrash, realia which could have pertained in the two last centuries BCE but not in the more recent period, better known to the rabbis. Suffice it to say that each of his proffered proofs has been critiqued before,[12] and none is convincing. But even if they were, we would still be left with only three "simple" midrashim, none of which exhibits the unique methods by which even early rabbinic midrash is characterized.

In fact, the only place where reasonable (though by no means definitive) precedents for the methods of the rabbis have been discovered are in the Hellenistic world, in contemporary readings of Homer and other Greek classics. Several of the interpretive methods attributed to Hillel find some parallel in the work of Greek rhetoricians of the first centuries CE, and Rabbinic Hebrew terminology pertaining to these methods is sometimes best understood as a translation of equivalent Greek terms.[13] But Lieberman argues that only two of the rabbis' characteristic methods finds a reasonable parallel, and his conclusion is that no definitive Greek influence may be identified (that is, on the methods themselves; he agrees that the terminology is sometimes borrowed).[14] At the same time, the Hellenistic character of some rabbinic forms is undeniable, and it is thus reasonable to see at least minimal Hellenistic influence behind rabbinic conventions and even methods of reading.

Yet identifying such influence is not enough. All scholars who have noted parallels have commented on the "hebraization" or "judaizing" of foreign elements.[15] And the native sources of rabbinic reading can also not reasonably be denied. The problem is, simply, that we cannot identify such sources, and, for this reason, we may also not say with any confidence which of the rabbinic methods may have been the rabbis' own innovation.

There can be no question that Jews before the rabbis read and interpreted scripture. But reading the ambiguities of scripture and arriving at the same solutions for these ambiguities as would the rabbis does not make such earlier reading proto-rabbinic (let alone rabbinic). What characterizes the rabbis' readings is not the substance of their interpretations, which sometimes demonstrably parallels that of earlier Jewish groups, but the precise and characteristic methods of interpretation which were employed. And, despite the attribution of rabbinic methods to earlier figures like Hillel, such attributions are extremely suspect, serving, as they do, the rabbis' self-interest by claiming greater antiquity (and therefore authority) for their methods and teachings. To be sure, it is probable that some of the rabbis' interpretive methods predate the rabbis themselves. But some were also surely their own innovation. The rabbis' readings of scripture find record in contexts where rabbinic discourse is internal and insulated, in documents where the rabbis speak to rabbis. Thus, the public sensibility which would demand recognition, and therefore traditionality, did not pertain here, and it is entirely conceivable that significant elements of the midrash of the rabbis were their own very unique invention. Whether the reader judges continuity, borrowing or innovation to be more likely, the precise contours of rabbinic interpretation will be described in the sections following.[16]

Notes

1. See Pesher Habakkuk, viii.3, ix.9, and xi.4 (assuming that the common interpretation of "the wicked priest"="one of the Hasmonean high priests" is correct) and cf. 4Q448 ("Paean for King Jonathan,") transcribed and translated in *The Dead Sea Scrolls Uncovered*, ed. and with commentary by Robert Eisenman and Michael Wise (Shaftesbury, Dorset and Rockport, MA: Element, 1992), p. 280.
2. See D. Goodblatt, "The Place of the Pharisees in First Century Judaism: The State of the Debate," JJS 20, n. 1 (June 1989):12–30, and Anthony J. Saldarini, *Pharisees, Scribes and Sadducees in Palestinian Society* (Wilmington, Delaware: Michael Glazier, 1988), pp. 128–132.
3. For other reasons, Henry A. Fischel also calls "the historical Hillel" into question. See "Studies in Cynicism and the Ancient Near East: The Transformation of a *Chria*," in *Religions in Antiquity*, ed. by Jacob Neusner, *Supplements to Numen* 14 (Leiden: E.J. Brill, 1968), p. 375, and "Stories and History: Observations on Greco-Roman Rhetoric and Pharisaism," in *American Oriental Society Middle West Branch Semi-Centennial Volume*, ed. by Denis Sinor, *Oriental Series* 3 (Bloomington, Ind.: Indiana U. Press, 1969), pp. 77–8.
4. Shaye J. D. Cohen calls the rabbis "latter-day Pharisees who had no desire to publicize the connection." See his detailed discussion of the relationship between the Pharisees and rabbis in "The Significance of Yavneh: Pharisees, Rabbis, and the End of Jewish Sectarianism," HUCA 55 (1984):36–42. The characterization quoted above is found on p. 41.
5. See Jacob Neusner, *Judaism: The Evidence of the Mishnah* (Chicago: U. of Chicago Press, 198?), pp. 241–250.
6. Anthony J. Saldarini writes that, during the period at hand, "scribes do not seem to be a coherent social class with a set membership, but rather a class of literate individuals drawn from many parts of society who filled many social roles and were attached to all parts of society from the village to the palace and Temple." See *Pharisees, Scribes and Sadducees*, p. 275.
7. *The Ruling Class of Judaea: The Origins of the Jewish Revolt Against Rome A.D. 66–70* (Cambridge: Cambridge U. Press, 1987).
8. P. 126.
9. Goodman argues cogently that the sanhedrin had not been a fixed, ongoing institution during the late second Temple period. See pp. 113–114.
10. As well as the book of Revelation.
11. See David Halivni, *Midrash, Mishnah and Gemara: The Jewish Predilection for Justified Law* (Cambridge: Harvard U. Press, 1986), pp. 30–34.
12. See Richard Kalmin's review in *Conservative Judaism* 39, n. 4 (Summer 1987):78–84.
13. See the discussion of David Daube, "Rabbinic Methods of Interpretation and Hellenistic Rhetoric," HUCA 22 (1949): 239–264.
14. Saul Lieberman, *Hellenism in Jewish Palestine*, 2nd ed. (New York: Jewish Theological Seminary, 1962), pp. 42–82. The judgments referred to here are found on pp. 54, 56, and 59–61.
15. See Daube, "Rabbinic Methods of Interpretation," p. 240, and Henry A. Fischel, "Studies in Cynicism and the Ancient Near East," pp. 407–411.
16. This chapter was written with the support of the Abbell research fund of the Jewish Theological Seminary of America.

Chapter Seven

Scriptural Interpretation in the Mishnah

Before discussing the Mishnah's approaches to the reading and interpretation of Hebrew Scripture, it is first necessary to explain why one would want to isolate this document in the first place. Why not speak simply of tannaitic/early rabbinic developments in scriptural hermeneutics? What justifies and/or requires that the Mishnah be dealt with on its own terms?

The answer to these questions points us to two of the most heated debates in contemporary scholarship of classical rabbinism, those being (1) Can attributions or other apparently historical claims in early rabbinic documents be taken at face value?, and (2) What is the relationship between the scriptural interpretations recorded in the halakhic midrashim, which purport to be tannaitic, and the laws of the Mishnah which apparently relate to these interpretations? Did such interpretations actually yield the laws of the Mishnah, which would make the substance of the halakhic midrashim prior, or are these midrashim really later apologia for the Mishnah's laws?

The view of what might be called "traditional" scholarship is that attributions are accurate and that rabbinic laws are in fact derived, by means of various accepted methods, from Scripture.[1] According to this view, it would be unnecessary to distinguish between the Mishnah's record of early rabbinic developments and the testimony of other tannaitic texts. The alternative view, propounded most vigorously by Jacob Neusner, rejects the historical claims of given documents and reads them as individual statements, each with its own integrity, in the unfolding canon of rabbinic Judaism.[2] Since the halakhic midrashim (as well as the Tosefta) are acknowledged to have come to final documentary expression subsequent to the Mishnah, and because their internal claims to tannaitic provenance cannot be accepted uncritically, Neusner will view the Mishnah as the earliest record of rabbinic readings of scripture. Moreover, since the claims of the halakhic midrashim to record the views of specific named sages must be viewed skeptically, we cannot supplement the evidence of the Mishnah with midrashic traditions attributed to the same sages. Neusner's approach, it will be clear, requires that we consider the Mishnah independently.

So this section assumes, to begin with, the methodological restrictions proposed by Neusner. However, its conclusions will suggest that Neusner's position, even on its own terms, is, as often articulated, too extreme. We will find that, despite radical differences in the relationships of the Mishnah and the halakhic midrashim to Scripture, there is no question that the methods of reading typified in the latter are also attested in the former. When the Mishnah did actually read Scripture, the methods it employed were largely the same as the early midrashim. Thus, though the Mishnah may have been redacted earlier, it is clear that the sorts of readings to which the midrashim give voice were developing at the same time as the Mishnah. Therefore, whatever the agenda of the halakhic midrashim as redacted documents, it is reasonable to suppose that, in limited instances, the rabbinic methods of reading indeed yielded the laws to which they are attached.

Popular introductions to Rabbinic literature have sometimes described the Mishnah as a record of rabbinic interpretations of Torah. Perhaps because the Mishnah has traditionally been approached through the lens of the Babylonian Talmud, which often seeks to find the source of mishnaic laws in Scripture, such a description generally evokes no dissent. But the simple fact is that the Mishnah quotes Scripture relatively rarely. To be precise, I count a total of approximately 265 quotations of Scripture in the Mishnah (excluding references to liturgical recitations of Scripture and excluding tractate Abot). There are 517 chapters in the entire Mishnah (again, excluding Abot), meaning that Scripture is quoted only slightly more than once every two chapters. If we recognize that there are certain chapters and tractates which are unusual for the quantity of Scripture they do quote, we will appreciate that, in the bulk of the Mishnah, quotation of Scripture is rather a rare occurrence (in fact, in a few tractates there are no quotations whatsoever). Therefore, not only is it incorrect to speak of the Mishnah as a commentary on the Torah, but it is only slightly hyperbolic to suggest, borrowing Neusner's words, that "superficially, the Mishnah is totally indifferent to Scripture."[3]

But this superficial description doesn't do justice to the actual relationship of the Mishnah to Scripture, which is far more complex than its formal independence would suggest. Neusner reviews the relationship of the Mishnah's laws to Scripture in some detail and suggests, in conclusion, the following three categories of relationship: (1) "there are tractates which simply repeat in their own words precisely what Scripture has to say;" (2) "there are... tractates which take up facts of Scripture but work them out in a way in which those Scriptural facts cannot have led us to predict;" and (3) "there are... tractates which either take up problems in no way suggested by Scripture, or begin from facts at best merely relevant to the facts of Scripture."[4] It is more than a matter of coincidence that Neusner's categorization recreates, in large part, precisely the possibilities suggested in the Mishnah itself, at Hagigah 1:8:

> [Laws concerning] the releasing of vows fly in the air, for they have nothing [in Scripture] on which to depend. Laws of the Sabbath, festival offerings, and the misappropriation of sacred things, they are like mountains hanging by a hair, for they have little Scripture and many laws. [And the laws of] judgments, the sacrificial service, purities and impurities, and prohibited sexual relations, they have [Scripture] on which to depend....

In other words, sometimes the Mishnah submits to Scripture's dictates, sometimes it reads Scripture aggressively, and sometimes it sets its own agenda, mostly ignoring what Scripture may or may not have to contribute to the subject. Behind the Mishnah, undoubtedly, lies the Torah, but how and whether it reads that Torah is, apparently, its own choice.

This complex and varied relationship suggests complex rhetorical purposes. Much of the vocabulary employed, the institutions assumed, and the occasional verse quoted, all suggest that the relationship between the Mishnah and Scripture is profound if non-specific. The less-educated reader will certainly hear the many Scriptural echoes behind the Mishnah and conclude that it is a powerfully traditional document. But readers with greater erudition will quickly appreciate that, even when the Mishnah reads Scripture, its reading is sometimes not so "traditional" (in the popular sense). They will see the Mishnah defining its own categories, even forcing Scripture into the mold which the Mishnah, alone, creates.

A superb example of the Mishnah's "misreading" of Scripture for its own ends is found in chapter three of tractate Baba Meṣia. The Mishnah, speaking of deposits given to one's neighbor and the obligations of the bailee in such cases, obviously assumes as its background Exodus 22:6–12. Verses 6 and 9 seem to make a clear and natural distinction: "If a man should give to his neighbor money or vessels to watch, and it be stolen from the man's house [there is no liability]... If a man should give to his neighbor an ass or an ox or a sheep, or any beast, to watch... if it be stolen from him he shall make payment to its owner." According to these verses, the law changes as a function of the nature of what is given to be watched; inanimate movables involve a lower level of liability and animals a greater level. This is clearly the simple and most natural reading of the verses at hand. But the Mishnah suggests a different category distinction, denying explicitly, in the process, the distinction offered in the Torah: "If one deposits with his fellow *an animal or vessels* to watch, and they are stolen or lost—if he paid and did not want to [instead] take an oath [eliminating his liability], for they have said, 'A gratuitous bailee may take an oath and go out [free of any liability],' if the thief is found..." etc. (emphasis added). For the Mishnah, the important difference is whether or not the bailee is paid—a distinction utterly without precedent in the Torah's law. The Torah's distinction, at the same time, is explicitly erased, without any reason offered to justify this shift.

Now, if pressed, there is no doubt that the rabbis behind this Mishnah could justify their proposed categorization with reference to Scripture. Some rabbinic author does just this, in fact, in the halakhic midrash to the same verses (see Mekhilta, Neziqin 15; Horowitz-Rabin, p. 301). But the reading in the Midrash is defensive and forced, and the Mishnah, in any case, typically does not bother with such a justification. A common reader might not pick up on all this, but the rabbinic reader would surely have realized the problems posed in the present Mishnah. He would have understood, in other words, that the Mishnah's law, even when related to the Torah, is not dictated by the Torah. The Mishnah's rhetoric of Scripture allows for greater rabbinic power and independence than might at first appear.

When we turn to the Mishnah's explicit readings and interpretations of Scripture, we already discover many of the characteristic assumptions and methods which would find more widespread expression in later rabbinic documents. Before illustrating these, however, it is important to note that the majority of the Mishnah's explicit references to Scripture simply quote a verse (or part thereof) to support an opinion or assertion. They say, in effect, "the law is such-and-such because Scripture says...." Of course, even such cases involve subtle interpretations. But these interpretations are not evident on the surface and readings of this kind tend to be quite straightforward. Far more interesting, for present purposes, are those cases which make their interpretive methods explicit.

The rabbis in the Mishnah (as later) do not insist upon literal or simple readings of Scripture, and their interpretations are sometimes quite inventive. An excellent example of the flexibility of Mishnaic reading is Berakhot 1:3, where the Houses of Shammai and Hillel argue the proper physical position for reciting the Shema. Based upon Deuteronomy 6:7 ("when you lie down and when you rise up"), the Shammaites propose that one should actually recline in the evening and stand up in the morning. Countering with a reference to another phrase in the same verse ("when you walk on the road"), the Hillelites say that the Shema may be recited in any position, claiming that the words "when you lie down and when you rise up" may be understood to require the recitation of these words when you would ordinarily be doing these things, that is, in the evening and in the morning. The Hillelites are less bound by the literal meaning of the words, whereas the Shammaites seem to require a more literal application of what the words say.

But, in truth, even the reading of the Shammaites is not all that literal. They do, after all, require recitation at specific times of day and not at all times, as the verse might be understood to require ("when you sit in your house and when you walk on the road, and when you lie down and when you rise up"). Moreover, any application of these verses to a specific liturgy called the Shema, to be recited, in precise form, twice each day, must be understood as anything but literal. The verses at hand say merely "these words," referring, apparently, to the words of the Torah in general. Indeed, the Shema as we have it is most likely a rabbinic formulation, and this midrashic dispute may be understood, therefore, as a self-conscious and somewhat fanciful re-reading of a Scriptural source.

Perhaps the most overarching principle informing rabbinic readings of Scripture, already in evidence at this stage, is the assumption that, divinely inspired as they are, all of Scripture's words, and even individual scriptural features, are meaningful. This assumption is illustrated in a homiletical reading at Berakhot 9:5, referring again to one of the verses which comprises the Shema (Deut. 6:5). Part of this midrash understands the doubling of the letter *bet* in the Hebrew word for "your heart" to imply that you should love God with *both* of your hearts, that is, with both your inclination to do good and your inclination to do evil. Behind this reading is the assumption that even individual letters of the Torah carry (potentially, at least) divine import, so if the letter is doubled, God must have intended this doubling to teach us something.

The latter part of the same Mishnaic midrash shows the rabbinic willingness to read Scripture creatively and perhaps even playfully. The last phrase of this verse in Deuteronomy requires that you love God "with all your might"—בכל מאדך. In one of two interpretations, the Mishnah reads this to mean "with each and every measure by which He measures you, you should thank Him very much" (בכל מדה ומדה שהוא מודד לך הוי מודה לו במאד מאד). This is all built upon the similarity, aural and orthographic, between Scripture's "מאד" and the words מדה, מודד, מודה, and מאד (with a different meaning than Scripture's term). On one level, this interpretation shows the assumed power of even individual Scriptural terms. But it also shows the inventiveness with which the early rabbis were willing to approach these terms.

Many of the rabbi's formal exegetical methods are already employed in the Mishnah. Relatively common is the קל וחומר (*a fortiori* reasoning), which sometimes serves as the building block for rather sophisticated disputes (see, for example, Pesahim 6:2). The principle limiting the application of קל וחומר, insisting that the derived case be no more expansive than the case upon which the proof rests, is also already known in the Mishnah (Baba Qamma 2:5). Similarly attested are גזרה שוה (the equation of common Scriptural terms used in different contexts; see, e.g., Sotah 6:3), בנין אב (the construction of a general category from specified scriptural examples; see, e.g., Baba Qamma 1:1), היקש (equation of principles or cases; Makkot 1:6), derivation based upon the juxta-position of scriptural discussions (סמיכות, see Hullin 8:4), דבר שהיה בכלל ויצא מין הכלל (a lesson based upon a specific example which already would have been subsumed under a general ruling; see Baba Mezia 2:5), the reconciliation of two apparently contradictory scriptures (Sheqalim 6:6), and others. Many of these cases are paralleled, sometimes almost exactly, in the halakhic midrashim.

This latter fact returns us to the issue mentioned earlier, that is, the question of the relationship between the Mishnah and those early rabbinic documents which offer themselves explicitly as commentaries on the Torah. In evaluating this question, we must account for three phenomena: (1) the midrash's characteristic methods are used in the Mishnah, if only infrequently; (2) parallels between the Mishnah and these midrashim are not uncommon; and, (3) there are rare blocks of Mishnaic text, such as large sections of Sotah chapters 5, 7 and 8, which are themselves clearly halakhic midrash, in both form and substance. Even if we grant, then, that the halakhic midrashim are post-Mishnaic compositions which, by tying the Mishnah's laws back to Scripture, serve as apologia for the earlier document (and there are reasons to believe that this characterization is overly-neat), we must still conclude that rabbinic-midrashic reading was already alive and well in the period during which the Mishnah took shape. Nor should this conclusion be the cause for surprise. Midrashic reading, though formally confessing the superior authority of scripture, is often, in fact, an extraordinary show of rabbinic power and even independence. In this respect, such methods of interpretation are well suited to the more general posture of the Mishnah as it relates to scripture.

One question which has drawn considerable attention, and which is relevant already with relation to these earliest rabbinic exegeses, is whether the rabbis were at all sensitive to what we would call "the simple sense" (the *peshat*) of Scripture.[5] This question is rendered acute by virtue of the fact that the rabbis so often seem either to ignore or to read against the apparent simple sense. Consider, for example, Baba Mezia 2:7 (with parallels at Mekhilta *dekaspa* 20 [pp. 324–5] and Sifre Deut. 223). The Mishnah offers itself as an interpretive reading of Deut. 22:2: "If your brother is not near to you, or you do not know him, then you shall gather it [the lost animal which you have recovered] into your house and it shall be with you until your brother claims it, then you shall restore it to him." Allegedly based upon this verse, the Mishnah rules: "A deceiver, even though he listed its [=the lost object's] indicative characteristics, you should not give it to him, for it is said, 'עד דרש אחיך אתו [=until your brother claims it]', [meaning] until you examine your brother [עד שתדרוש את אחיך] to see whether or not he is a deceiver." Relying upon various possibilities of meaning in the verbal root, this midrash reverses the direction of the action in the sentence, making "your brother" the object instead of the subject. This is done in complete disregard for the structure of the sentence and despite the fact that the verse, as it stands, is not ambiguous.

Now, do examples like these mean that the rabbis did not know the simple sense of what they were reading? Mishnah Shabbat 8:7 makes it evident that the rabbis behind the Mishnah did at least distinguish between different levels of proof from Scripture. There, R. Meir introduces his proof of a particular opinion (from Isa. 30:14) with the phrase, "even though there is no [bona fide] proof of the matter, there is a hint for it...." Admittedly, this does not mean that bona fide proofs relate to the simple sense of the source text, but at least these rabbis perceived different levels of straying from the text.

A midrash at Sotah 8:5 shows that rabbinic reading, at this stage, was even more appreciative (when it chose to be) of the simple sense of Scripture. There, the Mishnah records a dispute regarding the law to be derived from Deut. 20:8, "And the officers shall speak further to the people and say, 'Who is the man who is afraid and fainthearted...?'" R. Aqiba suggests that the words "afraid and fainthearted" should be taken "according to their meaning," that is, to exclude someone who is afraid of the horrors of war. R. Yose the Galilean, by contrast, suggests that the verse means to exclude someone who is "afraid of the sins which are in his hand"—presumably, if someone is a sinner, he cannot be assured of God's protection in war, and he will thus be afraid. This Mishnaic midrash is clearly aware of the plain meaning of the verse at hand, as it indicates explicitly. This does not mean, however, that the simple reading is necessarily preferred. Whatever the value of simple reading, it has no presumed authority in questions of rabbinic halakha.

We see, then, that the first record of rabbinic reading already shows the rabbis methods to be well developed. These are, it must be recognized, often aggressive methods, permitting the rabbis to build significantly upon the scriptural base-texts they choose to employ. This independence of spirit which is evident already at this earliest stage of rabbinic interpretation helps to explain the considerable developments in interpretive methods to be found in the following period.[6]

Notes

1. The assumption that attributions may be accepted at face-value is widespread. The strongest argument for the priority of Midrash to Mishnah is David Halivni's *Midrash, Mishnah, and Gemara: The Jewish Predilection for Justified Law* (Cambridge: Harvard U. Press, 1986).
2. Neusner's method and its defense have been articulated repeatedly. Perhaps its most powerful (and polemical) statement is found in *Reading and Believing: Ancient Judaism and Contemporary Gullibility* (Atlanta: Scholars Press, 1986). See my detailed discussion of these questions in chapters one and two of this book.
3. Neusner, *Judaism: The Evidence of the Mishnah* (Chicago: U. of Chicago Press, 1981), p. 217.
4. Ibid., pp. 221–2.
5. This question has been addressed more broadly by David Halivni in *Peshat and Derash: Plain and Applied Meaning in Rabbinic Exegesis* (New York: Oxford U. Press, 1991). Halivni's examination of the early rabbinic evidence is not sufficiently detailed, making his treatment of the rabbis' scriptural readings during this period incomplete.
6. This chapter has been written with the support of the Abbell Research Fund of the Jewish Theological Seminary.

INTRODUCTION TO CHAPTER EIGHT

This article represents the first product of my "mature" method. The foundations of this method are two-fold: (1) Whether or not rabbinic documents may be "mined" to discover historical evidence concerning the generations during which they were purportedly produced (concerning which see part I of this book), they must finally be read sequentially, as the formulations of a final "authorship," precisely as Neusner suggests. This is because the only period for which these documents provide indisputable evidence is the period of their final formulation. Hence, they may serve as evidence for the composition of religious/intellectual histories. (2) Each document must be read for its rhetoric, the reader seeking to expose the persuasive elements of the formulation, ever-cognizant of the nature of the original reader (and therefore reading) assumed by the "author." A detailed exposition of this method may be found in the first chapter of my *Reading the Rabbis*.

In the present article, I conduct such a reading to explore the relationship of each cohort of rabbis to the "canon" they inherit. I ask about the precise outlines of the canon assumed by each. I consider how the canon changes and how later versions of the canon affect earlier canonizations. Finally, I offer the history of the rabbis and their canons as a heuristic model on the basis of which other canonical models can be judged and other canonical histories critiqued. Among a variety of important conclusions, I critique the work of Sid Leiman, whose interpretation of the history of the masoretic biblical canon cannot—or so I argue—be maintained. (Unfortunately, Leiman's work continues to be cited by many scholars without an awareness of the difficulties I expose here.)

I hasten to add that, in recent work, Jacob Neusner has confirmed the conclusions of the present piece while employing a different method; see *What, Exactly, Did the Rabbinic Sages Mean By "The Oral Torah"?* (Scholars Press, 1998).

Chapter Eight

The Formation of Rabbinic Canon: Authority and Boundaries

In an extremely thoughtful essay on canon and canonization, Gerald T. Sheppard distinguishes between two understandings of canon, relating to two poles in the canonization process.[1] The first "canon" is that of rules, ideals, norms, traditions, etc., that are believed to possess a certain elevated authority. It is generally this meaning of canon that is intended when we speak of a text or rule being "canonical," that is, possessing a certain recognized authority within a particular community. This canonical characteristic may be present in either religious or secular contexts, and thus, just as there is a "canon law," so too are there literary or artistic values that are canonical in any given society. Because, as is clear, there might be various levels of such authority admitted in a community, different texts or traditions can be canonical to a greater or lesser degree at the same time.

The second usage of canon is in connection with standard lists or enumerations, such as in "the biblical canon" or "the canon of classics of Western literature." Subsumed in this meaning as well is the definition of the accepted boundaries of a given text. At this level, the canon enumerates, in effect, the chapters or stories or traditions that are to be included in the document in question. For example, it is this canon that we speak of when we contrast the various canons of the book of Daniel.[2]

According to Sheppard, and supported by others,[3] traditions or texts that attain certain levels of authority (type 1) are often subsequently defined by the boundaries of a recognized delimited scripture (type 2).

> The recognition of canon [= type I] materials, defined as traditions offering a normative vehicle or an ideal standard, occurs in most world religions and usually

contributes momentum to an impulse within the history of religion to totalize, to circumscribe, and to standardize these same normative traditions into fixed, literary forms typical of canon 2.[4]

James A. Sanders further explains, "A canon begins to take shape... because a question of identity or authority has arisen, and a canon begins to become unchangeable... somewhat later, after the question of identity has for the most part been settled."[5]

While the matter is relatively clear in theory, important problems are encountered when we seek to apply this theoretical construct to real cases. The first problem is the practical difficulty of tracing the development of a canon from one canonical pole to the other. For example, there are significant differences of opinion regarding the history of the development of authoritative biblical traditions and books (canon type 1) into closed books and uniformly recognized canons (type 2). Some argue that the canonization (1→2) of at least the Torah and Prophets was relatively early (by the mid-fifth century BCE) and that even the Writings, with the exception of minor details, were canonized long before the so-called council at Yabne.[6] In contrast, encouraged by the discoveries at Qumran, many are now of the opinion that the ancient Hebrew canon was more fluid at a far later stage than had previously been believed.[7]

This debate is partially a consequence of the fact that Jews did not, until at least the first or second century CE, have a precise or equivalent term for canon.[8] Moreover, the phrase employed by the early rabbis ("rendering the hands impure," m. Yad. 3:5) and understood by some to be their expression of canonical definition is not unambiguous, and Leiman, at least, denies that it has any direct bearing on the question of canonization.[9] As a consequence, the Yabnean debate that, in the opinion of many earlier scholars, represented the rabbinic canonization of the Hebrew Scripture, is presently subject to various alternative interpretations. Beckwith sees the claims that Canticles and Ecclesiastes do not render the hands impure to be merely individual opinions, unimportant in connection with books that the community had long held to be canon.[10] Leiman, approaching the problem from a different direction, argues that the debate only concerned the question of whether the books under discussion were divinely inspired but not whether they were canonical. It is demonstrable, he claims, that even those who questioned whether they were inspired nevertheless accepted them as canon.[11]

The second problem with the stated theory is its limited picture of canonical process, admitting the crucial importance of development in one direction but not the other. It is emphasized that traditions or teachings, once attaining a certain level of authority, usually generate an impulse to define and to standardize those traditions, that is, to canonize them. But is this necessary? Granted, it is reasonable to believe that canonical definition is preceded by the recognition of a certain authority. But must this authority lead to such precise definitions? Moreover, even if such definitions are at some point achieved, is this to say that the closure of a canon is the final stage of canonical development? What of the possibility that—perhaps as a consequence of new questions of identity—canons might be reopened?[12] As we shall see, the example of rabbinic literature suggests that traditions for which the community comes to claim new and greater authority can challenge the integrity of earlier delimited canons. Surely, alternative pictures are available.

Below we will trace in some detail the development of the canon of rabbinic literature. This history is instructive for two reasons. First, compared to the case of Hebrew Scriptures, the history of the canonization of this literature—in both senses of the term canon—is far better documented. The developing authority of specific rabbinic texts or traditions within the rabbinic community is reflected in the various commentaries that responded, at relatively short intervals, to these texts, as are the precise boundaries that were recognized at any given stage.[13] In addition, there is explicit testimony to the level of canonical authority ascribed to the literature at each step in the presence or absence of the term "*torah she-be^{c}al pe*" ("Oral Torah") in various rabbinic documents. By claiming that rabbinic traditions, too, were part of the Torah revealed at Sinai, this term reflects the self-conscious willingness of the rabbinic authors to equate the authority of their own teachings with written scripture and indicates the self-assured admission of these teachings into the canon of "Torah."

Second, as mentioned, the rabbinic model will offer an alternative to the narrower view of canonical development stressed by Sheppard and Sanders. We will see that as rabbinic Judaism matured it sought to ground its authority in the revelation at Sinai. As the canonical authority of rabbinic literature was thereby enhanced, the boundaries of the earlier defined canon became blurred. In consequence of the ever more precious status of rabbinic tradition as a whole, traditions that had earlier presumably been excluded from the canon were subsequently readmitted. Furthermore, with the claim that even rabbinic opinions yet to be enunciated were part of the original revelation, the theoretical distinctions between the authority of different elements of the ever-expanding canon were largely eliminated.

This same phenomenon will yield one further lesson, to be spelled out below. I will argue that one of Leiman's central arguments concerning the development of the biblical canon, that is, that there was a distinction between "inspired" and "uninspired" canon, is—at least in the community that finally defined that canon—not tenable. In the later rabbinic community, at least, the literature that embodied the norms and values of Jewish society had finally to be understood as being inspired. If the earlier rabbinic community at Yabne shared this same impulse, then the solution Leiman proposes becomes, as a consequence of what follows, very difficult to accept.

II

There can be little question that the Mishna (ca. 200 CE), at a very early stage, was deemed canonical; its boundaries were clear and unambiguous, and these boundaries represented the exclusion of other contemporary traditions from its corpus. At the same time, at least in rabbinic circles its authority could not be ignored. This is evidenced in the variety of commentaries and responses that, already in the century following its promulgation, the Mishna stimulated (the Tosepta, the Amoraic commentaries, the redacted halakic midrashim).

Still, vis-a-vis the canon of Mishna, this same literary response had ironic consequences. The Tosepta and the halakic midrashim were compilations of (at least purportedly) tannaitic traditions, and the Amoraim too seem to have given ample attention to non-Mishnaic tannaitic texts. That is to say, while the formal boundaries of the Mishna were respected in the several generations following its closure, the choice that the Mishna's author had made to exclude certain traditions was undermined by the recovery of many such traditions into other soon-to-be canonical documents. Moreover, the precise level of the Mishna's canonical authority was, in the opinion of some, still open to dispute and dissent—its authority was far from absolute even in the rabbinic community.[14] At the very least—as has recently been demonstrated[15]—the status of the Mishna as "Torah" had at this time not yet been formulated, and so its full canonical authority had not yet emerged.

This latter claim requires clarification. It is true that rabbinic tradition is, in some ill-defined manner, subsumed under the rubric of "Torah" at the beginning of Abot (at its redactional level, at least, a post-Mishnaic document), but it is not clear yet that the Mishna or other specific rabbinic traditions are meant to be included in this category. The claim for authority that is articulated in this text may refer more precisely to the sages of the Mishna and then, only by derivation, to the traditions that they teach.[16] In the halakic midrashim, by contrast, clear reference is made to an Oral Torah, though only on two occasions (Sifra, *Behuqotai* 8, 12 [to Lev. 26:46], and Sifre Deut. 351). The precise object of these references is unclear, however, and in at least one of the two cases Martin S. Jaffee has shown that the redactor was uncomfortable with the notion of "Oral Torah" altogether.[17] In any case, these midrashim evince an essential tension. As Neusner has demonstrated, the words of the sages are claimed in these documents to be Torah.[18] On the other hand, in their implicit critique of the Mishna (which does not generally justify its rulings by reference to scripture, as the midrashim deem proper) these same texts seem to suggest that the Mishna. without the enhancement of midrash at least, is not.

The Yerushalmi (ca. 400 CE), in a careful, extended commentary that overwhelmingly respects the agenda established by the Mishna,[19] does apparently pay homage to the canon of Mishna—both to the boundaries that it defines and to the authority that it claims. Its concerns are addressed to the law of the Mishna and to its language, and, as Neusner has properly argued, the similarity of the Yerushalmi's approach to the Mishna with the approach of the midrash to scripture unambiguously suggests that the Mishna, like scripture, is deemed in this Talmud to be Torah.[20]

The same conclusion is supported by the explicit reference to an "Oral [Torah]" in the Yerushalmi (though not employing the full term *"torah she-be^{c}al pe"*), now not only generally but also in specific connection to the Mishna. The Yerushalmi's discussion of Oral Torah (a single discussion found, with slight differences, in Pe'a 2:17a, Hag. 1:76d and, in somewhat abbreviated form, in Meg. 4:74d) makes the following points: (1) Several [nonscriptural] laws were stated to Moses at Sinai, all of which are included in the Mishna (this general point is evident in the Mishna itself, but the characterization of these laws as "Torah," suggested clearly in the points that follow, is found here for the first time). (2) Most of the Torah revealed to Moses at Sinai was not written (and therefore must have been oral). (3) The revelation to Moses was both written and oral, and the oral component is more precious than the written. (4) Every bit of wisdom ever to be pronounced by a rabbi or rabbinic disciple, past, present, and future, was already revealed to Moses at Sinai. These points, in chorus, leave no room for doubt: The Mishna is canonical as the Torah is canonical—that is, both are inspired. But we must be careful; as Neusner has suggested, this is canon in the first sense, not in the second. The same traditions that enhance the status of the earlier texts eliminate, for purposes of this enhanced authority, the effective boundaries that the earlier texts define.[21]

With the exception of the first point listed above, all of these traditions speak of an Oral Torah that clearly goes well beyond the Mishna alone. This is especially clear in the last point, where all rabbinic traditions of any age are included in the inspired Oral Torah. The same expansion is achieved in the Yerushalmi's overall commentary, where not only the Mishna but also extra-Mishnaic tannaitic traditions and even the traditions of the Talmudic sages themselves are subject to the same nature of commentary and scrutiny. What we witness in the Yerushalmi, therefore, is an enhancement of the canonical authority of the Mishna and other rabbinic traditions (canon type 1) and a concomitant dissolution of the canonical boundaries of the Mishna as a distinct authoritative document (canon type 2).

The same may be said with respect to the Bavli (ca. 600 CE), where each of the trends evidenced in the Yerushalmi is even more extreme. Though the Bavli formally respects the foundation of the Mishna in its commentary, it is willing to ignore that foundation far more often than the Yerushalmi.[22]

Moreover, its extensive resort to tannaitic sources outside of the Mishna and its frequent positing of an Amoraic foundation often subvert the canonical limits of the Mishna and suggest, resoundingly, that all of this tradition, Mishnaic and beyond, is Torah.

The status of that expanded Torah is elevated indeed. Though the Bavli speaks explicitly of the Oral Torah on a total of only four occasions,[23] the ideology of Oral Torah it expresses is without parallel in earlier rabbinic documents. The two instances that devote significant attention to the notion are formulated with painstaking care and so can be appreciated only with patient, extended analysis. With the reader's indulgence, I shall detail such analyses below in order that, in the end, we shall be able fully to appreciate the considerable distance that the perceived authority of the rabbinic canon traveled from its relatively humble beginnings.

The first Bavli text in which the concept of Oral Torah forms a central concern is the oft-quoted story of Shammai, Hillel, and the convert in Shabb. 31a.[24] Relevant portions of the text follow:

> 1. a. Our Rabbis taught: It happened that a gentile came before Shammai and said to him "how many Torahs do you have?"
> b. He said to him: "Two, a Written Torah and an Oral Torah."
> c. He said to him: "With respect to the Written one, I believe you, but with respect to the Oral I do not believe you. Convert me on the condition that you teach me [only] the Written Torah."
> d. [Shammai] rebuked him and sent him out in anger.
> e. He came before Hillel [and stated the same condition, and] he converted him.
> f. On the first day he said to him [in naming the letters of the Hebrew alphabet] "*aleph, bet, gimel, dalet*." The next day he reversed them.
> g. He said to him: "But yesterday you didn't say it to me this way!"
> h. He said to him: "*Have you not [inevitably] depended upon my [words]? With respect to the Oral [Torah] also depend on me.*"
>
> II. a. It happened at another time that a gentile came before Shammai and said to him "convert me on the condition that you teach me the whole Torah while I stand on one foot."
> b. He pushed him with the beam of the building that was in his hand.
> c. He came before Hillel [and said the same thing, and] he converted him.
> d. He said to him "That which is hateful to you do not do to your fellow—*this is the whole Torah and the rest is interpretation*. Go and learn." [emphasis added]

The subject of both of these exchanges, beyond the superior character of Hillel, is the relationship of Written and Oral Torah. This is explicit in the first story. The potential convert approaches Shammai and Hillel, asking them both about the existence of a second, Oral Torah, and they both insist that the oral component is Torah just as is the written. For present purposes, the manner in which Hillel persuades his interlocutor is of particular interest. Hillel demonstrates that, on the most basic level, Written Torah is dependent on oral teachings. The written signs do not reveal their own meaning; that meaning is available only through the (oral) tradition of reading. First we must be told the pronunciation of the letters; next we must be taught to combine them and to make sense of those combinations. Only thus does the written text begin to have any meaning at all. On account of this, it is nonsensical to insist on the Written alone; the Oral must, by definition, be prior.

A related point is made in the second exchange. There Hillel's claim is that, aside from one particular teaching, "that which is hateful... ," the rest of the Written Torah is interpretation. Of course, the Oral Torah is also, in good part, interpretation,[25] and so this response may be understood as a fundamental equation of the two kinds of Torah. But when we consider that "the whole Torah," embodied in the maxim "that which is hateful... ," is also interpretation, we are led to understand that there is nothing in the Written Torah that is not interpretation, and the Written and Oral Torahs are, therefore, intrinsically equal. Both practically (in the first story) and essentially (in the second), the Bavli unites the two Torahs and hints that it would be a mistake to suggest the ultimate superiority of one over the other. Both together comprise the full divine revelation.

The same point is made, at greater length and with significant artistry, in Gittin 60a–b. To appreciate its rhetoric, we require extensive portions of that text. To prevent the analysis from becoming unwieldy, I divide the talmudic deliberation into smaller units, but full understanding demands that we finally view the text as a unified whole.

The relevant deliberation is introduced by a lengthy discussion of the question of whether the canonical limits of individual scriptural books or units (such as the Pentateuch) are, for ritual purposes, inviolable. The Talmud begins with two questions, the first regarding the permissibility of reading scrolls of individual books of the Torah in the synagogue and the second regarding the permissibility of reading scrolls containing the liturgical portions from the prophets (*haptarot*). In both instances, the larger concern is the problem of writing or reading portions of scripture that are smaller than some canonical whole; scrolls of individual books are smaller than the whole Torah of Moses (containing five books), and the liturgical prophetic portions are, with a couple of possible exceptions,[26] all smaller than canonical prophetic books. In the first case, reading sections that are less than some canon is prohibited, but, in the second, ingenious argumentation leads to a positive ruling. The Talmud's reasoning is this: Though ideally books of *haptarot* should be prohibited, we see elsewhere that R. Yohanan and R. Shimeon b. Laqish would refer to a book of aggada (narrative midrash) on the Sabbath despite the fact that, being Oral Torah, its writing should have been proscribed. How could these authorities have justified their actions? Since *it was impossible to do otherwise*—because, in the absence of a written record, this element of the Oral Torah would have been forgotten—it is judged that a relatively minor infringement of the ideal is justified. So too, then, in the case of liturgical prophetic portions should the infringement of the ideal be justified (if we required whole books rather than smaller liturgical portions many communities would not be able to afford this ritual), and, consequently, the canonical boundaries cannot here be respected. As we shall see, both this reasoning and the specific reference to the book of aggada will find meaningful echo below.

The same concern for writing sections of scripture that are less than their canonical whole dominates the next part of the discussion as well:

> a. Abbaye asked Rabba: Is it permissible to write a scroll [containing less than a full book of the Torah] for a child to be instructed with?
> b. Ask [this question] of the one who said the Torah was given in scrolls [and] ask [this question] of the one who said the Torah was given sealed.
> c. Ask the one who said the Torah was given in scrolls since it was [originally] written in scrolls it may [now] be written [in scrolls], or since it was [finally] joined, it is joined [and should not resume its scroll-by-scroll status]?
> d. Ask the one who said the Torah was given sealed: since it was given sealed, we do not write it [in individual scrolls] or perhaps *since it is impossible* [not to write smaller scrolls, because without them it will be impossible to educate children] we may write?
> e. He said to him: We do not write [scrolls of smaller scriptural portions].
> f. And for what reason?
> g. Because we do not write. [emphasis added]

The immediate question here is whether it is permissible to write scrolls of small portions of the Torah to use in the instruction of children. The Talmud tells us that there are two opinions regarding the original giving of the Torah that might predispose one to analyze this question in a certain manner, but the question is valid according to both presumptions. Of course, if one begins with the opinion that the Torah was originally given in smaller, individual scrolls, then one is more likely to answer the present question in the affirmative. Nevertheless, one could still conclude that since the Torah was finally, at the end of the forty-year sojourn in the desert, combined to form the single Torah of Moses, it should remain combined and not be disassembled into its smaller segments. On the other hand, if one begins with the opinion that the Torah was originally given "sealed," then one is more likely to answer the present question by suggesting that it remain sealed. Nevertheless, recognizing that prohibiting the writing of such scrolls might make it impossible to teach children, one might disregard the "ideal" law and permit the writing of smaller portions of the Torah.

This is not an innocent, even-handed analysis of the question and its possible answers. As we said, if one begins with the presumption that the Torah was originally given in smaller scrolls, then one is more likely to answer the present question in the affirmative. But even if one begins with the "sealed" opinion, one is nevertheless more likely to answer this question in the affirmative because it may reasonably be analyzed as a case of "since it is impossible [to do otherwise]." The text above already identified two matters that should probably have been prohibited, but because it would have been unrealistic, because self-destructive, to maintain such prohibitions the law turned out to be permissive. So too here, we are now predisposed to think, the law should be permissive, and according to both analyses, therefore, we should expect an affirmative answer.

That is precisely why the negative answer, given at e., is so surprising. Just as surprising is the manner in which that answer is justified. Avoiding any recourse to logical or authority-based justification, the Talmud simply asserts that such scrolls may not be written because they may not be written ("because I said so!"). Though such a response might be thought to be weak, lacking any outside source or justification, it is, in fact, the strongest manner that an answer may be asserted—there is no room here for challenge because no room has been left for challenge.[27] There is no logic to offer an alternative to and no source to interpret differently. The simple strength of the prohibition allows virtually no opportunity for subsequent comment.

Yet the text confounds our expectations and proceeds immediately in what follows to offer objections. Though Jewish tradition had long before defined the boundaries of its canonical books, the desire to defend the defined boundaries against dissolution—represented in Rabba's negative ruling at e.—will not be respected. The objections that are raised, moreover, are striking indeed. Taken from a Mishna and two related, purportedly contemporaneous traditions, the objections all refer explicitly to a case where a small portion of Torah text was written and the early authorities approved of this fact. While the opinion that prohibits such writing is then defended in each instance, on balance it is clear that the interpretations required for such defense are rather forced. Formally, the negative ruling is salvaged, but we are unable to escape the impression that the counter-evidence brought in the objections themselves is considerably more impressive. Furthermore, to make sure that we are not tempted to accept the negative ruling as conclusive, the Talmud concludes this immediate deliberation by revealing that this question remains a subject of (unresolved) tannaitic debate.

The text below, returning to the question of how the Torah was originally revealed, persists in confounding the boundaries of scripture that we have come to know.

> j. R. Yoḥanan said in the name of R. Bana'ah: The Torah was given in scrolls, as it is said "Then I said, behold, I have come with the scroll of the book that is written

for me" (Ps 40:8).

k. R. Shimeon b. Laqish says: The Torah was given sealed, as it is said "[And it happened, when Moses completed writing the words of this Torah in a book, until they were finished, that Moses commanded the Levites... saying,] Take this Torah book... (Deut 31:24–26)"

There is little here to suggest an interpretation of these opinions, but the scriptural proof texts, at least, offer a direction. The text employed by R. Shimeon is taken from a context in which it is unambiguous that Moses completed the writing of the Torah only at the end of the forty-year sojourn in the desert. This leads the well-known rabbinic commentator, Rashi (1040–1105), to interpret the term "sealed" in this way:

It [= the Torah] was not written until the end of the forty years, until all of the portions were revealed, and those that were revealed to him [= Moses] in the first years were recalled by memory until [at the end of the forty years] he wrote them.

Other commentators dispute details, but they agree that the Torah was revealed—even according to the "sealed" opinion—piece by piece over the course of forty years. The same must be true, therefore, of the "scrolls" position, and the only difference between them, then, is whether each section of Torah was written by Moses as it was revealed or whether some sections, at least, were preserved orally, by memory, until some later time when they were finally written down.

The impact of these opinions is crucial. Why, in a larger tradition that speaks of the whole Torah as having preexisted creation (see b. Pes. 54a and b. Ned. 39b), would the notion that the whole Torah was revealed in one event at Mount Sinai not at least be considered here? And why would one of the opinions that is considered insist that the Written Torah was originally, at least in part, preserved orally? Why decompose the "sealed" whole and flirt with the possibility that it was, during the forty years in the desert, in no essential way different from the Oral Torah (which, as the contemporary myth would have it, was also revealed at that time)?

After a brief elaboration of the opinions quoted most recently, the Talmud begins to make clear the meaning of these factors in the context of its larger concern. The deliberation continues:

l. ...

m. R. Eleazar said: The Torah, most of it is in writing and the smaller portion [of it] is oral, as it is said "Though I write for him greater parts of my Torah, they are reckoned as strange" (Hos 8:12, translated for the present context).

n. R Yoḥanan said: Most is oral and less is in writing, as it is said "for by word of these things..." (Exod 34:27, translated for the present context).

Here, for the first time in this text, "Torah" means something other than the five books of Moses. With no forewarning, "Torah" suddenly encompasses other teachings and traditions, apparently what is known by the rabbis at this stage of development as the Oral Torah. The debate is not whether such a Torah was indeed revealed to Moses at Sinai—that is apparently taken for granted—but which of the Torahs, Oral or Written, is larger.

There is reason to doubt, however, whether or not this is, in fact, the precise question. Rashi interprets the phrase "in writing" in this way:

> Most of the Torah is dependent on midrash, for [the Written Torah] is written to be interpreted by my means of... the rules of Torah interpretation.

For Rashi, the Torah "in writing" means not the Written Torah but the Written Torah and all that is derived from it, that is, much of what is commonly called by the rabbis "Oral Torah." What forces Rashi into such a position? The answer, I believe, is the obvious absurdity of Eleazar's claim that most of the Torah is in writing. It must certainly be evident to Eleazar—who lived after the promulgation of the Mishna and in the period during which the Tosepta and halakic midrashim likely took shape—that most of rabbinic Torah is included not in the Written Torah document but in the extensive rabbinic traditions that define Jewish practice. The Yerushalmi, long before Rashi, understands that this must be so, and in its version Eleazar himself challenges the possibility that most of the Torah is written, suggesting instead that "more numerous are those things that are derived from the Written than those derived from the Oral" (y. Pe'a 2:17a and y. Hag. 1:76d). According to both the Yerushalmi and Rashi, there-fore, the dispute is one of ultimate source: Is the majority of the law connected to the Written Torah in some way or was it revealed to Moses independently, without any direct connection to the Written Torah?

If this interpretation is correct, then the "Torah in writing" here means not the Written Torah but that part of Oral Torah that is called "written" by virtue of its derivative origin in the Written Torah. In this usage, any distinction between what is conventionally known as Written and Oral Torah is rhetorically eliminated and, while we may debate the sources of law, various laws with these different sources ultimately blend into a single continuum of divine authority.

The sense that the conventional categories finally disintegrate is similarly evident in the discussion that follows:

> o. ...
> p. R. Judah b. Nahmani, the spokesperson (*meturgeman*) of R. Shimeon b. Laqish expounded: It is written "write for yourself these things" (Exod 34:27) and it is written "for by word of these things" (ibid.). How can these be reconciled? Things that are written [=Written Torah] you are not permitted to say them orally [and]

things that are oral you are not permitted to state in writing.

q. It is taught in the school of R. Ishmael: "[Write for yourself] these" (Exod 34:27)—These you may write but you may not write laws [= legal traditions of the Oral Torah].

r. R. Yohanan said: The Holy One, blessed be He, established His covenant with Israel only on account of things that are oral, for it is said "for by word of these things did I establish with you a covenant, and with Israel" (ibid.).

Here, ironically, Written and Oral Torah are for the first time definitively distinguished: what is oral may not be written and what is written may not be kept orally. But, upon closer inspection, it becomes clear that this distinction is illusory. To begin with, we already have evidence, at the beginning of this long deliberation, that the prohibition enunciated here is being disregarded (by R. Yohanan and R. Shimeon b. Laqish who, it will be recalled, referred to a book of aggada (= written Oral Torah). Not only that, but the prohibition itself is the opinion of one "R. Judah b. Nahmani the spokesperson of R. Shimeon b. Laqish." Ordinarily, such a spokesperson would be expected simply to repeat the exact words of his master. At the very least, we can be sure that the opinion of a spokesperson circulated in the school of his master and most likely had his approval. And yet it is the very master of this spokesperson, R. Shimeon b. Laqish, who is described as being one of the two people who disregards this prohibition. If this prohibition was ever heeded, in other words, its power was lost in a mere instant. Though in theory Oral should remain oral and Written written, in fact Oral was quickly written, and this distinction, like others in theory, did not last.

The reason for all this becomes clear in the end. The covenant with Israel, we discover, was established primarily because of the Oral Torah. The centrality of Oral Torah is here articulated clearly, and there can be no doubt that it was toward this end that the Talmud was leading all along.

By refusing to respect the immutable boundaries of canonical books—smaller scrolls, defined by the scribe or the liturgical community, may be written—the Bavli challenged also the conceptual integrity of these boundaries. Allowing scripture to be recorded in smaller and smaller pieces, scripture ultimately approached disintegration. Large texts became small and small texts became mere words; words, of course, are the stuff of Oral Torah. At the same time, we learned, Written Torah was originally, at most, smaller scrolls—again approaching units of speech—and, according to one of two opinions, Written Torah was originally oral. In effect, the only difference between Written and Oral Torah during the life of Moses was what they would one day become; for most of that period the form of the two Torahs was literally identical.

Similarly, the Oral Torah is also written—this on two accounts. First, that part of Oral Torah that is derived from the Written is called written in this text. Second, the Oral Torah is literally written because "it is impossible" to do otherwise; to assure its preservation, it must be written. Just as the Written Torah was once oral, the Oral Torah is now written. Boundaries disintegrate. The categories merge.

So we see, in the Bavli, that the Oral Torah is canonized as Sinaitic revelation in the fullest sense. At the same time, as the authority of rabbinic canon is thus enhanced, the canon of scripture or, much later, of Mishna essentially disappears. In fact, if the first point is taken seriously, then the second, as its consequence, seems inevitable. On the level of myth, if it was all part of the original divine revelation, then there can be no reason to distinguish the fundamental authority of one from that of the other. Neusner is in some measure correct, therefore, in his claim that there is in rabbinic Judaism no canon other than the whole Torah.[28]

However, it must be admitted that the erasure of boundaries is not complete, despite the theoretical thrust of the texts examined above. The Talmudim both, after all, often seek to justify rabbinic traditions by reference to scriptural proof. Why do so if what is scriptural is not distinct and authoritatively superior?[29] Furthermore, the Mishna too seems to be preferred as a source of proof or objection; again, why the preference if its heightened canonical status relative to other parts of the canon is completely obliterated? In truth, the evidence is contradictory and both tendencies are indeed supported.[30]

It seems to me that the spirit of the Bavli, and perhaps even the Yerushalmi, prefers to deny a canon that is smaller than the whole. It may even be true that ideally, for both of these documents, the canon should never be closed. This, certainly, is the upshot of the tradition that claims that anything a disciple would one day rule before his master was already revealed to Moses. But history did not agree. In fact, the Talmud was ultimately closed and, following that closure, all subsequent teachers had to respect the superior authority of the Talmudic sages. The right to further dispute their opinions was denied. The Torah that the Talmudic masters had reopened was effectively canonized with their own contribution.

III

The history of the development of the rabbinic canon, as examined above, sheds light on several current controversies in the study of the biblical canon. First, the debate concerning the canonical status of the Qumran Psalms scroll or the Temple Scroll might find its solution in the dual level of canon that the rabbis tolerated. As we saw, in the Talmudim the greater authority of the canonically delimited Hebrew scripture was, on the one hand, respected by the rabbinic authors. But, on the other hand, they also wanted to claim that the corpus of rabbinic teachings was similarly Torah and, according to the stated theory, the canonical boundaries of Hebrew scripture are inconsequential. Thus, we see, a universally recognized, more authoritative canon might coexist with a second-level canon which, though in some measure derivative from the first, nevertheless stands in tension with it—claiming a common divine source and exhibiting independence that often belies its derivative nature. By the same token, perhaps the Qumran texts in question were understood, in some measure, to be a second-level, derivative canon for which, at the same time, the community wanted to claim equivalent canonical status.[31]

A second aspect of the development of the rabbinic canon—the fact that inspiration finally came to be claimed for all rabbinic teachings—calls into question Leiman's proposed solution to the problem of Yabne and the definition of the biblical canon. Seeking to explain the various claims recorded in Mishna Yad. 3:5 that Canticles and Ecclesiastes "do not render the hand impure," Leiman notes, with others, that similar claims are made in connection with other biblical books well over a century later. Yet these very same books are admitted by all to have been canonized long before. How is this apparent contradiction to be resolved? Leiman suggests that the argument represented in the "rendering the hands impure" debate is not over the canonical status of the books in question but only over whether they are inspired. Even those who denied their inspired origin, Leiman claims, continued to admit their place in the canon.[32] In effect, Leiman reverses the canonical process described by Sheppard and Sanders. Not only is it not true, in his opinion, that a commonly recognized level of canonical authority must precede canonical definition, but it is even the case that inclusion in the defined canon can in certain cases be independent of an accepted minimum canonical authority.

In large part, Leiman's argument is a matter of semantics. Though generally Leiman is imprecise about what he means by "uninspired canonical books" on one occasion, at least, he reveals precisely what he is proposing:

> There is evidence that some Tannaim of the first-third centuries C.E. denied the inspired status of the Song of Songs, Ecclesiastes, and Esther. They suggested that these books *be removed from the biblical canon* and be included among the uninspired canonical books.[33]

In other words, uninspired books are not biblical and are canonical only to the same extent as other authoritative non-biblical books, such as *Megillat ta'anit* or early rabbinic documents. But, of course, the canon question that is raised by these books is precisely the question of biblical canon, and so Leiman has in essence agreed with those who argue that the final definition was at this time not yet agreed upon. Of course, that there might be authoritative but non-biblical books is no novelty.

Returning to the lesson of the rabbinic canon—the status of which

Leiman uses to support his proposed solution—it should now be emphasized that Leiman's scenario contradicts not only the picture suggested by Sheppard and Sanders (a picture that I too challenge, though from a different perspective), but also the rabbinic model itself. As it turns out, while it may be so that early rabbinic documents were considered both uninspired and canonical (= authoritative to a certain degree), the community apparently found this status to be intolerable. In a society where canon/authority was equated with Torah, the claim had finally to be made that all religiously authoritative works were Torah, and therefore inspired. This process, whereby increasing authority came to be equated with inspiration, progressed over the course of several centuries in rabbinic circles. But the biblical books whose status was questioned had also been around for several centuries at the time of the Yabne debate. It seems highly unlikely, therefore—given the sensibilities of this community—that the challenge to their inspiration could have been divorced from the question of their inclusion in the canon. Leiman's single explicit statement must therefore be correct: the question was whether these books were biblical. Whether this was a serious challenge or, as Beckwith claims, merely the opposition of individuals is a matter of judgment. But the essential nature of the question seems beyond doubt.[34]

A third lesson of this study is the recognition that canonical process does not transpire in one direction only, as the theoretical discussions of Sheppard and Sanders might lead one to conclude.[35] It is clear that, by sometime in the early rabbinic period at the latest, the canon of Hebrew scripture was commonly recognized and respected. Little more than a century later the Mishnaic canon was similarly closed. In the generations immediately following, neither of these canons was seriously challenged—no one in the rabbinic community thought to reopen the canon of Torah and to admit to its company, for example, the Mishna. Nor did anyone in this community claim for subsequent teachings the right to be included in the canon of the Mishna. But as rabbinic teachings of all kinds came to be called Torah—tentatively at first and then with greater confidence—the boundaries that defined the earlier canons gradually became less secure. Ultimately, at the theoretical level, at least, it all became Torah, and the canons that were once closed were forced to admit a wealth of new traditions and documents. In retrospect, the revelation at Sinai came to be a far more fertile event than had previously been realized. Thus, in the course of a community's seeking its self-definition, canons not only come to assume precise forms; the quest for new definitions can also cause earlier boundaries to be redrawn.[36]

Other implications of this study remain to be explored. Clearly, caution is warranted before proceeding to extend the lessons of the rabbinic history to other literatures. But despite differences between this literature and others, we have shown that the rabbinic model can be used to make critical comparisons.

Undoubtedly, others who examine this history will have much to add to what we have proposed above.[37]

Notes

1. G. T. Sheppard, "Canon," *The Encyclopedia of Religion* (New York: Macmillan, 1987) 3. 62–69.
2. Various schemes of definition have been proposed by different writers. See, e.g., James Barr, *Holy Scripture: Canon, Authority, Criticism* (Philadelphia: Westminster, 1983) 76; Barr suggests a threefold distinction: (1) canon as a list of books of holy scripture, (2) the final form of a book, and (3) a principle of finality and authority. Sid Leiman proposes a definition that corresponds closely to Sheppard's first meaning of canon (*The Canonization of Hebrew Scripture: The Talmudic and Midrashic Evidence* [Hamden, CT: Connecticut Academy of Arts and Sciences, 1976] 14). Many of the debates over the canonization of Hebrew Scripture and its various parts have been mostly semantic, the parties to the debate being unwilling to admit their different uses of the term "canon"; on this, see Gerald H. Wilson, "The Qumran Psalms Scroll Reconsidered: Analysis of the debate," CBQ 47 (1985) 625.
3. See Sheppard, "Canon:" 64 and 66; James A. Sanders, *Torah and Canon* (Philadelphia: Fortress, 1972) 91; idem, *Canon and Community* (Philadelphia: Fortress, 1984) 31–32, 34; and Brevard S. Childs, *Introduction to the Old Testament as Scripture* (Philadelphia: Fortress, 1979) 370.
4. Sheppard, "Canon," 66.
5. Sanders, *Torah and Canon*, 91.
6. See Sid Z. Leiman, *The Canonization of Hebrew Scripture*, 125–35; and Roger T. Beckwith, *The Old Testament Canon of the New Testament Church* (Grand Rapids: Eerdmans, 1985).
7. This is supported, for example, by the discovery at Qumran of noncanonical psalms, some previously unknown, interspersed with canonical psalms in a way that does not distinguish the former from the latter. For a review of the debate concerning the Qumran Psalms, see Wilson, "The Qumran Psalms Scroll Reconsidered" In this connection, see also Yigael Yadin, *The Temple Scroll* (Jerusalem: Israel Exploration Society, 1983) 1. 390–92 n. 8; and Edward L. Greenstein, "Psalms:" in *The Encyclopedia of Religion* 12. 39. If Yadin is correct about the status of the Temple Scroll at Qumran, it is possible that even the superior canonical status of the Torah itself was not respected in certain communities. On this, see Yadin, *Temple Scroll* 1. 390–97; and Michael Fishbane, "Interpretation of Mikra at Qumran" in *Mikra* (ed. Martin Jan Mulder; Philadelphia: Fortress, 1988) 362–66. See also Sanders's discussion of these matters in *Canon and Community*, 11-16, 33.
8. See Sheppard, "Canon," 63.
9. See Leiman, *Canonization of Hebrew Scripture*, 103.
10. See Beckwith, *Old Testament Canon*, 275
11. See Leiman, *Canonization of Hebrew Scripture*, 15, 112–14, 132; and see my discussion below.
12. I do not wish to deny Sanders' concern for the reception of a canon into a community and for the *relecture* of that canon in the new canonical community. This too is part of the canonical process that Sanders' canonical criticism addresses. Nor does it elude the present writer that the fixing of a canon generates often massive projects of exegesis, exegesis that effectively reopens the canon that it addresses. But, still, there is no extended and explicit consideration in this scholarship of the possibility that an earlier closed canon might actually break down, not merely to be supplemented but, for all practical purposes, to be radically redefined. Sanders' adaptable canon retains its adaptability through reinterpretation, not through redefinition.

13. It should be clear that the history that follows pertains only to the canonization of this literature within the rabbinic community as such. No conclusions should be drawn for the canonical status of this same literature in contemporary non-rabbinic Jewish communities.
14. See David Weiss Halivni, "The Reception Accorded to Rabbi Judah's Mishnah," in *Jewish and Christian Self-Definition: Aspects of Judaism in the Greco-Roman Period* (ed. E. P. Sanders, with A. I. Baumgarten and Alan Mendelson; Philadelphia: Fortress, 1981) 2. 204–12.
15. See Jacob Neusner, *Torah: From Scroll to Symbol in Formative Judaism* (Philadelphia: Fortress, 1985).
16. Ibid., 54–56.
17. Martin S. Jaffee, "Oral Torah in Theory and Practice: Aspects of Mishnah-Exegesis in the Palestinian Talmud," *Religion* 15 (1985) 390–92.
18. See J. Neusner, *Midrash in Context* (Philadelphia: Fortress, 1983), 125–37.
19. See J. Neusner, *Judaism: The Classical Statement* (Chicago: University of Chicago Press, 1986), 80–87.
20. Neusner, *Midrash in Context*, 53–107, 128–35.
21. Ibid. 135–37.
22. See again Neusner, *Judaism: The Classical Statement*, 80–87, 222–23, but cf. D. Kraemer, "Scripture Commentary in the Babylonian Talmud: Primary or Secondary Phenomenon?" AJS Review 14, no. 1 (Spring 1989) 1–15 (chapter 12 in this volume).
23. Sabb. 31a, Git. 60b, Qid. 66a and Tem. 14b. The mention at Yoma 28b is not supported by manuscripts.
24. Though this tradition claims tannaitic origin in the Bavli, there is reason to be dubious. The parallel quoted in Abot R. Nat. does not include the second part of this sequence and the part that it does include seems to be an enhancement and a clarification of the prior Bavli version. Confirming this judgment is Burton Visotzky, "Hillel, Hieronymous and Praetextatus," JANESCU 16–17 (1984-85) 223 n. 35; and J. Neusner, *The Rabbinic Traditions About the Pharisees Before 70* (3 vols.; Leiden: Brill, 1971) 1. 322. The sequence, as it appears in the Bavli, appears in no other primary rabbinic document, and on those grounds it may be considered to illustrate a view that pertains uniquely to the Bavli.
25. Note the tradition attributed to R. Joshua b. Levi at y. Hag. 1:76d: "Scripture and Mishna, talmud [= sophisticated deliberation and interpretation], laws and narratives [aggadot], even that which an experienced disciple will one day teach in front of his master, [all of this] was already said to Moses at Sinai." Clearly, the rabbinic tradition in all of its aspects, including both law and interpretation, is here included in the Oral Torah.
26. According to b. Meg. 31a, the whole book of Jonah is to be read as the *haptara* during the afternoon service of Yom Kippur. In later practice. the whole book of Obadiah is read as the *haptara* for *wayišlah*.
27. See the opinion of E. Dupréel, quoted in C. Perelman and L. Olbrechts-Tyteca, *The New Rhetoric: A Treatise on Argumentation* (Notre Dame and London: University of Notre Dame Press, 1969) 55. See also the Bavli's own awareness of the consequences of offering or not offering justifications at Abod. Zar. 35a: "Ulla said, 'When they issue a decree in the West [= Palestine] they do not reveal its reason for a full year lest there be a person who doesn't agree and come to disregard it.'"
28. Neusner, *Midrash in Context*, 135–36; see also idem, *Writing with Scripture: The Authority and Uses of the Hebrew Bible in the Torah of Formative Judaism* (Minneapolis: Fortress, 1989).
29. Other differences also support this hierarchy, e.g., the fact that textual criticism is applied by the rabbis to the Mishna but not to scripture. In general, it seems to me that Neusner

overstates his case for the elimination of canonical distinctions in the rabbinic "Torah." Supporting this critique, see Donn F. Morgan, *Between Text and Community: The Writings in Canonical Interpretation* (Minneapolis: Fortress, 1990) 106–7.

30. It may be suggested that this apparent contradiction is to be resolved in line with James Barr's conception of the condition of the biblical canon at the turn of the Common Era. He writes: "Possibly we have to think of something more like a backbone, securely established... and beyond that a placing of other books at greater or lesser proximity..." In the case of rabbinic canon, scripture and the Mishna would be the backbone, and other traditions, though claiming like canonical authority, would in practice be at various distances from the authoritative center. See Barr, *Holy Scripture: Canon, Authority, Criticism* (Philadelphia: Westminster, 1983) 57–59.

31. See again Barr, *Holy Scripture*, 57-59; and see Fishbane's explanation of the status of the Temple Scroll in the Qumran community in *Mikra*, 365-66. See also n. 29.

32. See Leiman, *Canonization of Hebrew Scripture*, 14–15, 103, 111–12, 114.

33. Ibid., 132 (emphasis added).

34. Leiman's analysis is flawed on several other counts as well. One is Leiman's unsupportable assumption of a normative Jewish view; on this, see J. A, Sanders's review in JBL 96 (1977) 590–91. Second, Leiman seeks to prove the plausibility of canonical but uninspired biblical books by showing that the same individuals who challenged the inspiration of certain works (according to Leiman's interpretation of "rendering the hands impure") nevertheless employed these same works elsewhere to supply biblical proof texts (see pp. 112–13). His proof rests on two highly questionable assumptions: (1) that attributions of traditions to specific individuals may be accepted uncritically as being reliable, and (2) that it is unnecessary to distinguish the different documents in which traditions attributed to a particular sage appear. Needless to say, these assumptions cannot be defended according to currently recognized methodologies.

35. See n. 12 above.

36. It is possible that a similar process transpired in the early Christian community as the OT came to be supplemented/supplanted by the NT. Whether this parallel should be admitted depends on one's view of the canonicity of the OT in this same community. In any case, at least in connection with the canon of rabbinic Judaism, Morgan's elegantly simple statement is apt: "Canons come and go... "; see *Between Text and Community*, 19.

37. I am grateful to my colleagues Baruch Bokser, Burton Visotzky, and Edward Greenstein for their many important corrections and suggested improvements in the revision of this work.

INTRODUCTION TO CHAPTER NINE

The following piece was written for *The Millennial Encyclopedia of Judaism, The Religion*, edited by W. S. Green, et. al. The section on rabbinic doctrine concerning evil and suffering is based primarily upon my own work, presented at length and in detail in *Responses to Suffering in Classical Rabbinic Literature* (Oxford, 1996). The other sections are largely based upon the primary scholarship of others. Nevertheless, remarkably, there are no works that consider the full range of doctrines and responses documented here. This, therefore, represents a genuine contribution to the study of an important set of Jewish beliefs through the ages.

The reader is directed to my aforementioned book for my more significant contribution to this subject. There, I examine rabbinic teachings relating to human suffering employing the method outlined earlier. Responses to this work have inevitably correlated with a reviewer's opinion concerning Neusner's documentary method, which—along with the rhetorical criticism I employ as a reader and interpreter—serves as the foundation of this scholarship. That being said, I must add that I have been particularly gratified by the responses of (mostly Orthodox) rabbis, many of whom have indicated how important my work has been in their own understanding of rabbinic tradition.

Chapter Nine

Judaic Doctrines of Evil and Suffering

1. Foundations

From the earliest canonical traditions of Israel to contemporary Orthodox Judaism, suffering has been seen as punishment for the wickedness and sins of humanity. The persistence of this connection is evidence of its ability to explain the suffering of Israel and to provide comfort to sufferers. But, however powerful the explanation, important questions would always remain: Why is there evil in the first place? Why do humans pursue sin with such resourcefulness? Why do the innocent also suffer? These questions and others would repeatedly challenge the religious imagination of Israel to refine or find alternatives to the classical scheme.

The opening chapters of Genesis narrate a series of "falls" which, in combination, explain not only the human condition in general but human sin and suffering in particular. Thus, in the well-known story of the temptation of Eve (Gen. ch. 3), the first humans transgress God's prohibition of eating from the fruit of the "tree of knowledge of good and evil" (2:17). As a consequence, they are cursed with the pain of childbirth (3:16), the sweat and toil of producing food, and death (3:19). In the space of this brief chapter, the nexus of transgression and punishment=suffering is firmly established. Crucially, so too is the root of human sin in temptation.

The punishment of an evil humanity by the waters of the flood (chapters 6–7) shows that the cause-and-effect established in the Garden of Eden will be oft-repeated. But, in this latter case, the source of human evil is more difficult to discern. According to Genesis 6:5, "the evil of humanity is great... for all the inclinations of the thoughts of his heart are evil all the day." Seemingly, there is a quality in the hearts of humans which inclines them to do evil. But why is this so? Though the text provides no clear answer to this question, the juxtaposition of the observation just quoted with the prior mythic narrative suggests that the cause of human evil may well be divine beings.

According to the myth only hinted at in the Torah's record (6:2–4), at some time prior to the flood, "sons of gods" took human women for mates and produced from these couplings "the mighty men of old." There were on earth at the same time *"nephilim"* (=fallen ones), who may be either the "sons of gods" themselves or their offspring. Whatever the precise meaning of this story, it is notable that the observation concerning human evil follows it immediately. It is difficult, therefore, to escape the conclusion that the transgression of the divine-human boundary by divine creatures is somehow at the root of human evil.

Evil and sin as the origins of suffering are abundantly in evidence in throughout the Torah. This is especially so in the promised blessings and curses which constitute the penultimate chapter of Leviticus, and even more in the covenantal scheme that defines the central ideology of Deuteronomy. Thus, for example, "if you (=Israel) fail to heed the voice of the Lord your God... then all of these curses will come upon you... The Lord will allow you to be smitten before your enemies... and your corpse shall be food for the birds of the sky and the beast of the earth... " (Deut. ch. 28). Unsurprisingly, the same explanation is repeatedly offered in the Bible's royal history. This is most dramatically illustrated, perhaps, in the bible's justification for the exiles of the kingdoms of Israel (II Kings 17) and Judah (ch. 21).

2. Alternative Biblical Approaches

But the gravity of these latter catastrophes and the suffering which accompanied them challenged the plausibility of the ancient explanation. Granted that suffering (such as exile) is punishment for sin. Why does Israel not learn the lesson of repeated suffering and, if she does not, will suffering ever end? In response to this dilemma, both Jeremiah (31:30–3) and Ezekiel (36:26–7) propose that the heart of Israel—a heart of stone, in Ezekiel's imagery—must be replaced with a new heart, one inscribed with the Torah of the Lord. Evidently, the sinful Israel was cursed with a sinful heart; sin was part of Israel's essence. Therefore, the elimination of sin, and hence of suffering, demanded a fundamental reworking of human (or, at least, Israel's) nature.

In the course of Israel's travails, other understandings of the root of suffering also found their way into the canon. One of the most important of these (by virtue of its place in Christian interpretation) is II Isaiah's "suffering servant," a servant of the Lord who suffers on account of—and to atone for—the sins of others (Isaiah 52:13–53:12). In this explanation, suffering continues to be a consequence of sin, but not of the sin of the sufferer himself.

The book of Job, of course, offers an extended critique of more "traditional" explanations of suffering, avowing that Job's accusers "do not speak rightly" (42:7). But the "right" explanation of Job's suffering is less clear or, perhaps more correctly, the subject of competing redactional understandings. If the narrative introduction is to be granted priority, Job's suffering is a product of Satan's (or "the adversary's") provocations of God (Job 1–2). But if the voice of God, in response to Job, is to be believed, suffering is simply beyond human understanding (ch. 38). In human terms, suffering and the God who brings it cannot be said to be just. But this is evidence of human, not divine, limitations.

3. Post-biblical Jewish Literature

The ancient explanations of evil and suffering would continue to play an important role in Jewish literature produced during the late second-Temple period (2nd century BCE–1st century CE). For example, the author of I Maccabees hints, through narrative juxtaposition, that the suffering of Israel at the hand of Antiochus is a consequence of their abandonment of traditional ways (I Macc. 1:11–24, 52–4). In II Maccabees, one of "the seven brothers" explains their torture at the hands of the Syrian Greeks as punishment for their sins against God (7:18).

But alternative explanations of sin and suffering flowered during this same period. The most striking such explanation, finding expression in both I Enoch and Jubilees, grew out of the Torah myth spoken of above. In this latter-day version, the "*nephilim*" are fallen angels who rebel against God by leaving heaven, taking human women as mates, and spreading a variety of evil teachings and curses. From these encounters, humans learn temptation and the art of war, amongst other evils. In addition, according to Jubilees, following the flood, "demons" remained to lead the children of Noah (=humanity) astray. And, though Noah beseeched God to imprison the malevolent creatures forever, Mastema (=Satan) prevailed upon God to allow him to remain free and wreak havoc forever. Finally, the suppressed myth has reasserted its power.

The most extreme Jewish expression of the mythical power of evil is offered in a sectarian scroll found near Qumran, known as the Code of Discipline. According to this scroll, God created two spirits—"the spirits of truth and of perversity." Those who follow the spirit of truth are "under the domination of the Prince of Lights," while those "who practice perversity are under the domination of the Angel of Darkness." This world is the battlefield on which the war between these two forces is fought, and all sin is a result of the (temporary) victories of the Angel of Darkness. This is the fate of the humankind "until the final age."

In literal terms, all of these various authors agree that our sin leads to our suffering. But ultimately, they claim, we are not at fault. We sin because there are evil forces more powerful than we. Still, none of these authors, even the most extreme among them, denies Isaiah's claim that God "creates evil" (45:7). Whether evil begins with rebellious angels, Satan, spirits of darkness, or a person's wicked heart, God created them all.

4. Following Destruction

The deterioration of conditions under Herodian and Roman rule, leading to the destruction of the second Jerusalem Temple, combined to force Jews to seek alternative explanations of the suffering that surrounded them. When he explained the destruction as a product of fate (*Jewish War* 6.250, 267–8), Josephus was probably reflecting a popular opinion among hellenized Jews. But even more popular, if the literary record is to be believed, were various imaginations of the apocalypse, assumed by many to be at hand. Nascent Christianity, claiming that the Messiah had actually arrived, testifies to this inclination. So too, in different ways, do the Apocalypses of Ezra and Baruch.

According to both of these books, the number of generations of humans was fixed at creation. When the last of these generations was born to life, history would come to an end and the final age would dawn. This dawning would be marked by unprecedented sufferings and catastrophes; much as a woman's labor is most painful immediately before birth, so too would the birth of the World-to-Come follow the most painful period in human history. There would be a final judgment. The wicked would suffer eternally, while the righteous would forever enjoy the rewards of the final era.

For the communities for which these writings spoke, the suffering of their generation was not necessarily punishment at all. Instead, most suffering could be seen as the "birth-pangs of the Messiah." Evil was a part of the human condition, and those who had done wickedly would be punished. But present suffering was redemptive. In their lifetime, they believed, the Messiah would come.

5. The Classical Rabbinic Canon

Writing a generation after the failure of the Bar Kokhba revolt, the early rabbinic authors could no longer imagine that the Messiah would soon arrive. Instead, they turned their attentions to systematizing the law of God and Israel (in a document called the Mishnah), and they explained suffering—in thoroughly traditional terms—as punishment for sin. So, according to R. Shimeon b. Eleazar, the pain humans experience while making a living is a consequence of our evil deeds (M. Qiddushin 4:14). In another illustrative teaching, women are said to die in childbirth for failure to observe three commandments specifically directed to them (M. Shabbat 2:6). The Mishnah's general rule is this: "According to the measure with which a person measures, with it do we measure him" (M. Sotah 1:7). If a person sins, he or she will suffer punishment in kind.

Though rarely straying from this opinion, here and there, the early rabbis gave expression to important expansions or alternatives. According to one tradition, oft-quoted in subsequent rabbinic compositions, suffering has superior power to atone for sin (second only to death, see Tosefta, *Yom ha-Kippurim* 4:8). Conceptually related, though rhetorically more powerful, is the claim that "sufferings cause God to pardon more even than sacrifices... Because sacrifices are with one's property whereas sufferings are with one's body" (Sifrei Deuteronomy 32). Subsequent to the destruction of the Temple, it was surely difficult for Jews to imagine what would take the place of the sacrifices ordained in the Torah. If suffering could perform the task, one could hardly cavil. It is not surprising, therefore, that the midrash from which this teaching is quoted repeatedly comments, "precious are sufferings."

At the same time the rabbis were extolling suffering—and condemning any who would question the place of suffering in God's justice—they maintained a guarded silence concerning the origins of evil. On only a few occasions in their earliest teachings did they speak of the human inclination to do evil (*yetzer hara^c*), borrowing from the language of Genesis to describe the cause of moral failure. From the traditions at hand, it is clear that they understood this inclination to lead to anger and transgression, seducing a person away from Torah and thus leading to his demise. But, at this early stage, the inclination for evil is not viewed as an independent force. Nor does Satan find more than an occasional place in the early rabbinic tradition, where he serves more as a literary trope than a force to be reckoned with.

The condition just described will change in later classical rabbinic literature, where the *yetzer hara^c* becomes a common reference, a force oft to be reckoned with. In the Babylonian Talmud, the evil inclination is described as speaking to a person, seeking to entice him to worship foreign gods. Not only does it incite a person to do evil in this world, but it also testifies against him in the World-to-Come. Stating matters with directness and clarity, Resh Laqish declares, "Satan, the *yetzer hara^c* and the Angel of Death are one and the same" (Baba Batra 16a).

Human suffering and the inclination to do evil are bound together in a massive apologia for God's justice, found in Genesis Rabbah (ch. 9). The midrash asks, at least by intimation, this question: Given the reality of human experience, how can we make sense of God's assessment that the created world is "very good" (Gen. 1:31)? In the course of defending this divine evaluation, the midrash argues for the goodness of death, suffering, hell (*gehinnom*), the evil inclination, and the oppressive earthly empire (Rome). Typical of the midrashic strategy is the justification of the evil impulse: if not for the *yetzer hara^c*, a man would not take a wife, build a house, have children and engage in business. In other words, the *yetzer,* equated with ambition and sexual lust, has favorable consequences. The force for evil, properly sublimated, yields good.

The only significant heterodox views concerning suffering in the classical rabbinic canon are preserved in the Babylonian Talmud (the Bavli). In one text (Shabbat 55a–b), the Talmud concludes that suffering and death can come about without prior sin. The ancient link of sin and consequent suffering (=punishment) is here definitively broken. In a related narrative (Ḥagiga 4b–5a), the Talmud illustrates the reality of death by accident, death bearing no relationship to divine justice. And in the Bavli's most extended deliberation on human suffering (Berakhot 5a–b), we find a repeated rejection of the classical apologia for suffering. Asked whether they find their sufferings "precious" (echoing the midrash quoted above), prominent sages reply: "neither them nor their reward." There is little rhyme or reason to our suffering; the beautiful elements of our lives are few and fleeting.

6. The Middle Ages

Exponents of the medieval Jewish philosophical tradition represent a range of opinions regarding suffering and evil. Saadia, writing in the early 10th century, follows a traditional path. Beginning with the uncompromising insistence that humans have free will, he offers that suffering may be either punishment for the few sins a good person commits in this world (assuring his place in the future world) or a test from God, later to be compensated. Judah Halevi likewise writes (early 12th cent.) that a man's troubles serve to cleanse his sins, and therefore recommends a pious attitude of acceptance and joy.

In his earliest relevant comment (Laws of Repentance, ch. 5), Maimonides (12th cent.) polemically insists that God has granted humans complete free will; he will grant no room to the opinion, evidently still popular, that God decrees the course a person will follow from his or her youth. Thus, evil caused by humans must be understood as the result of their freely chosen path. Those who fail properly to repent will, as the tradition suggests, die as a consequence of their sins. Speaking from an obviously philosophical perspective, Maimonides nevertheless employs the voice of Torah.

But in his *Guide for the Perplexed* (pt. 3, chapters 10–12), Maimonides forges a distinctive philosophical position. He begins with the assumption that God's created world is thoroughly good. Contrary to the claim of Isaiah, then, God cannot have created evil in any of its forms. If not, then how can the obvious evils of creation be explained? He answers that evil is privation and privation, being not a thing but the absence of some thing or quality, is not created. By his enumeration, there are three species of evil: (1) evils that befall people because they possess a body which degenerates; (2) evils which people, because of their ignorance (=the absence of wisdom), cause one another; and (3) evils which people, because of their ignorance, cause themselves. God creates none of these evils (=sufferings). According to Maimonides' system, all are caused by natural forces, by essential human failings, or by human ignorance.

The opinions of medieval Jewish mysticism (Kabbalah) regarding evil (and consequent suffering) are varied and sometimes at odds. Early Kabbalistic texts already record the belief that evil is a product of the unchecked growth of the divine power of judgment. Judgment, untempered by mercy, is wicked. This domain of judgment gone awry is called the *sitra aḥra*, "the other side." The great classic of the Kabbalah, the *Zohar*, gives credit to the view that evil originates in leftovers (*kelippot*) of earlier worlds that God destroyed. Alternatively, it suggests that evil was contained, *in potentia*, in the Tree of Knowledge (of Good and *Evil*), but was suppressed by the Tree of Life, to which the Tree of Knowledge was bound. When Adam "cut the shoots," separating one tree from the other, he activated the evil which the tree had contained.

Perhaps the most enduring contribution of Kabbalah to Jewish understandings of evil is that of Isaac Luria (16th cent.). According the interpretation of Gershom Scholem, Luria's views, contained in his highly original cosmology, are a response to the great tragedy of the prior generation —the expulsion of the Jewish community from the Iberian peninsula. Struggling to understand why they had suffered so, they found unparalleled comfort in the interpretation which Luria promulgated.

According to Luria, in order to create the world, God—the *ein-sof* ("the limitless one")—had to contract into Himself, leaving space for creation. In this space remained sparks of the Divine light, preserved in special vessels. This light contained concentrated "shells" of stern Divine Judgment which, when the vessels were shattered (due to a flaw in the plan of creation), were scattered throughout creation. This, in the system of Lurianic Kabbalah, is the root of all evil. Its popularity lay not only in its explanation of the suffering of Israel, but also in its recipe for redemption: Redemption required that the vessels be repaired, and the tools of reparation were the mitzvot of the Torah performed even by common Jews.

The most extreme persecutions of these centuries provoked profoundly ambivalent responses, or so the evidence of contemporary liturgical suggests. On the one hand, Jewish poets returned again and again to the notion that suffering is punishment for sin. In one of the most exemplary (and best known) of these poems, the "*Eileh ezkera*" (composed shortly after the first crusade in the late 11th century), the author justifies the Roman torture and execution of ten talmudic rabbis as punishment for the sin of Joseph's brothers who had "kidnapped" him and sold him into slavery. Of course, for the author and his readers, this is not history but theodicy; it explains their own suffering as well as that of their rabbinic ancestors. It is appropriate, therefore, that in liturgical performance the reciter ends each stanza by declaring "we have sinned... forgive us."

But, on the other hand, this and many similar compositions from the same broad period exhibit a considerable degree of horror and even anger, some complaining against the God who is "mute" or who "hides His face." This is a God who bids His children slaughter their own children on the altar, as Abraham prepared to do to Isaac so long before. Still, the act of sacrifice—whether of Isaac or of their own sons and daughters—is justified as "sanctification of God's name." It is an act both meritorious and cleansing.

Crucially, neither the availability of alternatives nor the memory of persecution caused Jews to abandon the ancient explanation of suffering as punishment for sin. Even Glückel of Hameln, a woman of relative comfort and culture, returns to this piety on several occasions in her memoirs. Writing near the end of the 17th century, she clearly believes that sin is punished with suffering which in turn atones the sin. God's judgment is just, she says, to be accepted in modesty.

7. The Turn of Modernity

Jews entered modern culture in fits and starts. But enter they did, and with entrance came modern opinions, dominated by science and humanism. Thus, suffering would more readily be seen as a consequence of natural law, the product of divine design, perhaps, but surely not of divine intervention. Without punishment, sin was a matter of pure theory, of little import to most but the clergy. The same could be said of the question of evil.

But the anti-semitic upheavals of modernity—the Russian pogroms followed, less than a half a century later, by the Nazi holocaust—made it impossible not to ask the question anew. Yiddish and Hebrew writers served as witnesses to the earlier of these crimes, employing the languages of traditional Judaism to critique and even betray that very tradition. H.N. Bialik, the great Hebrew poet, provides powerful examples. He mocks the cowering Jews who "crammed by scores in all the sanctuaries of their shame, So sanctified my Name!" These pious cowards, crying out "We have sinned!" do not even believe what they say—so Bialik writes. No God of might is listening; death for "for the sanctification of the name" is therefore an obscenity.

If evil is a human quality, suffering the product of natural forces, human and natural, then only the struggle for human dignity and freedom would suffice as a response. This view, already well-established in the rhetoric of early Zionism, would gain greater power following the holocaust. For many Jews, the holocaust meant that all hope in God, even if imaginable in modernity, was now lost. Secular power was the only power a Jew could have. For some, the turn to the exercise of human power would find theological underpinnings, the holocaust and the founding of the State of Israel being interpreted according to prophetic paradigms. Needless to say, the effort to make sense of the horror of the holocaust would long remain the central challenge to Jewish faith.

Eliezer Berkovits's *Faith After the Holocaust* remains illustrative of common directions. Like almost all Jews outside of extreme Orthodoxy, Berkovits categorically rejects the notion that the Holocaust was divine punishment. He calls it, instead, absolute injustice. The God of the Holocaust is again the silent God, the God who hides His face. Jews are, following Isaiah, servants suffering by divine decree. But, Berkovits adds, "the world is sustained by the suffering of the guiltless." In this, presumably, some will find comfort. So, too, will they in the assurance that there will be "a dimension beyond history in which all suffering finds its redemption through God." Strikingly, for those who insist on faith, tradition contains whatever explanations and promises might be needed.

But for modern Jews unfamiliar with the theological tradition, a God whose might is demonstrated in silence or who hide's His face, is a cruel God, and thus unacceptable. As the sales of Harold Kushner's *When Bad Things Happen to Good People* show, the God these Jews (and non-Jews!) are prepared to consider is a God who is not all-powerful and is therefore not the source of their suffering. This God doesn't punish them, but He may help them, and He will surely provide them with comfort. The appropriate question to address to this God, writes Kushner, is not "Why are you doing this to me?" but "Can you help me?"

INTRODUCTION TO CHAPTER TEN

This modest piece was written for a symposium on Prozbul in the short-lived journal, *S'vara*. (The journal, subtitled "A Journal of Philosophy, Law and Judaism was co-published by the Columbia University School of Law and the Shalom Hartman Institute. Unfortunately, the journal was thoroughly dependent upon the editorial energies of Prof. George Fletcher of Columbia and, when Prof. Fletcher was no longer able to carry the weight of its publication, the journal folded.) In this piece, I apply the method described earlier to the texts that deliberate on the well-known legal institution attributed to Hillel. Once again I discover that each text approaches the topic at hand in a way that conforms to its more general "personality." The present essay therefore exposes another important example of the particular documentary biases of individual rabbinic texts, especially the Bavli.

Let me be more specific. Typically, most scholarship on the Prozbul has assumed as accurate the various rabbinic reports concerning Hillel and the his institution (other pieces in this same issue of *S'vara* are typical). They have "solved" conflicting accounts of how Hillel justified his institution by privileging one rabbinic explanation or another, and the result has been—frankly—bad history. In contrast, this essay shows that each rabbinic document justifies Prozbul according to broader ideological preferences and prejudices. Thus, no one of these "explanations" of Hillel's move can be considered historical. The only history we have here is the history of the documents and their ideologies. So the Mishnah quietly allows for rabbinic prerogative, the halakhic midrashim insist that it is all justified by scripture, the Yerushalmi declares that no relevant Torah law was in force to be offended, and the Bavli baldly states that, one way or the other, Hillel disregarded the law of the Torah—and a rabbi has every right to do just that. Hence, this case provides additional evidence for the characterizations I have suggested in *The Mind of the Talmud* and elsewhere.

Because *S'vara* did not survive for long, and was read by very few when it was published, this will be the first time many readers have an opportunity to consider this case (I have not re-published it or referred to it elsewhere). It should be read in the larger context of my work on the Bavli, not only in *The Mind of the Talmud* but in *Reading the Rabbis* as well.

Chapter Ten

Prozbul and Rabbinic Power

The prozbul attributed to Hillel—a legal device designed to circumvent the Torah's requirement to forgive debts in the Sabbatical Year— has long attracted the attention of historians of Halakhah. Yet we would be wise to eschew historical conclusions concerning the origins of this institution; the earliest literary sources that testify to the prozbul derive from two centuries after its supposed promulgation. Still, there is a great deal to be said about the theoretical problem that prozbul represents and the meaning of the responses recorded in various rabbinic documents. This is, after all, one of the few times that a Sage is reported to have used his power apparently to contravene an explicit requirement of the Torah.

By examining the responses of different rabbinic sources to Hillel's decree and considering whether they uphold the evident meaning of the first reports of the prozbul, we will gain insight into their attitudes toward rabbinic authority vis-a-vis Torah. We find that rabbinic self-confidence grew significantly as rabbinic Judaism itself gained a larger following, to the point that rabbinic prerogatives relative to the Torah came to be asserted explicitly and without apology.

The first reports of the prozbul are found in the Mishnah. At Gittin 4:3, we read "Hillel established prozbul in order to repair the world." The justification *mipnei tiqqun ha 'olam* [in order to repair the world] is unusual for the Mishnah, but it in fact adds little clarity to the matter; what is meant by "repairing the world" and how the prozbul accomplishes this is left to our interpretive imaginations. The text at m. Shevi'it 10:3, however, goes a distance toward clarifying what Gittin leaves unelaborated. According to this Mishnah:

> When he saw that the people refrained from giving loans one to another [in anticipation of the Sabbatical Year] and transgressed what is written in the Law, "Beware that there not be a base thought in thine heart," [saying "the seventh year, the year of remission, is approaching," so that you are mean to your needy kinsman and give him nothing] (Deuteronomy 15:9), Hillel established prozbul.

Hillel's enactment thus gives greater weight to one biblical concern than to another. Noting that observance of the remission of debts led to the "harboring of base thoughts," Hillel thought it better to find a loophole that would make repayment of debts permissible, thereby assuring the constant availability of loans to the needy. In a society where the collection of interest was prohibited and there was, therefore, little motivation to give loans in the first place (beyond the mitzvah, that is), Hillel understood the serious consequences of the Sabbatical cancellation and saw fit to circumvent it. By introducing the verse from Deuteronomy 15, this Mishnah suggests that prozbul does less violence to the Torah's law than might otherwise be imagined. Still, it does not claim that the prozbul itself is actually justified by the Torah, and the language describing Hillel's action (*hitqin* [established]) leaves little doubt that the enactment is fundamentally rabbinic. Thus, we have here a clear example where a Rabbi, though perhaps motivated by the Torah's own concerns, legislates in a manner that contradicts the letter of the Torah. The Mishnah allows us to be sympathetic with Hillel's enactment. It does not, however, ask us to ignore the essential nature of that enactment.

The earliest response to the Mishnah is found in Sifrei Deuteronomy 113.[1] The Midrash reads Chapter 15, verse 3, in this way:

> "That which you have with your fellow you should forgive"—but not one who transfers his bills of obligation to a court [for by doing so he need not forgive that which is owed him].

The Midrash continues by quoting Mishnah Shevi'it 10:3, which perpetuates the use of the term "established" to describe Hillel's enactment, thus suggesting that the act is an assertion of rabbinic prerogative.

It is clear that the Midrash itself wants us to believe that prozbul is justified biblically. It seems to me that we are meant to overlook the implications of the Mishnah's language—the Midrash was "stuck" with that language, so it had to make its point in another way. By tying the Mishnah to a source in the Torah, the Midrash argues that Hillel's undertaking is not what it appears. Whatever the language of the Mishnah, prozbul gains its strength from the Torah. Indeed, the Midrash claims, Hillel did nothing beyond what the Torah itself would permit.

The Yerushalmi (Shevi'it 10:2–3=Gittin 4:3) similarly diminishes the apparent presumptuousness of Hillel's enactment, though employing a very different strategy. Without reproducing all of the details, we may summarize the Yerushalmi's treatment of the matter in this fashion: after pointing out that Hillel's enactment seems to contradict the law of the Torah, it is suggested that the obligations relating to the Sabbatical Year are not in force at this time (the time of Hillel and beyond). This position is defended on the basis of midrash. What this means is that the obligation to forgive debts, as any of the Sabbatical obligations, is in rabbinic times only rabbinically required. Hillel, therefore, is not uprooting the law of the Torah; he is merely redirecting the law of the Rabbis.

Here again, as in the Sifrei, the authors want to deny that Hillel exercised the kind of authority that the Mishnah seems to suggest. Apparently uncom-fortable with this possibility, the Rabbis behind these texts want us to believe that Hillel's enactment was rather mundane— either because prozbul is itself justified by the Torah, or because the law seemingly set aside by prozbul is not in fact a law of the Torah at all but only (at this time) a rabbinic requirement. Whichever way we have it, Hillel offers no model for the forceful assertion of rabbinic prerogative. The Torah's law, if it applies in a given case, must be respected.

When we come to the Bavli (Gittin 36a–b), we discover a radically different approach. The Bavli's deliberation, to be fully appreciated, requires close analysis. We will paraphrase or quote, as necessary, to give a sense of the fine development of the Bavli's argument. The Bavli, after quoting Mishnah Shevi'it, asks, "and is there something [a debt] that is forgiven according to the Torah and Hillel established that it should not be forgiven?!" The problem is enunciated in its starkest form; the issue cannot be avoided. The Gemara then quotes (in the name of Abbaye) the opinion also found in the Yerushalmi: we are dealing with the Sabbatical law in this time, which is only rabbinic in authority. A source is offered to support this position. But the Bavli does not permit things to rest here. Unlike its Yerushalmi counterpart, the Bavli now points out that if the Sabbatical laws are at this time only rabbinic, then the rabbinic requirement to forgive debts in the rabbinic Sabbatical (before Hillel's enactment of prozbul) contradicts the Torah's requirement that debts be repaid. In effect the rabbinic Sabbatical law would permit borrowers to steal from those who loaned to them. Thus, the Bavli insists, there is no way around the problem. Whether the Sabbatical in this time is rabbinic or from the Torah, there is still some way that the Rabbis (those before Hillel or Hillel himself) are opposing the law of the Torah.[2]

Two answers to the dilemma are proposed. The first is the claim that "it is [a case of] 'sit and do not do,'" that is, a passive transgression (one which involves the failure to perform a particular act), which is assumed not to be a problem. No justification for such an assumption is offered; the Gemara's "solution," attributed to Abbaye, is merely asserted. But even if we accept this position as justified, we must recognize its implications. The claim is that the Rabbis have the power, when their wisdom so suggests, to command that a positive commandment (such as repayment of debts) not be performed. Yet, according to the well-known tradition, 248 of the Torah's 613 commandments are positive. The Rabbis here are thus arrogating to themselves the right to annul a significant minority of the Torah's commands. This supposed resolution, which arguably renders Hillel's prozbul less "radical," turns out to be quite radical indeed.

The second response, applicable whether the obligation to relinquish debts derives from Torah or rabbinic authority, is that "the *hefqer* [abandoned property] of the court [= declared by the court] is *hefqer*." In other words, the court assertedly has the power to declare property ownerless, allowing another party to take rightful possession. In this case, if the obligation to forgive debts derives from the Torah, then the prozbul, in effect, declares the borrower's property [= the worth of the loan after the Sabbatical cancellation] to be *hefqer* and thus enables the lender to recover the loan. If the obligation to forgive debts does not derive from the Torah and the borrower is obligated to repay, then the initial rabbinic demand for the remission of loans declares the lender's property to be *hefqer* and thereby enables the borrower to retain the loan without incurring guilt.

Two scriptural sources are offered for the principle that courts have the authority to confiscate property. The first is Ezra 10:8, where Ezra, representing the court, demands the returnees to assemble in Jerusalem and threatens those who fail to comply with the confiscation of their property. If Ezra has the right to do this, the Gemara assumes, then so do later courts. The second derives the principle by a fanciful reading of Joshua 19:51.[3] Whichever is accepted, the point is clearly made: Scripture (though not the Torah itself) recognizes the authority of courts to interfere with ownership rights. Thus, though no direct justification of the prozbul can be found (*pace* the Sifrei), a general rabbinic power understood to be grounded in Scripture may be at work here.

We should hesitate to think that rabbinic power is somehow diminished because the power of Torah is enlisted for support. There is a vast difference between claiming that the prozbul is derived from the Torah (as in the Sifrei) and claiming that the court (the Rabbis) has a generalized power to perform a certain kind of act. The first claim subordinates the Rabbis to Torah, the second asserts that they have the God-given right, at least in certain circumstances, to circumvent the Torah. Needless to say, the Rabbis were quite adept at discovering verses which could be construed to support their prerogative; mere mention of the verse "It is not in Heaven" (Deuteronomy 30:12 and cf. Baba Metzia 59b) graphically illustrates this point. In the case of prozbul, the Gemara requires us to recognize that the Torah yields to the

Rabbis, not the other way around.

The Gemara, at this point, goes off in a related but apparently distinct direction:

> A. They asked: When Hillel established prozbul, did he establish it for his generation or did he establish it for all generations?
> B. What difference does it make?
> C. [It affects whether later courts have the right] to annul it.
> D. If you say that he established it for his [own] generation, then we may annul it.
> E. But if you say that he established it for all generations, behold, "a court may not annul the decisions of its fellow court unless it is greater than it in wisdom and in number." (Mishnah Eduyot 1:5)

What is the point of raising this question here? One answer would be to assert, now in a different way, the weight of rabbinic power in comparison with the power of the Torah. In the previous section, the Gemara has just finished demonstrating that, one way or the other, the Rabbis have succeeded in putting aside the law of the Torah—though, presumably. the law of the Torah was declared for all generations. Now, we learn, if a Rabbi intends to issue a law for all generations, it will be extremely difficult to set aside that law. The law of the Torah may be uprooted even if the later court is not greater than the lawmaker (God); because of the restriction enunciated in Mishnah Eduyot, this freedom is not available in cases of rabbinic law.[4]

In contrast with the earlier sources, the intent of the Bavli here has been to emphasize the innovative boldness behind the prozbul and to assert, in a broader way, rabbinic prerogative vis-a-vis Torah. Before offering some general conclusions based upon this finding, we should briefly describe the other text in the Bavli where the present question is addressed. In Yevamot 89b-90b the question explored at length is whether the Rabbis have the authority to "uproot" laws of the Torah. The technical conclusion is that there is no such authority, but this conclusion is undercut by the many examples of legitimate uprooting that are collected there and by the several principals of exception that may be applied. These principles include not only the two offered in Gittin ("sit and do not do" and "the *hefqer* of the court is *hefqer*"), but also the notion that "fencing the thing is different." This means that the court has the authority to do anything that, in its wisdom, will serve the greater good of Torah by "establishing a fence" around it (N.B.: No scriptural justification is offered for this principle).

The illustrative examples of securing the Torah with a fence are, first, a case where the court executed a man found riding a horse on the Sabbath and, second, a case where the court ordered the lashing of a married couple who had sex out-of-doors (at 90b). In the first case, the act for which the man was executed is prohibited only by the Rabbis, not by the Torah. Yet because it was a time that the Sabbath was commonly being disregarded, the Rabbis deemed the execution justified. In the second case, there is no explicit prohibition at all. Yet because it was a time of general moral laxity, the punishment was believed warranted.

The first case is more extreme: in effect, the Rabbis justify their murder (taking life without legal warrant) of this man for an act that the Torah does not prohibit. Overall, the exceptions spelled out in this passage are far more powerful than the rule and, though the right to uproot the Torah is formally denied, in reality it is perfectly clear that the Rabbis reserve this authority. The Yevamot text, like Gittin, leaves no doubt concerning the extent of rabbinic power. The Torah directs and instructs; it does not necessarily restrain.

Why would the Bavli want to state its support of rabbinic power so forthrightly? Why would it not wish, as do its predecessors (excluding the Mishnah), to hide the assertion of rabbinic power behind the veil of scriptural justification?

The answer lies in the Bavli's broad theory of rabbinic "Torah" and its relation to Written Torah. As I have shown elsewhere, the Rabbis asserted that their contribution was essential, at the most fundamental level, for establishing the meaning of Torah.[5]

At the same time, the application of their own reason was deemed in no way inferior to the explication of Written Torah. To make this point, the Rabbis of the Bavli did not hesitate to emphasize the distance of some of their laws from Written Torah.[6] Moreover, in one notable text (Gittin 60a–b), the authors of the Bavli assert the equality of their Torah (the Oral Torah) with the Written Torah in the most uncompromising way, declaring that the Written Torah was once (in Sinai) oral (at least in large part) and that the Oral Torah has long been written.[7] In the end, the Rabbis behind the Bavli are confident of their own prerogative. Their treatment of prozbul is but one of many emblems of this confidence.

Prozbul offered rabbis of different periods an opportunity to reflect upon themselves and upon the Torah. It challenged them to consider what they were really undertaking; were they submissively or assertively traditional? What we discover by tracing their various musings on this matter is that rabbinic Judaism grew immensely in strength and confidence as it established itself through the centuries. Finally, as it emerged from Late Antiquity into the Medieval world, it concluded that the single, seamless Torah included the words of the Rabbis as well as those of God. This consciousness explains why, when asked to identify the source of, say, "Hear O Israel, the Lord our God, the Lord is One," the educated Medieval Jew would reply, "Berakhot 13a."

Notes

1. *Sifrei on Deuteronomy*, L. Finkelstein (ed.) (New York: Jewish Theological Seminary of America, repr. 1969), p. 173.
2. Notably, the Bavli does not consider the possibility offered in the Sifrei that prozbul is itself justified according to the Torah. Halivni proposes that the Bavli is unfamiliar with this Sifrei; see *M'qorot u'm'sorot* (Tel Aviv: Dvir, 1968), p. 539, n. 1. Be that as it may, it seems to me that even if the Bavli knew the Sifrei it would have no interest in it. The Bavli seeks not to diminish the problem of the conflict between the authority of the Torah and that of the Rabbis, it seeks to emphasize it.
3. "These are the territories which Eliezar the priest, and Yehoshua the son of Nun, and the heads of the fathers of the tribes of the children of Yisrael divided for an inheritance by lot in Shilo before the Lord, at the door of the Tent of Meeting. So they made an end of dividing the country."
4. Maimonides articulates precisely this distinction in his outlining of rabbinic power; see *Mishneh Torah, Hilkhot Mamerim*, ch. 2.
5. See D. Kraemer, *The Mind of the Talmud: An Intellectual History of the Bavli* (New York: Oxford University Press, 1990), pp. 146–156 [hereinafter KRAEMER].
6. See KRAEMER, pp. 130–138, and my analysis of Baba Qamma 83b–84a in *Reading the Rabbis: The Talmud as Literature* (New York: Oxford U. Press, 1996), pp. 33–48.
7. See my analysis of this text, at length, in "The Formation of Rabbinic Canon: Authority and Boundaries," *Journal of Biblical Literature*, 110(4), 1991, pp. 620–626 (chapter eight of this volume), and *Reading the Rabbis*, pp. 20–32.

Part III

Literary Studies

INTRODUCTION TO CHAPTER ELEVEN

The essays in this section form a history of the development of my scholarly method, from my graduate training to the preferred method of my mature scholarship. I have not included all of my most important articles here; I have omitted pieces that have already been substantially reprinted in one of my books. Still, the reader will gain a good sense from these pieces of where I have been and where I have come.

The first piece is effectively a restatement of one of the most important findings of my Ph.D. dissertation, "Stylistic Characteristics of Amoraic Literature." My dissertation advisor was Professor David Weiss Halivni. At the time I was engaged in my research, Halivni had begun to argue—as he has, indeed, continued to argue—that the named sages of the Talmud, the Amoraim, were uninterested in the preservation of argumentation. In Halivni's view, it was the unnamed "redactors" of the unattributed gemara text, whom he called the "stammaim," who first evinced an interest in argumentation. It was they who first preserved what earlier argumentation may have survived or, when it did not, reconstructed argumentation to support the "apodictic" teachings that constituted the vast bulk of Amoraic tradition. In fact, the intent of my dissertation was to test and confirm Halivni's thesis. I therefore examined the forms of Amoraic teachings, from generation to generation, to consider the extent to which they were either "apodictic" or "argumentational." In the first few Amoraic generations, my findings did confirm Halivni's suspicions.

However, beginning in the fourth Amoraic generation, the evidence did not fully support Halivni's picture. In fact, as the reader will see, the testimony of this generation evinces a subtle but distinct turn of interest toward argumentation, including its preservation. Here, in other words, I take issue with Halivni and, though he has moderated his claims slightly, he has never fully accounted for the evidence I offer here and elsewhere (see, in particular, *The Mind of the Talmud*, chapter 3). Let me be more specific. In *Midrash, Mishnah, and Gemara*, Halivni first speaks of the "indifference" of the Amoraim with respect to argumentation. He insists that the discursive materials "were not considered worthy enough to be transmitted to posterity" (p. 70). But later he modifies his view, writing:

> Since the Amoraim did not deem it important enough to have the discursive material committed to the transmitters with the same exactitude and polish... most of the discursive material did not survive, and what did survive was cryptic and truncated.

In response to this condition, the following generations of sages, the Stammaim, "set out to reclaim what was left of the argumentational material..." (P. 77). Now, if they did not preserve it, there could have been nothing left to "reclaim." Moreover, if it was "committed to the transmitters," even without the same "exactitude and polish" as the apodictic material, it was still committed! And if we preserve it without "exactitude and polish," it is just as reasonable to suppose that this was a consequence of the form of the discursive material which, by its nature, is more difficult to preserve with exactness. This is not evidence of lack of interest, it is simply a reality that will affect any such materials when preserved orally.

In my opinion, Halivni's "traditions history" remains inadequate, as it continues to ignore important evidence. Upon consideration of the account that follows, I am confident that the reader will agree.

Chapter Eleven

The Beginnings of the Preservation of Argumentation in Amoraic Babylonia

The agenda defined by the Mishnah is to a significant extent the subject of the Gemara's deliberations as well.[1] But the manner in which their common agenda is addressed is radically different, and this difference is perhaps most evident in their dissimilar styles of presentation. The Mishnah presents simple opinions or differences of opinion. It does not record the deliberations that produced these opinions. The Gemara, on the other hand, expresses itself primarily through the deliberations that produced the final opinions. In order for us to understand the development of the Gemara as a literary text, and before we can consider the motivations of its authors, we must ask when these deliberations joined the conclusions as objects of preservation.

Of course, this question has been asked before.[2] But finding a solution has been complicated by a variety of difficulties. First, the anonymous Gemara text, that segment of the text that is most replete with the deliberations whose source of preservation we seek, is of unknown origin. The chronology of the anonymous sections is at least in doubt, and according to recent consensus they are post-Amoraic.[3] This material is unlikely, therefore, to yield useful information concerning the origins of the preservation of argumentation. Attributed Amoraic material is no more generous in providing evidence that bears on our question. The vast majority of Amoraic deliberations are extremely brief, and the introductory formula "Rabbi X said to Rabbi Y" reveals little concerning their origin. Technical indications of dialogue are so fluid in the manuscripts and versions as to call into question the preservational status of such texts. Unfortunately, the literature was not sufficiently self-conscious to address the process of the formulation of these traditions. As a consequence of this general condition, scholarly conclusions have depended upon subjective analyses of evidence that admittedly yields a variety of interpretations.

I would like to suggest, however, that a crucial body of evidence has been ignored, and that the road to discovering the origin of the preservation of argumentation is not as cluttered as it might appear. What has been overlooked is the fact that when the Amoraic sages acted to preserve their traditions they did, on a good number of occasions, admit to this fact. This, if anything, is the intent of the formula "Rabbi X said Rabbi Y said." The first name in such a couplet, "Rabbi X," reveals to us the name of the authority who repeated a tradition as its primary Tanna. The Tanna, it has been noted,[4] served a function similar to a published book; that is, he assured that the published subject would be preserved. When Amoraim act in this position, then, they are stating their commitment to the preservation of such traditions. Moreover, these formulas reveal that it was not only anonymous academic functionaries who acted in this fashion, but some of the most prominent sages of the Amoraic era.[5] Even were we to consider the possibility that such chains of tradition are sometimes artificial constructs, we would still be forced lo admit that such attributions serve to enhance the position of the Tanna. In doing so they also assure that traditions whose survival is dependent upon this process will be preserved.

But at the same time it is crucial to note that the form of traditions that the Amoraim admit to preserving is limited. What is restricted from this process, apparently, is Amoraic argumentation. While any student could point to dozens of examples of Amoraic preservation of brief, categorical traditions, even the most seasoned scholar would be hard-pressed to quote an example of explicit Amoraic preservation of argumentation. Not that such cases do not exist—they do. It is these few rare cases, where Amoraim actually quote Amoraic argumentation, that are most instructive with respect to our question of the origins of the preservation of argumentation.

In a review of the entire Babylonian Talmud, I have discovered only thirty-three cases[6] of explicit preservation of argumentation from the first four Amoraic generations. By "explicit preservation" I mean traditions that approximate the model referred to above, that is, "Rabbi X said Rabbi Y objected to Rabbi Z." Both the chronology of these cases and the precise model of argumentation that was preserved in this way reveal a great deal concerning the beginning of the Babylonian Gemara style.

There are no cases of explicit preservation of argumentation from the first two Amoraic generations.[7] This supports the general observation that stylistically these generations quite closely followed the model established by the Mishnah.[8] The first cases occur in the third generation, and they represent a rather modest beginning.

Third generation sages who explicitly quote earlier argumenlation are

Zeira,[9] Joseph[10] and Rabba.[11] The traditions quoted are generally brief questions, and they are typified by the direct participation in the earlier argumentation of the individual now quoting it.[12] This suggests that the earliest motivation to repeat argumentation was a kind of self-consciousness, a thesis that can be supported from other contemporary factors.[13] There are exceptional cases of longer preservation,[14] but these too are characterized by direct personal involvement. The only near-exception to this rule is the preservation by Joseph at B. Hul. 36b, where after beginning with his own involvement, Joseph goes on to quote several steps in which he himself was not directly involved. Still, the beginning of this exchange, and therefore the general motivation, conforms to the previously noted rule.

There are relatively many cases of explicit preservation by sages who are contemporary with the third and fourth generations. Without exception these sages are individuals who served also as messengers of traditions between Palestine and Babylonia. This factor, I will suggest, is central to their position as preservers of argumentation, and not merely coincidental. These cases deserve more lengthy attention, and I will deal with them, therefore, after a brief description of explicit preservation in the fourth generation.

Fourth generation sages are no more prolific in quoting argumentation than their predecessors. While Abbaye quotes one deliberation in which he himself was involved (B. Eruv. 45b), he also sees fit to quote the argumentation of others (B. Eruv. 12a and B. B.M. 10a). Rava preserves argumentation on four occasions, though in two[15] the preserved deliberation is in a less typical narrative form. In one of his other two cases (B. B.M. 10a) Rava is joined by Abbaye in the preservation of argumentation, and this example is particularly significant because the preserved traditions have been transported from Palestine, and because they are very finely formulated. This phenomenon finds numerous parallels, and it leads us now to consider the factor of transport.

In sixteen of the total of thirty-three cases of explicit preservation of argumentation, the preserved argumentation has been transported between Palestine and Babylonia (in either direction, though usually the tradition has originated in Palestine). Six of these traditions are introduced with the formula "when Rabbi X came (from Palestine) he said..." When compared to the traditions preserved within Babylonia, these cases are often far more elaborate, and many exhibit fine literary formulation and reworking. Reference to a few select examples will help to illustrate.

At B. Yeb. 11b–12a R. Ḥiyya b. Abba repeats an exchange of four steps between R. Johanan and R. Ammi. The deliberation is initiated by R. Johanan's question, and what follows is simple dialogue. What is significant in this case is that R. Nachman b. Isaac, a Babylonian sage (the others are Palestinian), offers an alternative version of the deliberation, which is introduced with the formula "R. Nachman b. Isaac taught it this way (*mtny hky*)." This formula is indicative of a formally constructed tradition, and it means that an exchange whose latest participant was a third generation Palestinian has already assumed a formal literary character in fourth generation Babylonia. It also means that R. Nachman knew Ḥiyya b. Abba's quotation as a formal preservation. Nor is this a one-time event. Precisely the same phenomenon, relating to a different subject but repeating the structure and participants of this case exactly, is found at B. Zeb. 85b. In neither of these examples does the fact that the tradition was transported to Babylonia from Palestine appear to be central. But equivalent examples of formulation and reformulation of quoted argumentation do not recur in traditions restricted to Babylonia. That fact, when considered in conjunction with related evidence, is certainly significant.

A second example, at B. Hul. 134a–b, is introduced with the "when R. X came from Palestine" formula, in this case R. Dimi being the one who preserves earlier argumentation. The deliberation that originated in Palestine, an exchange between R. Johanan and R. Laqish, is only three steps in length, but the initial step involves a question concerning two contradictory Tannaitic sources, and the steps that follow are also not simple. It is clear that the present formulation is the one repeated by R. Dimi; Rava and Abbaye, both later contemporaries, address it directly. This is significant in that the parallel Palestinian traditions[16] do not retain the dialogical character present here; they are stated as typical categorical Amoraic traditions. We must assume, therefore, that either R. Dimi preserved an exchange that the Palestinians themselves did not see fit to preserve, or that R. Dimi, for some reason, chose to formulate these traditions in a dialogical form. In either case, what stands out is the fact that when transported from Palestine to Babylonia, Dimi quotes not independent traditions, but traditions that relate to one another in argumentational dialogue. Again, a similar phenomenon, with equal elaboration, is not present in exclusively Babylonian traditions.

A third example, at B. Hul. 57a–b, is in certain ways less significant than the previous two. It is, first, a case of explicit preservation in which the individual who repeats the argumentation is personally involved. This is apparently the least sophisticated model of such preservation, as witnessed previously. Second, the whole matter here is not formulated with the same literary exactness as the previous examples. It is part of a longer narrative, and as is the case with Talmudic narrative in general, it is difficult to evaluate the conditions and chronology of its formulation. On the other hand, the argumentation is repeated quite explicitly on account of transport, in this case from Babylonia to Palestine, and the quoted exchange is far longer than anything we have seen previously, extending to a full eight steps.[17] Here it would be impossible to deny that transport of traditions is somehow significant in motivating the preservation of relevant argumentation.[18]

But why should this be the case? Why, when it is transported, does a conclusive tradition need the elaborating argumentation, while, when it remains in the environs of its creation, it does not? One possible answer is suggested by in the gemara itself, at B. Hul. 51a. In this case, a legal decision that originated in Palestine is reported without elaboration before Abbaye. Confused by the tradition, Abbaye pursues to great lengths the individual who brought it from Palestine, and, when he finally hears the full story, he discovers that the original report had been an incorrect representation of the fuller picture. Brief statements or reports are likely to become confused, in other words, precisely because of their brevity. Brief traditions require interpretation, and in the openness to such interpretation confusion is likely to result.[19] Argumentation, on the other hand, provides a context. Deliberation is itself interpretation, and though it may be more difficult to preserve, in the end it assures more accurate repetition.

When simple traditions were repeated in their home context, interpretation was more secure and confusion less likely to arise. But there was apparently some recognition that simple traditions, when transported over a long distance and to a different milieu, were more open to such confusion. On those rare occasions when it was deemed essential to avoid such confusion, something of the original context was also preserved. For this reason, it would appear, preserved argumentation more often accompanies traditions that were transported between the two great centers of Rabbinic learning.[20]

However, if this is the motivation for preserving argumentation, this means that argumentation has not yet attained a status that demands independent attention. It is quoted in the service of other traditions—to provide a context or to suggest a clarifying interpretation. Because its independent worth is as yet dubious, preservation of such traditions is not yet frequent or systematic. The same may be said, of course, of the more simple preservations found in exclusively Babylonian sources. There, the prevalent model of personal involvement suggests that a sage might quote a deliberation in support of a present opinion. The earlier deliberation, though, is not remarked upon for its own sake. This is, of course, not true of the gemara text in general, where attention to argumentation is often central. Both in scope and intent, then, this is a modest beginning.

Concerning the chronology of this preservation, it is noteworthy that the individuals who were responsible for the transport of traditions, Dimi, Ulla and Rabin in particular, were Palestinian sages of the third–fourth generation (that is, students of R. Johanan; earlier contemporaries of Abbaye and Rava). If their repetition of Palestinian traditions in Babylonia motivated the occasional preservation of an argumentational exchange, then this factor may also have acted as a catalyst for the preservation of argumentation by Babylonian sages themselves. The awakening self-awareness in formulating traditions would certainly have provided fertile ground for such a response, and as we noted, this was precisely the period during which the first explicit preservation is found in Babylonia. It appears to me that the coincidence of these factors is more than a matter of chance.

Moreover, another phenomenon that follows immediately upon this period is indicative of a significant change in sensibilities concerning preservation. What I am referring to is two cases, at B. Git. 25a–b and B. B.M. 55b–56a, where Abbaye comments at length about details of earlier argumentation. The form and nature of his comments is extremely revealing.

In the Gittin text, Abbaye's comment is preceded by three stages of argumentational exchange. Abbaye's tradition, referring to this exchange, is this: "Abbaye said: He asks him X and the other answers Y and he then objects X." I have not translated in full because what is stated in three words in the Hebrew (the language of X and Y; the rest of the comment is in Aramaic)[21] would require many words of explanation in an English translation. The original tradition is as brief as I have here represented it. In the Baba Metsia text Abbaye's comment is longer, but the length is required by the difficulty and sophistication of the argumentation that he is referring to and of the insights that he suggests.[22]

What is true of both traditions is this: both are formulated in the typical categorical Amoraic style (spoken of as "apodictic" by Halivni), and both are entirely dependent upon the retention of the earlier argumentation to which they refer. The categorical form means that these are published traditions. To say that they were "published" means that they were intended to be formally preserved for transmission to future generations. But in these particular cases that preservation could not have been independent. As I said, without the referent argumentation, these traditions are entirely incomprehensible. That means that those who published these traditions of Abbaye (and of Rava, who in each of these two cases responds to Abbaye's observation) assumed that the argu-mentation would also be preserved.

Furthermore, unlike the previous examples, in each of these texts the primary focus and concern of the author of the traditions is clearly the argumentation itself. Particularly in the Baba Metsia case, it is difficult to posit any function other than commentary on argumentation. This was not the case in the examples of explicit preservation, where the deliberation was not clearly the primary focus. This transition is of extraordinary significance. Because these published traditions are primarily concerned with the argumentation itself, we may conclude that the preservation of that argumentation was also a primary intent of the authors. This is the first time that such a phenomenon occurs, and it is the first time, therefore, that a comment in the true spirit of gemara has been composed.

Abbaye and Rava are Babylonian sages of the fourth generation (early-to-mid fourth century). They did, therefore, have the opportunity for direct exchange with and considerable influence by the Palestinian messengers of whom we spoke earlier. Is the chronological proximity of these two phenomena—explicit preservation and published, detailed commentary—a mere coincidence, or was there some kind of direct influence of one on the other? Explicit evidence is not, as far as I am aware, available, yet we might suggest a possible relation by reference to a similar, better known phenomenon.

All would agree that commentary follows the initial publication of a text. It would be absurd to publish a commentary unless one were secure in thinking that the text to which it referred would survive. A text must demonstrate its viability before a commentary is to be composed. That was certainly true of earlier Rabbinic materials. The power of the Mishnah motivated its commentary. Simple Amoraic traditions were preserved before later sages could refer back to them. In all cases the viability of preservation comes first.

This is certainly also the reason that there are no early Amoraic comments on Amoraic argumentation; there were no such comments because argu-mentation was not formally preserved during that period. But in the third generation for the first time, and particularly in connection with texts that had been transported between Palestine and Babylonia, argumentation was preserved in a formal, intended way. The viability of preserving argumentation was now finally established. And it was precisely at this time, therefore, that the first extended comments on argumentation were published.[23]

Of course, when speaking of a tradition as vast as that of the Bavli, a relatively small number of cases such as this does not, on its own, make for convincing conclusions. But is does open a window to inquiry. It now becomes relevant to ask whether other evidence supports these conclusions. Is there some other feature that characterizes the product of these Amoraic generations that would lead us to believe that it was at this point that argumentation was first formally preserved? For example, considerably more argumentation is recorded in the Bavli in the names of sages of these generations than of previous generations. Could this be explained by our proposal that it was now, for the first time, that the value of such traditions was recognized? What is the nature of the many argumentational traditions attributed to these generations? Do they exhibit evidence of intentional, primary formulation? Are they, on the other hand, different from similar traditions in other generations? Do they tell us anything of their preservation at all?

Whatever, in the end, is the answer to these questions, we may still, at this stage, be confident in making the following claims: Formal preservation of argumentation, on at least a very limited scale, began in the third Amoraic generation and continued modestly thereafter. The transport of traditions between Palestine and Babylonia played a significant role in this process. Its fruit may be seen in the fourth generation in the first published commentaries on argumentation. These cases are very few in number, and this reflects the fact that attention to argumentation as an independent object of interpretation did not gain complete support in rabbinic circles until several generations later.

What we have discovered in the mid-Amoraic era, then, is merely the seeds of what would later typify gemara. It may not yet be spoken of as a comprehensive method, but only as a relatively modest proposal; something that would be tested, but not yet widely employed. It was only the authors of the anonymous gemara who would finally extend the implications of what we have seen here to all of Rabbinic tradition. It was they, in the end, who for the first time understood the functions that argumentation could truly be made to serve.[24]

Notes

1. But see Jacob Neusner, *Judaism: The Classical Statement* (Chicago, 1986), pp. 94–114 and 222–240. I have taken issue with Neusner's precise conclusions in my "Scripture Commentary in the Bavli: A Primary or Secondary Phenomenon?," in *AJS Review*, Spring, 1989, 1–15 (chapter 12 of this volume). Of course, the broad approaches of these two documents are so clearly distinct as to reflect different overall agendas. For a lengthy discussion of the significance of these differences see D. Halivni, *Midrash, Mishnah and Gemara: The Jewish Predeliction for Justified Law* (Cambridge and London, 1986), pp. 38–92.

2. R. Sherira Gaon (10th cent.) in his famous epistle already offers one suggestion concerning the beginning of the preservation of deliberations in the Gemara; see ed. Levin, pp. 62–64. Most modern scholars of Rabbinic literature have also proposed solutions to this question, generally by seeking the "antiquity of the sugya." See, e.g., A. Weiss, *On the Literary Production of the Amoraim* (Hebrew) (New York, 1961), p. 7ff.; H. Albeck, *Introduction to the Talmuds* (Hebrew) (Tel Aviv, 1969), pp. 576–596; B. DeVries, *Studies in Talmudic Literature* (Hebrew) (Jerusalem, 1968), pp. 181–199.

3. See a review of the relevant literature in D. Goodblatt, "The Babylonian Talmud," in J. Neusner, ed., *The Study of Ancient Judaism*. Vol. 11 (Ktav Publishing, 1981), pp. 154–7 and 177–181. See also Richard Kalmin, "The Stam and the Final Generations of Amoraim: Assessing the Importance of Their Relationship for Study of the Redaction of the Talmud," in A. Avery-Peck, ed., *New Perspectives on Ancient Judaism*, v. 4, *The Literature of Early Rabbinic Judaism: Issues in Talmudic Redaction and Interpretation* (Studies in Judaism, Lanham, MD: University Press of America, 1989), pp. 29–35.

4. See S. Lieberman, "The Publication of the Mishnah," in *Hellenism in Jewish Palestine* (New York, 1950), pp. 83–99. Lieberman astutely points out that the question is not whether Rabbinic traditions were ever written, but whether authoritative versions took a written form or not. He concludes that they did not, and I remain convinced that published authoritative traditions were preserved orally. See also J. Neusner, *The Pharisees: Rabbinic Perspectives* (New Jersey, 1973), pp. 225–27, and "Tannaim," in *The Encyclopedia of Religion* (New York, 1987), vol. 14, p. 272.

5. Note especially the activity of R. Judah in this regard. See B. Kosowsky, *Otsar Hashemot Latalmud Bavli*, (Jerusalem, 1977), vol. 2. pp. 637–54.

6. This was the number that I discovered in my dissertation research. Since that time a few more have come to my attention. They do not change the analysis that I suggest below.

7. I have followed the generational divisions proposed by Albeck, op. cit., p. 144ff.

8. See I. Halevy, *Dorot Harishonim*, part II, p. 591; A. Weiss, op. cit., pp. 10–11; and David Kraemer, *Stylistic Characteristics of Amoraic Literature*, (Ph.D. diss., Jewish Theological Seminary, 1984; hereafter referred to as SCAL), pp. 47–79.

9. B. Ber. 48a, B. Men. 7a.

10. B. Ber. 25b, B. Hul. 36b.

11. B. Eruv. 17a. 40a and 40b; B. Suk. 17a–b.

12. See e.g. B. Ber. 25b, 48a and B. Eruv. 17a.

13. See SCAL, p. 81ff.

14. See Rabba at B. Eruv. 40b and particularly at B. Suk. 17a–b.

15. B. Pes. 103a, B. B.M. 48b.

16. See Y. Hal. 3:4 (59b), and Y. Peah ch. 4 end (18c). For a fuller discussion of this example, see SCAL, p. 162ff.

17. On manuscript variants in the quotation segment, and my evaluation that the printed text ought to be depended upon, see SCAL, pp. 170–171, n. 29.

18. Of the other cases of transported argumentational traditions in quotation, five are quite brief (one or two steps). One of these (B. B.B. 27b) repeats a simple question (a semi-apodictic form, see SCAL, pp. 312–318) and the response, one (B. Meilah 21b) a brief textual contradiction (*rmi lih*) and the response, and one (B. Nid. 29a) merely a simple objection. The other three such cases are quite long and elaborate. One (B. Men. 7a) is ten steps or longer, and the other two (B. Bes. 38a–b and B. Hul. 19b) are motivated by provocative points of narrative.

19. See B. Hul. 124a for an excellent—and amusing—example of this phenomenon.

20. If transport itself was truly the crucial factor, then we would expect the same phenomenon to have occurred in the transport of traditions from Babylonia to Palestine. The Babylonian Talmud records that this was in fact the case in a number of instances, and the text referred to above from B. Hul. 57a–b is only one such example. The Yerushalmi also ought to record similar evidence. Though I have not made an extensive search of that document, several examples have come to my attention. For a review of these, see SCAL, p. 167.

21. The sharp delineation between Hebrew and Aramaic in Amoraic sources, suggested by some contemporary scholars, needs to be considered with caution. Particularly when quoting earlier sources or employing technical terms, Hebrew and Aramaic might be used in the same tradition.

22. For a more detailed description of these texts, as well as full textual analysis, see SCAL, p. 216ff.

23. The comments of Abbaye do not refer to argumentation preserved from Palestine. But this does not, I think, effect the viability of what I am proposing. Once the viability of preserving argumentation was demonstrated, any argumentation became a potential object for such comments.

24. My gratitude is due to the Abbell Fund for its assistance in supporting this project.

INTRODUCTION TO CHAPTER TWELVE

The following piece is a sort of extended footnote, though one with more profound implications. At approximately the same time I published my *The Mind of the Talmud*, Neusner published what appeared to be his definitive work on the Bavli—*Judaism: The Classical Statement*. The book, published by University of Chicago Press, seemed to conclude a "Chicago Series" on the great rabbinic classics, beginning with the Mishnah (*Judaism: The Evidence of the Mishnah*) and coming to culmination with the Bavli. Having been persuaded, in significant measure, by Neusner's Mishnah work, I came to the Bavli volume with great eagerness. I was taken aback, therefore, by one of the book's central conclusions.

In *Judaism: The Classical Statement*, Neusner examines, above all, the focus of the Bavli's extended discussions. Of what and in relation to what, he wants to know, does the Bavli speak? Using selected tractates as a representative sample, Neusner concludes—among other things—that the Bavli is as significantly a scripture commentary as it is a Mishnah commentary. He states his conclusions in this language:

> The importance of the Bavli's distinctive contribution now becomes entirely clear. The Bavli carried forward a long-established enterprise, namely, the forging of links between the Mishnah and Scripture. But the organizers and redactors of the materials compiled in the Bavli did something unprecedented. *They allowed sustained passages of Scripture to serve, as much as sustained and not merely episodic passages of the Mishnah served, as main beams in the composition of structure and order.* In a single document, *the Mishnah and Scripture functioned together and for the first time in much the same way.* (p. 239, emphasis added)

For reasons that should be clear, I understood these conclusions to be offered as definitive, characterizing the Bavli as a whole. But these same conclusions contradicted my own experience as a student of the Bavli, so I wanted to know whether I might test them based upon other evidence I then had in hand (from my dissertation research) and some I had yet to gather. As the reader will see from what follows, I quickly discovered that my intuitions were correct and there was little doubt that Neusner's sample was not representative. Yes, the Bavli does include significant scripture commentaries here and there, but such commentaries do not characterize the Bavli as a whole. The Bavli remains, at least on its surface, a "commentary" on the Mishnah. (I put the term commentary in quotation marks because, in my estimation, the Bavli is not a commentary in any common sense of that term; see *Reading the Rabbis*, pp. 142–4 and 146–7.)

In private communication, Professor Neusner suggested that I misunderstood his intent and conclusions. He insisted that his work was meant to be a first exploration. He sought to test a thesis and set his conclusions "out there" for others to refine. Indeed, in later work, Neusner came to characterize the Bavli as a Mishnah commentary, setting aside the apparent purport of this earlier work. In recognition of the direction of his developing scholarship on the Bavli, I think it fair to say that I did, indeed, misunderstand his larger intent, being misled by the factors described above. Still, if I was misled, I imagine that others might similarly be misled, and my essay therefore constitutes an important corrective on the limited conclusions of *Judaism: The Classical Statement*.

Chapter Twelve

Scripture Commentary in the Babylonian Talmud:
Primary or Secondary Phenomenon?

Virtually without exception, the Bavli is described by its students as a commentary on the Mishnah. This definition is such a commonplace that it is difficult to imagine the need to test or defend it. Its accuracy seems so self-evident that the question "what is the Bavli?" is itself rarely, if ever, asked.

But even if the definition is correct (and this has recently been challenged; see below), this does not mean that scholars are exempt from testing it, if only to offer it anew. The task of proposing an adequate definition of the Bavli is, despite all appearances, not a simple one. The text is extraordinarily vast, and because of its vastness it is often difficult to grasp more than its details. But it is precisely such a grasp that is necessary before a definition can be offered. The challenge, therefore, is to seek the large structures upon which the Bavli is erected, requiring the sort of reading to which the document is perhaps least well suited.

Despite its difficulty, the exercise of definition promises much. If we describe a document we begin to gain access to those who composed it. Who were they? What was important to them? How did they view the world? Choices of subject and form are ideological choices, and so inquiry into these and other literary considerations will yield explicit evidence regarding the broad ideological assumptions of a document's authors. Furthermore, the more we are able to nuance a description, the more insight will be gained into the community that produced a given document. Though a broad definition might appear adequate, the substrata of details must be probed as well.

For these reasons, the Bavli ought now to be subjected to fresh studies of description and definition. Being the grandest and most complete expression to emerge from Babylonian Judaism in late antiquity, its testimony to the nature of that Judaism is without parallel. Its pages embody the sinew and spirit of its community and age, and its definitions exemplify, to a significant extent, the self-definitions of that same community. It is only through describing, and thereby understanding, this document that the Judaism of that period and place may truly be grasped.

But in this instance definition promises even more. By gaining a fuller understanding of the Bavli as a religious and intellectual composition, something may also be said about the communities into which it was received. The Bavli became, of course, the foundation document for virtually all of (rabbinic) Judaism to follow. What made it so influential and convincing? Was its success merely political, or is there something in the power of its ideas and the design of its composition that accounts for its ultimately universal reception in late antique and medieval Judaism?

Having framed the question this way, a response must also account for the Bavli's "competitor," the Yerushalmi. Both are, after all, understood to be commentaries on the Mishnah. But the communities that produced them were hardly identical. In order to distinguish the Judaism of early-fifth century Palestine from that of sixth-century Babylonia, it is necessary to seek the characteristics by which the Yerushalmi and Bavli are distinguished from one another. Furthermore, if there is interest in comprehending the forces that cause a document of this sort to be received as authoritative, it is imperative to ask why the Bavli ultimately came to be preferred. What, if anything, makes the Bavli unique?

It is in recognition of precisely these issues and questions that Jacob Neusner defined the program of his recent book on the Bavli, *Judaism: The Classical Statement*.[1] His findings in that study are of extraordinary note. Based upon his taxonomy of "units of discourse" in tractates Sukkah, Sotah, and Sanhedrin in both Talmuds, Neusner concludes that the authors of the Bavli chose, when framing that document, not only to follow the order of the Mishnah and to compose a commentary upon it (as had been the case in the Yerushalmi), but to allow Scripture, as well, to form the organizational outline upon which the Bavli's commentary would be based.[2] In significant proportion the Bavli is also a Scripture commentary, Neusner claims, and its previous characterizations now require significant revision.

If Neusner is correct, then our understanding of the Judaism that produced the Bavli must also undergo revision. Briefly, both Scripture and the Mishnah having been posited as its foundation, the Bavli will now be seen as the definitive summa of classical Judaism, and this not merely on account of historical accident, but by design. It will be the comprehensive synthesis of all of rabbinic Judaism that preceded, including Midrash, Mishnah, and Gemara. It might even be suggested that this redactional choice mirrors an ideological choice to equate written and oral Torah, an equation which, as Neusner has shown, was made *explicitly* (that is, by use of the term "oral Torah," in full) in the Bavli for the very first time.[3]

But Neusner's conclusions require careful evaluation, particularly since the sample upon which he bases his conclusions does not uniformly speak in his support. Distinguishing "Scripture units of discourse" from all others, including those that employ Scripture to comment directly on Mishnah, Neusner shows that in tractate Sotah, 32.1 percent of the total units of discourse are based on Scripture, in Sanhedrin 35.3 percent are, but in Sukkah, only 2.9 percent of the total address Scripture independent of Mishnah.[4] It is this latter number that requires that we proceed with caution.

Why ought we to suppose that Sukkah is anomalous and that Sotah and Sanhedrin are typical of the Bavli? Perhaps both are representative of a type that appears in equivalent proportions, in which case the claims for the whole will have to be phrased more modestly. Or perhaps, in the end, it will turn out that Sanhedrin and Sotah are less typical, and though they might include significant Scripture commentaries, this is not true of the Bavli as a whole. There is nothing in the data that Neusner adduces, as far as I can see, to indicate which of these possibilities is more likely. Until we make this determination, it seems premature to argue for a total revision of the "traditional" wisdom.

It is not necessary to actually replicate Neusner's procedure for a substantial portion of the Bavli to evaluate the reliability of his sample. There are other ways to test the likelihood that either Sotah and Sanhedrin, on the one hand, or Sukkah, on the other, are/is more typical of the Bavli as a whole. One way—tedious but nevertheless available—would be simply to count the total number of scriptural citations per tractate (or per page in a given tractate) for a significant proportion of the Bavli. If it turned out that Sotah and Sanhedrin have a significantly higher proportion than most other tractates, then we would have to conclude that Sukkah is more likely to reflect the norm. If, on the other hand, it turned out that Sukkah has a significantly lower proportion, then we would have to favor Sotah and Sanhedrin as normal. I have not conducted such an accounting (nor am I aware that anyone else has), but I have reason to believe, based upon other data, that the former is the case, and not the latter. It is these data that I will present below.

In earlier research[5] I conducted a detailed analysis of the nature of the traditions attributed to the most prominent amoraic sages of the first four generations[6] (Rav, Samuel, Johanan, Resh Laqish,[7] Judah, Huna, Nachman, Sheshet, Ḥisda, Joseph, Rabba, Abbaye, and Rava). In the course of this analysis I enumerated traditions that articulated legal opinions, those that interpreted earlier rabbinic texts (usually either Mishnah or baraitot), and those that interpreted Scripture.[8] These latter traditions can form the basis of an accurate test for the representativeness of the tractates under consideration.

The reliability of a test based upon this body of amoraic traditions can be justified in this way: First, a quick review of the texts that embody the majority of Scripture units of discourse in Neusner's study will indicate that amoraic traditions, of which those of these sages form a sizable proportion, are relatively prominent in the samples. Their contribution is supplemented significantly only by baraitot, and in a far more limited way by interpretations of the anonymous gemara. By way of a concrete example, in the lengthy section of Scripture units of discourse at Sotah 9b-14a (M. Sotah 1:8–9), of a total of eighty-seven units delineated by Neusner, only five are clearly attributable to the anonymous gemara,[9] and four are more difficult to identify.[10] All other units are formed around either amoraic traditions (the vast majority) or baraitot. In these, the anonymous gemara comments only modestly, for the most part, and in all respects is subservient to the identified (amoraic or tannaitic) tradition.[11] Because of its prominence, therefore, the amoraic contribution may be taken to be representative of the whole.

Furthermore, though my sample includes not only traditions that treat Scripture independently of Mishnah, but also those that employ Scripture in the service of Mishnah, this difference should not be taken to invalidate the relevance of the sample. Since finding a source for Mishnah in Scripture is a general objective in the Talmud's Mishnah exegesis, we must assume that Scripture units related to Mishnah are distributed with relative uniformity through the Bavli (or at least with greater uniformity than Scripture units that are independent of Mishnah). In fact, Neusner's own analysis supports this conclusion. In his detailing of the use of Scripture in Sotah, units independent of Mishnah are grouped in few distinct sections (pp. 96–97). Units that elaborate Mishnah, on the other hand, relate to almost all Mishnah paragraphs (pp. 88–89). This being the case, in order more closely to approach Neusner's sample we may, at the outset, subtract a certain number from the base of units found in each tractate. What this means is that discrepancies between tractates should be considered to be even more extreme than they appear. As can easily be seen in table 1, even as a preliminary test the numbers suggest that Sotah and Sanhedrin should not be taken to be representative.

Table I
Total Number of Comments on Scripture, by Tractate

Sage	Ber	Shab	Eruv	Pes	R.H.	Yom	SUK	Bez	Meg	Tan	M.K.	Hag
Rav	12	27	7	5	5	6	3	3	18	4	4	7

Samuel	9	7	4	3	0	3	0	1	8	1	0	3
Johanan	31	25	7	17	13	18	4	0	18	18	3	3
Judah	3	4	1	1	1	3	0	0	1	3	1	0
Huna	5	3	2	0	1	2	2	0	3	1	2	2
Nahman	3	0	1	3	0	1	0	0	3	1	0	0
Sheshet	2	2	0	0	0	1	0	0	1	0	0	0
Hisda	3	4	4	2	2	1	1	1	1	1	0	0
Joseph	5	0	0	3	1	2	0	1	2	1	0	1
Rabba	1	3	1	2	0	0	1	1	2	0	0	0
Abbaye	3	2	1	7	2	6	5	0	2	2	2	1
Rava	5	10	8	13	3	9	4	0	25	5	3	4
Total	82	87	36	56	28	52	20	7	84	37	15	21

	Yev	Ket	Git	Kid	SOT	Ned	Naz	B.K	B.M.	B.B.	SAN	Shv
Rav	15	6	1	5	18	9	1	3	5	12	46	2
Samuel	2	1	4	2	9	4	0	0	2	3	17	4
Johanan	7	3	5	6	26	8	7	10	4	23	89	2
Judah	2	3	2	1	0	2	0	1	0	2	18	0
Huna	2	4	1	1	2	0	1	3	0	3	7	0
Nahman	0	3	0	3	3	1	0	1	0	3	11	0
Sheshet	0	0	0	0	1	1	0	1	0	1	2	0
Hisda	4	4	1	1	6	2	0	1	3	3	8	1
Joseph	0	1	1	1	0	1	0	1	2	1	5	0
Rabba	3	0	0	1	2	2	0	2	0	3	2	0
Abbaye	3	3	1	4	2	0	1	3	1	4	13	5
Rava	27	4	1	8	14	11	4	15	10	11	28	7
Total	65	32	17	33	83	41	14	41	27	69	246	21

	Mak	A.Z.	Hor.	Zev	Men	Hul	Bek	Arak	Tem	Ker	Me'	Nid
Rav	3	9	0	4	1	6	8	2	2	1	0	2
Samuel	1	1	0	4	0	12	1	3	1	0	0	3
Johanan	1	6	3	15	7	9	2	4	1	2	2	5
Judah	0	1	0	1	2	0	1	1	0	0	0	0
Huna	0	2	0	6	2	0	0	0	0	1	0	0
Nahman	0	1	0	1	1	1	0	0	1	0	0	0
Sheshet	0	1	0	0	2	0	0	0	0	0	0	1
Hisda	0	1	1	4	4	6	2	0	0	1	0	1
Joseph	0	1	0	2	2	1	0	0	0	0	0	1
Rabba	0	0	1	4	0	1	1	1	0	0	0	0
Abbaye	3	2	3	9	2	2	6	1	2	4	0	2
Rava	2	9	7	14	8	15	15	9	8	5	1	4
Total	10	34	15	64	30	53	36	21	15	14	3	19

A number of things may be said about the numbers shown in the tables. First, there is some variation based upon the individual contributor.[12] Joseph, for example, contributes relatively few scriptural comments. The same may be said for Judah, though his contribution on Sanhedrin is quite pronounced. Johanan, on the other hand, is rather prolific in this area, though his traditions are especially preserved in tractates from Moʿed. Second, earlier sages seem to have contributed more than later sages, but the fact that Rava is an exception suggests that the most crucial factor is the total quantity of a sage's contribution (Rava and Rav are the most prolific sages in the Bavli, followed by Johanan). In any case, the general picture, by tractate, comes through quite clearly.

Both Sotah and Sanhedrin are obviously in the upper end of scriptural units, and are perhaps even exceptional. This certainly seems to be the case for Sanhedrin, which, even given its length, preserves scriptural comments in a quantity well above other tractates (see table 2). The same, I would argue, is the case with Sotah, which, despite its moderate length, nevertheless includes more such traditions than nearly any other tractate, including many which greatly exceed it in length. Berachot is similar to Sotah in both quantity and length, and Megillah, though relatively short, includes a great many comments on Scripture. But these four (Shabbat, when adjusted for its length, will not be equivalent to the others) are obviously out of the ordinary. Accounting for their respective lengths, in comparison to other tractates, will only reinforce this conclusion.

Table 2
Total Number of Scriptural Comments Attributed to Sages
Accounted by Tractate

No. of Comments per Tractate

1–9   Bezah, Me'ilah

10–19 Moed Katan, Nazir, Gittin, Makkot, Horayot, Temurah, Keritot, Niddah

20–29 Sukkah. Rosh Hashana, Hagigah, B.M., Shevuot, Arakhin

30–39 Eruvin, Taanit, Ketubot, Kiddushin, A.Z., Menachot, Bekhorot

40–49 Nedarim, B.K.

50–59 Pesachim, Yoma, Hullin

60–69 Yevamot, B.B., Zevachim

70-79 —

80–89 Berachot, Shabbat, Megillah, Sotah

90+   Sanhedrin

In table 3 I consider the number of scriptural comments by the sages listed in table 1 per page of printed Bavli text. Of course this is not a precise measure, but with a few exceptions (that I have indicated) the amount of text per printed page is approximately equivalent over the whole, and for purposes of such a comparison we are certainly within the realm of reason.

Table 3
Number of Scriptural Comments per Page of Printed Bavli Text (Vilna Edition)

Note: + or - indicates whether pages should be added or subtracted in order to account for differences of quantity of text per printed page.

Tractate	No. of pages	No. of comments per page
Ber.	64+	1.29/1
Shab.	157	0.55/1
Eruv.	105	0.34/1
Pesachim	121	0.46/1
R.H.	35	0.8/1
Yoma	88	0.59/1
Sukkah	56	0.36/1
Bezah	40	0.17/1
Megillah	32	2.6/1
Ta'anit	31	1.2/1
M.K.	29	0.51/1
Chag.	27	0.77/1
Yev.	122	0.53/1
Ket.	112	0.28/1
Ned.	91-	0.45/1
Nazir	66-	0.21/1
Sotah	49+	1.6/1
Gittin	90	0.19/1
Kid.	82	0.4/1
B.K.	119	0.34/1
B.M.	119	0.23/1
B.B.	176-	0.39/1
Sanh.	113+	2.2/1
Shev.	49	0.43/1
Makkot	24	0.42/1
A.Z.	76	0.45/1
Horayot	14	1.0/1
Zev.	120	0.53/1
Men.	110	0.27/1
Hullin	142	0.37/1
Bechorot	61	0.59/1
Arakhin	34	0.62/1
Temurah	34	0.44/1
Ker.	28	0.5/1
Me'ilah	22+	0.13/1

Niddah	73	0.24/ 1		

Adjusted for the length of the tractate, again the exceptional nature of Sotah and Sanhedrin (as well as Berachot and Megillah) can be seen. These are the only tractates (along with Ta'anit, which, because of its brevity, finds its proportion a little skewed) in which the ratio of scriptural comments per page is greater than 1/1. In particular, the ratio for Sanhedrin is noteworthy because one would expect, on account of its length, that its ratio would be more even (much as the ratio for Megillah is higher because of its brevity). In fact, the majority of tractates have a ratio of 0.5/1 or less, and in light of these data, it appears more likely that Sukkah represents the norm, while Sotah and Sanhedrin are distinct from the norm.

Another measure confirms the same conclusion. In general, the number of non-Scripture-related traditions contributed by the sages listed above is far greater than those that are Scripture-related. It will be of interest to consider whether this is the case in the tractates that we have termed exceptional. I have chosen, for illustration, those sages whose contribution to the scriptural comments is most prolific. (Four other tractates will serve for a comparison. If this same accounting were to be conducted in all tractates, it would be easily demonstrated that the numbers for these tractates are far more typical.)

Table 4
Number of Scripture Comments Compared with Other Traditions
(Scripture Comments/Law or Legal Commentary)

Name of Sage	Exceptional tractates	No. of comments per page	Other tractates	No. of comments per page
Rav	Berakhot	12/42	Sukkah	3/34
	Megillah	18/15	Eruvin	7/81
	Sotah	18/16	Kiddushin	5/39
	Sanhedrin	46/36	Hullin	6/82
Johanan	Berakhot	31/49	Sukkah	4/23
	Megillah	18/11	Eruvin	7/59
	Sotah	26/10	Kiddushin	6/34
	Sanhedrin	89/49	Hullin	9/114
Rava	Berakhot	5/49	Sukkah	4/45
	Megillah	25/27	Eruvin	8/58
	Sotah	14/8	Kiddushin	8/49
	Sanhedrin	28/85	Hullin	15/75

As shown in table 4, while there is some individual variation, it is certain, again, that the tractates that we have previously defined to be exceptional are in fact just that. They are the only tractates in which the contributions of major amoraic sages comprise an equal or greater quantity of scriptural comments. In other tractates, such traditions do not even begin to approach the number of legal or legal-commentary traditions. The norm, again it seems clear, is closer to Sukkah, and not to Sotah, Sanhedrin, Berachot, or Megillah. These latter, rather, are not typical, but are, with relation to the Bavli as a whole, out of the ordinary.

For this conclusion to stand, it is not necessary that we be able to suggest why these tractates admitted different principles of overall composition. Even so, if we are able to venture a suggestion or two concerning why Sanhedrin and Sotah are out of the ordinary, we will have gone some distance in explaining why the authors of these texts chose to set for themselves a task that was distinct, at times, from the one pursued in the rest of the Bavli.

What, then, might the explanation be? The answer to this question would require a much lengthier study, but in a preliminary way we may suggest this: There is something about these tractates (what, we shall consider below) that generates the inclusion of usually lengthy, but quite distinct, excurses on Scripture. For example, something in Megillah elicited the inclusion in the latter part of chapter I of a lengthy commentary on parts of the "scroll" (megillah) of Esther, as well as other related scriptural texts. Notably, when one eliminates the number of scriptural comments attributed to Rav, Johanan, and Rava that are found in this block of text (10b–17a), the number of scriptural comments in the tractate (attributed to the sages considered, out of a preliminary total of sixty-one) is only sixteen—far more typical of the Bavli in general. These blocks are in fact relatively unusual in the Bavli, and they are by no means distributed throughout. Rather, they are to be found, for the most part, in precisely the tractates that we have defined as exceptional.

What then about these tractates precipitated the inclusion of these larger blocks devoted to scriptural exegesis? It seems most likely, when we examine the Mishnah paragraphs to which these texts are connected, that there is something in the character of the Mishnah that determined, for the most part, where these blocks were to be included. This may be demonstrated in a number of ways, including reference to the very numbers that Neusner gives.

Distinguishing his "Scripture units of discourse" by their relationship to the "larger redactional purpose" of the gemara, Neusner lists those units of discourse that illustrate "a point of law or theology in the antecedent analytical composition" and those that are "autonomous of the point of law or theology in the antecedent analytical context" (pp. 102–4). In Sotah only 6 percent of the total units of discourse are fully autonomous Scripture units, in Sukkah only 1.2 percent, and in Sanhedrin (more significantly) 17.6 percent. In other words, in only a minority of cases does the Scripture unit of discourse serve needs that are totally independent of the Mishnah's agenda. In all other cases, even if it does not relate to the Mishnah directly, its inclusion is nevertheless generated by a "point of law or theology" that is itself directly related to the Mishnah. And even if we grant that in Sanhedrin Scripture is often addressed as a wholly independent focus of commentary, the 17.6 percent of its units that are fully autonomous Scripture units will still not allow us to claim that the Bavli is a Scripture commentary in the same measure that it is a Mishnah commentary.

A further demonstration of the same conclusion will result from considering directly the nature of the Mishnah at hand. Following, I have singled out those mishnaic portions which, by Neusner's accounting, have attracted the most Scripture units. Attention to their content is, with a few exceptions, telling.

Sotah

1:1–2. Beginning of the discussion of the "jealousy" ceremony for the suspected wife.
1:8–9. An application of the "measure for measure" principle of justice to several biblical figures. Proof-texts are quoted.
7:1–6. Things to be recited in any tongue or in the holy tongue. Mishnah quotes proof-texts.
8:1. Same as above.
9:5–6. Ceremony for the "breaking of the neck of the heifer." Again, quotation from Scripture.
9:11–13. An accounting of the diminution of God's presence in this world, and of the world's quality, over the course of time. Explicit statement of rabbinic theology.

Sukkah

4:9–10. The "water-pouring" celebration.

Sanhedrin

1:1–6. The number of judges required for different cases. Proof-texts are quoted.
4:5. Warning to witnesses in capital cases. Discussion of meaning of creation of Adam. Quotation of scriptural texts.
6:2. Midrash in the Mishnah. Biblical figures and proof-texts.
6:4–6:6. Execution. God regrets the loss of life of the wicked and righteous. Text quoted.
7:5–6. Blasphemer; worshipper of idols. 8:2. The "rebellious son"; proof-text.
11(10):1–3. Those with portions in the world-to-come and those excluded from the world-to-come. Proof-texts.

In most of these cases, there is something about the Mishnah itself that is sufficiently unusual or provocative to have generated the inclusion of the scriptural block. To begin with, many of these quote two or more verses of Scripture in close proximity, a phenomenon that is rare in the Mishnah. Some tractates are entirely devoid of this phenomenon, such as Eruvin or Ketubot, and most others do so on only one or two occasions. Sotah and Sanhedrin, which include texts that are dense with quotations from Scripture, stand apart in this regard, and it is reasonable to propose that this factor alone might engender the scriptural echo in the Bavli. But the presence of scriptural quotations is only one element of a larger phenomenon, for these quotations tend to cluster around topics of particular interest in the rabbinic corpus. The matter of divine justice and its relation to biblical figures (and, by extension, to others) is the central theme at the beginning of Sotah. Rabbinic "historiography" is the theme at its end (where the conclusions, speaking of God's gradual withdrawal from contact with humanity, are in tension with the beginning of the tractate). Sanhedrin's discussion of the death penalty and of the value of human life, in connection with the model of Adam, is unusual in form and content for the Mishnah, and again is of unique interest in defining rabbinic ideology. The "rebellious son" is a difficult institution in the rabbinic world, and the Mishnah relating to it is unusually dense in midrash halacha. Finally, the discussion of the world-to-come is not only unusual in form, but it also, of course, holds a crucial place in the rabbinic canon.

In order to test the part played by the Mishnah and its precise characteristics in attracting Scripture units, it is instructive to consider the whole of Mishnah Sanhedrin and the characteristics of its individual parts, and to compare this description with the presence or absence of Scripture units in the gemara. In all of Mishnah Sanhedrin, the only texts that quote two or more verses of Scripture in close proximity are as follows: 1 :1–6 (specifically 4 and 6), 2:4,[13] 4:5, 6:2, 8:2, 8:4, and all of chapter 10 (11). It is in connection with these Mishnah texts, and these alone, that the clusters of Scripture units of discourse that Neusner describes are to be found. That is not to say that they are all accompanied by such a cluster (2:4 and 8:4 are not). But that is not essential to the argument. What is crucial is that no text outside of these is accompanied by one. And even if elsewhere an occasional Scripture cluster is to be found in proximity to a Mishnah that does not share these features, deeper analysis would still probably yield, in many cases, less obvious but crucial connections to the Mishnah. Be that as it may, it is clear that the nature of the Mishnah may not be dismissed. At the very least, the nature of the Mishnah is highly influential in determining whether a cluster of Scripture units will accompany it in the gemara.

On the basis of what we have seen, we have good reason to doubt whether Sotah and Sanhedrin, as opposed to Sukkah, can be considered representative of the Bavli as a whole. It appears likely, rather, that Sukkah is more typical, and that Sotah and Sanhedrin, in their inclusion of extended blocks of commentary on Scripture, are less so. This being the case, it is unnecessary to revise totally what I referred to earlier as the "traditional wisdom," that is, that the Bavli is primarily a commentary on and supplement to the Mishnah. What is necesssary, given the material that Neusner has drawn to our attention, is to add a footnote—to keep in mind that, despite the Bavli's general organizing principle, there are nevertheless relatively unusual but still significant blocks of text that follow the direction of Scripture and not of Mishnah. Scripture is only secondary as an independent concern of the Bavli, but it is one that should not be ignored.

This means, to begin with, that the Bavli, like the Yerushalmi, defines its task to be the broad explication of Mishnah. Its purpose and direction are largely dictated by that text, and, with some exceptions, the Mishnah's displacement of Scripture as the focus of extended inquiry is sustained in its pages. This is, however, no less profound a move than would have been the case if Mishnah and Scripture served side by side in the Bavli; which is more radical after all—implied equation or explicit displacement?

On the other hand, these conclusions also suggest that the horizons of inquiry of the Bavli's authors were wider than those of their Palestinian counterparts. They were willing, from time to time, to diverge from the directions outlined in the Mishnah, and this independence is reflective of the spirit of the document as a whole. For even when the Mishnah is the spine of the Bavli's deliberation, the precise program that it pursues is wholly its own. The virtuosity with which this program is addressed, and the painstaking, convincing manner in which it is presented, may very well be at the root of the Bavli's final triumph.

My gratitude is due to Baruch Bokser and Leonard Gordon for their kind suggestions in the revision of this paper.

Notes

1. Chicago and London: 1986.
2. See Neusner, pp. 223 and 233.
3. See *Torah: From Scroll to Symbol in Formative Judaism* (Philadelphia, 1985), pp. 144 f. The equation is also made in the Yerushalmi, as Neusner shows, but the explicit phrase "oral Torah" does not appear there; see pp. 75–77.
4. See Neusner, *Judaism*, pp. 96–100.
5. For the primary results of this research, see "Stylistic Characteristics of Amoraic Literature" (Ph.D. diss. Jewish Theological Seminary, 1984), hereafter cited as SCAL.
6. The "generations" are conventions, and there is some difference in arrangement among scholars. The sages to whom we are referring flourished in the mid-third to the mid-forth centuries.
7. The statistics for this sage have been misplaced, hence his absence from the following tables. His contribution was not as large as that of many others, however, and the sample is large enough that this will not affect the outcome.
8. These traditions were the "apodictic" traditions attributed to these sages, and not statements found in argumentational exchanges. Argumentational contributions are extremely rare in the earliest generations, and are considerably fewer in number than apodictic traditions even in the later generations that I include. Furthermore, comments on Scripture are rare in the argumentation. For this reason, our choice of data can be considered reliable. See SCAL, chaps. ii–iv.
9. Nos. xxxiii, xlviii, lvii lviii, lxxiv.
10. Nos. xl, li, lxiii, lxviii—the language of composition of these units makes it likely that they are simply baraitot that are not identified as such.
11. Professor D. Halivni, in personal consultation, has confirmed this conclusion on the basis of his own studies with respect to the rest of the Bavli. The anonymous gemara rarely generates comment on Scripture independently.
12. I do not assume that traditions attributed to a particular sage were necessarily composed by that sage. That is in no way necessary for the data herein examined to be deemed reliable for present purposes. Even if the attributions are an absolute fiction (which I do not assume), they may still be used as a test for the distribution of Scripture comments through different Bavli tractates, for the reasons that I described above. The language I use below in reference to these attributions is more literal merely for purposes of brevity.
13. Depending upon the reading of the Mishnah, 3:7 may or may not quote two. In any case, the two that might be quoted are nearly identical, rendering them, for present purposes, a single text.

INTRODUCTION TO CHAPTER THIRTEEN

This article is my first formal defense of the thesis and interpretations set forth in *The Mind of the Talmud*. In that book, I offered a "strong" interpretation of the meanings of the Talmudic form. By "strong," I mean an interpretation that made clear claims concerning the ideologies of the Talmud's authors, claims that were in significant respects contrary to the "common wisdom." I was therefore very pleased that the book generated considerable response and discussion, both assenting and dissenting. As the dissenting arguments began to appear, it seemed fitting for me to respond in defense of my interpretations. This article is one such defense. (Other defenses, both explicit and implied, may be found in "The Ideal Reader as a Key to Interpreting the Bavli," *Prooftexts* 13 (1993): 1–17; and *Reading the Rabbis*, chapters 1–6).

Briefly, in this piece I defend my assertion that the Bavli recognizes that Divine truth (=an exact and accurate interpretation of God's will) is humanly unavailable (truth is indeterminable but not indeterminate). If this is correct, then definitive decisions, both affirmative and negative, should be relatively rare in the Bavli. Yet, by appearances at least, definitive refutations are to be found in the Bavli with some frequency. If my interpretation of the Bavli's form is correct, how can this be? The answer, I show, is that such refutations are not nearly so common as might appear and that, in fact, the common failure of apparently definitive refutations serves as further support of my thesis.

This article first appeared in a special issue of the journal *Shofar* (for which I served as guest editor) dedicated to the memory of Baruch Bokser. The journal is a minor one, and it is my expectation, therefore, that this will be the first opportunity for many readers to consider the present arguments.

Chapter Thirteen

Rhetoric of Failed Refutation in the Bavli[1]

In my recent book, *The Mind of the Talmud*, I make certain claims concerning the underlying ideologies of the Talmud's authors based upon analyses of the Bavli's distinctive forms of expression. Trying to understand the Bavli's characteristic preference for argumentation and process over settled conclusions, I argue that this quality of the Talmud's argumentational form bespeaks a recognition on the part of its authors, that Divine truth is ultimately indeterminable.[2] The form itself suggests that Divine truth may be approached but never determined with confidence, and for this reason the Talmud is more concerned with theoretical argumentation than with halakhic (practical) conclusions.[3] Underlying this position, I suggest, is the recognition that God's will, recorded in Torah, is accessible only through profoundly human and therefore fallible acts of interpretation.[4] Affirming this flaw, the Bavli's authors place the act of interpretation, in the application of human reason, at the very center of their enterprise.[5]

This ideological position is implicit, I suggest, in many of the Bavli's common forms. For example, when the Bavli begins a deliberation with two or more opinions or interpretations—as it does so often—it will typically seek to maintain the viability of all expressed opinions, even when those opinions are contradictory. What, other than the ideology described briefly above, could lie at the foundation of such an approach? Certainly, if the Bavli's primary concern were the actual determination of halakha or divine truth, such a preference would be indefensible. Similarly, the Bavli pursues alternatives—alternative explanations, alternative answers, alternative interpretations—with a zeal that is difficult to comprehend.[6] Again, how could alternatives be so important if divine truth resided in a single known position? The Bavli's extensive attention to opinions that are known to be rejected in practice, such as those of the school of Shammai, is another well-known illustration of this ideology. In fact, the Bavli's argumentational form itself—so I argue—with its incessant questioning and search for justifications, shows the recognition of its authors that the truth may not finally be determined. The authoritative tradition does not, the Bavli shows, speak with a single, unambiguous voice.

But there are certain features in the argumentation of the Bavli that might appear to contradict the thesis that I have laid out. The most obvious of these are the Bavli's common willingness to support given positions, the record of conclusive halakhic decisions in some talmudic discussions, and the presence, at the Bavli's final compositional layer, of definitive refutations. I will comment on the first two of these phenomena briefly in the paragraphs below. The third phenomenon—definitive refutations in the Bavli—is the subject of the extended exposition that follows.

As stated, the first apparently problematic evidence is the simple fact that, though the Bavli often avoids definitive conclusions and persists in maintaining alternatives, it also often finally supports particular conclusions. In such instances, is the Bavli not supporting what it perceives to be divine truth? In light of multiple other features in the Bavli, I contend that this would be a mistaken reading of this phenomenon.

Needless to say, the fact that one supports a particular position does not necessarily mean that one believes that position to correspond with "the truth," divine or otherwise. This may perhaps best be seen by reference to collegiate or forensic debate. Spokespersons for either side of such debates clearly support their positions with enthusiasm, even with zeal. But they recognize that such preference is a matter of judgment and that the opposing position may also, with some reasonableness, be supported. If this were not so, there would be no justification for engaging in such debate in the first place. The point in debate is not the determination of a single undebatable truth—this would require formal demonstration, not reasoned, partisan argument. The form of debate argumentation itself shows the recognition by its participants that judgment—not undeniable truth—is at the center of such discourse.

By the same token, the Bavli, in the way it goes about expressing its support of its preferred positions—not through philosophical, let alone mathematical, demonstrations and not through mere authoritative proclamations but, instead, by means of deliberation and multivocal persuasion—shows its alliance with this same basic recognition. In fact, the sorts of questions that are asked and the kinds of alternatives that are considered, as the Bavli goes about building its support of one opinion or another, often serve as much to weaken the reader's confidence in the Talmud's preferred conclusion as they do to strengthen it.[7] The very recourse to argumentation and rhetoric shows the authors' recognition that the position finally supported may not be God's absolute truth.

A second possible problem is the fact that the Talmud does record definitive halakhic decisions. In truth, however, this is not a serious difficulty. To begin with, there are, in relation to the total number of halakhic questions that arise in the Talmud, relatively few such explicit definitive decisions.[8] Second, it is widely recognized that halakhic declarations in the Talmud are often post-Talmudic additions to the original Talmud text, and this has been shown to be so even when such declarations are apparently recorded in the names of amoraim.[9] Furthermore, I have argued in my book, and Halivni supports the same position in his recent book, *Peshat and Derash*, that the Talmud evinces a gap between halakha and Divine truth.[10] If this is so, of course, then the determination of halakha in the Bavli would represent no problem for the thesis that I have presented. Finally, it will be readily understood that, even (perhaps especially) in the absence of divine truth, a community will have to make decisions concerning its practices. It is possible, therefore, to understand halakhic decisions as signposts for practice in a world where divine truth is ultimately indeterminable. According to this approach, it is by no means necessary to construe halakha as the divine truth itself.

A third problem, not easily dismissed, is the Talmud's willingness to offer definitive refutations of given opinions, most explicitly using the term "*tiuvta d'R. Ploni tiuvta*," usually translated, "the refutation of R. Ploni is a [definitive] refutation." The problem is that if no particular position can be shown to be definitively correct, then it should also be relatively more difficult to declare a given opinion definitively incorrect. Wrong must be in relation to what is right—what is true and correct—and if the latter is finally indeterminable the former, too, should be difficult (though obviously not impossible) to determine. How, then, can it be so that the Talmud does (seemingly) often record such definitive refutations?

In order to respond to this problem, let me first say more about its nature and scope. To begin with, when I say that it should be difficult to declare a position definitively incorrect, I do not mean to say that it should be impossible. Theoretically, at least, in given instances we may have enough information to declare an opinion incorrect while still not possessing sufficient information to determine the actual truth. So small numbers of such refutations will not be a problem; only if the Talmud commonly records such refutations will it be reasonable to insist that the Talmud is far more confident about its access to Divine truth than I have claimed. The more crucial question, therefore, is the precise scope of this phenomenon. Consideration of the details is extremely telling.

Objections from more authoritative sources are suggested in the Talmud 1500 times or more.[11] On most of these occasions, the objection is countered with a response readily and immediately. In only 297 instances is language used that hints that the objection might finally be definitive ("*tiuvta d'R Ploni?*" and related expressions) and, again, in the majority of these instances, a response is immediately offered to make it clear that the intended refutation is, indeed, no refutation at all. In only 118 cases does the language of the Talmud suggest that the refutation is conclusive (*tiuvta d'R Ploni tiuvta*).[12]

Even if we go no further in our analysis of these cases, these few statistics already speak volumes regarding the Bavli's approach to what is definitively wrong and correspondingly to what is definitively right. If, of the thousands of times that the Talmud brings an objection from a more authoritative source (the most powerful objection that the Talmud might bring), at most 1 in 12.4 turn out to be definitive, we must conclude that, as a matter of principle, the Talmud prefers not to speak definitively, even in negation. Because of the frequency of such objections and the simultaneous infrequency of such conclusions, we must understand this as a crucial element of the Talmud's rhetoric; the Talmud's reticence is not specific but symbolic. It says, in effect, "do not be so quick to conclude that you have eliminated this opinion or that. Such confident dismissal is misguided."

But the story of the Talmud's hesitance to suggest definitive refutations does not stop here. As it happens, even many of what appear, at first blush, to be definitive refutations turn out to be either what might be called "failed refutations" or what might be called "compromised refutations." By "failed refutations" I mean cases where, in the very context where the definitive refutation is declared to stand ("*tiuvta d'R. Ploni tiuvta*"), the gemara suggests precisely the information one would need to counter the refutation. I do not include, in this category, cases where extreme ingenuity or the methods of modern critical scholarship might show how the refutation is unnecessary. I restrict myself to cases where the Talmud's typical reader—intelligent, questioning but pious[13]—could easily show, on the basis of immediately available information, why the refutation does not necessarily stand. By "compromised refutations," in contrast, I mean cases where the refutation is noticeably weakened by the information at hand, but where the refutation, nevertheless, formally stands in the end. Needless to say, it is occasionally difficult to distinguish these two categories and in a few cases an evaluation might have gone the other way.

Of the total of 118 cases in which the gemara explicitly supports such a refutation, I have found 44 to be failed refutations. Another 23 are compromised refutations, and only 51, in the end, stand without any compromise.[14] That is, fewer than half of even those cases in which the language suggests definitive refutations are, in the end, unambiguous and definitive. Let me describe more precisely how this is so.

Of the so-called failed refutations, 13 fail because the refuted opinion turns out to be only one of two recorded traditions of that opinion.[15] The alternative tradition is not similarly refuted in these cases, and, in several instances, what was a refutation for one version is a support for the other. At most, one might conclude on such occasions that one version of the tradition should be preferred above the other. Other cases of *tiuvta* refutations disappear because of alternative readings in the deliberative Talmud text—sometimes recorded in manuscripts or in the medieval commentators[16]—and sometimes what might, according to a particular interpretation, appear to be a refutation can just as easily be construed, according to a slightly different interpretation, to be a support.[17] On four occasions, after declaring that an opinion is refuted on the basis of one tannaitic source, the Talmud records another tannaitic text that will support the allegedly refuted opinion.[18] Other such refutations fall away for various other reasons and, finally, six are the well-known cases of *"tiuvta v-hilkheta"*—instances where, following the declaration of refutation, the gemara goes on immediately to say that, nonetheless, the halakha follows that same opinion.[19] The gemara defends this decision, on each of these occasions, by explaining why the refutation was not, in fact, necessary. The explanation shows either that an alternative authoritative source or an alternative interpretation or reasoning was actually available to support the very same, now not-refuted, opinion.

Concerning what I have called compromised refutations, there are various ways that they are compromised; it is impossible to categorize this phenomenon with the same precision as we may the failed refutations. Still, one source of such compromise deserves comment. I am speaking of those cases where the gemara declares that the refuted authority reached his now-refuted opinion because "the Mishnah misdirected him."[20] In each of these instances it will be clear to the reader that a simple reading of the Mishnah will, in fact, support the refuted opinion and so, though the refutation stands as far as the gemara's explicit language is concerned, the refutation has certainly been called into question in the reader's mind. Which is to be preferred, after all, the simple meaning of a Mishnah or its secondary interpretation?

Permit me now to demonstrate what I have been describing by quoting two cases of failed refutations. The first is a sugya at Temurah 25a–b. For present purposes, the essential elements of the text are these:

> a. R. Johanan said: If one set aside a pregnant [animal for a] sin-offering and it gave birth, if he wants he can atone with it [or] if he wants he can atone with its offspring.
> b. What is the reason?
> c. R. Johanan holds that if he left it over [declaring the mother to be hallowed but not the offspring in its womb] it is left over [and] a fetus is not [regarded as] the thigh of its mother.
> d. [In this case, therefore,] it is as though he has set aside two sin-offerings for security's sake. If he wants [then] he may atone with it [or] if he wants he may atone with the other...

> e. They object: "If one says to his bondwoman, 'you are a bondwoman but your offspring [in your womb] is free,' if she was [in fact] pregnant she has obtained [freedom] for it."
> f. This is fine if you say that if he left it over it is not left over [and that] a fetus is [regarded as] the thigh of its mother—for this reason she has obtained [freedom] for it, because it is as one who frees half one's slave, and whose [opinion does this follow]? It is R. Meir, as it is taught, "One who frees half of his slave, he goes out to freedom..."
> g. But if you say [as R. Johanan did, above at a.–c.], then why has she obtained [freedom] for it? Has it not been taught, "a slave may obtain a writ of manumission for his fellow from a master who is not his own but not from a master who is his own."
> h. Rather, learn from it (from e.) [that] if he left it over it is not left over, and the refutation of R. Johanan is a [definitive] refutation.
> i.[But] say that [the question of status regarding the case] "if he left it over, is it left over?" is a [matter of] tannaitic dispute...
> j. R. Johanan would say to you: [No, in this case] everyone agrees that if he left it over, it is left over, and here, this is the reason...
> k. Rather, you may certainly say that there is here a tannaitic dispute...
> l. R. Johanan would say to you... etc.

The collapse of the alleged definitive refutation is clear here at many steps. In fact, each of the tannaitic texts quoted following the purported refutation (i. and k.) may be claimed to support R. Johanan completely—at the very worst, there are several individual opinions that provide tannaitic support for his position and show that the refutation is not at all necessary.

In fact, this very sugya moves Tosafot to remark, at Zebahim 114a (s.v. "*v'kasavar*") that "this is the way of the gemara, when the opinion is not the preferred one, it says '*tiuvta*' even though it can find tannaitic opinions that dispute [such a conclusion]," and which, I would add, actually support the allegedly refuted view. In other words, in the opinion of this Tosafot, the gemara will remark "*tiuvta*," even definitively, as an expression of judgment even when the refutation is unnecessary. "*Tiuvta*" may not mark a definitive refutation at all, therefore, but only a statement of preference.

A second case, of which I quote but a bare minimum here, is the sugya ending with "*tiuvta v'hilkheta*" at Erubin 15b–16b. The steps necessary for demonstration are these:

> a. It is said: If that which is open [in a barrier that is intended to act as a Sabbath boundary] is [in measure] the same as that which stands
> b. R. Pappa said: it is permissible...
> c. Come and learn: These walls which are mostly doors and windows are permissible, on the condition that that which stands is greater than that which is open...
> d. [Suggesting that] if it is the same, it is forbidden
> e. [Thus] the refutation of R. Pappa is a [definitive] refutation
> f. And the law is according to R. Pappa.
> g. A [definitive] refutation and the law?!

h. Yes, because a careful reading of the Mishnah supports him, as we learn: "the open should not be greater than that which is built up"—but if it is the same [in measure] as that which is built up, it is permissible [thus supporting R. Pappa].

The text well points out, in the end, that, in spite of the fact that the baraita (c.) certainly contradicts the opinion of R. Pappa, an exacting reading of the Mishnah supports the same opinion. Clearly, whoever decides the halakha here believes that support from a Mishnah is more powerful than refutation from a baraita.

It is not only the details of this case that make it notable, but what its method represents. The cases of *"tiuvta v'hilkheta"* collectively suggest, as indicated earlier, that another tannaitic source may almost always be found, or that an alternative reasoning may virtually always be applied. The canonical spring from which the gemara draws its sources is so diverse and the canons of its reasoning so pliable that it is extremely difficult to imagine many cases where a given opinion may not, in the end, be salvaged. It may be necessary, on rare occasions, to declare a particular opinion definitely wrong, but such occasions are rare indeed.

Again, in concrete terms, of the 297 cases in which a refutation is proposed only 75 finally stand as definitive refutations. Only 51 are entirely uncompromised.[21] This is out of a total of perhaps thousands of cases in which objections of this sort—that is, those from more authoritative sources—are suggested. Needless to say, this number of truly definitive refutations is almost unimaginably small when considered in light of what might have been anticipated in a traditional system such as is presumably represented in the Bavli.[22]

What is the meaning of the phenomenon that I have here outlined? As stated earlier, the centrality of refutation to the Bavli's approach and the frequency of refutations of this sort to the Bavli's argumentation make this phenomenon an important element of the Bavli's overall rhetoric. What this rhetoric of failed refutation is saying, I contend, is that complete confidence either in or, here, against a particular opinion is ill-conceived. "If you think that you have proven an opinion wrong," the Bavli seems to be saying, "think again. Don't be so sure. Support for the same opinion may not be difficult to find."

Two final observations are in order. First, as might be expected, this phenomenon is subject to an entirely different sort of analysis by the source-critics. Halivni's comments on the text at Bezah 25a are typical of this approach:

> ...it appears that the sugya here is composed of two sources; in one source they objected from the baraita... to R. Hisda and left it with a refutation and in the second source they objected from this baraita to a second baraita [noting the contradiction

between the two]... and R. Naḥman resolved [the apparent contradiction]... According to R. Naḥman's resolution of the contradiction between the two baraitot, the objection from the baraita to R. Ḥisda would also be resolved. But the source where this objection was raised against R. Naḥman did not know R. Naḥman['s resolution] and for this reason said "*tiuvta*." But the one who combined the two sources either did not sense this [that the resolution now became available] or did not want to add to the language of the sources and left them as they were—and this is the basis of the difficulty in the sugya.[23]

In my opinion, even if one assumes the sort of textual history that might be posited by the source critic, this approach does not adequately explain the present phenomenon. If one imagines, as does Halivni here, that a final redactor inherited two complete and formulated deliberations, one must still ask why both were recorded side-by-side. It is inconceivable that any such redactor did not detect the contradiction in the two presumed sources—any intelligent student, let alone someone entrusted to redact the Talmud, would immediately notice this contradiction (or others like it in similar texts). We would still have to explain, therefore, why he preserved both sources side-by-side. As described, this sort of thing happens often enough to be noteworthy. We must assume, therefore, that the redactor's juxtaposition was either naive—unlikely, in my mind—or intended. If it was intended, this demands that we make sense of the final, combined text. Furthermore, if we assume that the final Bavli is a product not only of preservation but also of selection, this would be all the more necessary.[24] Why would a redactor have chosen to preserve two contradictory sources when he could have selected between them? Only if we imagine that the redactor was entirely subservient to his inherited tradition—exercising virtually no judgment at all—can we avoid the problem represented in these texts, and the evidence, as understood by recent scholarship, does not support such a picture.[25]

If, instead, these texts are best understood by positing an earlier source to which an author/redactor appended an alternative text that he formulated, we would still, of course, have to explain the final product. Why would someone so revere a text that he sees need to preserve it even though he disagrees with its conclusion, yet feel at liberty to record his alternative which renders the first conclusion moot? Clearly, mere subservience to an inherited tradition would in no way explain this phenomenon. So, again, we are back to explaining the final text as it stands before us. Needless to say, this is also true if the contradictory approaches are both formulated at some final stage of composition-redaction. Whichever way we reconstruct the textual history, we cannot escape the rhetorical-critical question.

A final problem with the source-critical solution is the fact that the purported sources from which these texts are alleged to be built are not distinguished from one another by essential textual criteria. That is, unlike other sources in the Bavli, which are set off from the deliberations in which they are embedded by different languages or formal conventions, or are identified by certain characteristic terms of introduction, the sources that are presumed to stand at the foundation of these texts bear no such distinctions. The move to identify different sources is motivated by the assumption that the Bavli cannot contradict or undermine itself in such short order; if, by definition, it cannot do so, then there must be two sources. Their existence is a matter of necessity, resting on the said assumption. But if one admits that the Bavli might have reasons for formulating texts that would, in fact, undermine certain conclusions—such as here where, we might posit, the Bavli wishes to communicate the rhetorical point we have identified—then there is no reason to assume different sources. The rhetorical-critical approach accounts for the final text and for the present phenomenon in its fullness. In light of the agreement of the message that emerges with the overall ideology of the Bavli, it seems to me that this approach is vastly preferable.

Second, it is essential to appreciate the impact this phenomenon has on our characterization of the traditionality of the Talmud.[26] Again, the types of objections that comprise the substance of what we have been discussing are those that are rendered from earlier sources of recognized higher authority. These include objections to amoraic (Talmudic) opinions from tannaitic traditions (the Mishnah or extra-Mishnaic sources of the same period) or, rarely, from scriptural texts. Of course, these are the most powerful objections that might be rendered because they depend upon superior sources, that is, upon "Torah." Yet even such objections rarely yield definitive refutations. It is almost always possible to interpret them in a different way or to find another source that might be interpreted to support, rather than to contradict, the opinion at hand.

Simply put, what this means is that, although the authoritative tradition always has a voice in the Talmudic deliberation, it rarely has a veto. Since it is never the source that declares its own meaning but only the later Talmudic reader who offers his interpretation, genuine, definitive authority rests, if anywhere, at the final stage of discussion (as it were, *hilkheta k'vatrai*). And the voice of this Talmudic master, receiving but not submitting to the earlier tradition, is vigorous in asserting its own prerogative. The source is almost always made to yield before the later opinion. Interpretation guarantees considerable, if not complete, freedom to shape the new tradition.

In the end, a phenomenon that might have been thought to pose a problem for my analysis of the Bavli's form turns out to be a resounding support. Not only when affirming, but also when refuting, the Talmud cautions against definitive conclusions. Not definitively knowing the Divine truth, the Bavli also hesitates to declare what is definitively false. Indeed, "indeterminable" is a term that may appropriately be applied both to truth and to falsehood in the Bavli.[27]

Notes

1. I am indebted to Richard Kalmin and Burton Visotzky for their critiques and advice in revising this paper.
2. Jacob Neusner has claimed that my characterization of the Talmudic form is incorrect (see *How the Talmud Shaped Rabbinic Discourse* [Atlanta: Scholars Press, 1991], pp. 147–153). I assume he cannot mean my speaking of the Talmud as "argumentational" (where "argumentational" means the presence of regular questioning, discussion, objections, search for reasons, etc.), for every page of the Talmud attests to its argumentational quality; this claim requires no demonstration. He must instead have a different conception of the nature of the Talmud's argumentation; the many texts and phenomena I identify he characterizes as "anecdotal" and therefore essentially irrelevant to the inquiry. Yet his confidence in his alternative is based, in the present context, upon the evidence of "Babylonian Talmud Tractate Zebahim Chapters One and Five" (p. 150); even assuming his understanding of that material is correct, is it reasonable to suppose that the evidence of two chapters speaks for the whole? I draw upon evidence distributed among many dozens of chapters! I shall have ample occasion to respond to Neusner's arguments in the future. At present, I merely offer the phenomenon analyzed herein as but one more support for the essential correctness of my characterization and conclusions.
3. *The Mind of the Talmud: An Intellectual History of the Bavli* (New York: Oxford University Press, 1990). For my arguments in favor of these propositions, see primarily chapter 5, but also chapter 6.
4. See pp. 120–127.
5. See, especially, pp. 146–156.
6. See ibid., pp. 95–96.
7. An excellent example of this phenomenon is the lengthy text at B.Q. 83b–84a which seeks a source from scripture for the Mishnah's requirement to make monetary compensation for personal damage done to another. The gemara's problem, of course, is that scripture speaks explicitly of payment in kind, that is, "eye for eye." Briefly, the Talmud records nine attempted derivations of the Mishnah's position, five of which turn out to be unsuccessful. Even those which do succeed, the gemara shows, are plagued by weaknesses. At the end, the possibility that scripture actually does require the payment of an eye for an eye is considered, and the way this possibility is rejected is obviously forced and implausible. The Talmud never hints that it will finally support anything but monetary compensation, but its overall consideration of the source of this position shows clearly the weakness of the foundation on which this opinion rests. For a fuller analysis of this text, see my discussion in *Reading the Rabbis: The Talmud as Literature* (New York: Oxford U. Press, 1996), ch. 3.
8. This claim is at present impressionistic. A simple counting in the concordance of the terms by which such decisions might be announced would be insufficient to support or deny this assertion; we are interested in cases where the Talmud conclusively supports halakhic decisions, not merely in those where such decisions are proposed but not finally accepted. I intend to make such a determination by reviewing all such cases individually.
9. See Yaakov Spiegel: "*Hosafot me'uharot (saboraiot) beTalmud Bavli*," Ph.D. diss., Tel-Aviv University, 1976, and "*Amar Rava hilkheta—piskei halakha me'uharim*," in *Diyunim besifrut h"zl bemiqrah uvetoledot yisrael*, ed. Y. D. Gilat, C. Levine, and Z. M. Rabinowitz, (Ramat-Gan, Israel, 1982), pp. 206–214.
10. For my discussion of this matter, see *The Mind*, pp. 139–146. Halivni discusses the same issue in *Peshat and Derash: Plain and Applied Meaning in Rabbinic Exegesis* (New York: Oxford University Press, 1991), pp. 101–125.

11. Counting, in the concordance, the appropriate forms of the root TUV (this being the verb that is commonly used to introduce such objections), I find 1462 such instances. The term *ta shema*, appearing over 1250 times, is often used interchangeably with TUV, and it is for this reason that I say "1500 or more."

12. Objections of this sort are distributed throughout the Talmud. The suggestion that an objection might be definitive—either followed by an answer or by the admission that it is definitive—is found in all tractates but three (Hagiga, Makkot, and Tamid). Seven others only suggest that an objection might be definitive when they conclude that that is in fact so. It is possible, therefore, that redactional characteristics of certain individual tractates may play a factor in this phenomenon, but it is sufficiently widespread and uniform to speak of "the Talmud's" approach to such objections.

13. See my "The Intended Reader as a Key to Interpreting the Bavli," *Prooftexts* 13, n. 2 (May 1993):125–140.

14. For examples of failed refutations, see Shab. 40a, Erub. 10a and 72b, Pes.26b and 101a–102a. Examples of compromised refutations may be found at Yoma 11a–b, Suk.4b, and Ket. 111b.

15. See Shab. 41a, 69b, Erub. 72b, Pes. 26b, 32b, Yoma 39b–41a, Suk. 55b, Meg. 2a, Sanh. 31a, Yeb.40a, Git. 28a, Qid.59a–b, Zeb. 34a.

16. Ber. 43b, Shab. 20b, Yoma 54a, 87b, Suk. 55b, Yeb. 72b.

17. Ber. 10b, Shab. 40a, 69b, Pes. 96b–97a, Meg. 2a, Git. 28a, Zeb. 34a, 84b–85a, Hul. 28a–b, 68b, Bekh. 28a.

18. Git. 53b, B.B. 132a–b, Zeb. 15a, Tem. 25a–b.

19. Ber. 23b, Erub. 10a, 15b–16b, Ket. 41b (=B.Q. 15b), Sanh. 27a. See also Bezah 25a with Halivni's comment and reference to the comment of Nachmanides' son (in *Meqorot umesorot*). It would appear that these cases of "hilkheta" are not post-Talmudic; they are each followed by brief discussion of why the refutation was inconclusive, always in the common voice of the anonymous Talmud.

20. Ket. 90a, 101b, Hul. 133b, and Bekh. 40b. See also Erub. 16b, Suk. 31a–b, and Yoma 48b–49a.

21. Ber. 23b, Shab. 29b, 40b–41a, 69b, Pes. 30b, Suk. 51a, 56b, R.H. 20a, Meg. 16a, Taan. 29b, M.Q. 20a, Yeb. 19a, 20b–21a, 110b, Ket. 13b, 48b, 57b, Ned. 51a, 79a, 90a–b, Naz 14b–15a, 19b, Sot. 36b, Git. 50a, Qid. 16b, 52a, B.Q. 128a–b, 129b, B.M. 13b–14a, 95b, B.B. 46a, 81a, 127a, San. 83a, 88b, Shev. 37b, A.Z. 58a, Hor. 3b, Zeb. 36b, 119b, Men. 9a, 29b, 84a, Hul. 5a, Bekh. 9a, 46b, Ker. 13a, Arakh. 36a, Tem. 7b, 32a, Nid.39b.

22. Neusner has argued that the Bavli is not a traditional system. In my opinion, the heuristic dichotomy that he constructs to suggest this conclusion is unnecessarily stark and is insensitive to much work on tradition in religious societies (see esp. Edward Shils, *Tradition* [Chicago: University of Chicago Press, 1981]). Because of the extremity of the definition of tradition that he insists upon, his conclusions are less valuable than they otherwise might be. When I speak here of a traditional system, I mean one that defines even its new directions employing the vocabulary of and often built upon the foundations of the traditions that it inherited. Still, it should be recognized that my conclusions have important consequences for characterizing the "traditionality" of the Bavli and, in obvious ways, support the conclusions suggested by Neusner. For other consequences, see my discussion below. For Neusner's approach, see *Tradition as Selectivity* [a very good definition of tradition indeed!]: *Scripture, Mishnah, Tosefta and Midrash in the Talmud of Babylonia, The Case of Tractate Arakhin* (Atlanta: Scholars Press, 1990).

23. *Meqorot umesorot, Yoma-Hagiga* (Jerusalem: Jewish Theological Seminary, 1975), p. 321.

24. In this judgment, I concur with Neusner's conclusions in *Tradition as Selectivity* and other related writings.
25. Cf. F. Gerald Downing, "Compositional Conventions and the Synoptic Problem," *JBL* 107, n. 1 (1988), pp. 69–85.
26. See above, n. 21.
27. Cf., on "indeterminacy of belief" in rabbinic Haggadah, Max Kadushin, *The Rabbinic Mind* (New York: Bloch Publishing, 1952; 3rd ed., 1972). pp. 131–147.

INTRODUCTION TO CHAPTER THIRTEEN

Unlike the other pieces in this volume, the following essay never appeared in a scholarly journal. Originally, the was an oral presentation, one of two classes that I offered at the annual convention of the Rabbinical Assembly in 1987. For purposes of inclusion in the *Proceedings of the Rabbinical Assembly* in that year, I transcribed my oral presentation from a recording and "cleaned it up" so that it could be read without too much difficulty (printed oral presentations, unedited, are virtually unintelligible). In that original printing, no other modifications were made.

    The present version has been more significantly modified. Sections have been rewritten for clarity. I have added or deleted materials to make my argument more coherent. Still, elements of its original quality remain, as the reader will notice, for example, that the opening refers to an "earlier analysis." Here, I was speaking of my earlier oral presentation, which I have not reproduced in the present volume. Where necessary, I have here added clarifications to explain such "oral residues," but I have not eliminated them entirely.

    This essay contains my earliest thinking concerning rhetorical criticism as it might be applied to the reading of Talmudic texts. My approach is not yet fully formed, but its future directions are already clear. The first of my oral presentations, exemplifying my emerging method, became the foundation of my article "Composition and Meaning in the Bavli," reproduced in the next chapter. In a more expanded form, the text elaborated in that article served as my focus in chapter 6 of *Reading the Rabbis*. But, for most readers, the reading offered here will be entirely new. It is a worthy illustration of a rhetorical reading of the Talmud.

Chapter Fourteen

New Meaning in Ancient Talmudic Texts
A Time Poem

Let me again introduce the intent of what I will be doing. As I stated in my earlier analysis, I am trying to read the Talmud text in a way that will be more familiar to Western readers—and less typical of common talmudic study. Typically, the Talmud is read (actually, *studied*) at the level of its details, for details are the substance of halakhah. But when read this way, the text is so atomized that we often lose the beauty of the forest for the individual trees. To change our way of reading, we must begin to change our way of thinking about the text. We must recall, above all, that the Talmud text was composed at some point to be viewed as a whole, and therefore it should be read precisely that way—as a whole. This approach, though conventionally deemed "unnatural" when applied to the Talmud, is precisely the approach that will make the Talmud more accessible to modern, Western individuals. They (actually, we) frequently don't attend to the individual details, and instead permit the text to make an impression on the basis of a much fuller reading. If we do the same with the Talmud, we will be accomplishing two things. First, we will make it more accessible to ourselves and our congregants (or students in general), because this is a manner of reading that is not quite so strange to them. Second, I claim that we will be recovering a layer of meaning from the text that unfortunately has been neglected in Talmud study for many years. If we do this, we will be doing a great deal.

Theoretically speaking, I am simply arguing that the lessons our colleagues in Biblical studies have learned in recent years must also be taken to heart by students of the Babylonian Talmud. Talmud scholarship is now at a point where Bible scholarship was two decades ago. At that time, the world of biblical scholarship had been greatly enlightened by the insights of form-criticism, a careful examination of the variety of forms embedded within the biblical text. There was, of course, a recognition that, whatever the meaning of these forms (and the different forms were often construed to suggest different sources), the text was put together at some time, and that its composition—whatever the sources of the final document—was meaningful. The authors of the text in its final form were composing a thesis on the basis of the sources, and scholars of Bible then, as well as students of Talmud now, frequently failed to ask what thesis the text was trying to present. It is my contention that this is the turn which Talmudic scholarship must now take, and that the benefit it will yield is just what I have described—it will make the text more accessible to those who are unaccustomed to learning it in the traditional way.

What I will do, then, is examine a significant section of a Talmudic text (part of the first three folio pages of tractate Pesaḥim), and read it in a manner that makes sense of the whole.

Before we begin to read the text, though, a few words of introduction are in order. To appreciate what the Talmud's authors are trying to do in this lengthy sugya, we must teach ourselves to disregard our prejudice regarding Jewish assumptions of time. This is necessary because, as we shall see, the text that we are examining asks us to consider a variety of definitions for cycles of time. The first Mishnah in Pesaḥim begins by defining the time when the process of searching for ḥametz on the day before Pesaḥ is to begin. It renders its decision in a manner that the rabbis of the Talmud, at least, consider to be provocative. To speak of the beginning of the evening of the fourteenth day of Nisan, the Mishnah uses the term "*or*," a good rabbinic Hebrew term meaning "evening," but one term that is not used widely and which, in other contexts, could also mean simply "light" (which the rabbis of the Gemara associate with "morning"). But the Gemara that accompanies this Mishnah, as well as the Mishnah itself perhaps, is not merely asking the simple question of when we begin checking for ḥametz. It is making a much larger comment on the meaning of time in rabbinic Judaism. There is, in this text, a recognition of the variety of ways we can view time, particularly the beginnings of cycles and, more particularly, the beginnings of days. And, of course, our view of when a day "begins" affects our view of the world in a very profound way.

In order to admit possibilities other than the one we are prejudiced to see, we must first recognize that the notion that the Jewish day begins in the evening prior to a specific day is not a definition that is obvious in the Torah or the rest of the Bible. Without exception, and usually very clearly (if one is willing to read as a non-apologist), the Biblical text thinks that the "Jewish" day begins in the morning. There are a variety of ways to demonstrate this, and I will make reference to two such demonstrations very briefly.

Let us begin with the creation story, which is the source most people would cite as proof that the Torah's day begins in the evening. The text is so well known that it is difficult to forget our prejudice when reading this story. But if we look at the interpretation of Rashbam, we will be introduced to a startling suggestion.

First, the text itself:

> In the beginning God created heaven and earth... And God said: let there be light, and there was light, and God saw that the light was good, and God divided between the light and the darkness, and God called the light day, and the darkness He called night. And there was an evening and there was a morning; one day (Genesis, chapter 1).

It is almost impossible for us to hear the words "and there was evening and there was morning; one day" without imagining a "cha-cha." We have stepped forward with the text, as it has described to us God's creative activity during the first day. We then assume we have taken a step backward, to the evening before, as the text, in summation, remarks "and there was evening and there was morning," the morning drawing us along with one more forward step. But this is not what this text means at all. As far as I know, Rashbam is the first major Jewish rabbinic commentator to make this point. His words are therefore noteworthy. He declares: "It is not written here 'and there was a night and there was a day,'" which is what the text would have said if it meant what we have understood it to say. "Evening" and "morning" are points of transition, not periods of time. Rashbam continues:

> but rather "and there was evening...," [meaning that] the evening of the first day came, and the light descended [and it passed into night], "and it was morning...," [meaning] the morning transition point of [= following the] night, for the morning light had broken: behold [at that very instant] one day of the six [of creation] was completed...[1]

According to Rashbam, what is the text trying to describe? The day comes first, with its details of God's creative activity. God, though, like any sane being, would not work at night. Thus, following the evening transition there is nothing relevant to the creation for the narrative to describe. Therefore, the Torah recounts the passage of the night simply by speaking of its beginning (the evening) and its end (the morning), and only then does the text begin describing the new creation activity of the next day. In the meantime, it has declared when the first day is finished—at the moment of the morning transition, just before the creative activity of the new day is to begin.

Rashbam goes on to make the point unambiguously:

> ...scripture did not come to say that the evening and the morning were one day... [rather, how does the day work?] The day broke, and the night was finished, behold [at that moment] one day was finished and the second day began.

The day begins in the morning. That is the system which the creation story assumes.

If one reviews the modern commentators on this text, one will find that it is Jews alone who interpret it as suggesting that evening precedes morning. All others, as far as I have been able to find, assume the same interpretation as Rashbam, and those who do mention the other alternative do so only to remark on the curiosity of the Jewish approach, which they all understand to be prejudiced by Jewish practice. Those who do not have such a prejudice—because they have no practice to defend—recognize, with Rashbam, the simple meaning of this text.

In deliberations on this matter, most modern Jewish commentators who insist that the Torah's day begins with the night make reference to Leviticus 23:26ff. as "definitive" proof. Speaking of the mitzvah of Yom Kippur, the Torah declares:

> And the Lord spoke to Moses, saying, "On the tenth day of this month is the Day of Atonement.... It is a great Sabbath to you, and you shall afflict yourselves (fasting) on the ninth day of the month in the evening, from the evening to the evening, you shall celebrate your Sabbath."

This clearly proves that *the fast* begins the evening before the tenth day. This very evening, however, is called "the ninth day of the month in the evening" and not "the evening of the tenth day," as it should have been if the counting of days actually did begin in the evening. This almost certainly reflects the assumption that the day begins in the morning, and that the night follows the day. This is why the evening when the fast begins is connected with the ninth day in the text, and not with the tenth.

Whether or not we are persuaded that the Torah's notion of counting time is different from our present notion of Jewish time, we must at least admit that neither of these systems is any more rational than the other. Our own modern American system, based ultimately upon the Roman system, begins the counting of the day in the middle of the night, and there are even systems that begin counting a new day in the middle of the day. Yet, though any system might be neither more nor less rational, the way time is perceived certainly has important psychological consequences. We will allude to the meaning of these differences briefly later.

Let us proceed now to the Gemara text. By the time of the rabbis, the authors of this text, it was of course already well established that the Jewish day began the preceding evening. It will be interesting to discover, therefore, that the very rabbis who composed this text had some interest (which we will consider below) in testing the limits of that definition.

The Gemara begins by ostensibly asking what the Mishnah means when it states "*or* of the fourteenth [of Nisan] we search for the ḥametz by the light of the candle." What is the meaning of the Hebrew word *or*? Evening or morning? I say "ostensibly" because there is in fact no question about what the Mishnah means. The Mishnah below in the same chapter (quoted also in this text of the Gemara) contrasts *or* to "shaharit." In that context, the only thing *or* could mean is evening. Further, if we look in the middle of the Gemara (on 3a), we see that the authors of the Gemara are in possession of a baraita which is directly parallel to this Mishnah, except that it replaces the word *or* with the Hebrew word for night. There too, there is no room for ambiguity concerning what our Mishnah also must mean. Thus, when the Gemara, written hundreds of years after the baraita was composed, asks the meaning of *or*, it is evident that it already knows the answer to its own question. We have to understand, then, that everything between the beginning of the Gemara and the point at which we arrive with this baraita is "playful," in the sense that the generative question is not a serious question.

This prior recognition is evident in the Gemara's framing of the question as well. When introducing the two possibilities (R. Huna says "morning" and R. Judah says "night") the Gemara remarks, "You might think that the one who says 'morning' means morning literally." This, of course, is the Gemara's way (by saying "you might think") of revealing that this will not be the final conclusion. The dispute is not a genuine dispute, therefore, and the exercise that we will now undertake, at the Gemara's direction, has, indeed, a second purpose. What this purpose is we shall see as we proceed.

If we review the variety of "objections" (actually proofs of one view or another) that are now adduced, with attention to the broad structure of these objections, we will find that the composition of this progression seeks to make a point. To understand how this is done, we will have to consider the relation of each of the objections to the previous ones, what each seeks to prove, and, in particular, the source of each objection.

The first "objection," is taken from a Biblical text (Genesis 44:3). The proof is straightforward. The words *or* and "morning" are used in close combination; therefore, the word *or* must mean "day (morning)." The response in this case, as in all of the following cases (until the objections from Rabbinic sources), is that this proof is not definitive. This is typical of the Gemara (preserving the ongoing viability of the dispute), but the responses do not concern us as much as the objections themselves. What is essential is that the proof comes from the Torah, that it is extremely simple, and that it proves that *or* means day.

The second objection is also from the Bible (11 Samuel 23:4). It, too, is based upon the presence of *or* and "morning" in combination. Here, again, *or* must mean day. A problem with this derivation is suggested, and we are drawn along to still another objection. Again a Biblical text (Genesis 1:5) is quoted to prove that *or* must mean day. The proof again is quite simple, in this case the simplest of all ("and God called the *or* day..."). As we would expect, there is a response to this derivation as well, and so further attempted proofs will follow.

The next several "objections" (proofs) are also from Biblical texts, but the derivation that each suggests is far less simple. Unlike the previous three instances, in which the proof is based upon the combination of the word *or* with another (either "morning" or "day"), requiring nothing but what the immediate context provides, the next several instances require either other parts of the verse to make their point, or some logical deduction on the part of the reader. The fact that they are less straightforward is what causes them to be ordered in the text following the earliest three, simple proofs. Despite this dissimilarity, however, what they bear in common with the first few is more significant. They are all based upon Biblical verses, and, with only one exception, they initially attempt to prove that *or* must mean day. If this were the case, of course, the Mishnah would require that checking for hametz begin in the morning. As we have seen, however, this is not a serious position. The point, based upon *seven*[2] Biblical verses, must be something else again, something that begins to become clear only when we listen to the effect of the statement repeated so often in this section of the Gemara: "therefore *or* must be day...." The full impact will be revealed only when we compare these proofs to those that follow, those that are taken from rabbinic rather than Biblical sources.

The next proof is precisely the Mishnah below in this same chapter (1:3) which leaves no doubt concerning the meaning of the word *or* in the first Mishnah. The Mishnah, quoted here, says: "R. Judah says that we check *or* of the fourteenth and in the morning of the fourteenth and at the hour of elimination [of the hametz]." By virtue of the contrast between *or* and "morning," it is clear that *or* must mean evening, as the Gemara recognizes, and it declares this to be a definitive proof.

This is obviously a point of transition in the Gemara. First of all, this is the first proof that is not a Biblical verse, but a rabbinic source. Moreover, once we have come to rabbinic proofs it is perfectly clear that the word *or* means evening. It seems to me—though this is not explicitly stated—that this transition represents, at the very least, the Gemara's recognition of the difference between the Biblical term *or* and one of the rabbinic meanings of *or*. But if they recognize this difference, why do they quote the Biblical verses, which clearly are "irrelevant" to the stated question, in the first place?

To answer this, let us review the cumulative effect of the Biblical proofs. With but one exception, the Biblical proofs want to claim that *or* means day. The moment we arrive at the first rabbinic proof, we see how different the Biblical usage (assumption) is from the rabbinic. What if we were to separate Biblical from rabbinic usage, and ask, at this point, when our days should begin according to the Bible? We would have to respond, almost by reflex, "in the day (morning)!" When, in our consciousness, do we consider beginnings to occur? The answer, Biblically, would have to be "in the morning."

Once the Gemara has declared a proof to be convincing (as it has with the first rabbinic proof), one would think that there is no reason to go further. But the Gemara does, and this persistence is important. It is not simply because there happen to be more proofs available—once you have one good proof, why do you need another? Rather, by accumulating rabbinic proofs, the Gemara obviously wants to make a point—to enhance its total impact. What that point might be, we shall consider as we proceed.

The second of the rabbinic proofs, another baraita taken from the context of Pesaḥ, also wants to prove that *or* means evening. Unlike the first, however, it turns out to be inconclusive. Why bother with it, then? Again, the message is not necessarily in the answers these proofs generate, but in the initial claim they allow us to make, that is: "therefore, *or* is evening."

The third (rabbinic) proof is like the first. It proves that *or* means evening, and it is taken to be definitive. Its subject is the holiday ritual (in this case, the fixing of the calendar), and it is simple and brief.

The next proof supplies a kind of transition. It is based upon a rabbinic source, but it is a misfit. It does not use the word *or*, but a different form of the word which clearly has a different connotation, as the Gemara admits. Because it is not fully appropriate, it is reasonable to ask why it is adduced here. The answer, I think, is its content, which is the sacrificial ritual. This is important because, in the proofs that follow, which also speak of the sacrificial ritual, we will see that a different notion of the cycles of time is clearly at work, even in rabbinic sources. This is true because, unlike the holidays which, with little effect, can be separated (with respect to their beginnings) from the details of scripture, the sacrifices are so tied to scripture as to make such a separation impossible. For this reason, Biblical time remains intact in the realm of the sacrifices, even when it is the Rabbinic sources which discuss them. The Gemara now proceeds to enunciate this very point.

The next proof, from the Mishnah (Edduyot 4:10 and Keritot 1:6), is very complicated, relating to a dispute between *beit Hillel* and *beit Shamai*. The dispute concerns a woman who has suffered an early miscarriage on the eightieth night after she had given birth (assuming that she had given birth to a girl). The night, in the context of purity laws, belongs to the next day. Thus, the miscarriage would render its impurity in connection with that day. In the context of sacrifices, however, the eighty-first day does not begin until the next morning. Will the night of the miscarriage be numbered with the previous eighty day impurity-following-childbirth cycle, or will it be numbered with a new cycle? The proof teaches conclusively that *or* (used in the Mishnah quoted) means evening. But, just as crucially, it teaches us that even according to the Rabbinic mind, the "purity day" begins in the evening, and the "sacrifice day" begins in the morning. This distinction, the second part of which is confirmed immediately below, will be the key to understanding this Gemara as a whole.

Allow me to reiterate. We have been introduced to two distinct ways of counting time, one way relating to purity and the other relating to sacrifices. In relation to purity, the count begins in the evening. In relation to sacrifices, the count begins in the morning. (Both of these are defined by the Torah. For purity, see, e.g., Leviticus 15:6ff.). This, given what we already know, is very powerful, for it leads to the question: How do we make use of these respective cycles? Concerning the holiday (and broader Rabbinic ritual), the count begins in the evening. As we have seen, this is also true for the purity cycle. Should there be any question concerning this halakhah, the Gemara goes on to demonstrate it definitively.

The next proof (also, incidentally, proving that *or* means evening) declares that, in the case of sacrifices, "the night follows the day." The following proof, which concerns Yom Kippur (and therefore the holiday ritual in general), declares that the observance cycle begins in the evening. Finally, the last proof. The beraita, which parallels our Mishnah but understands *or* as "night," leads to the conclusion of this argument (as though it were an argument in the first place). Still, the impact of the intervening process is deeply felt, and its lesson appears to be strong.

In sacrificial observance, the night follows the day. Since the world of sacrifice is a Biblical world, its definitions line up with those of the Bible. The world of Rabbinic ritual, on the other hand, is a world of purity. We know from elsewhere, of course, how central purity was to early Rabbinic observance. By declaring that the day begins when a person's purity begins, these sources declare something about a more ideal world, a world in which purity reigns. Furthermore, though the shift from counting from the morning to counting from the evening may have occurred before the Rabbinic period[3], the Rabbis still had an option in the presence of different models. Their decision to side with a model which was not the one offered most generally by the Biblical text must be taken to be significant.

But the point is not that resolution has been achieved, together with the clarification of simple meaning. What we have witnessed is the claim that there is no single cycle of time, but a variety of cycles. Echoes of this same point continue to be heard below, even after this discussion is apparently over. We see below, for example, that the Gemara continues testing the beginning of the period during which hametz should be searched for. At 4a, the Gemara asks:

> ...since we now hold that all agree that *or* is evening, still, being that hametz is only prohibited beginning at the sixth hour of the day, why not check at the sixth hour? And should you say that scrupulous people hurry to perform mitzvot early...

Abraham arose in the morning [and not the evening before, as is being required here]!

Again, the morning transition is begin tested as a viable option, and though an explanation for the evening is found, the presence of such attempts does not allow this option (the morning), at least for the Pesaḥ ritual, to be forgotten.

Other such sources continue to make the point:

> Abbaye said (4a): therefore a rabbinic student should not begin his regular study on the evening of the thirteenth which is the dawn of the fourteenth, lest he...be led to ignore the mitzvah [of checking].

By the time of Abbaye, who lived in the mid-fourth century, the fact that the night preceded the day was certainly well established. Why does he attach the night to the previous day here? Again, it is our assumptions of time which are confounded. And, finally, at the bottom of 4b:

> you might think [that when the Torah says "you should not find leavening in your houses for seven days"] *it means days and not nights....*

Days, in their connection to Pesaḥ, will not disappear. What is it about Pesaḥ that causes the Gemara to want to do this?

Let me repeat this point. The lesson is not only that Rabbinic ritual is aligned with purity, as we noted above. There is also something about Pesaḥ itself that causes the authors of this Gemara to upset our assumptions about Jewish time cycles in precisely this context. What might that "something" be?

The answer which suggests itself to me is one that the Torah itself, I believe, makes about Pesaḥ. If we trace the beginning of the Exodus cycle as it is described in Exodus Chapter 12, we find that the time of redemption is not a moment, but a series of moments—a process. The redemptive process begins (according to Rabbinic tradition) on the first day of the month (Exodus 12:2), and its first action is directed to the tenth day of the month (verse 3). The actual redemptive event begins with the slaughter of the lamb on the fourteenth (verse 6), and that is followed by the eating of the lamb in the evening (verse 8). The last plague occurred at midnight (verse 29) and the exodus itself began in the morning (verse 41). Pesaḥ is the symbol of redemption. In redemption, time is not a moment, but a progression. It may be for this reason, therefore, that the Gemara wants to confound our relation to time, and to lead us to reconnect to a variety of cycles of time. Time, in the Passover, should not be focused on a moment: it should be spread over a continuum.

Of course, this is merely a proposal for the meaning of the Gemara, and it may, in the end, be one of many. Be that as it may, if this is not the point of the Gemara, it is certainly its effect. Having created a "time poem," the authors have reawakened our awareness to meanings that we may long ago have forgotten.

NOTES

1. This comment will not be found in Mikraot Gedolot. Rashbam's comments on the beginning of Genesis were censored by the printer because of this very comment. The whole commentary has been printed elsewhere from manuscripts.

2. The fact that there are seven such proofs from biblical verses also significant, particularly when we see the effect of the first proof from a Rabbinic source. See below.

3. There is a scholarship on this matter that I cannot review here. Suffice it to say that some claim the shift occurred in the Babylonian exile, while others point to verses in the New Testament which apparently suggest that beginning in the morning was still in practice in the first century.

INTRODUCTION TO CHAPTER FIFTEEN

In this article, my method for reading the Bavli (as other rabbinic texts) reaches nearly full maturity. My claim, in short, is that the method most appropriate for analysis of the Bavli is a sort of rhetorical criticism. The principles of this criticism, as it pertains to the document at hand, are these: the Bavli needs to be read at the level of its final composition, accounting for its sources but ever aware of their formulation into relationship. To appreciate the rhetoric of the text, we must focus on the Talmud's rhetorical unit, the sugya. Furthermore, because the text communicates through the manipulation of details, we must give acute attention to those same details. Finally, the Talmud is a communication of process, not conclusion. It's concern is primarily for the path to the destination, not for the destination itself (indeed, in the Bavli, there often is no definitive "destination"=conclusion). Hence, we must be aware of, and interpret, the steps along the way—the turns and reversals and contradictions, etc. Only thus will the meaning of the Bavli truly be understood.

In the present piece, only one crucial component of my preferred method remained unrealized. What I did not yet appreciate is that, if the text is viewed as a rhetorical expression—communicating with an intended reader or learner—then it is essential to account for the responses of that reader before the communication can be properly interpreted. This last step I take in my article, "The Ideal Reader as a Key to Interpreting the Bavli," appearing in *Prooftexts* 13 (1993):1–17. That later article does not appear in the present volume because it is already expanded and re-presented in the first chapter of my book, *Reading the Rabbis*. The reader is directed to that book for the "final chapter" of the methodological story told here.

In the present article, I read and interpret two talmudic sugyot. The first reading is expanded in chapter 6 of *Reading the Rabbis*. The second reading, examining the sugya on teshuva in Yoma 85b–86b, has never before appeared in a book.

Chapter Fifteen

Composition and Meaning in the Bavli

Literary form analysis of the Babylonian Talmud (the Bavli) has resulted in considerable progress in our understanding of its composition.[1] One important result of this approach has been the recognition that the anonymous text of the talmudic sugya is the product of post-amoraic author-redactors.[2] These conclusions have forced a revision in the manner that we view the text, and if it was at one time possible to imagine the Talmud as the record of a developing debate in a rabbinic academy, this is no longer the case. Sensitive now to the frequent compositional interventions of the Talmud's authors,[3] scholars have been able to recover many an original amoraic meaning. But despite the immense value of this approach, it has not provided the key for characterizing the Bavli as a complete document. What is needed for that task is a method that explores not only the meaning of the sources in contrast to the voice of the anonymous author, but also the meaning created by that author as he shapes his sources to make a final statement.

The method to which I am alluding became a central concern in biblical scholarship nearly two decades ago.[4] In his presidential address to the Society of Biblical Literature (1968),[5] James Muilenburg criticized the form-critics for their "too exclusive employment of the form-critical methods,"[6] and proposed that the time had arrived for a new approach to the text:

> What I am interested in, above all, is in understanding the nature of Hebrew literary composition, in exhibiting the structural patterns that are employed for the fashioning of a literary unit, whether in poetry or prose, and in discerning the many and various devices by which the predications are formulated and ordered into a unified whole. Such an enterprise I should describe as rhetoric and the methodology as rhetorical criticism. (p. 8)

The text, Muilenburg argued, is not merely to be broken down into its various and sundry units. It is equally crucial to consider the manner in which the units constitute a whole, and how they are employed within that whole to communicate the author's (redactor's) meaning. The final goal of rhetorical criticism, as Muilenburg defined it, is to "grasp the writer's intent and meaning" by discerning "the configuration of its component parts... [and] not[ing] the various rhetorical devices that are employed" (pp. 9–10).

In an exemplary exercise of rhetorical-critical technique, George A. Kennedy recently applied his expertise in classical rhetoric to an analysis of the New Testament. In the introduction to his *New Testament Interpretation Through Rhetorical Criticism* (Chapel Hill and London, 1984), Kennedy defines rhetorical criticism in a manner reminiscent of Muilenberg (and under his admitted influence). He writes:

> Rhetorical criticism takes the text as we have it, whether the work of a single author or the product of editing, and looks at it from the point of view of the author's or editor's intent, the unified results, and how it would be perceived by an audience of near contemporaries. (p. 4)

The concern of the rhetorical critic is to comprehend the meanings of the text at the level of its final composition. For what purpose was the text put together in this way? How does its arrangement impact upon the reader (listener) to create a meaningful impression? How are rhetorical turns employed to affect the development of a thesis? What in the synthesis of the parts into a whole influences one's understanding of the composite message? Stated simply, how does the author (editor/redactor) seek to communicate his intent to his audience?

It is precisely this series of questions that I believe must presently be asked of the Babylonian Talmud. As the form and source critics have made evident, the Talmud is a text in which the redactor's (more correctly, author's) hand remains always at or close to the surface, leaving both his own contribution and his sources readily discernible. Moreover, that author actively shapes his sources to create a composite whole. It is at this stage essential, therefore, to speak of "the view of the Gemara," as well as of the view of individual Amoraim or of generations of Amoraim. This is, of course, the explicit goal of rhetorical criticism.[7]

Because the Talmud of Babylonia was composed at a time when rhetoric as a form was a central scholastic interest, it is reasonable to consider whether rhetorical criticism as applied to the Talmud might be related to the rhetorical discipline practiced in the Greek and Hellenistic academies.

The works of Aristotle—author of one of the most significant Greek treatises on rhetoric—were translated into Aramaic under Shapur I (whose reign began ca. 240) and Khusrau I (532), and Greek philosophy in general was appreciated by the Persians.[8] Nevertheless, there is no evidence that these works influenced talmudic forms. The conventions of classical rhetoric were subject to an ancient, formal tradition, with well-defined technical categories,[9] none of which am I able to discern in the "rhetoric" of the Talmud.[10] Also, classical rhetoric was an oratorically-based discipline—it considered the manner in which an orator influenced his audience. On the other hand, it is reasonable to assume that at the final stage of its development—that stage with which rhetorical criticism is concerned—the Talmud was a written work. This is suggested both by the sequential, analytic quality of the talmudic deliberation[11] as well as by the fact that it leaves so much unexplained, a feature more typical of written than oral compositions.[12] In addition, Greek theorists of rhetoric made a distinction between rhetoric and dialectic, and the Talmud is clearly the latter, not the former. It seems unlikely, therefore, that rhetorical criticism of the Talmud would allow for more than coincidental reference to the categories of Hellenistic rhetoric.

But rhetorical criticism, as evidenced by Kennedy's work, does employ many of those categories. If the text of the Talmud is so much unlike the texts of that rhetoric, ought we hesitate to use its tools? I think not.[13] Even if the Talmud was a written composition, it still clearly preserves a significant "oral residue."[14] For this reason, it is perfectly conceivable that a text such as the Talmud might be considered both written and oral; "written" in the nature of its analysis and "oral" in significant elements of its mode of expression. Therefore, even if its origins are written, its manner of composition can often be understood by making reference to the primarily oral categories of classical rhetoric.

But the very need to respect the categories of classical rhetoric in order to make use of its lessons has been called into doubt. Muilenburg has commented that rhetorical scholars were too much dominated by Greek prototypes.[15] Others have made the same point. The Belgian philosopher, Chaim Perelman, in conjunction with L. Olbrechts-Tyteca, argued that rhetoric ought to be understood as the "study of the methods of proof to gain adherence."[16] Furthermore, "the very nature of deliberation and argumentation"—that is, the very form by which the Talmud is typified—"is opposed to necessity and self-evidence, since no one deliberates where the solution is necessary or argues against what is self-evident." The Talmud is, then, by its very nature a text that seeks to convince and is tied intimately to the purposes and forms of rhetoric.[17] Finally, readers, and not only listeners, may constitute an "audience," and written texts, like orations, attempt to persuade. In both its form and style, therefore, the Talmud is a text that may justifiably be approached with the questions that rhetoric defines. Kennedy confirms this when he states—despite his grounding in classical rhetoric—that all genres are (potentially) rhetorical and, in particular, all religious systems (as systems which seek to win adherents) are rhetorical.[18] The Talmud then, as an argumentational treatise of religious intent, is well-suited to the questions and definitions that this system can present.

Focusing upon our specific concern, let us articulate some of the questions that should direct a rhetorical-critical examination of the Bavli. Having first employed the source-critical method to isolate the compositional layer of the text, how is the intent of the author to be comprehended? This will require attention to the unique contribution of that unattributed author: What does he actually say? What part of his statement of meaning is embedded in the structure and ordering of the text? What is the nature and authority of his proofs? Is the logic cogent, or are there contradictions? What is the function of rhetorical tropes, and in particular (because of their prevalence in the Bavli) rhetorical questions?

But this will not be enough. The vocabulary of the Gemara is not merely independent terms or phrases, Hebrew or Aramaic, but whole units of opinion or discourse from earlier authorities. We must also ask, therefore, how the compositional shaping of these earlier tannaitic and amoraic traditions creates a new statement of meaning. This is particularly true because the redactor often changes the meanings of his original traditions. The choice and arrangement of earlier amoraic traditions is more than an editorial convention or convenience. But if there is intent, then what is its meaning? How does the author-redactor of the talmudic sugya shape his raw materials to create a coherent thesis?

It is the sugya, ultimately, that is the focus of this study, that being the term applied to the unit that is shaped by the Talmud's final authors. The sugya, in general terms, may be understood to correspond to the "rhetorical unit" spoken of elsewhere in rhetorical criticism. This is the unit to which a given analysis will be limited, and so its parameters must be defined at the earliest possible stage of the inquiry. This definition is, however, a circular one. Having determined the limits of the sugya, its meaning is made clearer; but the reader's sense of the meaning will in part direct his definition of those limits. Cognizant of this circularity, there should still be no hesitation in seeking the boundaries of the sugya, directed by the following questions: How does the author introduce his discourse? How does it conclude? How do the elements that highlight this definition effect the meaning of the whole? How does definition of the unit (the sugya) define the interest of the text as a whole?

To demonstrate this method I will analyze two sugyot from the Babylonian Talmud, chosen because they employ both halakhic and aggadic elements. My hope is that these illustrations will generate interest in using this method to analyze many talmudic texts, for I am confident that the phenomenon described here is widespread in the Bavli.

Literary Studies 213

The first text to be examined, at Yevamot 13b–14b, is a typical halakhic deliberation that reveals how rhetorical considerations may be applied to the most common of talmudic forms.

The sugya begins with a discussion of the mitzvah "do not separate yourselves into factions" (based upon a fanciful reading of Deut. 14:1). In addressing the application of this law, the Gemara makes reference to the Mishnah (Yevamot 1:4) which describes the different opinions of the House of Shammai and the House of Hillel with respect to Levirite marriage and purities. Before responding to the apparent contradiction between the prohibition of factions and the conflicting opinions of these two houses, the Gemara considers, at length, the possibility that the House of Shammai never practiced according to their opinions. That deliberation. and the subsequent attempt to resolve the contradiction, follows:[19]

> a. Do you think the School of Shammai acted on the basis of their opinions? The School of Shammai did not act on the basis of their opinions.
> b. And R. Johanan said: They certainly did!
> c. And [they are engaged] in the [same] dispute as Rav and Samuel, for Rav says "The School of Shammai did not act on the basis of their opinions" and Samuel says "They certainly did!"
> d. When [does this dispute apply]?
> e. If you say [that they are arguing about the period] before the heavenly voice [in Yavne announced that the law follows the School of Hillel], then what is the reason of the one who says they did not act [why not, being that no heavenly decision had yet been made?]?
> f. But if after the heavenly voice, then what is the reason of the one who says they did act [being that the heavenly voice had already decided against Shammai]?
> g. If you wish, I will say [that the dispute applies to the period] before the heavenly voice, and if you wish, I will say [to the period] after the heavenly voice.
> h. If you wish, I will say before the heavenly voice, and in a case where the School of Hillel is the majority. [Under those conditions] the one who says [the School of Shammai] did not act [on the basis of their opinions says so] because the School of Hillel were the majority [and the law generally follows the majority]. And the one who says that they did act [said this because] we go according to the majority where [the competing parties] are equivalent, but here [the Gemara posits] the School of Shammai are "sharper."
> i. And if you wish, I will say after the heavenly voice. The one who says they did not act [says this] because the heavenly voice had come out [and announced a decision]. And the one who says they did act, it is R. Joshua['s opinion that he follows], for he said that we pay no heed to a heavenly voice.
> j. And the one who said they did act, why do we not read here "*lo titgodedu* (Deut. 14:1), [meaning] don't separate yourselves into factions?"
> k. Abbaye said: We say *lo titgodedu* only with respect to two courts in one city, these teaching according to the opinions of the School of Shammai and these teaching according to the opinions of the School of Hillel, but [with respect to] two courts in two cities, we have no objection.
> l. Rava said to him...

m. Rather, Rava said: We only say *lo titgodedu* with respect to a court in one city, in which half teach in accordance with the School of Shammai and half teach in accordance with the School of Hillel, but [with respect to] two courts in one city, we have no objection.

n. Come and hear [an objection]: "In R. Eliezer's place they would, on Shabbat, cut the wood to make the coals to make the iron [to make the knife to perform the circumcision]; in the place of R. Jose the Galilean they would eat fowl with milk." In R. Eliezer's place they would [do so, but] in R. Akiba's place they would not, for it is taught [in Mishnah Shabbat 19:1] "R. Akiba stated a general rule: Any labor that it is possible to do before Shabbat does not supersede Shabbat." [This objection is directed, apparently, against the opinion that claims that the School of Shammai did not act on the basis of their opinions, which may be equated with the view "don't subdivide into factions."]

o. What sort of objection is this? [Haven't we already learned that, even according to the more restrictive interpretation of *lo titgodedu*,] different places are different [and are not subject to the prohibition of factionalism].

p. And the one who taught it (the objection), why did he teach it [being that it was obviously not a good objection]?

q. You might have thought that, on account of the severity of Shabbat, [the whole world] is like a single place; this text (quoted in the "objection") comes to teach us otherwise].[20]

r. Come and hear [another objection]: R. Abbahu, when he went to R. Joshua b. Levi's place he would handle a lamp [on Shabbat, despite the fact that the kindling of the lamp would have been prohibited], but when he went to R. Johanan's place he would not handle a lamp.

s. And so what is the problem? Do we not say that different places are different [and not subject to the prohibition of factionalism]?

t. This is what we are saying: How could R. Abbahu have acted this way in this place and this way in this place?

u. R. Abbahu was of the [same] opinion as R. Joshua b. Levi [who permitted], and when he went to R. Johanan's place he would not handle [a lamp] because of R. Johanan's honor.

v. But isn't there his attendant [who, seeing R. Abbahu's contradictory actions and not understanding the reason, might become confused]?

w. He informed his attendant.

x. Come and hear [a final objection]: "Even though these prohibit and these permit, the School of Shammai did not refrain from marrying women of the School of Hillel, nor did the School of Hillel [avoid] those of the School of Shammai (Mishnah Yevamot 1:4)."

y. It is fine if you say that [the School of Shammai] did not act [on the basis of their opinions], for this reason they did not avoid [marrying]. But if you say that they did act, why did they not avoid [marrying]?

z. (At this point the Gemara establishes that the Schools of Shammai and Hillel agree on the definition of a mamzer—a child of blemished status whom another non-mamzer Israelite may not marry—and that, in the present dispute, the School of Shammai would be producing children whom the School of Hillel would consider to be mamzerim.)

aa. So do we not learn from this that they did not act [on the basis of their opinions, being that they did intermarry? This must mean that the mamzerim whom they might in theory have been producing were not being produced in fact].

bb. No! They certainly did act [on the basis of their opinions. How so?] They informed them [in cases where there were problems] and they separated [in only such instances].
cc. This also makes sense, for it is taught in the end [of the Mishnah]... Rather, is it not [obvious] that they informed them? Learn from it!
dd. (This step briefly shows why the latter part of the Mishnah was a more obvious proof of "they informed them" than the former.)

In order to appreciate the full impact of the Bavli's argument, it is useful to consider how this same problem might otherwise have been handled in rabbinic circles. The Yerushalmi (Yevamot 1:6, 3b) begins its deliberation on this issue by quoting a baraita (Tosefta 1:10) which clarifies the severity of the halakhic differences between the Houses of Hillel and Shammai, yet speaks of the great peace that existed between them. The Gemara, however, objects ("there is the condition of mamzer between them, and yet you say this!?"), and proceeds to list several possible solutions, all of which restrict or eliminate the possibility that the Shammaites acted on the basis of their opinions. Finally, after quoting a related tradition, the Gemara twice declares that the law follows the Hillelites. Though it begins with a tolerant tradition, the whole thrust of the Yerushalmi is to eliminate the option of tolerance. This is clear both in the nature of the solutions that it quotes, as well as in its emphatic conclusion—the law follows Hillel. The tolerant position of the Mishnah is, in the end, annulled, and the declaration of a single definitive law rests secure.

The argument of the Bavli, on the other hand, favors toleration. This is evident, first, in the overall structure of the text. In contrast to the Yerushalmi, the Bavli begins with intolerance ("you shall not separate into factions") and concludes with tolerance. Whereas the Yerushalmi raises the mamzer objection almost immediately, explicit mention of this problem waits, in the Bavli, to the very end (z.), there only to be resolved. And the tradition affirming the heavenly decision in favor of the Hillelites, which so resoundingly concludes the Yerushalmi's deliberation, is never quoted explicitly in the Bavli. When it is, however, referred to (e.–i.), the potential impact of such a reference is immediately nullified, the text preferring to support a view that ignores heavenly voices.

By setting the context for the opinions of Abbaye and Rava that follow, it is the unattributed section of the sugya, asking whether and when the Shammaites actually followed their opinions (d.–i.), that is the key to the argument of the text as a whole. The Gemara answers its central question—"When [does this dispute apply]?" (d.)—by proposing (in typical "talmudic" fashion) that the dispute can be understood to refer to the era either before or after the declaration of the heavenly voice. If it is referring to the earlier era, then the dispute must assume that even then the School of Hillel constituted the majority. Therefore, since rules of rabbinic procedure declare that the law follows the majority, the party who holds that the Shammaites did not follow their views can easily justify himself: the law followed the majority (Hillel)! The opinion that holds that they did follow their views, on the other hand, believes that the rule of the majority only applies where both parties are equally insightful; if the minority is "keener" than the majority then they may nevertheless follow their own opinions.

The effect of this definition is—both technically and in terms of content—unsettling. First of all, it turns the burden of proof on its head. Before the heavenly voice the one who argued that the Shammaites followed their opinions should have needed no justification. But by positing that the Hillelites were in the majority it is all of a sudden the one who says that the Shammaites did act in accordance with their opinions who must defend himself. Of course, by this reversal the defense is rendered more difficult, and any effective defense is rendered that much more notable. And what a defense, indeed! The position is justified by the claim that the Shammaites were keener than the Hillelites. This means that the heavenly voice would not finally support the party that was more likely to be "correct," and, furthermore, that rabbinic Jews had, for many centuries by this point (that is, the time of the composition of the Gemara), been following the views of the less "sharp" party (!).

The second part of the Gemara's analysis is no less bold. If the dispute pertained to the era following the declaration by the heavenly voice that the law follows Hillel then, of course, those who hold that the Shammaites did not act on the basis of their opinions need no justification. But what of those who claim they did? The affirmative opinion, the Gemara suggests, follows the view of R. Joshua who, in the well-known story of the oven of Akhnai (b. B.M. 59b), declares that the law is "not in heaven" and that heavenly voices, therefore, need not be heeded. This, to be sure, is the definitive conclusion of that story, and it is apparently the stronger conclusion of the analysis here.

Having established such a context, the traditions that follow are rendered—in practical halakhic terms—well nigh revolutionary. The opinions of Abbaye and Rava (k.-m.) resolve the conflict between the prohibition of sectarianism and the opinion that the Shammaites actually followed their views by claiming that the prohibition "don't become sects" applies in only very limited circumstances. Given the Gemara's introduction, the permissive consequences of their definitions now pertain even to Shammaites who follow their opinions after the heavenly voice in Yavne! Though they might originally have been more modest, in their present context the halakhic definitions proposed by these Amoraim become tools of the broadest possible toleration.

The series of "objections" that follows serves the same rhetorical purpose. To begin with, the first two objections (n. and r.) are directed, despite reason to expect the contrary (rabbinic history and sociology; cf. the Yerushalmi), against the opinion that restricts diversity in practice (= the

School of Shammai did not act). This might itself be surprising enough, but the fact that the objections are inadequate to the task—as the Gemara itself admits[21]—is even more perplexing. The objections refer to cases where different laws were practiced in different locations (hence the objection: "see—they did act on the basis of their opinions!"), but following the interpretations of Abbaye and Rava this would represent no problem. Even according to Abbaye there can be no objection to different practices in different towns. So what is the point?

Rhetorically, these flawed objections accomplish two things. First, they illustrate prominent cases in which, even in matters as serious as Shabbat and kashrut, a variety of practices was tolerated. Secondly, by pointing out that, in light of the interpretations of Abbaye and Rava, the opinion that demands "don't separate into factions" applies only (possibly) in the same town, the "restrictive" opinion turns out to be very tolerant indeed. By means of the qualifying remarks of Abbaye and Rava, which the Gemara, in these "objections," insists that we notice, the denial of legitimate alternatives in practice is far more restricted. The objections don't work precisely because the other party already agrees that alternatives should be supported.

It is only the last objection, referring to the mamzer problem (y.–aa.), that grants the serious consequences of factionalism. The Gemara at first seems to admit the severity of this problem, but by means of a simple suggestion even this is resolved, and its final opinion, like what preceded, is permissive.

But given the nature of the solution, this final objection, too, turns out not to have been a good one. For an objection to be effective it must be supported by convincing logic and it must not admit an obvious answer. Lack of logical support is the problem with the first two objections, as we noted. The final objection is undone by a failure to satisfy the second criterion.

This "undoing" is accomplished in the following way: following a response to the second "objection," and immediately preceding the third, a seemingly irrelevant "rhetorical" question is asked concerning the servant of R. Abbahu (v.). How can R. Abbahu, the Gemara wants to know, act in different ways in different places in a manner that is perfectly consistent with the halakha but might, nevertheless, lead his attendant to draw the wrong conclusion? The answer: "he *informed* his attendant [of the reasons for his actions]." This, it turns out, is also the answer given to the final objection (the two schools could act in accordance with their views because they *informed* one another of any problems). The same Aramaic verb is used to answer both objections (adjusted only for number), and the echo of one in the other is unavoidable. The result of this repetition is that at the very moment that the third objection is raised the response to it is already at hand. Far more than a mere "rhetorical question," then, this brief exchange concerning the servant has served, rhetorically, to render this single "good" objection ineffective.[22]

The penultimate step of the sugya (cc.) confirms that tolerance and trust is the appropriate response to even serious problems that might result from pluralistic practice (the final step is a mere technical addition). By declaring in conclusion that "this also makes sense"—a statement that is sufficiently unusual to be noteworthy[23]—the Gemara assures that there will be no mistaking the thrust of its argument. This final emphatic repetition, the context established by the Gemara, and the overall deliberation, with its careful turns and mani-pulations, together serve to create a surprisingly forceful statement on behalf of the legitimacy of different practices in different rabbinic communities. Given the care with which this argument was formulated, there can be little doubt that this was the author's purpose from the very beginning.

A second sugya (b. Yoma 85b–86b), concerning teshuva (repentance) and its efficacy, allows us to expand upon our first analysis by showing how halakha and aggada can serve one another in pursuit of a common rhetorical purpose. More precisely, in this case it is the halakha that gives the aggada its rhetorical power.

The central issue to be addressed in the Gemara is defined by the Mishnah. The Mishnah (8:8) speaks of teshuva in connection with other means of effecting atonement:[24]

> A. A sin-offering or a definitive guilt-offering effect atonement.
> B. Death and the Day of Atonement atone [in combination] with teshuva.
> C. Teshuva atones for minor transgressions, for positive and for negative [commandments], but for serious [transgressions] it suspends until the Day of Atonement comes and causes atonement.

Despite Rashi's claims to the contrary,[25] the meaning of the Mishnah, in consideration of its structure, is clear: sacrifices, defined by the Torah, were absolutely effective. They could be performed perfunctorily and yet still they had power to atone. Death or the Day of Atonement (without sacrifice) effected atonement only in combination with teshuva, and teshuva itself was effective as a primary means of achieving atonement only in connection with minor transgressions; for more serious offenses it required the Day of Atonement (or, presumably, death) ,[26]

The Mishnah, beginning with sacrifice as the most effective method for achieving atonement and only then proceeding to less effective methods, was underlining with simple power the crisis that the Jews whom it was addressing faced.[27] The Temple, of course, had been destroyed, and so sacrifice, the only method of atonement that was not conditional, was no longer possible. This meant that weaker devices had to be employed. For people for whom God's graces were of utmost concern—but who, at the same time, had recently experienced an event (the destruction) that could be interpreted as the withdrawal of Divine grace—this situation must have been frightening indeed.

Moreover, although teshuva was the most accessible method of effecting atonement, it was, as a primary method, the least effective. Death and the Day of Atonement were associated with all transgressions for which sacrifice had been effective; teshuva as a primary method pertained only to minor transgressions.[28]

It should not be doubted that the rhetorical intent of the Mishnah was to underline this crisis. Because compositions that seek to gain adherents, like the Mishnah, address a living audience, rhetorical criticism considers the impact of such discourses as "it would be perceived by an audience of near contemporaries" (Kennedy, p. 4). This means that the reader's (listener's) contribution to the rhetorical situation is as important as the author's. In this specific case, it is inconceivable that a reader/listener could ignore the consequences of the Temple's destruction upon his experience and fail to sense the contrast between that experience and the more ideal world that the Mishnah describes. If the Mishnah (and the Gemara, which was even more distant from the world of the Temple) was composed for a contemporary audience, then the impact of this disjunction on the audience cannot be minimized.

The Gemara, certainly, understood this to be the problematic of the Mishnah, as is evident in its commentary:

> a. [With respect to clause A. in the Mishnah, the Gemara asks] a definitive guilt-offering does [effect atonement, but] a conditional guilt-offering does not? But "atonement" is written in connection with it (see Lev. 5:18)!
> b. These [things mentioned in the Mishnah] effect complete atonement, [but] a conditional guilt-offering does not effect complete atonement;
> c. alternatively, these [things mentioned in the Mishnah], another thing (the Day of Atonement) cannot effect their atonement, [but for] a conditional guilt-offering another thing can effect their atonement,
> d. for we learned [in Mishnah Keritot 6:4]: "Those obligated to bring sin offerings or definitive guilt-offerings who lived through the Day of Atonement are [still] liable... [but if they were obligated to bring] a conditional guilt-offering they are [after the Day of Atonement] exempt."
> e. (clause B. of the Mishnah)
> f. [In combination] with teshuva, yes [they do atone], but not by themselves?
> g. Should it be said that [this opinion] is not like [that of] Rabbi [Judah the Prince], for it is taught [in a baraita]: "Rabbi says: The Day of Atonement atones for all transgressions of the Torah, whether or not he repented, with the exception of...?
> h. [No,] you could even say [that this mishnaic clause is the opinion of] Rabbi. [What the Mishnah means to say is that] teshuva requires the Day of Atonement, but the Day of Atonement does not require teshuva.
> i. (clause C. of the Mishnah)
> j. Now [you say that teshuva] atones for [the transgression of] a negative precept; is it necessary [to say that it also atones for transgression of] a positive precept?! (This would be obvious, and so it is unnecessary for the Mishnah to say it. When the Mishnah says something unnecessary, the Gemara considers there to be a problem.)
> k. R. Judah said: This is what is being said [by the Mishnah]: "for positive [precepts]

and for negative [precepts] that [through their transgression] are transformed into positive [precepts]."

l. But [do you really mean to imply that teshuva does] not [atone] for bona fide negative [precepts] ? But there is a contradiction [t. Yoma 5:5]: "What are minor [transgressions, for which teshuva is said to atone]? Positive and negative [precepts] with the exception of 'Thou shalt not take [the name of the Lord thy God in vain] (Exod. 20:7).'"

m. [This does not contradict R. Judah's interpretation. What is meant is] "Thou shalt not take..." and anything that is like it [meaning any bona fide negative precept].

n. Come and hear [another objection to R. Judah's interpretation]:[29] "R. Judah (the Tanna, not the Amora to whose opinion we are objecting) says: Anything that is from 'Thou shalt not take' and below, teshuva atones [for its transgression, but] from 'Thou shalt not take' and above, teshuva suspends [the transgression] and the Day of Atonement atones."

o. [What is meant is] "Thou shalt not take..." and anything that is like it.

p. Come and hear [another objection]: "Since it says [that there is] teshuva by Horeb (Mt. Sinai, i.e., in the Torah) [in the word] 'He shall forgive (Exod. 34:7),' is it possible that this is true with respect to 'Thou shalt not take... (Exod. 20:7)?' Scripture says 'He will not forgive (Exod. 20:7).' Is it possible that this is true also with all other negative [precepts]? Scripture says 'His name (ibid.)' [meaning that for] His name He will not forgive, but He forgives [for] all other negative [precepts]."

q. [So, being that we have found a contradiction to R. Judah's interpretation of the Mishnah, how can we now defend him?] It is a tannaitic argument, for it is taught [in another baraita]... (a baraita follows that explicitly supports R. Judah's reading of the Mishnah).

r. The Master said: "Since it says [that there is] teshuva by Horeb [in the word] 'He shall forgive.'"

s. Where do we know this from? For it is taught [in a baraita]...

The destruction stands at the center of the Gemara's interpretive rhetoric. Though it is nowhere mentioned explicitly, its consequences are spelled out in detail. Each successive interpretive paragraph serves the same end: to underline the severity of the crisis precipitated by the elimination of sacrifice as a means of atonement.

The first paragraph begins (a.) by addressing a technical problem in the Mishnah's claim. In order to respond to this problem, it offers two solutions, the second of which (c.–d.) quotes the following Mishnah (Keritot 6:4):

> Those obligated to bring sin-offerings and definitive guilt-offerings who lived through the Day of Atonement *are [still] liable*, [but if they were obligated to bring] conditional guilt-offerings they are [after the Day of Atonement] exempt [my emphasis].

What is the point? The absence of sacrifices is more serious than one might have thought. There are certain kinds of liabilities for which, as the Gemara says, "another thing (the Day of Atonement) cannot effect their atonement."

If the Day of Atonement, which is clearly delineated in the Torah and, as the Mishnah admits, is prior to teshuva in terms of effectiveness, cannot replace these sacrifices, then this is obviously so for teshuva as well.

As the Gemara continues it only makes matters worse. Asking which authority is represented in the second clause of the Mishnah (g.) the Gemara quotes the opinion of R. Judah the Prince (Rabbi) which grants a great deal of power to the Day of Atonement. But his view contradicts the one recorded in the Mishnah. So, in order to propose a resolution between the opinion of Rabbi and the Mishnah, the author of the Gemara suggests that this is actually the meaning of the Mishnah: "teshuva needs the Day of Atonement, the Day of Atonement does not need teshuva." In other words, to avoid the apparent contradiction the Day of Atonement is strengthened, but teshuva, which is the primary concern of this text, is weakened further still.[30]

Nor is this the end of the process. The next segment in the Gemara (j.–k.) comments directly on the phrase in the Mishnah which defines the parameters of the effectiveness of teshuva (C. above). Again responding to a technical problem in the Mishnah, the Gemara suggests, in the name of R. Judah (Amora, third cent.), that teshuva achieves atonement only for "positive [precepts] and for negative [precepts] that [through their transgression] are transformed into positive commandments,"[31] but not for negative commandments in general. Severely reducing the category of commandments for whose transgression teshuva effects atonement, at this point it would appear that teshuva has relatively little to offer Jews who have lost their Temple and sacrifices.

The Gemara resumes by objecting, on the basis of various baraitot, to R. Judah's suggestion that teshuva is ineffective following the transgression of standard negative commandments. Two[32] objections are brought, but both are answered (l.–o.). Then a third objection (p.), claiming that teshuva is effective for all transgressions aside from swearing falsely by God's name, appears to be irrefutable. To defend R. Judah against this objection, the Gemara suggests that "it is a tannaitic argument," that is, that there are some who consider teshuva to be very effective and others who consider it to be only slightly effective. A baraita demonstrating the latter view (and therefore supporting R. Judah) is then quoted.

At this point (r.) the Gemara takes a remarkable turn. Using the technical term "the master said (*amar mar*)," the Gemara quotes one part of the previous deliberation, to comment upon it at length. What it chooses to address is the one baraita that definitively supported the power of teshuva. It completely ignores the lengthy interpretation of the Mishnah that so severely reduced its power, proceeding instead to deliberate at length on teshuva and its efficacy. The skeptical opinions expressed earlier are put aside, and claims on behalf of the power of teshuva, beginning modestly, become more and more incredible.

The tension and anxiety created by the initial interpretations are now resolved into a kind of triumph, and the crisis introduced by the Mishnah, and expanded upon by the initial Gemara, is eliminated thoroughly.

Retrospectively, we here come to understand the intent of the Gemara's preliminary commentary. Its point, in reality, was a rhetorical one, recognizing that the more severe the problem, the more powerful a solution will appear. By deepening the crisis of Jewish observance after the destruction, therefore, the Gemara assured that the solution embodied in teshuva could not be taken for granted. Having made the reader aware of the extreme consequences of the events that had transpired, the Gemara guaranteed that its remedy would be impressive indeed.

This deliberate heightening of the power of teshuva, prepared with such care in the Gemara's halakhic commentary, continues—and even intensifies—in the aggadic deliberation that follows. The Gemara first quotes a baraita which details the various gradations of transgressions, the means of attaining atonement for each, and the place of teshuva in each stage. At this point, teshuva is necessary for all manner of atonement, but it is by itself sufficient only for the non-performance of positive precepts. Next, following a lengthy "digression" on "profanation of the Divine name" (which was introduced in the final section of the baraita), the Gemara returns to a series of traditions that are united by the theme "great is teshuva...." These traditions, unlike the baraita, allow for the absolute effectiveness of teshuva, and they are worthy of close examination.

The collected traditions praising the worth of teshuva (86a bottom–86b top) may be outlined as follows:

> a. R. Hama b. R. Hanina said: Great is teshuva, for it brings healing to the world...
> b. R. Hama b. R. Hanina raised a contradiction: it is written...
> c. R. Judah raised a contradiction...
> d. R. Levi said: Great is teshuva, for it reaches the heavenly throne...
> e. R. Johanan said: Great is teshuva, for it pushes aside negative precepts of the Torah...
> f. R. Jonatan[33] said: Great is teshuva, for it hastens (or: "brings") the redemption...[34]
> g. Resh Laqish said: Great is teshuva, for [by means of it] intentional transgressions are accounted as unintentional...
> h. Is this so? But has not Resh Laqish said: Great is teshuva, for [by means of it] intentional transgressions are accounted as worthy acts...?
> i. There is no problem, here (h.) it is from love and here (g.) it is from fear.
> j. ...teshuva lengthens a person's days...
> k. ...the Holy One, Blessed be He, if a person transgresses in private, [a.] He will be satisfied with [mere] words [of teshuva]... and not only that, but [b.] it is accounted to him [the transgressor] as a good [thing]... and not only that, but [c.] Scripture accounts it to him as though he had sacrificed bullocks...
> l. It is taught (in a baraita): R. Meir[35] used to say: Great is teshuva, for on account of an individual who did teshuva, the whole world is forgiven... .

What is the organizing principle of this text? It is clearly not chronology; many of the authorities to whom opinions are attributed were contemporary Palestinian sages, and the others do not appear with chronological reason. In some instances the traditions of a single sage are arranged together, but that is insufficient to explain the overall structure. Rather, as we suggested, the purpose of the sequence is the progressive intensification of the power of teshuva.

This empowerment is most evident in the final steps (which I have underlined). In e., teshuva annuls negative precepts. In f., it brings the redemption. In g. and h. we find that teshuva has the power to change the reality of a previously committed act, so much so that (with the proper intent) transgressions might in the end be accounted as meritorious. k., in its final phrase (c), makes the most remarkable claim, given the stage that was set by the Mishnah and the initial Gemara. Now, we discover, teshuva actually has the power of sacrifice! But no, we learn in the final step (l.), teshuva is more powerful, for sacrifice is only effective for the individual, or, at best, for the nation of Israel. Yet the teshuva of a individual, this final tradition claims, is sufficient to bring forgiveness for the whole world! Teshuva has, in the end, been transformed from the least effective method into the most effective, with cosmic implications.

Considering the text as a whole, we are able to see that two levels of structure have been employed with rhetorical intent. The first is found in the detailed development of the substantial subsections, one of which heightens the crisis of the destruction by weakening teshuva, and the other of which denies the crisis and establishes the independent potency of teshuva. The second is the relationship of these subsections, the former creating tension and the latter resolving it. In fact, this broad structural intent continues even into the next segment of the text, for the Gemara now asks: "how may a penitent (baʿal teshuva) be described?" Why has this primary question been left to this point? It is because of a basic factor of the psychology of persuasion: before describing to someone how to repent he must understand why he ought to repent. He must be convinced of the value of teshuva before he will want to know how it is done. For this reason the text first demonstrates the value of teshuva and only after its demonstration is complete does it explain how teshuva might be accomplished.[36]

The final concern of the Gemara is the triumph of teshuva. Its claim, in conclusion, is that its triumph is indisputable. Sacrifice has disappeared, the Day of Atonement is but a shadow of its former self, yet we are in no way at a disadvantage in recovering God's favor; teshuva remains to us and its power is incomparable.[37]

Having ventured a rhetorical examination of these texts, let me conclude with general observations concerning the methodology, its assumptions, and its potential value.

Though the Babylonian Talmud, unlike many other rabbinic texts (Mishnah, Tosefta, etc.), explicitly indicates its sources,[38] the text, nevertheless, represents a final composition that not only has its own agenda, but often employs its sources precisely to advance that agenda. In my view, it is legitimate to construct a history of traditions and to consider developing rabbinic ideologies on the basis of such histories.[39] Yet such histories require extraordinary care, and in the end all we can be certain of is the document as it stands before us. Because a sugya wants to make a claim, we must ask what that claim is, and how it uses the evidence to support that claim.

Discovering the relevant questions is, of course, a circular process. We can only know the thesis of the text by examining it as a whole, that is, as the sum of its parts. But as we begin to perceive a pattern in the progression of the parts we are then led to ask how the parts support this pattern. Nevertheless, this is a valuable enterprise; it is precisely the "hermeneutical circle" that will be at work here.

Of course, we have assumed that the text in question—the Bavli— wants to make a claim, and that it is, therefore, subject to rhetorical analysis. On the one hand, even such an assumption is not necessary in order to apply this method. The methodological definitions of Muilenburg and Kennedy are extremely broad; any text can be examined with an eye to how it is "formulated and ordered into a unified whole," in order to understand "how it would be perceived by an audience of near contemporaries." All texts employ a "rhetoric" that can be isolated and interpreted.

However, I also want to claim that the Bavli is, by its very nature, rhetorical. By this I mean (as stated in the introduction) that the Gemara, as a text that examines religious norms and seeks to justify or ground those norms, is fervently interested in persuading its readers. If persuasion were not the point, then there would be no need to deliberate at such length. This being so, rhetorical analysis, as the "study of the methods of proof to gain adherence" (to reinvoke Perelman and Olbrechts-Tyteca), is a natural path by which to approach the Bavli. By this definition it is not merely rhetorical, it is explicitly so.

By means of the rhetorical method we will, I would argue, be highlighting a level of meaning that has previously been largely ignored in scholarship of the Bavli. This meaning is that of the sugya—larger than individual traditions, but far more modest and discrete than the document as a whole (or even its defined parts, e.g., the tractate and the chapter). Being inherent in the sugya and its structure, it must be sought in the Gemara's tightly formulated claims and in its careful orchestration of details. The meanings that emerge from this analysis, advanced by a circle of rabbinic scholars who lived in Persia sometime between the early fifth and the mid-seventh centuries, reflect a particular experience—one that must be addressed on its own, unique terms. But just as crucially, these scholars, through the texts that they composed, intended (by persuading their audience) to generate particular conventions. On account of their success, they influenced the shape of Jewish practice, in the most fundamental way, until the dawn of modernity and beyond.[40]

NOTES

1. For a review of the literature, see D. Goodblatt, "The Babylonian Talmud," in *The Study of Ancient Judaism* 2 (New York, 1981): 144–81. See also *Semeia* 27 (1983): 37–116.
2. For the most comprehensive support of this view see both intros. to D. Halivni, *Meqorot umesorot* [*Sources and Traditions*] (Yoma-Hagiga) (Jerusalem, 1975), and *Meqorot umesorot* (Shabbat) (Jerusalem, 1982). Also of great value is Shamma Friedman's methodological introduction to *pereq ha'isha rabba bebavli* [*A Critical Study of Yevamot X*] (Jerusalem, 1978), pp. 7–15 (reprinted from *Meḥqarim umeqorot* [*Studies and Sources*], New York, 1978).
3. See Friedman's methodological introduction and "Literary Structures in Sugyot of the Bavli" [Hebrew], *Proceedings of the Sixth World Congress of Jewish Studies*, 3 (Jerusalem, 1977): 389–402.
4. Similar methodological observations and proposals were made earlier by Meir Weiss in *Hamiqra kidemuto* (Jerusalem, 1962), revised, expanded and translated as *The Bible From Within: The Method of Total Interpretation* (Jerusalem, 1984). Weiss also notes similar tendencies in the work of Buber and Rosenzweig; see *The Bible From Within*, pp. 35–37.
5. Published as "Form Criticism and Beyond," *JBL* 88 (1969): 1–18.
6. See pp. 4–8.
7. In recent years Neusner has emphasized the need to consider the statement of the final document. For a concise statement of this view, see his "Talmudic History, Retrospect and Prospect," intro. to the Third Printing of *A History of the Jews in Babylonia*, 1, The Parthian Period (Brown Judaic Studies 62, Scholars Press Reprint, 1984), pp. xix–xxxvi, in particular, pp. xxix and xxxv.

In connection with rhetorical criticism and the Babylonian Talmud, it is worth noting Kennedy's remark in New Testament Interpretation:

> Redaction criticism might be viewed as a special form of rhetorical criticism which deals with the texts where the hand of the redactor, or editor, can be detected. It is concerned with the intent of that editor, and especially his theological intent, as revealed in his use of sources. (P. 4)

Though this statement is well suited for describing this activity as it might be applied to the Bavli, "redaction criticism" of the BT has not, to this point, asked these questions. Its primary concern, rather, has been merely the identification of the redactor's contribution and, to the extent possible, of his historical provenance. To underline the additional concerns I have in mind, I prefer to use the term "rhetorical criticism."

8. See *The Cambridge History of Iran*, ed. Eshan Yarshater, 3 (1) (Cambridge, 1983): 583.
9. For the early history of Greek rhetoric, as well as a description of its categories and conventions, see George Kennedy, *The Art of Persuasion in Greece* (Princeton, N.J., 1963), pp. 3–25. A more detailed and technical description of rhetoric according to prominent Greek authors is to be found in James J. Murphy's *Rhetoric in the Middle Ages* (Berkeley, 1974), pp. 3–42.
10. On the other hand, the argument for meaningful parallels can be made in the case of tannaitic texts. See Henry A. Fischel, *Rabbinic Literature and Greco-Roman Philosophy: A Study of Epicurea and Rhetorica in Early Midrashic Writings* (Leiden, 1973).
11. See Walter J. Ong, *Orality and Literacy* (London and New York, 1982), p. 9.
12. See Kennedy, *New Testament Interpretation*, p. 64.

13. Y. Gitay has made the case for applying the categories of classical rhetoric to the study of biblical prophecy; see *Prophecy and Persuasion: A Study of Isaiah 40–48* (Bonn, 1981), esp. pp. 34–49. Prophecy, however, is clearly oratorical. and is therefore more obviously appropriate for such an approach.
14. See Ong, *Orality and Literacy*, p. 119.
15. "Form Criticism and Beyond," p. 12.
16. *The New Rhetoric: A Treatise on Argumentation* (Notre Dame and London, 1969), p. 1.
17. Pp. 1 and 11.
18. *New Testament Interpretation*, pp. 97 and 158.
19. My translation, based upon the Vilna edition. Manuscript variants are mostly technical and do not affect the essence of the text to which my analysis is addressed.
20. R. Solomon Aderet records the following variants in his commentary:

> q1. You might have thought that... it is like two courts in one city.
> q2. You might have thought that... it is like one court in one city.

According to q1., the Gemara suggests that the objection was originally directed against Abbaye's interpretation of the *lo titgodedu* prohibition. According to q2., it was directed even against Rava's.

21. On this point, see Halivni, *Meqorot umesorot* (Tel Aviv, 1968), pp. 15–17. Halivni notes: "The ordering of these objections after the statements of Abbaye and Rava doesn't work well (p. 15)," and suggests that the person who originally raised these objections didn't know the opinions of Abbaye and Rava. Gilat reaches a similar conclusion; see "lo titgodedu," *Bar-Ilan Annual* 18–19 (1981): 83.
22. Given the larger rhetorical picture, I would venture that such questions are often far more important than they at first appear.
23. This phrase appears a total of 124 times in the Bavli, and only 8 times in the Yerushalmi.
24. See below, n. 37.
25. With respect to the offering of sacrifices, Rashi argues that "presumptively there is teshuva, for if he was not repenting he would not bring a sacrifice." Rashi is too influenced by rabbinic assumptions, perhaps, to admit that the sacrificial ritual can be performed with total disregard for its meaning, yet the Torah can admit the efficacy of such a sacrifice.
26. Supporting this interpretation, see E. E. Urbach, *The Sages: Their Concepts and Beliefs*, trans. Israel Abrahams (Jerusalem, 1979), p. 465.
27. Certainly the authors of the Gemara heard the Mishnah this way, as will become apparent in our analysis of their rhetoric. In connection with the Mishnah and its response to the disappearance of sacrifice, see Baruch M. Bokser, *The Origins of the Seder* (Berkeley, 1984), pp. 2–3 and 89–94. For an excellent review of rabbinic responses to the destruction of the Temple in general, see Bokser's "Rabbinic Responses to Catastrophe: From Continuity to Discontinuity," *PAAJR* 50 (1983): 37–61. Bokser includes extensive references to related literature.
28. This interpretation is supported by the structure of the Mishnah. While it might be argued that teshuva is required in combination with death and the Day of Atonement, it is still secondary in each of those instances. By itself teshuva is clearly the least effective of the methods described in the Mishnah.
29. Manuscripts include here:

> Come and hear [another objection]: "What are major [transgressions, for which teshuva does not atone? Transgressions that are punishable by] divine excommunication and capital crimes, and 'Thou shalt not take...' is included with them (suggesting, however, that other negative precepts are not)."

nn. [What is meant is] "Thou shalt not take..." and anything that is like it.

nnn. Come and hear [another objection]:

Vilna seems to have eliminated these steps through homeoteleuton. See *Diqduqei Soferim*, ad. loc., and note 60 there.

30. See footnote 28. The Gemara's present interpretation reveals that, at least in its eyes, the Mishnah's structural devaluation of teshuva is convincing.

31. That is, transgressions whose immediate and specific amelioration is commanded in the Torah itself. For example, the Torah requires that if one has robbed his neighbor (Lev. 19:13) then "he shall make restitution (Lev. 5:23)." See b. Hullin 141a.

32. Or three; see above, n. 29.

33. Or "R. Natan"; see *Diqduqei Soferim*, ad. loc

34. MS Munich includes at this point: "Resh Laqish said: Great is teshuva, for it hastens salvation..." See *Diqduqei Soferim*.

35. MS Munich does not mark this tradition to be a baraita, and records it in the name of Rabbi (Judah the Prince). There are also a variety of other versions; see *Diqduqei Soferim*, note 6.

36. Cf. Arakhin 15a–b for a similar rhetorical construction. There, only after a lengthy excursus on the gravity of *leshon hara* (the "evil tongue") does the Gemara ask how it might be defined.

37. A word is in order on the limits of this rhetorical unit as I have understood them. One might naturally assume that the first section of this text—the technical exposition of the Mishnah—and the latter section—including extensive aggadah on teshuva—should be considered distinct units. The forms of the respective sections would certainly support such an alternative. But allowing form to dictate, and ignoring content, would be extremely shortsighted in this case. The problem defined in the Mishnah is the apparent lack of effectiveness of teshuva. The Gemara's commentary, utilizing various forms, addresses this problem at length. My definition of the rhetorical unit, therefore, has been directed by this problem and its solution, and not by the forms as such.

38. Goodblatt, "The Babylonian Talmud," reviews the sources of the Babylonian Talmud and recent scholarship relating to these sources; see pp. 148–60 (285–97). The conventions for identifying these sources have generally been thought to be late— perhaps Saboraic—but Richard Kalmin has recently called this assessment into question, at least with respect to amoraic quotations; see "Quotation Forms in the Babylonian Talmud: Authentically Amoraic or a Later Editorial Construct?," *HUCA* 59 (1988): 167–87. Even without the technical formulae, the sources are generally perfectly evident; see Goodblatt, p. 148 (285).

39. Neusner, in *Judaism in Society: The Evidence of the Yerushalmi* (Chicago, 1983), comments that "if... we knew that there was a characteristic mode of formulating ideas... we should have a solid, because superficial, criterion for sorting out valid from invalid attributions." I have found that precisely this sort of external stylistic criteria characterizes the traditions of individual generations of Amoraim in the Bavli. For a review of these characteristics see D. Kraemer, "The Origins of the Sugya as a Literary Unit," *Proceedings of the Ninth World Congress of Jewish Studies*, division C, 3 (1986): 25–28. A fuller exposition may be found in my Ph.D. dissertation, *Stylistic Characteristics of Amoraic Literature* (Jewish Theological Seminary, 1984) and *The Mind of the Talmud*, chapter 2.

40. My profound appreciation is due to Baruch Bokser, Richard Kalmin, Ruth Fagen and, in particular, to the editors of *Prooftexts*, for their kind suggestions in writing this paper. I also wish to thank Dvora Shurman for her painstaking editorial suggestions.

Part IV

Applied Scholarship

INTRODUCTION

In the following section, "Applied Scholarship," I collect many of my popular pieces. Like many scholars, in the course of my studies, I am often struck by the "relevance" of scholarly insights for Jews who are not interested in academic scholarship as such. I have consciously chosen *not* to restrict myself to arcane scholarly research, and, as a result, I frequently happen upon discoveries that I want to share beyond the company of scholars. Most often, I communicate these discoveries in lectures and classes for the general public and, indeed, I have (as yet) not written a book for the same audience. But I have taken upon myself the responsibility to write brief pieces for non-academic audiences, many of which are included below.

There is no single thread that unites these essays. They are presented in chronological order for lack of a better organizing principle. In these pieces, the reader will see reflected my various non-academic interests over the course of the last fifteen or so years.

Introduction to Chapter Sixteen

This, my earliest piece, exhibits a common concern of scholars of Judaism at the Jewish Theological Seminary and elsewhere, that is, the development of halakha. This is, in truth, a methodologically primitive piece. The reader will see that I here accepted the attributions offered in rabbinic texts to establish my chronology; I had not yet learned that there was an alternative. Moreover, the work is entirely "internal," examining the development of Jewish tradition from the perspective of "insiders," with barely a nod to the wider contexts in which these perspectives were expressed. Still, the general direction of development described in this essay, from the Torah to early rabbinic to Talmudic and thence to medieval, is accurate. This remains one of the most interesting topics in the development of halakha, one which, despite many treatments, calls for even more studies.

After offering a detailed analysis of the internal development of the laws of Niddah, this article leaves the reader with a question: Why did the laws pertaining to the menstrual impurity of women become more and more stringent over the centuries? Reference to the blood tabu would seem to offer no key; there is no reason to believe that the tabu was any stronger in the rabbinic period than in the earlier biblical period. In the essay as originally published, I am able to venture not even a reasonable guess concerning the cause of the development of the law.

In retrospect, it is clear to me that the reason for my earlier failure was my absolute reliance on the categories and definitions of the internal rabbinic tradition. I naively thought that I would solve this dilemma if I could discover a source for the "eleven days between one Niddah and the next," a rabbinically defined institution which the rabbis see as the cause of greater stringency in the observance of female impurity. I hoped that a parallel might be found in Zoroastrianism (the religion of the Babylonian world in which the Talmud came to expression) or elsewhere, but, in the absence of such a discovery, I threw up my hands. What I should have done, I now realize, is go outside of the rabbinic system entirely—to disbelieve the rabbinic explanation and seek other factors that might have influenced such a development.

It now seems to me that, ironically, the key to understanding the law's development resides in the teaching, attributed to R. Zeira at Niddah 66a, which reports that "the daughters of Israel were stringent with themselves [requiring] that even if they should see only a drop of blood the size of a mustard seed, they would wait seven clean days [before immersing]." When

I first considered this tradition, I assumed it was a fabrication of the most outrageous sort. "Of course," I said, "the rabbis invented this to justify their adding stringencies to the laws that control a woman's cycle." By claiming that "the women did it," they hoped the stringencies would be more readily accepted—or so I judged at that time. But I have come to believe that R. Zeira's report is "accurate," in the sense that it was actually the women who directed the law in the direction of greater stringency. Why so?

Thomas Laqueur, in *Making Sex* (Cambridge and London: Harvard U. Press, 1990), documents the fact that, until recent times, common belief held that women were most fertile at the ends of their periods, as close as possible to the cessation of their bleeding (p. 212). By contrast, "standard medical-advice textbooks recommended that to avoid conception women should have intercourse during the middle of their menstrual cycles, during days twelve through sixteen" (p. 9). If the original Niddah restrictions were to be observed, a couple would have their first post-separation relations at the end of the woman's bleeding, precisely the point—according to this belief—that pregnancy was most likely to result. Now, it is widely recognized that "birth-control" is in the interests of women and primarily motivated by them. Pregnancy can be exhausting in its own right, and child-birth was, in the pre-modern world, dangerous and often life-threatening. Given these realities, *of course* women would be interested in limiting pregnancies. Against this background, we may readily understand the stringency reported by R. Zeira (extending the period of separation and permitting sexual relations only after the period of highest fertility had—again, in their understanding—passed) as an act of birth-control. This explains why it was *the women* who insisted upon this stringency. Indeed, it is reasonable to believe that it was they who forced the development of the law in the direction I have described.

Of course, I can't actually prove that this is the historical explanation of the development in the law. But it is better than any other I have found. I invite the reader to "insert" this possibility into this essay's final section and perhaps speculate upon alternatives.

I have made only one change in the original piece. Unfortunately, I was not given the galley proofs of the first printing to check for accuracy and, as a result, the article was printed in *Conservative Judaism* with an unfortunate and misleading error. Evidently, the editor, knowing later practice and therefore misunderstanding the Torah's law, imagined that I was wrong when I described the Torah's law as requiring a counting of seven days from the beginning of bleeding and not from its end. He or she therefore "corrected" my manuscript to conform with the later halakha. This caused a confusing contradiction in the printed piece, one which set many readers astray. I have corrected that error in the version that appears below.

Chapter Sixteen

A Developmental Perspective on the Laws of Niddah

Jewish law has thrived through history as a consequence of interpretation and development. Because of its flexibility, the law was not restricted to the specific concerns of the Torah, and even laws of great difficulty or obscurity could be adapted to the dictates of an ever-changing reality. Among the most outstanding examples of radical development is the institution of *niddah*—the ritual impurity of women during their menstrual flows. But unlike the vast majority of cases of halakhic development, the modern law of niddah stands in blatant contradiction to the spirit of the original Torah text. For this reason it is particularly interesting as a case study in development. A review of its evolution, beginning with the Torah and progressing through the Rabbinic period, follows below.

Niddah in the Torah

The Torah clearly delineates the rules by which a woman or man becomes ritually impure by virtue of a "flow," and how that condition is to be reversed.

> When any man has a running issue out of his flesh, because of his issue he is unclean (Lev. 15:2).

> And when he that has an issue is cleansed of his issue then he shall number to himself seven days for his cleansing... (Lev. 15:13)

> And if semen goes out from a man, then he shall bathe all his flesh in water, and be unclean until evening. (Lev. 15:16)

> And when a woman has an issue, and in her flesh be blood, she shall be seven days

in her menstrual separation... (Lev. 15:19)

And if a woman has an issue of her blood many days not in the time of her menstruation, or if it run beyond the time of her menstruation, all the days of the issue of her uncleanness shall be as the days of her menstruation: she shall be unclean... (Lev. 15:25)

But if she be cleansed of her issue, then shall she number to herself seven days, and after that she shall be clean. (Lev. 15:28)

A man or a woman who experiences an unnatural flow becomes unclean. For a man no minimum requirement is described; any "running issue" seems to be sufficient to impart purity. If such a genital flow has occurred the man must count seven clean days before he can perform the cleansing ritual. However, because a woman naturally experiences certain monthly flows, she must "have an issue of her blood *many days* not in the time of her menstruation" to reach the state of impurity for which she requires seven clean days. As a result of menstruation itself, though, a woman becomes unclean for only seven days *from her first flow*. For an unnatural issue the individual must bring a sacrifice at the end of the clean period; following menstruation no sacrifice is required.

Menstruation, the Torah recognizes, is a natural bodily function. For that reason the stringencies pertaining to unnatural flows do not apply. That menstruation is considered natural is evident from the structure of the text. The Torah's account of these laws uses the common chiastic structure (A-B-B-A, where A = unnatural flows and B = natural flows). Menstruation, here equated with seminal emission, is clearly the less severe of the potential flows which a woman might experience.

Rabbinic Expansion

(Sources for what follows, where not otherwise indicated, can be found in Maimonides, *Issurei Biah*, chapters 6 and 11, and in his respective sources.)

According to the midrash halakhah, as repeated variously in the gemara *Niddah* (especially the last two pages), a woman who begins to menstruate is impure for seven days regardless of the actual duration of her flow (cf. Lev. 15:19). If her period lasts three days, she is unclean seven. Following that period she may immerse immediately, without waiting seven clean days. If her period lasts longer than seven days she must count one clean day for each that has exceeded the seven. If her blood flow continues for "many days" (Lev. 15:25), that is—according to the Rabbis—three days not during the time of her period, then she becomes unclean to a greater degree. A man's uncleanness is dependent upon "sightings," a woman's upon the counting of these three days.

Therefore, if a man witnesses two flows in a single day (three to require a sacrifice) he becomes severely impure. A woman, on the other hand, may witness dozens of flows in a single day and still not acquire the state of severe impurity until she witnesses an issue for three consecutive days. Only after this has occurred is she required to count seven clean days prior to immersion.

Of course, these conditions do not describe practice today. The cause of the present stringencies is a matter of dispute in interpretation. It is impossible to understand the development of the law, however, without examining this dispute in some detail.

"The eleven days between one period And the next"

The Torah recognized a seven-day duration for a woman's menstruation. Regarding the lapse between one menstrual period and the next it says nothing, aware, apparently, that a woman's menstrual cycle is quite individual. The Rabbis, however, possess a tradition which suggests that there are *eleven days between one menstruation and the next*. Maimonides reads this phrase literally and suggests that a complete cycle is eighteen days (!) by definition. The Rabbis, of course, could not have conceived of this cycle in so literal a manner. They were, after all, married to women whose monthly periods recurred, on the average, approximately every twenty-eight days. Rabbinic sources, too, reflect a familiarity with the realistic norm. At Niddah 9b R. Laqish reports in the name of R. Judah Nesiah that an average cycle lasts thirty days. Rashi there explains the cycle in this manner: "The days of impurity are ten—seven for menstruation and three for 'unnatural flow,' and twenty days of purity." While his explanation is admittedly problematic, he clearly recognizes that, on the average, the days of purity (i.e. between periods) are twenty and not eleven. Even Maimonides recognizes that eleven days is not the norm, suggesting in his commentary to the Mishnah (to Niddah 38b) that eleven days is the very shortest time that might normally pass between one menstruation and the next. Yet, according to Maimonides, the eighteen-day "rabbinic cycle" became determinant for purposes of the laws of Niddah, and as a consequence of this institution, and the so-called "confusion" which it engendered (see below), practice moved unavoidably in the direction of stringency.

The gemara (Niddah 72b) reports in the name of R. Elazar ben Azariah that the "eleven days between one period and the next is a law (halakhah) to Moses from Sinai." This supposed origin is challenged, however, on the basis of a quotation from the Sifra which derives this eleven day period in typical midrashic fashion. To resolve the apparent conflict, the gemara concludes that "to R. Akiba it is scriptural, to R. Elazar ben Azariah it is halakhah."

Leaving aside for a moment the problem of the source of these eleven days, it is essential to recognize their effect according to Maimonides' interpretation. A woman's cycle, he explains, must be counted in the following fashion. From the very first time she sees blood she must count seven days of her cycle, followed by eleven days during which an issue brings severe uncleanness, followed by another seven days followed by eleven, and so forth. This counting regards her natural cycle as absolutely irrelevant! Assume a woman had a twenty-eight day cycle (an approximate norm). Her first seven day period would initiate her cycle. By the time her next period began, however—twenty-one days after the end of her first—another eleven and then seven days would have passed in her Jewish cycle, and her natural menstruation would then occur during what the Rabbis considered a non-menstrual time, rendering her severely impure and requiring seven clean days before her immersion. Despite the extreme difficulty and confusion which this cycle would impose, Maimonides claims that at one time Jewish women counted these cycles very carefully, and acted appropriately depending upon the correspondence of their own periods to this cycle. Problems were bound to develop, of course, and in order to be "safe" Rav relates that Rabbi Judah the Prince (end of second century C.E.) instituted certain stringencies which would help prevent mistakes (Niddah 66a and Rashi there). Finally, Rabbi Zeira (third generation Palestinian Amora, end of third century) reports that the daughters of Israel themselves were so concerned about this matter that even were they to see only a drop of blood the size of a mustard seed they would wait seven clean days before immersing—an unnecessary stringency by any definition. Still, this stringency came to be accepted as common practice, and today, therefore, a woman must wait seven clean days following her period regardless of when it occurs. The source of this practice, according to Maimonides, may be found ultimately in the artificial eighteen-day cycle. Had this eleven day period never been suggested then the law concerning menstruation would, as we have seen, maintain a condition of leniency for women.

Two sources of confusion ...

Nachmanides, among others, has a very different understanding of the "eleven days ...," leading to another justification for the stringencies described at Niddah 66a. According to Nachmanides (Laws of Niddah, ch. 1), the phrase "Eleven days between one Niddah and the next" must not be read literally as proposed by Maimonides. For Nachmanides, rather, the eleven days are a time during which a blood flow is considered as unnatural, but following which a blood flow is considered natural (that is: Niddah). According to this approach, after a woman's period, she must count eleven days. If she experiences an extended flow during this time, she becomes a *zavah* (one who has had an unnatural flow). But after that time, any flow is considered natural. A new Niddah period begins whenever, after the eleven days, new blood is sighted, whether on the twelfth day (the nineteenth day of her monthly cycle) or the twentieth (the twenty-seventh day of her monthly cycle). The result of this interpretation is, at least in theory, a leniency, and in this sense Nachmanides stands in sharp contrast to Maimonides.

Since only unnatural blood leads to the more severe degree of impurity, it is "better" to restrict, as much as possible, the possibility of considering a flow unnatural. By saying that only blood sighted within eleven days from the completion of the last period can be considered unnatural, the tradition is declaring that any other blood must be viewed as natural—a clear leniency in the law. This means that if a woman ordinarily has a twenty-eight-day cycle, even if she begins to sight blood on the twentieth day—which for her would be quite unnatural—the law will define this blood as Niddah blood and require of her only the less stringent demands made of a Niddah.

If for Nachmanides the "eleven days" is intended to be a leniency, whence the stringent direction that the law followed? Nachmanides explains that the stringencies associated with Rabbi Judah HaNasi and Zeira can be attributed to two possible sources of confusion: one a matter of counting and the other a matter of distinguishing different kinds of flows.

The fear of error in counting is this: a woman might sight blood on day eleven of the "eleven days" and mistakenly think that it is the twelfth day, the day on which her Niddah begins. She will begin counting the seven days of her Niddah too early and will consequently think that her Niddah has ended before it is actually over. Alternatively, it is possible that a woman counting the seven clean days required of her when she has become a *zavah* (having first seen unnatural blood for three consecutive days) will see some flow on the seventh day and mistakenly suppose that it is the eighth day. Since any sighting during the "seven clean days" necessitates that the counting begin anew, she will assume that she has just begun a new niddah, whereas in fact she remains a *zavah*. Obviously, if it is possible to confuse a *zavah* and a niddah, clean days must be required even of a niddah.

The fear of error in distinguishing flows is connected to the fact that not all kinds of blood or other secretions are considered impure (see Mishnah Niddah 2:6). Presumably, this is also intended to provide a leniency in the law. If all blood flows or secretions were considered impure, then many women would constantly be in a state of impurity, since many women experience different kinds of staining throughout their cycles. Restricting that which can be considered impure would protect women from this intolerable consequence. But, in fact, the result of this "leniency" is quite the opposite. The problem is this: because we no longer have "experts" who can distinguish between pure and impure blood, a woman might sight blood for seven consecutive days and think that they are all to be counted as days of her Niddah. After this, of course, she will consider herself pure. But what if the blood during the first six days was in fact "pure" blood, so that her Niddah actually only began on what she thought was day seven? Niddah would continue for seven days from what she thought was day seven, and as a result she would consider herself pure during what are actually the days of her niddah. Obviously, this is a situation that the Rabbis thought it proper to avoid.

Nachmanides' interpretation avoids the discord between nature and tradition that is established by Maimonides. But the consequence is the need to attribute later stringencies to a variety of largely obscure fears. For Maimonides the source of these stringencies is obvious and necessary; for Nachmanides it requires defining the legal norm by cases that are presumably abnormal.

The Spirit of the Law

The effect of the laws as currently constituted is this: a man and wife may not enjoy sexual relations for fully one-half of the month, that is, for half of their married life. Alternative sources exhibit a contradictory spirit, however—one which values sexuality and which would likely not tolerate the Niddah law as presently defined.

The Mishnah in Ketuboth suggests the proper frequency of sexual relations, taking into account the requirements of different occupations (5:6). According to its provisions, absence of sexual intimacy for fourteen days would be acceptable only for a husband who travels out of town. Otherwise it would be too long. When offering an explanation for the seven days of niddah (Niddah 31b) R. Meir says that abstention for a period of this duration will cause a woman, when she rejoins her husband in sexual relations, to be beloved to him as the day of their wedding. The same reason would, I suspect, be untenable if the period were extended to fourteen days. Finally, in a dispute (Ketuboth 5:6) concerning the length of time a husband who has sworn not to have sexual intercourse with his wife may remain married before he must give her a divorce, the School of Shammai describe a 14-day maximum, while the School of Hillel allows for a maximum period of abstention of only seven days (the length of her state of niddah). The longer duration would, according to Hillel, be offensive to the institution of marriage, and is therefore unacceptable. To express it otherwise, the School of Hillel could not permit the present practice of waiting fourteen days.

Searching for a Source

If, in light of the spirit described above, we consider the present situation to be untenable, we must consider what responses are available to each of the primary interpretations. For Maimonides, it is the eighteen-day cycle that creates our problems. How are we to understand its origin and authority?

The Sifra (midrash halakhah to Leviticus), which is quoted in the gemara, derived the eleven days through midrash (it does not discuss the alternative tradition that it is "halakhah to Moses from Sinai"). Yet, despite the midrash, Rashi recognizes that eleven days is not the simple meaning of the text, as reflected in his comment to Lev. 15, vs. 25. There he first describes the differ-ence between a menstruant and one who has had an unnatural issue as the Torah understood it, and only then continues by stating "and they expounded in this section the eleven days between the end of one period to the beginning of another period." This structural bifurcation reflects his opinion that the latter is not inherent in the text. We have seen, moreover, that for Maimonides the effect of the eleven days is in fact contradictory to the original intent of the text. These factors must lead us to question the origin of the midrash; it is surely not the Torah text itself that requires these conclusions. Rather, the midrash is most likely a "corroborating midrash" (according to the categories suggested by M. Elon in *HaMishpat HaIvri*)—one which seeks to justify through scripture a pre-existing law. If so, the alternative tradition, reported in the name of Rabbi Elazar ben Azariah. which describes the "eleven days" as "halakhah to Moses from Sinai" must be considered seriously. This proposed origin is also, however, not without its problems.

In order for a particular law to be considered *halakhah le-Moshe mi-Sinai*, Maimonides contends, it must not be derivable from scripture either by logic or by way of other midrashic devices (see his Introduction to the Mishnah). If this is true, then the eleven days cannot be *halakhah le-Moshe mi-Sinai* because, as the Sifra demonstrates, it *can* be based on a source in the Torah. Even if we do not accept Maimonides' definition (or if we think that the dispute is precisely whether the "eleven days" can be derived or not), the institution of "halakhah to Moses from Sinai" retains its inherent difficulties. A case in Mishnah Yadaim (4:3), for example, reflects that a law which is labeled "halakhah" is in fact a rabbinic injunction. Elsewhere (Shabbat 11a) a law which is accounted by R. Elazar as "halakhah" is praised by R. Ishmael in the statement "Great are the words of the sages." Aware of these and similar cases R. Asher suggests that the phrase "halakhah to Moses from Sinai" often refers to a law which is as clear *as though* it had been given to Moses at Sinai (Laws of Mikvah 1). Even the midrash (Menachot 29b) recognizes that Moses did not in fact receive the laws which possess this appellation, but nonetheless they are to be respected because they lend strength to the tradition. "Laws to Moses from Sinai" are typically either ancient traditions which have no basis in scripture (black, squared tefillin), or laws, sometimes rabbinic in origin, which might be difficult to accept without the authority of Moses' name (tithing in Ammon and Moab). The eleven-day period, it would appear, falls into this latter category.

But again, if not midrashic in origin, whence the 11/18 days? Maimonides, we noted, suggests that eleven days is the very shortest time which might pass between one menstruation and the next. Regardless of the biological accuracy of this proposal (*Our Bodies, Ourselves*, by the Boston Women's Health Book Collective, remarks [p. 18] that a normal cycle might range between 20–36 days) it is nonetheless valuable because it retains a "rational" origin for the Rabbinic cycle. Yet considering the Torah's appreciation of menstruation as a natural event, it is perplexing that the law should ultimately be defined by the abnormal extreme of the normal. If, on the other hand, Nachmanides' interpretation is more likely, then response to its effects must be more a matter of judgment, not an analysis of legal systems and institutions. The fear for counting is, in the context of this interpretation, an ironic one. The beauty of Nachmanides' system in the first place is that it is so much more in accord with natural cycles—cycles which, presumably, a woman would have far less trouble counting. In this system, a woman would ordinarily have to count the seven days of her Niddah, followed by eleven until she again sighted blood, generally at the beginning of her next period. She would rarely sight blood during her "eleven days"—unlike the Maimonides' system where her period would by definition frequently fall within her "eleven days"—and so both of the situations of confusion described above would be very unlikely events. This is not to say that they would never occur, but halakha has never been intolerant of errors of this sort, and it certainly does not define itself in anticipation that they might occur. Quite the contrary, from the Torah forward provision has always been made for atoning for just this kind of error. Why should the realm of sexual purity be different?

The matter of being unable to distinguish pure blood from impure blood is more difficult. Here we must be left, again, only to notice the irony. The fear that Nachmanides expresses is that pure blood might mistakenly be considered impure. The result of this mistaken "stringency" would be a tragic "leniency," in that her Niddah should actually begin later than she began counting it. But the point of defining some secretions as being pure was to lend leniency to a condition that might otherwise be intolerable for some women. Has this grant to some women led to an intolerable situation for all women? Would it not be better, in fact, to allow for the possibility that a rare mistake might be made rather than penalizing all women because of this fear? As we have noted, the law is amply prepared to handle such errors.

The study of niddah is incomplete while the mystery of the origin of the "eleven days" and its related consequences remains unsolved. It represents, nonetheless, a striking example of halakhic development which has been significantly influenced by popular fears (the blood tabu—remember Rabbi Zeira's report of the "daughters of Israel"). Cultural anthropologists have confirmed the power of this fear in many a "primitive" society—a power which persisted and prevailed in Jewish society despite the contradictory instruction of Torah. Perhaps, having been released from these tabus by the enlightening influence of modern science, we might finally permit the tolerant preference of the Torah (which requires no clean days following menstruation) to gain ascendance.

INTRODUCTION TO CHAPTER SEVENTEEN

This essay is, in effect, an extended apologia on behalf of the religiously meaningful qualities of academic study of rabbinic texts (in this case, the Bavli). In this respect, it is of a piece with much of Halivni's writing in English (see, in particular, *Peshat and Derash*, pp. 103–4). This should occasion no surprise, of course, since at this stage in my career, I was very much under the influence of Halivni and his scholarship. My purpose, in this essay, is to say, "Look! This method of study does matter for something! There are religious messages and meanings to be found in these texts that can be uncovered only through the methods of modern scholarship and no other way."

To make my case, I explicate two pieces of contemporary textual scholarship—one of Shamma Friedman and one of David Halivni—and show how their work, when subjected to a certain kind of questioning, can teach crucial and unexpected lessons. The lesson I learn from Friedman's analysis—a lesson I have documented at length elsewhere—is that the authors of the Talmud saw fit to equate the Torah of the rabbis with the Written Torah of God. From Halivni's analysis, I learn some of the consequences of the diaspora condition upon the religious assumptions and mind-set of the Babylonian rabbis. Both of these lessons are my own extension of each scholar's groundbreaking work, intended to illustrate the kinds of questions and interpretations that are fruitfully addressed to this sort of scholarship.

The second lesson, relating to the Babylonian rabbis' views concerning sacred territory and space, is an undeveloped topic of inquiry. In this, the 1998-99 academic year, I taught a course at the Jewish Theological Seminary entitled "Rabbinic Constructions of Space." In this course we studied and interpreted the rabbis' constructions of space in tractates Eruvin, Sukkah, Ohalot and Middot, along with briefer passages elsewhere. While engaging in this study, I returned with my students to the second example explicated below. I was encouraged by my earlier interpretation, and energized by the realization that the question of space—religiously significant as it is—has yet to receive a proper treatment in contemporary rabbinics scholarship. It is my intent to devote a book-length study to this topic in the near future.

Chapter Seventeen

The Scientific Study of Talmud

Study has long been a central act of religious expression and inspiration in Judaism. The Yeshiva, with its combination of piety and intellectual inquiry, has been the primary venue for pursuit of the word of God. In the company of the God-fearing, a (male) Jew could pass his days in a combination of prayer and Talmud Torah, and come—if the spirit moved him—tantalizingly close to recovering the experience of the revelation at Sinai. Though the demands were great, the reward was assured, and access could be found by any (male) Jew who was willing to assume the task. And, of course, the Yeshiva and its methods of study still beckon, as the growth of the *ba'al teshuva* Yeshiva testifies. The heart of the Jew—even the secular Jew—understands that this is the place where Judaism still "happens," and though it might be mysterious, its mystery is not so great as to be forbidding. To the contrary, the mystery of the Yeshiva is a source of its beauty and its strength.

In contrast, "modern" scientific study of religious texts has generally been thought to offer esoteric entertainment for the scholarly few, but precious little of true meaning for those who are not involved in scholarship. What is worse—or so the common wisdom goes—this peculiar form of study not only fails to communicate religious inspiration (which, in any case, is not its intent), but often serves to destroy it instead. Why, according to this same wisdom, is this the case? Because the methods of scientific study are cold and exacting, its practitioners are dispassionate and uninspired, and the community that it serves is exclusive and self-selecting. As a result of this not entirely unfounded reputation, those institutions that espouse this method of study have failed, to a great extent, to win the commitment of their students to Talmud Torah as a life's endeavor. In turn, the alienation of these students from text has meant that non-Orthodox Jews in general—for whom these students will be teachers—have no serious relationship with the varied texts of our tradition.

But the failure is not in the concerns of these methods of study themselves, nor even with those who practice them. Instead, there is somewhere a failure to communicate—a failure to communicate that the choice to devote one's life to the study of a text, by whatever method, is a religious choice (why else would someone be crazy enough to give his/her life to something?), and a failure to illustrate the meaning that is imparted by scientific study, and which can be discovered in no other way. Those who employ these methods have taken for granted that by studying how our ancestors expressed their religious sentiments in their own contexts, we, in our context, would be similarly inspired. But we cannot make such assumptions; the point must be illustrated.

Let us take, as an example, the Babylonian Talmud—that text to which most of the time and energy in the Yeshiva is devoted. The Talmud has traditionally been understood to be the close—if not literal—record of the deliberations of the Babylonian (Persian) Rabbinic academies between the third and fifth centuries. The primary concern of these academies was the determination of the halakhah (law) through interpretation of the precepts described in the Mishnah (Palestine, c. 200 C.E.). Needless to say, this is no longer the view of modern scholarship.

The first question raised by modern study is whether there were academies in the proper sense at all.[1] True, such academies were described in Rabbinic histories written in a later period (the "Geonic," from the Muslim conquest until the 11th century),[2] but these descriptions may be anachronistic retrojections from the Geonic experience. The Talmud itself seems to support a picture of scholarly circles that centered around certain respected teachers who were, however, not located in established institutions.[3]

The second problem is the question of "record." Sensitivity to the composition of the text has demonstrated that the Talmud is a finely conceived literary document that employs many of the conventions of its literary genre. Legal traditions generally assume a literary form that was dictated by the Mishnah,[4] and the uniformity of style of these traditions suggests that they cannot be literal records of original expressions.[5] In addition, the larger composition of the text demonstrates a commitment to tripartite structuring, affinity for rhetorical questions, the borrowing of traditions from one context to another, and a willingness to create artificial argumentation.[6] This being the case, it is of course impossible to speak of a literal (or even semi-literal) record.[7]

More crucially, a major part of the Talmud is a non-attributed deliberation which, though traditionally assumed to be the contemporary discussion in the academy, has now been shown to be the interpretive work of later authors who were separated from the traditions upon which they comment by as many as 300 years or more.[8] The agenda of these authors was, in part, to recover and preserve the traditions of their predecessors. But their innovation was far more significant than their conservation, and the period of their creative activity can now be spoken of as an independent era in the formation of the Talmud.

This picture, of course, greatly influences our understanding of the Talmudic text and its messages. Through attention to its chronological and literary development we are able to discover not only the development of many Jewish rituals and observances, but also the development of the Jewish psyche and Jewish ethical heart. A couple of examples should suffice to demonstrate this approach.

But before considering examples, a word of caution. Because of the elaborate nature of Talmudic discourse, discoveries of the sort described above require painstaking analysis—analysis that will be difficult to recreate in the space of this article. Nevertheless, illustration of the method is crucial, and the reader's patience will be necessary before we can realize the fruit of such an effort. The insights we have promised can become available in this way alone.

In his study of the tenth chapter of tractate Yevamot, Shamma Friedman[9] shows that the law of the Mishnah is changed, through a variety of methods, by later sages who considered its law to be unjust. The first Mishnah of that chapter describes a case in which a woman's husband traveled abroad, and witnesses came and reported that he had died. If she went ahead and remarried with permission, and her first husband then showed up, she must be divorced from both men, she may collect support from neither, and a great many other penalties follow. If, on the other hand, she married *without* permission, she may return to the first husband and none of the negative consequences are incurred. The reason for this difference is a simple legal one—marrying with permission is equated with performing the prohibited act (in this case, the second marriage) with intent, while marrying without permission is like performing the act mistakenly. Intended acts incur liability, unintended acts may not.

Of course, despite the legal justification, the law that derives from the theory is patently unfair. If the woman takes the trouble to marry with legal permission, she is punished, but if she has remarried without taking that trouble, she is unaffected. Both the named sages of the Gemara (the Amoraim) and the later anonymous sages responded to this injustice by trying to change the law. The ways in which they did so, Friedman points out, are significantly different, and that difference is meaningful.

Amongst the Amoraim, Rav changes the law by declaring that the law of the first part of the Mishnah ("with permission") is limited to a case where the initial report of his death had been by the account of only one witness, but if two witnesses have given the testimony, then she may stay married to the second husband. Samuel suggests that the law applies only where she does not deny that this returning man is her first husband, but if she claims that he is not her first husband (regardless of testimony), then her denial is confirmed. In both cases the law of the Mishnah is not denied outright, but it is restricted through limiting interpretation. The law of the Mishnah is, on its face, respected. The claim is made, however, that its intent is a limited one. In this way, both Rav and Samuel succeed in rendering the inequity of the Mishnah less onerous.

The anonymous author of the gemara takes a radically different approach. He suggests that when the Mishnah speaks of remarrying "without permission," it means that two witnesses (proper testimony) have come and, therefore, no permission of the court is required. For this reason, when the first husband reappears, she incurs no penalty. If she married "with permission," on the other hand, it was because there was only one witness (inadequate testimony), and permission of the court *was* necessary before she could remarry. Nevertheless, this permission came with a hitch—since the testimony was invalid, she was marrying at her own risk. If her first husband showed up again, she would be penalized in the ways that the Mishnah describes.

This approach, too, responds to the inequity of the Mishnah, and actually succeeds in eliminating it. But it does so by turning the Mishnah on its head. Now "permission" means "conditional permission because full legal permission (proper testimony) could not be obtained," while "without permission" means "without permission of the court because proper legal permission through genuine testimony was available." The law is now just, but the plain meaning of the Mishnah is completely violated. What is the meaning of this approach, as compared to that of Rav and Samuel?[10]

Rav and Samuel, and the Amoraim in general, approached the Mishnah with extraordinary reverence. Being the record of the oral Torah, the Mishnah was hallowed to an extent second only to written Torah itself. When responding to it, therefore, much like responding to Torah, reverence required (as much as possible) conservative interpretation; interpretation that respected the simple meaning of the text. This is not to say that radical interpretation could not be employed; it was (both for Scripture and Mishnah). But where there was an alternative, it was preferred.

For the anonymous Gemara, however, other considerations were equally crucial, and radical interpretation was, therefore, an everyday event. This is not to say that Mishnah was any less holy. But the relationship of these later sages with the holy was far more liberal. In this case, because of the ethical problems valued by the law of the Mishnah, the ethical element of the holy was permitted to take precedence. As a consequence, the letter of the holy text became a secondary concern.

Regarding the comment of Samuel (see above), Friedman suggests one further analysis that is worth highlighting. In its deliberation of Samuel's opinion, the Gemara quotes two traditions that speak of "any place where *the Torah* believed one witness[11] (my emphasis)." But there are two major problems with the suggested parallel of these traditions to the case spoken of by Samuel: 1) it is not the Torah that believed a single witness here, but the Rabbis, who established this rule to assure that the woman would not be left unable to remarry; 2) the literal parallel suggested by the Gemara is so difficult that Rashi is forced to comment at great length, and is unable, in the end, to explain the text adequately. Friedman solves these difficulties by proposing that the problematic traditions are borrowed from elsewhere in the Gemara, where the texts are totally appropriate, and that the problem is caused because the editor here did not adapt the traditions to their new context. As far as it goes, this suggestion is extremely helpful; the source of the difficulty has been pinpointed.

But Friedman does not go on to consider the implications of this borrowing. Earlier, he had already shown another case of such borrowing, but in that instance the tradition was modified to meet the needs of its new context. Why was the same not done here? Why were traditions that originally commented on *the Torah's* intent when it (according to Rabbinic interpretation) permitted the testimony of a single witness (or even of a woman) not appropriately modified when they were used to illumine a case where it was the *Rabbis* who established the rule? If, in other instances, modifications were permitted, the absence of such modifications here, particularly when their absence creates such difficulties, must be deliberate. What, then, is the intent of the Gemara's author here?

We know well from elsewhere that the Rabbis laid claim to immense power for themselves, even when this assertion of power contradicted the law of the Torah.[12] Could it be that precisely this kind of assertion is intended here? The equation, surely, is between laws whose source is in the Torah and laws whose source is Rabbinic. By leaving the borrowed traditions without change, is the author of the Gemara claiming that on some level this equation can be taken literally? Such a claim would not be outrageous, but it also could not be taken for granted. By borrowing freely from the realm of the Torah to that of the Rabbis, the Gemara is reminding its readers that Rabbinic law, too, is "canonical." Both realms share a place in the law of a "living God."[13]

At the beginning of the Gemara in tractate Shabbat chapter 10 (96b), "carrying out [from one domain to another on Shabbat]" is described as a "principal category" of Shabbat work, whereas "carrying in" is termed a "subcategory." In his critical commentary to this text, David Halivni[14] points out that no named Amora, in the Babylonian or the Palestinian Talmud, can be demonstrated to have subscribed to this distinction. In fact, the only source that explicitly holds this view is the anonymous Gemara in the Babylonian Talmud. How is the distinction defended? Because, the Gemara explains, there is a scriptural source that is understood to speak of "carrying out" in connection with the work of building the Tabernacle, but no verse that speaks of "carrying in."

But this is a strange justification because, in general, work that was performed in the Tabernacle is considered to be a "principal category" of work prohibited on Shabbat regardless of whether it is actually mentioned in scripture. So why is carrying different, that it requires explicit scriptural mention as well? Because, Tosafot suggests, carrying is an "insignificant [act of] work," and it therefore requires more before it (or any of its various forms) can be considered a "principal category." The Amoraim, who failed to make this distinction, apparently felt that "carrying out" and "carrying in" were the identical act; "out" and "in" merely depends upon where you are standing. The anonymous Gemara, on the other hand, was bothered enough by the fact that carrying is so minor an act that it was led to require more of it than of other, more significant, categories of work.

Again, as was the case with the text examined by Friedman, the anonymous Gemara can be seen to have taken a new approach to the tradition. What is particularly interesting about this latter case is the fact that, as for many of us, it was difficult for the anonymous Gemara to conceive of "carrying" as work in the same fashion as "lighting fire" or "planting." But why was this the case?[15] The following suggestion might be made. For the Gemara, the "domains" that were relevant for the labor of "carrying" were one of the ways in which space could be defined.[16] (The other metaphors for space were Sukkah, which defined three-dimensional space and, in a similar way, *Ohalot*, the space that was rendered impure by a dead human body.[17]) The Palestinian texts, that is, the Mishnah and the Palestinian Talmud, never questioned the viability of this definition of space because, for them, holy space and its gradations were an everyday concern. The space of the Land of Israel was different from the space of "outside the land"; the space of Jerusalem was different from the space of the rest of the land; the space of the Temple was different from the space of the rest of Jerusalem; and so forth.[18] But the anonymous Gemara, the Talmudic text that was most separated, both in terms of distance and time, from the holy space of the Temple and the land, is no longer fully at ease with the definitions of space defined by the Tabernacle (or, so according to tradition). It is with regard to these definitions that we hear a quiet word of protest here, and it may be the experience of alienation from holy space (again, much like our own), that provoked this protest.

These are but two specific examples that illustrate a trend concerning which a great many general observations may be made. For example, by considering the chronological development of the text we see that, though in the earliest Amoraic generations halakhah was the almost exclusive concern of the Amoraic sages, in later generations interpretation for its own sake also became prevalent, and by the time we reach the non-attributed level of the text we find that halakhah often takes a back seat to theoretical speculation even when it might contradict the law. The best example of this phenomenon is also the most commonly known, that is, the Gemara's extensive attentions to the opinions of the School of Shammai despite the fact that these opinions had long before been rejected as irrelevant for purposes of halakhah.[19] The willingness to address these "irrelevant" opinions was so pronounced at this level of the Gemara that it was even willing to consider the possibility that the sages of the School of Shammai were "sharper" than those of the School of Hillel (Yevamot 14a). Halakhah notwithstanding, theoretical speculation in the law had acquired a status that was perhaps without competition.

How could study that intentionally ignored the halakhah be justified? Because—the theory goes—study of the word of God, even when not relevant for practical law, is always praiseworthy. In the words of David Halivni:

> To the [authors of the anonymous Gemara], theoretical learning was a main mode of worship, worth pursuing even if it does not lead to practical decision making... the rejected view [in terms of practical halakhah] was not false; it is no less justifiable than the view that is being accepted... religiously, even the rejected view was acceptable.[20]

It is study as a religious act that becomes crucial at this point; for this reason theoretical speculation had to be released from its practical moorings. Torah study was an act at least equivalent to prayer.[21] In contrast, practical application was often too mundane.

It is only the historical, developmental analysis of modern scholarship that has revealed for the first time this remarkable model of religious inspiration—one in which pursuit of the word of God, as recorded in Torah, is so central—so *pure*—that Torah study takes on a life of its own. And it is precisely this model that is so crucial for understanding modern "critical" study of the Talmud (or of other traditional Jewish texts[22]) as a religious act. For, in the end, both traditional learning and modern learning are devoted to discovering the meaning of the word of God. The difference lies in the methods and questions employed to discover that meaning, and the assumptions that inform the answers that might be suggested. In the traditional approach, though study is understood (very seriously so) to be a Mitzvah, still, the assumption is that the literature is generally concerned with the halakhah, and answers that do not serve this end are often deemed unacceptable.[23] The modern approach frees itself from this restriction, and finds support for doing so in the text of the Gemara itself. Study of this nature may also be the worship of God, and its pursuit is no less a devotion to discovering the divine plan than is traditional study. But modern study assumes that this discovery can only be understood by examining that divine plan as it unfolded in full partnership with human beings. In such partnerships, I would contend, we can find immense inspiration.

Notes

1. For the conclusions suggested here, see David Goodblatt, *Rabbinic Instruction in Sasanian Babylonia* (Leiden: Brill, 1975). The dissenting view can be found in I. Gafni, *The Jews of Babylonia in the Talmudic Era* (Hebrew)(Jerusalem: The Zalman Shazar Center for Jewish History, 1990), ch. 6.
2. See, e.g., *Iggeret Rav Sherira Gaon*.
3. This should not be taken to contradict the associations made in the Talmud between certain scholars and specific locations, such as Rav in Sura or Samuel in Nehardea. The point is that schools of study were dependent upon specific individuals, and did not survive independent of those personalities, as do colleges in our own day.
4. See D. Kraemer, *Stylistic Characteristics of Amoraic Literature*, Ph.D. dissertation, Jewish Theological Seminary of America, 1984, chapters 2–4.
5. See William Scott Green, "What is in a Name, The Problematic of Rabbinic 'Biography'" in *Approaches to Ancient Judaism*, v. 1., W.S. Green, ed. (Missoula, Montana: Scholars Press, 1978), pp. 80–84.
6. See Shamma Friedman, "'al derekh heker ha-sugya," in *perek ha-isha rabba b'bavli* (New York: J.T.S.A., 1978), pp. 40–42.
7. See the introduction of D. Halivni to *Meqorot u'mesorot, moed* (Yoma-Hagiga), (New York: J.T.S.A., 1975), pp. 8–10.
8. For a review of the relevant scholarship, see David Goodblatt, "The Babylonian Talmud," in *The Study of Ancient Judaism*, v. 11, (New York: KTAV, 1981), pp. 155, 160–164. Halivni terms the sages of this period *Stammaim* ("*stamma-d'gemara*" being the term used by medieval Rabbis to speak of the anonymous gemara text. "*Stam*," in this context, is translated "anonymous"). The other scholars referred to by Goodblatt generally identify these sages with the Saboraim, on the basis of their understanding of R. Sherira Gaon's description of the Saboraic enterprise.
9. See Friedman, op. cit., pp. 47–59.
10. The analysis up to this point is Friedman's. This question and the proposed answer are mine.
11. Such as here, where she may remarry on the basis of the testimony of one witness.
12. E.g., the second day of Festivals, despite the Torah's command "thou shalt not add thereto," and the fact that on these days men do not perform the mitzvah of tefillin, despite the Torah's obligation to do so.
13. The Rabbis' assertion of their power, even to this "radical" extent, was essential to the survival of Rabbinic Judaism. In Palestine, where the Rabbinic movement was born in the first and second centuries, there were many other groups of Jews who made similar claims to religious and political leadership. In Babylonia, Rabbinic Judaism imposed itself upon a Jewish community that already had an independent history of over 500 years. In neither case could the success, let alone the ascendency, of Rabbinic Judaism be taken for granted. Even at the time when the anonymous Gemara was composed (and later) the Rabbinic interpretation and implementation of scripture was subject to the attacks of frequent rivals and, so, defensive claims of the sort that we see here were always relevant. The fact that it is made less explicitly than such claims had been earlier may reflect the relative confidence of Rabbinic Judaism at this later stage of its ascent to power in the Jewish world as a whole.
14. *Mekorot u'mesorot, Shabbat*, pp. 267–272.
15. Again, this question and proposed answer are mine.
16. See e.g. Eruvin 92a–b.
17. See e.g. B.T. Sukkah 20b–21b.

18. See Mishnah Kelim 1:6.
19. See Halivni, *Midrash, Mishnah, and Gemara*, (Cambridge: Harvard U. Press, 1986), pp. 76–7.
20. Ibid., p. 77.
21. See Berakhot 5a, where prayer and Talmud Torah are equated as the two acts which connect a Jew most intimately with God. For that reason, suffering that led to the inability to do either could not be considered "suffering of [God's] love." See also Mishnah Shabbat 1:2, B.T. Shabbat 11a, and P.T. Berakhot 1:2 (1:5, 3b), where one who is involved in Torah study is exempted from prayer. This would of course suggest that study is even more praiseworthy than prayer.
22. See Halivni's demonstration of how the thesis of study exemplified by the anonymous Gemara influenced the study of Bible as well (op. cit., chapter 7).
23. By "traditional" here, I mean study in the Yeshiva. Medieval commentators were often willing to offer solutions that were not in accord with the halakhah.

INTRODUCTION TO CHAPTER EIGHTEEN

This piece was written to expose my developing method and its meanings to Conservative rabbis (hence my choice of publication venue: *Conservative Judaism*). The present textual readings were greatly expanded and published in *Reading the Rabbis*, chapter 7. There is nothing in the readings as such that is not more finely explicated in that later version. Still, I include this essay in the present volume because of its explicit statement of the religious conclusions I draw from these readings. Simply stated, if the Talmud means to expose the conventional and imperfect nature of halakhic categorization of women—as I here claim—then we may call upon its imagined theoretical alternatives for practical ends. I expand this point, in a personal way, in the latter part of this essay.

In response to my explicit "confession," just explained, the reader might be tempted to remark, "So! You have admitted the personal prejudice that influences your scholarly conclusions! Have you not thereby called into question the objectivity of your scholarly work?" To this I answer, "absolutely yes, but...!" By this I mean to say, yes, the questions I ask and the interpretations I am willing to consider are indeed a product of my subjective self. But I am quite sure this is true of all scholarship. All of it is as "tainted" and none more "objective" than mine. The only difference is whether we, as interpreters, are willing to admit our subjective prejudices and consequently "correct" for them in our interpretations. In fact, I would argue that those who are aware of the part the subjective self plays in interpretation are likely to get closer to the "truth" then those who naively imagine that they approach their evidence "objectively." The excellence of interpretations must rest on the case that is made, whatever the prejudice of the scholar who undertakes the scholarly enterprise.

Chapter Eighteen

Critical Readings and Religious Insight: New Readings in the Bavli

The well-established tendency of those who study rabbinic literature—and the Talmud in particular—is to examine the trees (the details) very carefully but to ignore entirely the beauty of the forest (the composite text) of which they are a part. Proceeding this way, it is easy to miss the immense power of the text as a composition and remain untouched by the meaning that emerges from the details as they work together to create a larger whole. Consequently, essential messages of talmudic texts have largely been ignored by even experienced students, and profoundly *religious* statements have gone unnoticed. If we approach the text seeking uniquely religious lessons, then an alternative approach to reading must be proposed.

I have developed precisely such an alternative over the last several years, a few examples of which appear in print. The essence of the method is this: As suggested above, I give primary attention to the talmudic *sugya* as a whole, accounting for the details as they work together in the broader context. Particular consideration is given to the rhetoric of the Gemara; that is, to the twists and turns of the Gemara's deliberations as they make an impact on the reader. I assume, in interpreting the rhetoric, that questions have a purpose and that alternatives, when proposed, are meant to be taken seriously. I understand that the Gemara's conventions are meaningful and that, in general, there must be a reason why someone wrote a text this way and not another. When the Gemara uses and interprets purportedly earlier traditions, as it so often does, I compare my sense of the meaning of that tradition with the interpretation offered in the Gemara itself, and I try to account for the frequent differences that emerge; the source is recorded so that I can make my own judgment about its meaning and compare it with the Gemara's judgment. Why, in this or that instance, does the Gemara want me to accept an interpretation that seems unnatural? Finally, I note that though the Gemara's vocabulary is a halakhic one, it employs that vocabulary to express a wide range of attitudes and opinions. What is the unifying theme on which any given halakhic deliberation makes its comments?[1]

In this essay, I intend to provide one further example of reading the Bavli according to this method, but with a particular emphasis on the religious lesson that emerges from such a reading. I hope that others will be able to return to the Gemara, on the basis of this model, to seek varieties of responses to their own religious questions. I will then comment on how this approach has affected my own personal religious outlook.

The text we will examine is the discussion at Berakhot 20b of the variety of practices that women, slaves, and minors are obligated or not obligated to observe. The Mishnah (3:3) states the law simply:

> A. Women, slaves, and minors are exempt from the reading of the Shema and from tefillin
> B. and are obligated in prayer (*tefillah* = the Amidah), in mezuzah and in *birkhat hamazon*.

The Mishnah, typically, does not justify its law or explain the categories to which particular practices are assigned.

The Gemara's commentary, as printed, appears to address each of the details of the Mishnah, bit by bit. However, if we consider that commentary more inclusively, we will see that certain strategies unite the Gemara's overall approach to the Mishnah:

> I. A. The reading of the Shema—this is obvious!
> B. It is an affirmative time-bound commandment and women are exempt from all affirmative time-bound commandments (see M. Kiddushin 1:7)!
> C. What might you have said [that would have led you to believe that this is an exception to the general rule]?
> D. Since it [= the Shema] contains the [acceptance of the yoke of the] Kingdom of Heaven [which is so important that women should also be obligated to perform this commandment].
> E. [The law of the Mishnah] comes to teach us [that this is not so].
>
> II. A. And from tefillin—this is obvious [since it, too, is an affirmative time-bound commandment].
> B. What might you have said [that would have led you to believe that this is an exception to the general rule]?
> C. Since it is equated [in Scripture, see Deuteronomy 6:8–9] with mezuzah [for which women are obligated, for this too they should also be obligated].
> D. [The law of the Mishnah] comes to teach us [that this is not so].

III. A. And they are obligated in prayer—for they [= prayers] are [petitions for] mercy.[2]
B. What might you have said [that would have led you to the opposite conclusion making this teaching of the Mishnah essential]?
C. Since it is written "Evening, morning, and at noon [I pray and cry aloud]" (Psalms 55:18) it [prayer] is like an affirmative time-bound commandment [from which women should be exempt].
D. [The law of the Mishnah] comes to teach us [that this is not so].

IV. A. And in mezuzah—this is obvious [since it is not a time-bound commandments why would we imagine otherwise?]!
B. What might you have said [that would have led you to the opposite conclusion, making this teaching of the Mishnah essential]?
C. Since it [mezuzah] is equated [in scripture, see Deuteronomy 11:19–20] with the study of Torah [from which women are exempt, they should also therefore be exempt from mezuzah].
D. [The law of the Mishnah] comes to teach us [that this is not so].

V A. And in *birkhat hamazon*—it is obvious [since it is not an affirmative time-bound commandment].
B. What might you have said [that would have led you to the opposite conclusion]?
C. Since it is written, "when the Lord shall give you in the evening meat to eat and bread in the morning to be filled" (Exodus 16:8), it is like an affirmative time-bound commandment [from which women should be exempt].
D. [The law of the Mishnah] comes to teach us [that this is not so].

VI. A. R. Ada b. Ahava said: Women are obligated in the sanctification of the day [= kiddush for Shabbat] as a matter of Torah... .

A quick overview of this text permits us to make several important observations: 1) Despite the fact that the Mishnah speaks of women in combination with slaves and minors, the Gemara's concern is primarily the status of women in these matters (the Mishnah in Kiddushin that states the general rule concerning affirmative time-bound commandments speaks only of women, not of slaves and minors); 2) The text as a whole is apparently an essay in exceptions, that is to say, the only way the laws enumerated in this Mishnah are not self-evident (which, according to the methodology of the Gemara, would be unacceptable) is to claim that those laws might with good reason have been included in the opposite category. Each ruling, therefore, is actually an exception to the general rule or, at least, a potential exception.

Let us explore this second observation in greater detail. In the first segment of the Gemara (I.) we see that the Mishnah apparently teaches us something that should be obvious, that women are exempted from the Shema, an affirmative time-bound commandment. Needing to argue that this exemption is not obvious, the Gemara proposes that the Shema might have been regarded as exceptional on account of its paramount importance; that is, it might have been perfectly reasonable to conclude that women should be obligated to recite the Shema. The Gemara goes on to point out that this is not, in the end, the law; nevertheless, one is left with the strong impression that it just as easily could have been.

The same approach is articulated in the second segment, but with potentially further-reaching consequences. In this instance, the proposed position that would have led us to a conclusion opposite the one recorded in the Mishnah is that tefillin should have been equated with mezuzah (by virtue of their scriptural proximity), thus making women obligated in tefillin. But, as is well known, the very justification offered in the Gemara (Kiddushin 34a) to support the general rule exempting women from affirmative time-bound commandments requires equating all such commandments with tefillin (which, in turn, is equated with the study of Torah, from which women are "obviously" exempt). If tefillin itself—the archetypal time-bound mitzvah—could just as easily have been compared to mezuzah, thus rendering women obligated, then the very foundation of the general principle, as proposed in Kiddushin, falls away. There would be no general rule, then, and all we would be left with are "exceptions."

The next several segments approach the same point from a different angle. First, the Gemara makes it clear that prayer (III.) might easily be considered an affirmative time-bound commandment (which, of course, it is; see Rashi on the Mishnah). If so, then women should have been exempt from this commandment. Nevertheless, they are obligated to pray, and we are left with the impression that this is despite the time-bound nature of prayer. The obligation of women here is an "exception." The same is true with respect to *birkhat hamazon* (V.), which similarly might have been considered a time-bound commandment. Here too, then, the obligation of women is not a natural conclusion.

Finally, in its discussion of mezuzah (IV.), the Gemara suggests that it (= mezuzah, a commandment that is not time-bound) might have been equated with the study of Torah on the basis of scriptural proximity, thus rendering women exempt. But it is precisely this kind of reasoning that has been used to justify, according to the Gemara (Kiddushin 34a), the exemption of women from time-bound commandments. This Gemara illustrates, then, that non-time-bound commandments, just as easily as time-bound commandments, could have been equated with the study of Torah (by virtue of scriptural proximity). It therefore becomes evident that there is nothing more systemically logical about exempting women from time-bound commandments than from non-time-bound command-ments. Nothing in the system is necessary, therefore, not even the general rule that defines categories of exemption or obligation. Again, everything is exceptional.

Lest we have missed the overall point (or perhaps merely to emphasize it) the Gemara now goes on (IV.) to discuss explicitly a matter (kiddush) that is an obvious exception to the general rule. Now there is no escaping the fact that the categories are not comprehensive; in fact, one is left with the impression that the categories are barely the point at all.

Notably, precisely the same point emerges from many elements of the deliberation at Kiddushin 34a–35a, dealing also with the question of a woman's obligation to perform affirmative time-bound commandments. The text there is too lengthy to analyze in detail here,[3] but a few observations will suffice. After establishing the alleged scriptural basis for women's exemption from such commandments, the Gemara goes on to challenge at length the validity of the alleged source. It begins by noting that the only reason that women are exempt from the obligation to dwell in the sukkah—an affirmative time-bound commandment—is because the Torah explicitly applies the obligation to "the citizen" (Leviticus 23:42) which is understood to exclude women. Had that unusual term not been used, however, then women would have been obligated despite the affirmative time-bound nature of the commandment. To explain this contradiction of the general rule both Abbaye and Rava argue that the exclusionary term ("citizen") was necessary. According to the former, we might have thought that the obligation to "dwell" in the sukkah should naturally have pertained also to women; hence, the exclusion was necessary. According to the latter, since Sukkot and Pesach both occur on the fifteenth of the month we might have thought that just as women are obligated to perform the latter (to eat matzah), so too are they obligated to perform the former; hence, the exclusion was demanded. Both of these arguments offer systemically legitimate options and the latter, in particular, points out that there are exceptions of major importance to the rule of exemption that the Mishnah describes. The Gemara that follows records similarly provocative exceptions or alternative reasonings that in combination leave us with the impression that though the general rule is in the end supported, it is neither without exceptions nor is it the best or most natural outcome even in cases which abide by the general rule.

What we witness in these texts is the inevitable consequence of seeking explanations and justifications. When, following the Gemara, we ask for a reason—rather than letting a statement stand on its own, wholly unchallenged and untested—we quickly discover that for each reason or justification there might have been an alternative. We learn that things are not the way they are because they must be that way but that various alternatives might be just as valid. We discover that the assigned ritual position of women is not the single best position they might occupy—because alternative analyses of the same issues might be equally convincing. True we might respect the law as recorded by the Mishnah (the Gemara in this instance does not challenge any of the

Mishnah's rulings) but we must be aware as we do so that this law is conventional; it is not, as the Gemara makes us aware, the best of all possible worlds.[4]

This awareness profoundly transforms my affective relationship to the halakhic system. It requires that I approach halakhic practice with modesty. Knowing that the system could logically just as easily have taken a different turn I respect the turn that it did take as just one possibility among many. There may be many good reasons—historical, sociological, and the like—to observe the halakhah as it has come down to us but not because it is the "best" halakhah and certainly not because it is the single "true" expression of God's will. This awareness also means that in specific matters where our consciousness has been transformed, such as in the question of the halakhic status of women, I am more likely to be swayed. If, after all, the law is built around exceptions, then further exceptions might be justified. To be sure, if the way things are is recognized as not being the way they must be—a recognition stated by the Gemara itself—then why not change them to make them better? If the Gemara, by asking questions and seeking justifications, subverts the absolute standing of the law of the Mishnah, then why not follow in the same course? "Creative betrayal" (to borrow David Roskies' term) is, as the Gemara testifies, a legitimate traditional Jewish/rabbinic strategy.

Notes

1. For earlier examples of this approach, as well as a more detailed exposition of the method, see "Composition and Meaning in the Bavli," *Prooftexts* 8, n. 3 (Sept. 1988), pp. 271–291 [chapter 15 in this volume], and "New Meaning in Ancient Talmudic Texts," *Proceedings of the Rabbinical Assembly*, 1987, pp. 201–225.
2. See the alternative version of this section recorded in Tosafot. That version does not substantially change the point as it relates to my analysis.
3. My detailed analysis of this text now appears in my *Reading the Rabbis: The Talmud as Literature* (New York: Oxford U. Press, 1996), pp. 95–108.
4. My claims in this paragraph, relating to the consequences of the Gemara's deliberative form, are spelled out at length in *The Mind of the Talmud: An Intellectual History of the Bavli* (Oxford University Press, 1990), chapters 5–6.

INTRODUCTION TO CHAPTER NINETEEN

This is the only piece I have written on Jewish ethics. In it, I bring to bear my rhetorical reading of Talmudic sugyot, and my growing awareness of social history, on the enterprise of "doing Jewish ethics." My posture here is highly critical, and I have seen little since the appearance of this piece to cause me to change that posture. Simply put, most writing on Jewish ethical issues is slavishly halakhic and hermeneutically naive. Writers mine the Judaic canon selectively, without awareness of the subjectivity of their selection. They privilege halakhic sources, though "Jewish" means far more than "halakhic." They speak for "Judaism" without recognizing that they can only interpret "Judaism"—offering one interpretation among several. And they fail fully to account for the context in which Jewish teachings were taught, rarely noticing the critical differences between our experiences, assumptions and beliefs and "theirs." There are exceptions to what I here describe, but not many.

I have been disappointed by the failure of writers on Jewish ethics to pick up on either my specific arguments here or on my broader methodological critique. This may be due to the "fleeting" quality of articles appearing in popular journals. Or it may be a product of the fact that there is a relatively insulated cadre of scholars who write on these issues—scholars who refer and respond to one another but not to "outsiders." Or it may be due to the fact that they dismiss my critique, in which case I would love to hear a reasoned exposition of their dismissal. Whatever the case may be, I re-present this piece to a readership that may have missed its first printing in *Tikkun*, inviting a lively debate of my claims and arguments.

Chapter Nineteen

Jewish Ethics and Abortion

Commentators have written repeatedly on the question of Jewish law/values/ethics and abortion, some supporting it and others voicing condemnation. But virtually without exception, even when they have claimed to be speaking of values or ethics, their discourse shows that they have really meant Jewish law (Halakha). For those who are primarily concerned with ethics as such (henceforth: "ethicists"), there is no reason to grant that the two are the same—and considerable reason to argue they are not.

The crucial differences between Halakha and ethics are fourfold. Halakha defines a narrow canon, ethics should not. Halakhists believe "Torah" (broadly defined) is eternal, contemporary; ethicists will understand the tradition contextually. Halakhists submit to the final authority of their sources, ethicists exercise their judgment. Perhaps most crucially, halakhists prefer clear, definitive conclusions, whereas ethicists will understand that complex ethical questions often do not yield univocal, overarching answers. It is obvious that the two are radically different enterprises, and the standards and assumptions of Halakha are obviously not appropriate for the ethicist.

At the same time, rejection of halakhic discourse does not require the abandonment of traditional Jewish sources; it is possible to do ethics with traditional sources without accepting the ways of Halakha. In what follows, I hope to show how this can be done, first by reviewing and critiquing the common halakhic approach to abortion and then illustrating the alternative.

The biblical text most often cited in connection with the abortion question is Exodus 21:22–3. The verses describe a case of two men who, in the course of a scuffle, unintentionally strike a pregnant woman, who then miscarries. The text continues: "If there be no catastrophe, he shall be punished according to what the woman's husband shall exact from him, it shall be determined through adjudication. But if there be catastrophe, then you shall give life for life...."

Rabbinic tradition understood "catastrophe" to mean harm to the mother. Thus, if the mother's life was lost, so too should the life of the perpetrator be taken. But if the fetus was lost, no such "life for life" penalty was demanded. On this basis, halakhists have argued that the fetus was not valued as a life; feticide is not a capital crime.

Citations of rabbinic literature relevant to this question begin with Mishna Ohalot 7.6:

> If a woman has difficulty in childbirth, we cut up the offspring in her womb and remove it limb by limb, because her life comes before its life. If most of it [the child; the Talmud's version is "most of the head"] has come out, we do not touch it, because we do not push aside one life for another.

This Mishna clearly teaches that, at least at certain times, the fetus's life must be taken in order to save the endangered life of the mother. Based upon the Mishna's stated reason ("her life comes before its life"), it may even be argued that this applies to any point in the pregnancy. The direction of the law as delineated here is permissive at least in cases of therapeutic abortion.

The Talmud suggests a new and possibly crucial justification for the mishnaic law quoted above. At Sanhedrin 72b, the text proposes that, even if most of the baby (or the baby's head) has already emerged, it should still be proper to save the mother's life by taking the baby's life because the child would be in the category of "a pursuer"—according to rabbinic law, if one pursues another with intent to murder, a Jew is required to save the pursued even by taking the life of the pursuer (The Talmud rejects the proposed reasoning, claiming that in this case it is actually "Heaven" that is doing the pursuing). Maimonides and others understand this to suggest that, in the earlier mishnaic case, where the child is still mostly in the womb, the child is indeed categorized as a "pursuer" and for that reason its life may be taken. Following this reasoning, the conclusion regarding therapeutic abortion suggested above would appear unimpeachable and, indeed, most halakhic authorities have ruled that such abortion is legitimate.

A final discussion always quoted in connection with abortion is the Mishna and accompanying Gemara at tractate Arachin 7a. According to the Mishna, if a pregnant woman is convicted of a capital crime, she should be executed before she gives birth; only if she is already in labor should the court delay the execution. Regarding this law, the Gemara comments:

> What is the reason [we wait if she has gone into labor]? Since it has been separated

[from her womb] it is considered to be an independent body [and no longer part of the mother]. R. Judah said that Samuel said: A [pregnant] woman who is on her way out to be executed, they strike her [on her belly] opposite her womb in order that the child die first, so that [at the time of execution] she not be brought to disgrace [through the spontaneous birth of the child].

The procedure R. Judah describes in the name of Samuel suggests the permissibility of abortion even in certain cases where the mother's life is not threatened by the fetus. Furthermore, the tradition at hand unambiguously assumes that fetal life, at whatever stage before pregnancy, does not merit the full protection of the law. Based upon this text, many authorities have justified abortion for reasons other than the mother's physical health. Critics of that interpretation have countered that the text deals with unusual circumstances and should therefore not be deemed normative.

The problem with this whole discussion, from the perspective of modern ethics, is that none of these sources has been subjected to the necessary critique. For example, there are several problems with the verse from Exodus. First, its reference is ambiguous. While it is possible that the "catastrophe" it speaks of is the mother's death, it might also be the death of the child; if this were so, of course, radically different conclusions would be required. Second, even assuming that the ambiguous term refers to the mother, it is not clear that this text is relevant to the abortion debate. It speaks, after all, of the unintentional taking of fetal life, not of direct intervention to terminate such life. At best, the text implies that the killing of a fetus is not considered murder, and even this is not clear since murder is intentional, and the killing described in the passage is unintentional.

The relevance of Mishna Ohalot is also questionable. In fact, the Mishna speaks not about danger to a mother's life early in pregnancy, but rather about danger to her life during childbirth. If by "abortion" we mean taking the life of a fetus mostly during the early months of a pregnancy, then this text has no direct bearing on the abortion question.

It is not surprising that classic rabbinic sources contain scant reference to abortion and focus instead on the dilemmas of childbirth. Danger to a mother's life in childbirth was extremely common in pre-modern society. For a variety of reasons (children were a financial asset; infant and child-mortality rates were extremely high; medical procedures were dangerous or unreliable), abortion must have been uncommon. For related reasons (children as a financial liability; low infant mortality; safe and effective medical procedures), abortion is a common and reasonable option for us. What this all means, of course, is that the halakhic authorities of old were not asking our questions about abortion. Can we justify deriving instruction when the analogies are so inexact and the circumstances so different?

For these same reasons, the talmudic discussion of Mishna Ohalot is also not substantively relevant. Nor is its theoretical extension of much use. To begin with, it is not clear that Maimonides is correct in applying the principle of "pursuer" to the fetus before birth. But even if Maimonides is correct, we learn nothing about abortion in general. As stated, according to rabbinic law, even an adult "pursuer" may legitimately be stopped through the taking of his life. Thus, it is possible that the fetus could be judged a legally protected life and still be subject to the law outlined in the Mishna. In fact, there are multiple reasonable interpretations, and while these sources speak clearly about a common problem (danger in childbirth), they convey nothing unambiguous about abortion as such.

The fourth quoted text (Arachin) does, finally, speak of what we would call abortion. But its reasoning is so troubling from an ethical perspective that we should hesitate to regard it as instructive. The Talmud's justification for abortion before execution is that such a step will avoid disgrace to the body of the woman at the time of her death? Actually, her humiliation would be even greater if Samuel's procedure were followed, for she would be alive to experience it, along with great physical pain. Does the avoidance of possible humiliation at death justify causing considerable pain during life? Furthermore, who should be making this decision? No one has asked this woman what she would prefer. Should Samuel have the right to impose his concern for disgrace at death and ignore the woman's welfare during the last moments of her life?

Finally, the fundamental assumption of this source is troubling. Even if the fetus technically merits no legal protection, would it still not be better to await birth and then execute the woman? The Greeks and Egyptians judged the potential value of the fetus as greater than the value of swift execution (see Plutarch, *De Sera Numinis Vindicta*, 552). Should Jews not do the same? I think it is safe to say that this source is so ethically problematic that we should avoid using it entirely. Undoubtedly, it is possible to extract halakhic rulings from this talmudic debate. But doing so requires that we read with ethical blinders, an approach we should shun. If such traditions provide our lone justification for abortion, we build on dubious ground.

Considered from the perspective of modern ethics, the conventional, halakhic approach to abortion leads to a dead end. But what is the alternative? If the task is not primarily deciding what is permissible and what prohibited, but discovering fundamental values embedded in the tradition that pertain to a given question, then our approach must change in several essential respects.

First, we must frame new questions—questions that relate not only to the former concern, Halakha, but also to the latter, ethics. Naturally, different questions will sometimes lead us to different texts—to precedents whose relevance is not simply in the analogues they offer but in the values and attitudes they assume. Second, we must look beyond the canon as defined by

Halakha. Third, we must feel free to critique and question the teachings that the tradition records. And, finally, we must insist that general conclusions are not always possible; we must be open to ambivalence where the complexity of an issue so warrants.

In the case of abortion, our questions must include, but not be limited to, how Jewish traditions view the life or potential life of a fetus, the relationship of the fetus to the mother (and father), and the prerogatives of a mother (and father) with respect to the fetus. These questions will lead us back to some of the texts reviewed above, but other texts will also suggest themselves. More important, we will find that the nature of discourse and analysis changes. What follows is intended to illustrate the alternative for which I am arguing.

We begin with two traditions commonly cited in connection with the question of abortion, the first because of the light it sheds on the status of the fetus. The Talmud, at Yebamot 69b, declares that "until the fortieth day, the fetus is mere water." The attitude of the author is clear: During the earliest stage of fetal development the fetus is not yet considered human life in any genuine sense.

For the halakhist, the consequence of this statement may be obvious; "mere water," after all, should not be protected by the law. Nevertheless, we recognize that this "mere water" will soon be far more; how do we factor in our concern for the ultimate potential of this primitive substance? Is such potential irrelevant (to my mind, an unreasonable position), or does it call upon us to respect this "water" more than other "mere water?" And, if we judge that potential is an important consideration, how does this balance against the mother's wishes and needs? Thus, this talmudic precept enables us to begin formulating essential questions. Despite its relative clarity, it does not direct us to a singular answer.

The second much-cited tradition, scattered through a related cluster of texts, relates to the question of the relationship between a fetus and its mother. The tradition records a dispute concerning whether a fetus is considered "its mother's thigh [limb]" or not. Certain texts seem to prefer the view that a fetus is indeed considered a limb of its mother, but this position is not clearly supported by the Talmud as a whole. On the contrary, what distinguishes these discussions—and what has gone unnoticed (or, at least, unnoted) by halakhists—is that both opinions persist and that neither is deemed obviously superior to the other. The talmudic deliberations tend to explore the consequences of each without privileging one over the other.

From the ethicist's perspective, the Talmud's inconclusiveness in this matter is its most notable feature. The inability of the sages to support one position firmly shows their dilemma in assessing the status of the fetus vis-a-vis the mother. If the fetus were "its mother's limb" it would be judged to have no independent existence and therefore no independent rights. But the talmudic sages are not willing to grant the necessary correctness of that opinion. Nor, however, are they confident of the opposite opinion.

This indecision is evidence of ambivalence—an ambivalence with which we readily identify. The fetus is not quite a person; it is (for most of a pregnancy) unable to survive independent of the mother's body. Thus, it is reasonable to conclude that its life is in no significant way separate from that of the mother. On the other hand, there is no doubting the fetus's essential personhood, at least *in potentia*. The fetus, for a large part of its development, looks like a person and, one day soon, it will be a person. (Remember, each of us began as a fetus.) Thus, we also feel strongly that at some stage—a stage earlier than birth itself—the fetus has attained at least existential personhood. The positions recorded by the rabbis mark the two poles of our own confused reflections on this matter. If I understand them correctly, the rabbis support such confusion, confirming that there are no simple answers to these questions.

A text that has, to the best of my knowledge, never been cited in this connection is the Talmudic deliberation (Bava Batra 141b–142b) that considers whether one may give a gift to a fetus. The issue is the degree to which a fetus may be considered a legal entity: If it is such an entity, then it should be possible to give it a gift; the more distant it is thought to be from real personhood the more difficult it should be to support the validity of such a gift. The discussion begins with the opinion that a fetus may not acquire property, but the Mishna which this deliberation accompanies suggests the opposite. In fact, although the first stated law is supported to the end, the deliberation goes out of its way to review the many parties who support the contrary opinion, believing that a fetus may acquire property.

Most interesting, for our purposes, is the last-minute modification of the first tradition by R. Yoḥanan: Yes, he agrees, a fetus may not acquire a gift, but there is an exception for one's own fetus (in the womb of one's wife), for "a person's feelings are especially close to his own child." In other words, while it might generally be true that a fetus is not "person" enough for another to have full and proper intent to give it a gift, one's own baby, even before birth, is certainly person enough. There are differences in our feelings for our own fetus and that of another—differences which have real consequences.

This Talmudic text is important to our deliberation for several reasons. First, it again records and gives credence to two contradictory views, suggesting that the question of a fetus's personhood does not yield unambiguous answers. Perhaps more important, it recommends that the personhood of a fetus may change as a function of our emotional connections to it; our own child, in utero, is indeed a person as far as we are concerned. It has a reality—a presence—that creates a genuinely human relationship even before birth. The relationship just described is not, in the estimation of the Talmud, limited to the mother. The deliberation speaks from the perspective of the father, showing that, in the opinion of its authors, the father as well as the mother may relate in significant ways to the fetus before birth.

The few texts reviewed here merely serve to illustrate an approach. But for this method to yield as much insight as possible, we ought to consult a wide variety of texts. For example, it is essential to examine those midrashim that describe the development of the fetus in its mother's womb. If, as in tractate Niddah 30b, the fetus is believed to study Torah from beginning to end, what does this tell us of the valuation of that fetus? Even if we assume that the midrash is projecting the child's potential value as a future student of Torah, surely this tells us how highly prized potential human life is in the rabbinic mind.

At the same time, we should not ignore the question of the mother's well-being and her prerogatives as (partial) life-giver. Surely, the Arachin text discussed earlier—however perverted in its attempt to protect the honor of the mother—at least shows that concern for the mother's well-being is a significant factor, sometimes coming before the life of the fetus. Other traditions might contribute to an exploration of the abortion question. However difficult and imprecise the exploration might be, and whatever lessons additional investigations might yield, we can nevertheless begin to draw certain conclusions.

The exploration we have initiated leaves an ambivalent legacy. It is unquestionable that prominent voices in the tradition support the belief that, subsequent to the first forty days of pregnancy, the fetus, in significant respects, is human life. Those who support that view would undoubtedly denounce abortion in most cases. At the same time, it seems clear that one who performs an abortion is not guilty of murder. But we should not make too much of this conclusion. Neither did the rabbis consider there to be liability for murder if one took the life of a terminally ill person; the limit defined by the law is sometimes not identical with its fundamental values.

In fact, this distinction between the law's technical limits and its ethical soul may well offer the key to formulating a Jewish ethical response to the abortion dilemma. It seems to me that the traditions reviewed above, in combination, recommend a distinction between legal proscription and what we might call ethical imperative.

It is difficult to build a case for actually outlawing all abortion based upon these traditions. In certain cases, they clearly support both the legality and the morality of such an option. Yet we are also meant to recognize and regard at least the fetus's potential personhood, and this requires our personal renunciation of abortion as a ready option. To borrow Bill Clinton's formulation in the 1992 presidential campaign, we should be pro-choice, not pro-abortion. Undoubtedly, there will be limited circumstances in which we will support abortion without hesitation. But hesitation should otherwise be the hallmark of our approach to this difficult issue.

The last of the texts considered also bids us to respect the father's interest in the fetus. The Talmud's conclusion there supposes that even a father can develop a significant relationship with his child before birth. Personal experience tells me that this is so. If we admit the wisdom of this assessment, then we should conclude that a father, too, has the right to be involved in decisions concerning the disposition of the fetus. But all of this comes with an essential caveat—for the Talmud, the father's emotional connection and intent are more important than his biological contribution. Therefore, the committed father should be treated differently with respect to his interests than the mere biological father.

These conclusions represent my personal judgment of what a critical, ethical analysis of traditional Jewish sources will yield; the reader may agree or disagree. But whatever the wisdom of any specific conclusions, there is a compelling ethical voice to be heard in these teachings. In my opinion, the lack of clarity and confidence—the admission that these are complicated, difficult questions—is the most important characteristic of these various rabbinic discussions. This indecision offers us proper advice; we should hear it as a caution.

The religiously concerned person cannot approach the question of abortion without some discomfort. Even if he/she believes that abortion is sometimes moral and proper, it should be a determination that does not come easily. Certainly, the opposite position also has merit. The advice of Jewish tradition, as I read it, is to maintain both opposing opinions in tension, allowing the other always to serve as critique of the opinion one holds at the moment.

INTRODUCTION TO CHAPTER TWENTY

The academic fields I draw upon in this article will immediately be apparent to many readers: ritual studies, the study of oral cultures, and the history of Jews in late antiquity all make their contribution. I synthesize these disciplines to engage in a critique of the lived culture of the contemporary synagogue. My claim is straightforward enough: our current condition, in which many Jews do not understand the language of the ritual (Hebrew), is not as new as we might imagine. But we have chosen many of the wrong responses to the contemporary challenge, failing to learn from the "ritual intelligence" of our ancestors. I propose that we learn their lesson well and reformulated contemporary ritual to restore its living, dramatic character.

This essay represents some of my earliest interest in the study of ritual. Since the time of its composition, my interest in ritual has been increasingly ignited, thanks, in particular, to my conversations with Vanessa Ochs. My most recent book, *The Meanings of Death in Rabbinic Judaism* (Routledge, 1999), is an outgrowth of this interest. In this book, I engage in a comprehensive examination of ancient rabbinic rituals pertaining to death, the funeral and mourning, interpreting the rituals to uncover what I can of the underlying belief-system. The rewards of this approach are, I have discovered, immense, and I do not imagine that my involvement in it will end soon.

Chapter Twenty

Dramatizing the Torah

Imagine yourself sitting in the audience at an avant-garde performance in a foreign language. On stage is a main performer, reciting quickly in a repetitive sing-song. He is surrounded by others who occasionally interrupt with brief interjections. You have been provided with a translation but, not understanding the language of performance, you have no way of judging precisely where your attention should be directed at any given moment. Chances are, you are tempted to walk out and never come back.

This is the experience of most American Jews—at least in non-Orthodox settings—during the Shabbat morning Torah services. There are many reasons for the situation just described, some of them obvious: Few American Jews understand Hebrew, few have adequate Jewish educations, few conduct their lives according to the precepts first suggested in the Torah, and so forth. But, such explanations (however true they might be) are just excuses for not acting to improve matters.

If we want to bring Jews back to the synagogue, to educate them and increase their commitment to Jewish religious expressions, we must recognize what has been demanded of them, and how intolerable it is. True, there is value to tradition on its own terms, and the Torah service as we know it does reenact, as best it can, a tradition of many centuries. But, as presently conducted, it no longer speaks meaningfully. It is not feasible, therefore, to maintain this practice without modification. Jewish tradition does not demand that Jews suffer through ritual that offers little, if any, edification.

The Power of Performance

Ours are not the first generations that have had little comprehension of biblical

Hebrew. Most Jews in the first centuries of the common era, in the Land of Israel as well as in the Diaspora, spoke Aramaic, some spoke Greek, and only a few spoke/understood Hebrew. How did religious leaders of that age respond to Hebrew illiteracy? They made oral translation a regular part of the Shabbat morning Torah reading.

According to the record of the Mishnah and other early rabbinic sources (Mishnah Megillah 4:4, Tosefta Megillah 3:20), the Torah reader would read a single verse, followed immediately by a translation into the vernacular. Hebrew, translation, Hebrew, translation—thus the reading would proceed until the weekly portion, far smaller than our weekly portions, would be completed. It was impossible for those present in the synagogue *not* to understand what was being read.

It may be asked, what essential difference is there between this practice and ours? After all, ancient custom was necessitated by the limits of their technology. Without printing presses and therefore without books, this was the only way that translation of the Hebrew original could be provided. We, on the other hand, can handle Hebrew illiteracy far more efficiently; with *humashim*, we have no need for the Mishnah's cumbersome procedure. Isn't our efficiency preferable?

When we think in terms of efficiency, we miss a more basic point. It is true that we can provide translation in a book, but the procedure described above is far more than translation. It is public ritual performance. By "performance" I mean two things: First, all ritual by virtue of being performed or enacted is a performance. But ritual is also drama; by enacting a ritual, we symbolically dramatize a set of meanings. Such performance is simultaneously ritual, drama, communication, and instruction.

Torah as Holy Script

Needless to say, a printed translation, lying inert on the surface of a page, is incapable of replicating performance of this kind. The transformation of public ritual performance into private book-reading has, therefore, important consequences. These are well described in a recent cultural history of Shakespeare, *Reinventing Shakespeare*, by Gary Taylor. Taylor details the effects on the audience/reader of making Shakespeare's plays into books:

> Shakespeare's plays had been, throughout the 17th century, actions. They happened; they enacted a story temporally; they were acted out by particular persons from beginning to end; they acted upon an audience assembled in a certain place at a certain time. In the 18th century, they became things, they became, primarily, books. Books are spatial, not temporal; any reader can skip backward or forward, dip in, pull out, pause, repeat. Books can be cut up and rearranged, as time cannot. The transformation of Shakespeare's actions into books thus permitted and encouraged

their disintegration into assemblages of quotable fragments... undertext of commentary repeatedly interrupts the reading of the uppertext... the experience of reading *Hamlet* in the late 18th century was an experience of directed action repeatedly interrupted, postponed by eddies of subsidiary meditation. Books abstract, impersonalize, idealize; what had been an interaction between a cast and an audience became a kind of message left by an unreachable author for any and all possible readers. The text became a thing... .

Disintegration, interruption, abstraction, impersonalization, an unreachable author—these words describe what happens to a dramatic performance when it is made into a book with commentary; these words also describe the experience of reading the ḥumash. The books on our laps create a gulf between our experience and the dramatic performance on the *bima*. What might be alive—a voice with presence and spirit—is reduced to print on paper, brought to life only in the mind of the individual.

In contrast, the ancient practice kept the performance aspect of the ritual alive, thus assuring genuine communication. Near-simultaneous verbal translation created a live connection between the reader and the audience. The reader acted as witness to the word of God. The congregation listened and understood as a community. The Torah's message was not merely recited as past history; it was present and alive. Its immediacy was such that the teacher of the day had to respect the community's own hearing of the text. The ceremony as a whole yielded genuine learning and communal involvement.

The connection between performance/drama and true instruction cannot be underestimated. Effective education requires that the message be conveyed in a way that commands the student's attention and interest. One of the most effective means of doing so is through live presentation. For this reason, it is generally easier to learn from a good teacher than from an academic article, and from a professor who speaks spontaneously than from one who reads lecture notes.

But, you might ask, isn't Torah reading just that—reading from a text (closer to reading lecture notes than to spontaneous performance)? Bible scholars have long recognized that the biblical text (including the Torah) preserves significant aspects of the original oral forms of the stories it contains. And for good reason! In ancient societies, it was difficult to produce books (or scrolls) in large numbers and books were therefore quite precious and rare. By necessity, for most people book reading was oral and public, and written texts continued to be characterized by common oral features (one scholar calls this the "oral residue"). More accurately, then, Torah reading was closer to dramatic reading from a script, where the words and form are intended for oral presentation.

Bringing the Text to Life

I first appreciated the difference between reading and listening to the Torah portion when I had my first child. With baby in arm, it was impossible to follow the reading in a *humash*, so I began simply to listen (I am fortunate to be able to understand the Hebrew without translation). And what a difference it made! I no longer felt that I was fulfilling an assignment—to follow the reader word for word in the printed text. More important, I was no longer distracted by the commentary or by interesting pieces of text, earlier or later, that diverted my attention from the words then being spoken. Instead, I could experience the story or teaching as it was related to me personally and directly. There was something immediate and fresh—something I had not felt when I was reading the text. In fact, I could often imagine the reader as one in a chain of lawgivers or storytellers. The teaching he/she now repeated to me had been related to him/her by an elder, who had learned it from a prior elder, and so forth. Before me stood a living participant in the ancient chain of tradition and, as the next listener, I too now stood in that chain.

To improve upon the present condition, we must begin to experiment with alternatives. Some congregations might want to close their *humashim* and try literally to recreate the classical practice by following each verse in the Hebrew with a public, verbal translation in English. If this method is too foreign, or too disruptive, a congregation might instead experiment with reading an aliyah in English once in a while—with appropriate chanting. Or, for a more radical change, it might be possible to offer a dramatic presentation of some of the stories in Genesis, with multiple voices speaking for the various characters. This could even be done in Hebrew. The introduction of different voices with different dramatic inflections would bring the event to life even if individual words are not understood.

INTRODUCTION TO CHAPTER TWENTY-ONE

In the present piece, I tell the story of my personal struggle with the death of my colleague and friend, Baruch Bokser. The scholarship I draw from is found, at length, in my book, *Responses to Suffering in Classical Rabbinic Literature*. This essay illustrates how that scholarship informs my personal religious life.

    I have been extremely gratified to learn, over the course of the last several years, that mine is not the only religious life that has been affected by this work. One rabbi after another has reported to me how what he or she learned from my scholarship has informed the manner in which he or she now counsels those who experience personal suffering. Scholarship should not remain the exclusive domain of scholars. It should *matter* enough that it is important to communicate (at least some of) its conclusions to educated non-scholars. If this is one reasonable criterion by which to evaluate a scholarly project, then the present chapter testifies to the success of my scholarly choice.

Chapter Twenty-One

When God is "Wrong"

It had been coming for a long time. But the morning I heard of Baruch Bokser's death, I was beyond consolation. I was at the Jewish Theological Seminary, where I had spent many hours with my friend and colleague, but when the news came, the protective walls of that institution provided me no comfort. I escaped their confines and ran up the hill to Grant's Tomb. There in the Tomb, my tears were overwhelmed by waves of anger. I cried out against God and against the injustice of God's world. For months following, I felt nothing but anger toward God. My prayer was an exercise in protest. I knew God was wrong, and I would not find rest until God knew it too.

During that period, I did not know whether my protest and anger removed me from the tradition where I made my home. Was a good Jew permitted to express such anger? Or was acceptance and submission the necessary stance? Of course, I knew of Job, but I also knew that Job was rarely referred to by the rabbis—the founders of Judaism as we know it—and when they did refer to him, it was mostly in less than sympathetic terms. Did I, in my anger, have a place in this Judaism, or did my anger alienate me from the piety of this two-thousand year tradition?

At the time, I was already involved in research on classical rabbinic responses to suffering. I knew that some rabbis demanded that "when a person sees suffering coming upon him, he should examine his ways" (Berakhot 5a), implying that suffering is punishment for sin. But I also knew that other authorities denied the necessity of this connection, and I had some hope, therefore, that my angry alternative could also find a place in the tradition. Not knowing what I would find, I set out to see whether or not this was so.

In the course of this exploration, I turned my attention to the various stories of the death of R. Aqiba. In the Babylonian Talmud (the Bavli), this story appears in two, possibly complementary versions. At Berakhot 61b, the Talmud describes the torture and death of the great master. There, as Aqiba's flesh is being ripped by iron combs, his students cry out: "Our master! [Are we required to go] this far?!" Aqiba explains that, despite all appearances, he now has the opportunity to fulfill the commandment to love God "with all of his soul." He then recites the Shema and expires. Thereupon, the Ministering Angels cry out before God: "This is the Torah and this its reward?!" God comforts them, responding that Aqiba was assured a place in the World to Come.

What struck me as I read this story was that both the disciples and the Ministering Angels question Aqiba's suffering—and they pull no punches. In fact, it is hard for me to imagine any more challenging question from a religious Jew than the one attributed to the Ministering Angels here. Yet, remarkably, no voice in the text condemns such questioning. Answers are provided but questions of challenge or protest are unhesitatingly allowed.

In the other Bavli story relating to the death of Aqiba (Menachot 29b), Moses is transported to Aqiba's school, where he finds himself immensely impressed by Aqiba's brilliance. Why, Moses wants to know, did God choose him instead of Aqiba to receive the Torah at Sinai? Not denying the conclusion implied in Moses' question (Aqiba ought to have received the Torah), God responds, "Silence. This is what it occurred to me to do." Taking the discussion one step further, Moses wants to know Aqiba's reward. God shows Moses Aqiba's flesh being weighed out in the market stalls. "This is the Torah and this its reward?!" exclaims Moses. Again, not challenging the truth of what Moses implies (=the injustice of Aqiba's death), God replies "Silence, this is what it occurred to me to do."

I do not take God's direction of "silence" to be a condemnation of Moses' questions. Silence is demanded because, in this version, there is no room for discussion. God admits that it is all quite arbitrary. Still, the questions are good and legitimate, and that is why they are put in the mouth of Moses "our Rabbi," the greatest of all rabbinic heroes. What was in Berakhot expressed by the Ministering Angels is here articulated by none other than Moses. The most challenging question imaginable is voiced by the giver of Torah himself.

But I had doubts. Was I right in seeing this as so significant? I had earlier discovered that the rabbinic tradition of the Land of Israel condemned such questioning. Was the same true of the Bavli and, if so, did this mean I was wrong in interpreting these texts as I did? And did the Palestinian rabbis, despite their condemnation, also provide opportunities for challenges this grave? My questions compounded. I still did not know whether I had truly found support for my own religious protest or whether I was merely misreading the model before me.

As I searched, I found that the rabbis of Palestine and those of Babylonia disagreed sharply concerning proper responses to suffering. The Babylonian rabbis, who place this awful, biting question ("This is the Torah and this its reward?") in the mouths of Moses and the Ministering Angels, nowhere claim that one may not question God's justice. They may support that justice themselves, but they also, from time to time, question it and—more importantly—they permit others to question it without condemnation.

Turning to the other side, I was at first surprised to find (as I searched through a concordance) that the Bavli's critical question is also voiced in the Jerusalem Talmud (the Yerushalmi)—in one location but repeated twice. Alas, I said to myself, it appears that Palestinian rabbinic tradition is confused in this matter. But when I discovered who purportedly expresses the challenge there, I realized that the Palestinian tradition is indeed consistent. It condemns questioning, and it repeats the challenging question only to illustrate the abysmal end of one who allows him/herself to voice such a heresy.

As it turns out, the questioner in the Yerushalmi is none other than Elisha ben Abbuya—the arch-apostate of rabbinic tradition. Seeing the tongue of a well-known sage being dragged along in the mouth of a dog, Elisha responds "This is the Torah and this its reward?" Allowing himself to express this doubt, Elisha turns away from God and tradition, ever after to be known as "Aher"— "the Other."

In other words, in the opinion of the rabbis of Palestine, if you question God's justice, you are likely to become an apostate, like Elisha. But in the opinion of their Babylonian counterparts, such questions are perfectly legitimate—not at all contrary to piety. In fact, if you challenge God's justice, you are, according to these authorities, in the company of Moses and the Ministering Angels. There is no better company than that.

So, I discovered, by expressing my anger and voicing my doubts, I did not remove myself from the tradition of my choice. On the contrary, I could be a "rebel" (in Camus' sense) and a good Jew at the same time. Thank God there is room for me inside. May others find the same.

INTRODUCTION TO CHAPTER TWENTY-TWO

In this brief essay, I draw upon what I (think I) know about the history and sociology of the rabbinic Jewish community in the early centuries of the Common Era to learn lessons for the divided Jewish community of the late 20th century. The question I ask is a simple one: How is it that the rabbis of the "talmudic period" could develop a culture of respectful dispute while we in the contemporary Jewish world suffer the slings of insult and repudiation? Or, to put it in slightly different terms, what is it about the world of the rabbis which held them together despite sometimes serious disagreements, and is it possible for us to recreate that same "something"? As the reader will see, my conclusions are not optimistic.

I should add here that this essay illustrates what has drawn my interest and scholarly devotions to the world of the rabbis. Despite differences, the world in which the rabbinic movement was born and grew is similar, in significant respects, to the world in which we live. There was a dominant "international" culture (Hellenism), many identities competed for loyalty, Jews experienced significant upheaval and even catastrophe (the wars with Rome and the Bar Kokhba fiasco), and so forth. If we can learn from history (as I believe we can), then this is a period from which contemporary Jews have much to learn. This chapter is but one of many lessons that can be drawn from a thoughtful comparison.

Chapter Twenty-Two

Disputes that Unite

Common stereotypes portray Jews as an uncommonly contentious people, and insiders (that is, Jews among Jews) know that the phrase "two Jews" is completed with the words "three opinions." That there is some truth to these characterizations is unarguable. Something in the nature of traditional Jewish discourse allows (or, perhaps more accurately, encourages) us to disagree passionately with one another, sometimes so passionately that the fabric of our community appears in danger of unraveling.

But the Jewish tradition of dispute, originating in the Talmud, declares that the benefit of "dispute for the sake of Heaven" far outweighs any imagined dangers. How could different rabbinic voices, differing so vigorously, find a peaceful home side-by-side? Why, in rabbinic culture, did dispute draw the disputants together, while in our day it seems destined to tear us apart?

Entering The Dispute

To answer these questions, let us take a specific talmudic example and see if we can understand what made such respectful dispute possible—even desirable—in traditional Jewish culture. The mishnah in chapter 8 of tractate Hullin records the following opinions:

> R. Akiba says: [The prohibition of mixing] wild animals and fowl [with dairy] is not from the Torah...R. Yosi the Galilean says: "Thou shalt not seethe a calf in its mother's milk"...excludes fowl, which has no mother's milk.

At first glance, R. Akiba and R. Yosi seem to be saying almost the same thing (at least with respect to the status of fowl) in slightly different ways; R. Akiba declares that the separation of fowl and dairy is not from the Torah, while R. Yosi provides the specific Torah-source for the exclusion of fowl from this prohibition. But according to the Talmud's interpretation of their teachings (found at Hullin 116a), they do dispute, and their dispute is not insignificant.

Framing The Dispute

As the Talmud understands him, when R. Akiba says that the prohibition pertaining to fowl "is not from the Torah," he means to suggest that it is from the Rabbis. Whatever the source, he agrees that chicken parmesan (for example) would not be kosher. But R. Yosi believes that fowl is completely excluded from this prohibition so, as the Talmud reports, "in the locale of R. Yosi the Galilean they would eat the flesh of fowl with milk." The Talmud follows this report with another one showing that this practice was not limited to R. Yosi's generation. Others later followed his position and their alternate practice was respected.

In the world of Jewish observance, such a difference of opinion and practice has potentially serious consequences. If I belong to a group of Jews who categorize poultry flesh as meat, I will probably not be able to eat at the home of my neighbor who views chicken as parve. If we have difficulty eating together, we will have a difficult time maintaining our common bond and we will grow apart socially. I may begin to claim that my more lenient neighbor is wrong, that he misinterprets the Torah, that he has little regard for Jewish unity. If I gain control of the community's kashrut-granting apparatus, I might refuse to certify his restaurant. Less significant differences might perhaps be tolerated, but kashrut is a central marker of Jewish observance and identity. How can we accept such differences when the stakes are so high?

Common Commitment As Common Bond

The probable explanations of the tolerant rabbinic attitude toward disputes range from the mundane to the profound. At first glance, it seems obvious that the fact that R. Akiba (presumably) and R. Yosi (explicitly) could both offer proofs of their positions (in this and other matters) based upon close readings of the Torah meant that they had to be taken seriously. Their source was the recognized, authoritative source of Jewish practice, so the foundation of their teachings was strong. But, in reality, this would have made little difference if they were not respected voices in the rabbinic community, for it is possible that a particular reading of Torah could be declared "wrong." So the question must be, why did the rabbinic community respect these and other voices, even when they were in serious disagreement?

To answer this question, again the example of R. Akiba and R. Yosi is instructive. Whatever their interpretation of the Torah in this or any other case, it is beyond question that they were profoundly committed to the Torah, its God, and its people. This common commitment allowed for respectful dispute where lesser commitment would not. These rabbis, who lived in the aftermath of the destruction of the Jerusalem Temple, shared a common history—an ancient history that included the revelation of Torah at Sinai and, as importantly, a more recent history of struggle against an insensitive, sometimes tyrannical imperial force. By virtue of this common history, they also shared a common sense of purpose—the need to uphold (and therefore transform) the covenant in the face of radical upheaval. And they understood the challenge and the risk; simply put, if they could not work together to forge an inclusive vision of Judaism after destruction, the Jewish community at large, leaderless and directionless, might disappear.

Overcoming Our Differences

There is another factor that we might easily overlook. At the beginning, in the decades following the destruction of the Temple, the rabbis were a small movement, composed of masters and their disciples, living, for the most part, in close proximity. And even when the rabbinic movement grew in number and spread, it remained a relatively small proportion of the Jewish population as a whole. Let us not forget, we preserve the disputes of rabbis, not of rabbis and common Jews. Moreover, the rabbis and their disciples instituted rituals of gathering and study (the kallot) which assured that they would be together, study together, live and express their common commitment and faith. In such settings, among loved and trusted companions, they could disagree even forcefully without risking a serious rift. Needless to say, the same disagreements they could allow in the company of rabbis they would not share with outsiders.

All of which demands that we evaluate contemporary Jewish disputes with considerable sobriety. I have argued that the rabbis could tolerate and respect dispute because of their common sense of history, purpose and fate—*and because of the lives they shared.* If we are honest, it will be difficult to claim that the same can be said of large segments of the Jewish community today. Our size and diversity make it difficult for us to share our Jewish experiences in any immediate sense. The size of the world we live in allows us to live separated lives—Israelis from American Jews, Orthodox from liberal Jews, *dati* Jerusalemites from secular residents of Tel Aviv. With different experiences, we will interpret our covenantal commitments differently (or not at all), we will develop different opinions regarding the purpose of Jewish existence and the fate of Jews and Judaism in the next century.

Leap Of Commitment

Our only hope for Jewish "unity" (understood as a relative and compromised term) is a "leap of commitment." Given the diversity of the contemporary Jewish community, we must commit to one another not merely because it is prag-matically necessary but as an act of faith. The problem with the purely pragmatic approach is that, though many of us would agree that we need the cooperation and support of Jews unlike ourselves, selected Jewish groups might conclude that they can survive without other Jews: Haredi without secular, Israeli without American. Pragmatism is a cold, uncaring calculation. But if we believe that we are all children of Abraham and Sarah, all receivers of the Torah of Moses, all fellow survivors of the massacres of Hadrian and Hitler, then we will be less quick to dismiss others who interpret their covenantal commitment differently. Of course, belief is not enough; if we do not act with covenantal commitment, we should be dismissed by those who have taken up the yoke of the covenant. But if we act on this faith, struggling seriously with the responsibilities of Jewish-ness, we will be compelled to respect our differences. We will disagree, but as covenantal partners.

I am aware that this is an idealistic vision, a dream that many will dismiss as beyond reach. It is for this reason that I offer it with sober hesitation. Still, the "realistic" alternative is too awful to speak.

INTRODUCTION TO CHAPTER TWENTY-THREE

One of the most serious—and most frequent—flaws with earlier historical scholarship on the "rabbinic period" is the assumption of many of its practitioners that the rabbis represent "mainstream" Judaism. Indeed, despite frequent critiques of this naive and indefensible assumption, too many contemporary scholars fail to distinguish the evidence of rabbinic literary testimony from "the world out there." The interpretations this failure forces, and the conclusions it demands, riddle histories of Jews in antiquity from the late second Temple period to the Muslim conquest (and beyond).

If one examines the ample historical evidence without such prejudice, one is apt to discover surprising things. Crucially, one of the things one will discover is the fuller significance of the rabbinic movement—and, following it, rabbinic Judaism—against the background of its own time and place. If, by definition, rabbinic Judaism is "mainstream," then its particular contributions will disappear against a background from which, again by definition, it cannot be distinguished. In such a system of assumed definitions, all non-rabbinic phenomena will be viewed as "sectarian." If, on the other hand, one simply examines the evidence for second Temple and post-Temple Judaism, assuming nothing about the hegemony of rabbinic forms, one will appreciate how the rabbis stand out from their background in significant ways. The consequent history is one of remarkable dynamism.

I introduce this essay with these observations because its method might appear to be utterly unremarkable. In this piece, I examine the history of a particular Sabbath law to discover what I can about the rabbinic contribution to definitions of Sabbath observance. I discover that the rabbis introduced significant innovations—innovations which may be interpreted for the ideologies they embody and represent. The history of practice I conduct here has no precedent and the conclusions are newly suggested in this piece. In the course of this history, I am also able to correct several fallacious interpretations or "corrections" suggested by others who made the error of assuming that earlier Judaisms had to be interpreted through rabbinic lenses.

Finally, I include this piece in this section because I draw upon my historical conclusions to suggest contemporary applications. Proposing that "Considered against the background of the historical alternatives, the Rabbinic approach is flexible and liberal," I suggest that contemporary rabbinic leadership would do well to emulate the ancient rabbinic model. Of course, I admit that historical scholarship *need* not affect contemporary practices. But I see no reason why it *should* not.

Chapter Twenty-Three

The Spirit of the Rabbinic Sabbath

When first learning of the details of traditional Sabbath Law, many assimilated or nonobservant Jews recoil in astonishment at the apparent pettiness of the system. Like the first maskilim thrust head-first into modernity, they view the law as restrictive in the extreme—even oppressive. How, they wonder, is it possible to reconcile the reputed lofty spirit of the Sabbath with the onerous letter of the law, a law that is presumably meant to embody and protect the spirit?

Frankly, it is often difficult for us, rabbis and leaders in a mostly unobservant community, to argue convincingly that such a reaction is unwarranted. Though we ourselves may be Sabbath-observant after our own fashion, we too feel the burdens of the traditional halakhic restrictions. If we do not travel on Shabbat, we know how difficult it may be to get together with friends. If we do not use the phone, we know how impossible it is to arrange for a last minute "play-date" for our children or to speak to our loved ones in another city. And while we may expound upon our feeling of liberation at not being enslaved to the call of the phone, or our sense of peace in the absence of the blare of electronic noise, we know that this is only half right. After all, what could be more relaxing than watching a good movie on the VCR, what more spiritually uplifting than listening to a symphony on the CD player?

In what follows, I will argue that, however and whenever the halakha of Shabbat turned in the direction described above, the Rabbinic Sabbath Law is, in its essence and intent, a system of humanitarian liberation. Considered against the background of the historical alternatives, the Rabbinic approach is flexible and liberal, seeking to lighten a day that for other Jews was dark and severe, to enliven an institution that for others affirmed not life but denial and even death.

To make this argument, I choose as my primary example what is probably the most notorious "culprit" in the traditional Sabbath law, that is, restrictions on carrying. With no evident source in the Torah, no clear connection to what we might reasonably describe as "work," the Mishnah and subsequent rabbinic sources elaborate a system plagued by details, one which seems to contradict any system of logic, prohibiting for the sake of prohibiting. For example, this system permits a person to move a bed or table inside his home but prohibits him from carrying a pin from his home to the outdoors or for more than a short distance out of doors. To avoid transgression in this system, one must be familiar with the four Sabbath "domains" (private, public, *carmelit* and neutral) and their precise definitions, with the laws regulating the establishment of an *eruv* and the construction of a *mechitza* (erroneously called "eruv" by many modern observant Jews), and so forth. I have rarely met a rabbi who understands the intricacies of these laws, let alone a lay person. In the face of such overwhelming detail and potential confusion, a person can choose to live in one of relatively few observant communities, to carry nothing anywhere outside her home on the Sabbath, or to ignore the law completely.

But the rabbis did not invent these laws out of a perverse love for complication or a desire to "increase the number of transgressors in Israel." In fact, the rabbis did not invent them at all. Though the prohibition on carrying has no evident source in the Torah, it is demonstrably one of the most ancient and widely defended (and, therefore, presumably transgressed) of all Sabbath prohibitions. If we trace the record of Sabbath Laws as preserved in Jewish works from the biblical and post-biblical periods—an extremely rich corpus—we find that there is barely a source which does not offer some version of the carrying prohibition as central to the observance of the Sabbath. Let us review the record.

In a prophecy accusing the residents of Judah of grave sin and threatening them with punishment and exile (the date is, therefore, c. 600 BCE), Jeremiah recalls his prior instruction to the people, instruction that they had resolutely ignored. What was his earlier instruction?

> Do not carry a burden on the Sabbath day and (or?) bring it in by the gates of Jerusalem. Do not bring a burden out of your homes on the Sabbath day.... But if you listen to me, says the Lord, and do not bring a burden in through the gates of this city on the Sabbath day, and hallow the Sabbath day by doing no work on it, then kings and princes will come in through the gates of this city... (17:21–5)

Clearly, Jeremiah is familiar with the general prohibition of labor on the Sabbath. But the only sort of work he sees fit to emphasize, rendering it symbolic of the fate of Jerusalem as a whole, is carrying. And, crucially, the prohibition already includes not only carrying from outside to inside the city, but even carrying from one's private home out into the streets of the city.

Those who fail these prohibitions are, in his opinion, rightly punished with exile. (Some scholars believe that this section of Jeremiah is a later insertion from the time of Nehemiah. This would mean that we could date this development with confidence only to the mid-5th, not the early 6th, century BCE. But such a chronological difference hardly makes a difference for the point I am making, so we need not detain ourselves with the question of precise dating here.)

The next mention of the Sabbath law is found in Nehemiah 13, in Nehemiah's speech to God recounting his good deeds as governor of Judah. In the course of his statement, Nehemiah reports:

> In those days I saw in Judah those treading winepresses on the Sabbath, and bringing in the sheaves and lading asses; and they even brought into Jerusalem wine, grapes and figs on the Sabbath day... and I said to them: What is this evil thing that you do, profaning the Sabbath day?!... And when the gates of Jerusalem became shadowed before the Sabbath, I said that the doors should be shut... in order that no burden be brought on the Sabbath day (vss. 15–9).

In this account, Nehemiah clearly associates the "bearing of burden" with common agricultural work and related trade. He therefore suggests a rationale for prohibiting what might not otherwise be construed as work. But it remains crucial that, of all possible activities that constitute work and trade, Nehemiah sees fit to include carrying and "bringing in" on his short list. Moreover, we should not forget that in Jeremiah, already, carrying and its permutations were already symbolic of such commercial activity. Thus, it was unnecessary for Jeremiah to justify his objections by reference to trade. Any carrying in or out, whether to the city or from a private home, was already prohibited *as such*. At the earliest stage of the history of Sabbath practice, at least as far as we can recover, carrying is already viewed as one of the most central, and therefore one of the severest, Sabbath prohibitions.

Composed probably c. 100 BCE, Jubilees is the next Jewish work to provide evidence concerning specific Sabbath practices. In chapter two of Jubilees, the author represents God's angel as sharing with Moses the history of God's creation, along with teachings and practices that are consequent upon that creation. Speaking of the laws that follow from the Sabbath of creation, the angel says to Moses:

> Proclaim the law of this day to the sons of Israel and tell them to keep sabbath on it... that it is not lawful to do any work that is unseemly or do their own pleasure on it, or draw water, *or carry any heavy load through their gates* on it... And *they shall not bring in or take out from one house to another* on that day, for that day is more holy and blessed than any jubilee day. (vss. 29–30, emphasis added. Translated by R.H. Charles, revised by C. Rabin.)

It is hardly necessary to comment on this extract, for we see here what we have already seen above. The persistence of this prohibition in ancient Jewish sources is undeniable. What is perhaps most important, as we review this record, is the absoluteness of the law—the absence of loopholes or compromise. As far as we can tell, carrying out or in is prohibited without exception.

This severe and uncompromising prohibition is found again, with only slight elaboration, in another work that probably derives from the same period as Jubilees—the so-called "Damascus Covenant" of the Dead Sea scrolls. There, on column 11, we read:

> A person should not carry from the house to the outside or from the outside to the house. And if he is in a booth, he should not bring out from it nor bring into it. A person should not carry upon himself [even?] herbs to go out or to come in on the Sabbath. One should not carry in a house stones or dirt.

Do not carry out or in on the Sabbath, even the smallest quantity. This is the status of the prohibition—at least in some circles of Jews—in the period immediately before the birth of the rabbinic movement.

How does the rabbinic law compare to what we just saw? In the rabbinic system, the four defined "domains"—formal categories that find no precedent in the earlier record—make all the difference. How so? Because, to begin with, by virtue of the demanding rabbinic definition, a "public domain" is extremely hard to find—if not impossible. (R. Yohanan's relatively "limited" claim in the Bavli [Eruvin 22a, bottom] is that "We are not liable for the public domain in the Land of Israel" [=it doesn't exist]. In the Yerushalmi, the claim is even broader; there we read: "There is no public domain in this world" [Eruvin 8:8].) If there is a bona fide public domain, it can sometimes be made into a *carmelit*. Most of the world is a *carmelit* in any case—a domain in which carrying is prohibited not biblically but only rabbinically (according to rabbinic understanding, of course!). And now the crucial step: a *carmelit* can be symbolically rendered a "private domain." Through the erection of symbolic boundaries (*mechitzot*) and the pooling of domains by establishing a symbolic shared dish (the *eruv*), residents of a common courtyard or even a common city can be said to live in a single "private domain." They may consequently carry from one home to another without restriction, either out or in or from here to there over a distance.

As I said, there is no precedent for this system of artificial, liberating "domains" in the earlier Jewish record. True, there is "the home" and "outside." But these are hardly the rabbis' "private" and "public" domains. As far as we can tell, in the opinion of the authors of the earlier texts, the only way to make the "outside" into a "home" is literally to build a home upon it. And then, for the duration of the Sabbath, what is in your home is stuck there.

There is no way to contribute to your host's Sabbath meal by bringing over desert, at least not if you have forgotten to bring it over beforehand. In the rabbinic system, by contrast, with the appropriate steps, you can combine your homes with the public thoroughfare into a single Sabbath domain, and you may then bring over not only the desert but even the salad—even on the Sabbath itself! In other words, the rabbinic system, through its artificial and narrow definitions, liberates the observant Jew to do many things he or she could not otherwise do. This is the consequence of definitions and details.

Where does the rabbinic system come from? As far as we can determine, from the rabbis themselves. But whether the rabbis invented their particular system regarding carrying on the Sabbath, or whether they chose it from among several such systems, some more restrictive and some less so, the direction of the rabbis' move is unquestionable. The question becomes, then, why did the rabbis chose to do as they did? Can we understand something of their motivations in this significant halakhic choice?

To answer these questions, we must put this particular rabbinic decision in the context of other Sabbath decisions that together suggest a powerfully determined rabbinic conception of the Sabbath. Two decisions that also distinguish the rabbis from other Jews of late antiquity relate to fasting on the Sabbath and saving life.

The prohibition of fasting on the Sabbath in rabbinic law is well known. The Sabbath is supposed to be a time for rejoicing (*oneg*) in rabbinic interpretation. Fasting would destroy this intended spirit. But "well known" should not be equated with "necessary," for equally well known among students of Judaism in Late Antiquity are the many remarks by pagan writers suggesting that at least some Jews fasted on the Sabbath. Almost comically, M. Stern, in his *Greek and Latin Authors on Jews and Judaism*, lists such references in his index under the heading "Sabbath, confused with Day of Atonement." Stern "knows" that Jews don't fast on the Sabbath, so obviously the pagan witnesses must have been confused. Similarly, in his translation of the Damascus Covenant, Theodor Gaster translates an admittedly enigmatic law to declare, "No one is to observe a voluntary fast on the Sabbath," clearly motivated by his "knowledge" that Jews prohibit fasting on the Sabbath.

But neither of these moves is justified. The pagan references to Jews fasting on the Sabbath are too many to allow that they are the products of mere confusion. There are more than two independent witnesses here; their testimony must be upheld. And Gaster's translation is based upon an emendation of the Hebrew word (from *yitarev* to *yitra'ev*) which is the outcome of prejudice and produces a Hebrew form ("to hunger" in the reflexive) that is otherwise unknown (Vermes translates the same word, without emendation, as "willingly mingle"). So there is no extra-rabbinic prohibition on fasting and ample testimony that Jews did fast. Moreover, even the rabbis, in a tradition preserved much later in the Babylonian Talmud (Berakhot 31b), admit that fasting on the Sabbath is so efficacious that it "rends a seventy-year verdict against him [=the person who fasts]." Thus, when the rabbis recommend against fasting, they are imagining the holiness of the Sabbath according to one of several possible interpretive traditions. Some Jews saw holiness in terms of severity and denial. The rabbis, in contrast, saw a holiness that would be expressed in affirmation and joy.

It is also "well known" that, in "Jewish tradition" (=rabbinic tradition), human life is supremely sacred. Therefore, if a person is ill or in danger on the Sabbath, his or her life comes first; the Sabbath is set aside. But we should admit that this priority is neither necessary nor obvious. We could easily argue, to the contrary, that the Sacred Sabbath—the covenantal sign of God's creation—is so important that the value of an individual life pales by comparison. What, after all, is the value of an individual's life compared to the sacred day which, in the much quoted modern expression, "has preserved Israel?"

But in the same "Damascus Covenant," quoted already above, we read the following law (translated as literally as possible):

> And any person [literally, "soul of a person"] who falls into a source of water [=well] or mikveh [=collection of water]—a person should not raise him with a ladder or rope or vessel.

This law clearly believes that using a "tool," that is, "a ladder or rope or vessel," is prohibited on the Sabbath. To use such a tool would be to profane the Sabbath. So, if it is impossible to save a person who has fallen into a well except by profaning the Sabbath, this law demands that the sanctity of the Sabbath be respected and the person be permitted to die. Better to allow one life to be lost than to transgress the sanctity of what is perhaps Israel's most holy day. (Again, because of what "they know" of the values and beliefs of "Judaism," some scholars have refused to accept what they see in this text. Geza Vermes emends the text and translates, "should any man fall into water or fire, let him be pulled out with the aid of a ladder or rope or (some such) utensil." This emendation—reversing completely the meaning of the original!—is without justification, motivated only by a misguided notion regarding what Jews *must* believe.)

To the community whose practices and beliefs are reflected in this law, the Sabbath was an unyielding and inviolate sacred institution. It was holy on its own terms, independent of human participation. Humans could profane it, but their future observance could not hallow it. Thus, what difference did it make if an individual was no longer around to observe it?

The rabbis, in contrast, viewed the Sabbath as a holy occasion in which human participation was essential. Without both the abstention and the joy of the living Jew, the Sabbath was partial, imperfect. For this reason, the rabbis declared that "it is better to profane one Sabbath in order that he [=the person in danger] may observe many Sabbaths." The human life take priority because, according to the rabbinic interpretation, the Sabbath is a time for the affirmation of life: in drink, in meals, even in sexual intercourse.

Against this background, we may now suggest an interpretation or the rabbis' *eruv* law. As we observed earlier, the rabbinic innovation allows residents of a common settlement to combine their various domains into a single common "private" domain. By means of this combination, the rabbinic law overcomes ancient prohibitions and allows Jews to carry from private homes into the public thoroughfare or from one home to another. Significantly, the symbol which serves to combine domains is a shared dish of food, the *eruv*. It seems to me that this choice of a symbol is an expression of the rabbis' motivation and meaning. If the Sabbath should be a time of joy, sharing, and the affirmation of life, then the restriction which largely binds one to one's own home and table is intolerable. True, one could still go over to another's home to partake of a meal—provided one did not have a child or elderly family member who could not walk. But the responsibility would still fall primarily on the inviter, and this might be onerous. At the very least, the community aspect of the Sabbath would be restricted and individual domains separated. On the basis of the rabbinic innovation, though, the Sabbath can become a time of genuine communal sharing. It is a day which brings the community together—for prayer, eating, singing, and rejoicing—rather than breaking it apart. In light of what we saw above concerning rabbinic choices and ways not taken, this interpretation of the eruv law strikes me as a necessary one. It is, as we now see, part of a comprehensive package of interpretations and halakhic choices.

Not long ago, as I was explaining to students in a rabbinical school class that, according to the halakha, Manhattan is not a "public domain," I ran into opposition. The students insisted that they had learned something different with Professor Eliezer Diamond. It just so happened that Professor Diamond was teaching a class down the hall so, during the break, the students ran to him to ask him about the conflict. According to their report, Diamond granted that I was technically correct but, as the students quoted him, "if Manhattan isn't a *reshut harabim* [=public domain], what is?!" My response: that is exactly the point! The rabbis of the Talmudic period did not want there to be a *reshut harabim*—at least not where significant populations of Jews live—as both the Yerushalmi and Bavli attest. They wanted to eliminate the public domain, leaving only a *carmelit*, because this would allow Jews to get together on Shabbat. The alternative—a severe, unyielding, life-denying Shabbat—was intolerable in their eyes. They thus did what was necessary to recreate the Sabbath in their own life-affirming image.

This, in my estimation, is the spirit of the rabbinic Shabbat. Notably, they were courageous enough to manipulate the law to assure that this spirit would be created and protected. Of course, they did not ignore the fact that prohib-ition, too, is essential to creating and protecting the spirit of the Sabbath, but not prohibition alone. Balance is essential and, as the evidence of other communities of Jews (including the later Karaites) demonstrates, the balance can become imbalanced; light can yield to darkness.

What does this mean for those of us who seek to set standards and provide examples in our communities? The individual reader will undoubtedly reach her or his own conclusions; it would be presumptuous of me to suggest specific conclusions for you, because we will have different estimations of what is wise. But there are two lessons that I am willing to propose based upon what we have seen above: First, the intended spirit of the rabbinic Sabbath is relatively clear. If, in your view, the letter of any particular law destroys the spirit, it is incumbent on you to interpret the law so that it allows the affirmation of community celebration, joy, and life on the Sabbath. Second, whatever interpretations you are or are not willing to make, you must take the responsibility of teaching the rabbinic "Sabbath-philosophy" to those who will listen—to those who are interested in Jewish practice but can't always find a way in. If you don't propose certain reinterpretations, perhaps they will intuit them on their own. You will then be in a position to debate the details, to try to strike a balance. The dialogue that will result will be good for you and good for Judaism.

INTRODUCTION TO CHAPTER TWENTY-FOUR

This paper was presented at a conference on "Judaism and the Natural World" held at Harvard University. When I was invited to present a paper, I was engaged in the final revisions of my most recent book, *The Meanings of Death in Rabbinic Judaism* (Routledge, 2000). It was only "natural," then, that I looked to my work-in-progress for something to present. I was aware, from my earlier research, of the meaningful association between a people's burial practices and their beliefs concerning the relationship of humans and the earth. I was thus able to apply what I had learned in my research into death-practices to a consideration of rabbinic beliefs concerning humans and their natural environment.

This piece is, for the most part, a "scholarly" paper, with all of the appropriate apparatus. I include it in this section for two reasons. First, it demonstrates how one's conclusions in an apparently limited field of scholarship can have far wider implications. Second, and more important, I do not pretend to be "merely" objective in the lessons I suggest here. I believe my present conclusions are supported by the evidence, but I do not hesitate to state my conclusions strongly, baldly declaring their political implications. I do not apologize for the political tenor of my conclusions, because these are matters of unparalleled import. If a religion is about our place in the world, then the subject of this chapter is the most "religious" of any in this book.

Chapter Twenty-Four

Jewish Death Practices: A Commentary on the Relationship of Humans to the Natural World

Writing about death practices of the Mambai people of the island of Timor, Peter Metcalf and Richard Huntington remark on "the constant reiteration in ritual language of the motif of the decaying corpse..." Commenting on the centrality of this motif, the authors suggest:

> The significance of this motif relates directly to fundamental ideas of Mambai religion and cosmology. These ideas are expressed in the most sacred and esoteric of their myths... It is a creation myth. Impregnated by Father Heaven, Earth Mother gives birth to the mountains, the trees, and the first people. Having instructed her children about mortuary rituals, she dies. But her body does not entirely decompose. An outer layer forms the "black earth," but beneath the topsoil formed out of her own body the Mother remains whole and pure, her white milk undiminished by death and decay. From this milk plants draw life, and in turn men and animals feed on the plants (Traube 1986: 38–40, 215–16).
>
> The debt that humans owe to the Mother for the gift of life is the underlying motivation behind Mambai death rituals. That debt must be paid back with their bodies, which return to black earth again. Failure to return the debt would throw the entire cosmos out of kilter; plants would not grow to nourish humans, and children would not be born.[1]

Death ritual is here an expression of the relationship of humans to the earth. The relationship established at creation is recapitulated in the ritual of returning-to-the-earth for the Mambai dead.

This example, meant by Metcalf and Huntington to represent one possible interpretive paradigm, suggests that death rituals might be one of a society's most significant expressions of their perceptions of the relationship of humans and the natural world. The foundation of such an interpretive paradigm is the recognition (1) that the relationship between humans and the earth is likely to be established in a people's creation myths (though it might, in theory, originate in myths concerning a subsequent age); (2) that the relationship might be re-lived in a variety of a people's rituals, but (3) that death-rituals are likely to be first among them. This recognition demands that serious consideration always be given to the possibility that death-rituals might serve as a lens through which to view and interpret a people's conceptions of this relationship.

Other examples, which I take from the ancient world, will buttress the plausibility of this interpretive approach. Ancient Egyptian religion assumed an essentially static world, in which nothing significant ever changes. In such a world, "creation is the only event that really matters supremely, since it alone can be said to have made a change." Because everything that is was established at creation, it is the story of creation uniquely that holds the key to understanding the present.[2]

Ancient Egyptian death-practices express complete fidelity to this belief in the unchanging quality of the created world. On the surface, death would appear to be the ultimate change in status—a radical challenge to the beliefs described above. But, as is well known, Egyptians fought this challenge by rendering death an "unchanged" state. In preparing their deceased for entombment, they sought, to the extent possible, to preserve the body from physical change (=decay). This might have been accomplished through mummification. Alternatively, a stone effigy could serve as a "replacement" for the body of the deceased, creating a permanent body that was immune to decay. The liturgy of burial, as well, was directed toward this end. Mortuary priests addressed the deceased by declaring (for example) "Thy bones perish not, thy flesh sickens not, thy members are not distant from thee."[3] In addition to these steps, each person was entombed along with his or her personal ornaments, toilet needs, pots and dishes containing food and drink, and sometimes with weapons and tools. All of this was evidence, of course, of the belief that nothing substantial had changed, for the needs of death were essentially identical to the needs of life. The body, without which the individual could not survive, continued to demand the same sustenance.[4]

In this system, death practices clearly served as a reflection of and commentary on the created world. In this static world, humans, like the rest of creation, were in their essence static, unchanging even in the face of death. An Egyptian who witnessed these rituals and experienced death in this way could have little doubt of this "fact."

Zoroastrianism, the ancient Persian religion, provides an equally powerful example. The Vendidad, a part of the Avesta, opens with the following words:

> Ahura Mazda spake to Spitama Zarathustra, saying:
> I have made every land dear (to its people)...
> The first of the good lands which I, Ahura Mazda, created, was Airyana Vaego, by the Vanguhi Daitya.
> Thereupon came Angra Mainyu, *who is all death*, and he counter-created the serpent in the river and Winter, a work of the Daevas...
> The second of the good lands and countries which I, Ahura Mazda, created, was the plain...
> Thereupon came Angra Mainyu, *who is all death*, and he counter-created the locust, *which brings death* unto cattle and plants.
> The third of the good lands and countries which I, Ahura Mazda, created, was the strong, holy Mouru.
> Thereupon came Angra Mainyu, *who is all death*, and he counter-created plunder and sin. [emphasis added][5]

And so forth. The creation of the world is enacted in a series of steps and counter-steps, the benevolent god, Ahura Mazda (=Ohrmazd; see below), creating good land and his evil counterpart, Angra Mainyu, creating suffering and death. The text is emphatic in its insistence that Angra Maiynu, who creates death, is all death.[6]

The creation of humanity itself proceeds in the following steps: The Just Man was created sixth in the order of creation (followed only by Fire). Man was created in five parts—"body, breath, soul, form and fravahr" (=that part of man "which is in the presence of Ohrmazd the Lord."). The tradition explains the reason for creation in these parts: "so that when during the Assault men die, the body rejoins the earth, the breath the wind, the form the sun, and the soul the fravahr, so that the devs should not be able to destroy the soul." The first man, Gayomard, met death because of the Evil Spirit, but, upon death, he emitted seed which was purified by the light of the sun. This seed led to the growth of special plants, from which all of humanity ultimately emerged.[7]

According to the system outlined above, there is a primeval enmity built into the very fabric of creation. Good and evil, products of different and antagonistic creating gods, are and will ever be in opposition to one another (until, that is, the end of history and the final defeat of the force of evil). Since, in this belief, evil and death are essentially equated, death must be seen as the greatest of mundane evils, to be hated and shunned. Indeed, Zoroastrian religious practice, as codified in the Vendidad, was as much as anything else a system for dealing with the danger of death.

The deceased, whose soul had departed and whose body had been possessed by the demon of death, the Drug Nasu, was to be disposed of as immediately as possible. But there were practical limitations on the disposal of the dead. As is well known, ideally, corpses were to be placed on Dakhmas, towers for the dead, where their bodies would be consumed by dogs and birds. In a territory where there were no Dakhmas, corpses were instead to be placed "on the highest summits, where they know there are always corpse-eating dogs and corpse-eating birds" (Vendidad, Fargard VI, V:45). If the season or weather made proper disposal impossible (in the winter, for example, there may be no dogs and birds about to consume the corpse), the dead were to be buried in the house until conditions changed, at which time they could be exhumed and properly exposed (Fargard VIII, II:4–10).

From even these few details, it is clear that Zoroastrian death practices recapitulate the enmity built into creation at its origins. Evil and impure death, brought into the world by the Evil God of creation and the demons who do the work of that God, must be kept separate from the pure earth. Humans must similarly maintain their distance from death impurity. Thus, death must literally be carried away; permanent interment of the corpse is a sin, bringing together, as it does, opposing forces. But to say that impure death and pure earth must be separated is not to say that humans, purified of death long after death, remain separated from the earth. Rather, the dust of the person, consumed and then scattered, will rejoin the earth, later to be reassembled for resurrection.[8] Earth and Death cannot be united, Earth and humans ultimately must be. In practice, the purity of the earth must always be protected. To fail to do so is, in Zoroastrianism, a sin of the highest degree.

We could multiply examples to demonstrate the claim made earlier, but these should already suffice. Death and creation are inextricably linked. Death practice, therefore, will serve as a commentary on the meaning of creation and the place of human's within it.

We may now turn to classical Jewish death practices, as described in rabbinic literature,[9] to consider the nature of their commentary on the relationship between humans and the natural world.

According to Mishnah[10] Shabbat 23:5, immediately following death, the "needs of the dead" must be attended to. These "needs" (nearly identical to contemporary Roman practice[11]) include closing the eyes of the dead, anointing and washing the body, removing the pillow (or mattress), placing the dead on the sand (=the ground) and tying the jaw in place. For present purposes, the most interesting of these practices is the removal of the body to the ground. What is the purpose, practically and symbolically, of this long forgotten practice?

The Mishnah explains that the purpose of this requirement is "so that he may remain" or, according to another version, "be cooled." Reasonably enough, in a warm climate where the dead might quickly begin to decompose, steps must be taken to delay the process, particularly if we interpret this requirement as pertaining only on Shabbat (when delay of burial until the next day is necessary). But the other practices described by the Mishnah are not restricted to the Sabbath, so such a limited interpretation is at least problematic. Moreover, as noted parenthetically above, the rabbinic customs closely mimic prevalent Roman customs, which include the laying of the deceased on the ground. Obviously the Roman custom was not motivated by Sabbath restrictions. It seems to me likely, therefore, that laying on the ground is a more popular Jewish custom, one which the rabbis behind the Mishnah endorse. The Mishnah's explanation of this practice may simply be a "rationalization" intended to deny popular explanations of the same practice. But, be that as it may, this doesn't change the fact that the placing-on-the-ground is the first step in a process which ultimately leads to the laying of the deceased in a cave under the ground. It is in this context that the practice must be interpreted.

Also crucial to interpretation is the more immediate mishnaic context. The Mishnah's discussion of the "needs of the dead" is part of a larger discussion of stringencies and leniencies pertaining to acts which are technically permitted on the Sabbath but still problematic. For example, immediately preceding its discussion of preparations for burial, the Mishnah prohibits a person from waiting at the boundary of Sabbath-settlement in order to be closer to his fields at the Sabbath's end. In fact, merely standing by the boundary is technically permissible. The Mishnah's prohibition is motivated by the problem-atic intent of the person who would perform this act. By contrast, in the next ruling, "the business of the bride" and "the business of the dead" (=bringing the casket and shroud) are permitted—though one who does these things runs the risk of actually transgressing the Sabbath—apparently because of the perceived importance of marriage and burial.

Which brings us to "the needs of the dead." These "needs of the dead" are distinct, in this Mishnah, from the "business of the dead"—the latter involving preparations for the funeral and the former acts directly relating to the deceased. The needs of the dead are apparently considered sufficiently important to warrant some flexibility with respect to acts that would under other circumstances be prohibited on the Sabbath. Why so? If we admit (as the rabbinic record broadly suggests) that the deceased person was considered sentient, then he or she would have bona fide needs—needs relating to what he or she was actually *feeling*. What the deceased "needs," in other words, is steps to diminish the discomfort of death. So "oiling" (=anointing) would be called for even on the Sabbath because it would help eliminate the discomfort that stiffness brings the deceased. Similarly, if the body is sentient, decomposition would hurt, and slowing the process—as this Mishnah suggests—would postpone discomfort. In this context, the question becomes whether separation of the body from the earth was also believed to be the source of discomfort. Evidence available elsewhere leads me to answer a tentative "yes."

Saul Lieberman documents the ancient Jewish belief (held by other peoples as well) that no fate was worse than lack of burial—lack of return to the soil.[12] If the dead would suffer by distance from the soil, then this practice may properly be construed as a "need of the dead," intended to avoid discomfort. This act, like others listed in the Mishnah, addressed or responded to genuine needs of the deceased, literally conceived. For this reason were these practices permitted on the Sabbath.

As mentioned, this placing on the ground was the first step in a long process of returning the body of the deceased to the soil. Of course, part of the process—a significant part—was the entombment of the deceased under the ground. But this was not identical to burial, and the difference is important. The Mishnah assumes, and archaeology has confirmed, that Jews would be buried in caves (see m. Baba Batra 6:8). The bodies would be placed in spaces carved in the walls of the caves, and these niches (or ditches carved in shelves) would be closed with stones (or covered with stone slabs). But, crucially, the stones could be removed, and those who visited the deceased could therefore know—because they would witness—the progress of the decay of the flesh and its return to "dust." It was important to know when the flesh had decayed fully because, when the bones alone were left, they would be gathered and reburied—an occasion for both sadness (because it recalled the death itself) and celebration (because the deceased was finally "gathered unto his ancestors") (see m. Moed Qatan 1:5). Only at this final point was death fully realized— atonement complete and peace in the world of the dead assured.

The centrality of the return-to-the-earth in rabbinic death ritual is reinforced in a long-forgotten mourning ritual. Among the various obligations/prohibitions which apply to the mourner is the obligation to overturn all of the couches/beds in his home (see Mishnah Taanit 4:7 and Tosefta Moed Qatan 2:9). Of course, if couches and beds (=places to sit and recline) are unavailable, the mourner will be forced to sit on the ground—close to and in striking imitation of the deceased. It is crucial that we be mindful of this latter factor: that is, the partial participation of the mourner, through ritual enactment, in the experience of the deceased. The parallel of the experience of mourner and deceased takes many shapes: the special quality of the first three days following death for each, the inability of each to participate in "the settlement of the world" (through work and sex), *both* mourning the death for seven days (see Talmud Bavli, tractate Shabbat, p. 152a, bottom), and so forth. The requirement that the mourner be on or close to the ground is another of these parallels, one which ritually emphasizes the importance of such terrestrial proximity. As we saw above, death is about returning to the ground, the flesh returning to dust. But life, too, is never far from the earth.

The relationship between the rituals just recounted and Judaism's creation myth will be obvious. In its brief description of the creation of the first human, Genesis 2:7 relates that "the Lord God formed the person dirt from the ground and blew into his nostrils the breath of life, and the human became a living soul." Humans (=this first human, later separated into male and female) are earth, and therefore, as the author of Ecclesiastes much later states, just as all life comes from dirt, so must all life return to dirt (3:20). At first reading, the association between creation-myth and death ritual is straightforward and the lesson of this association matter-of-fact. We are, in our essence, one with the earth, as our ritual of return-to-the-earth will ever remind us.

But the associations and ritual choices are not as simple as they initially seem. To begin with, as has oft been noted, the Torah commences with not one creation story but two, and the accounts of the creation of humans differ significantly. In contrast with the story of Genesis 2, which we just considered, Genesis 1 emphasizes that God created humans by God's word, created them "in the image of God." This account allows for no essential connection between humans and the earth, for God did not create humans out of a pre-existent substance. Moreover, the claim that humans are "in the image of God" seems to suggest that humans are "above" the earth, and certainly essentially different from it. So, by a critical reading, the Torah offers a choice of creation stories, a choice that will lead to drastically different conclusions concerning the relationship of humans and the natural world.

I am sensitive to the fact that traditional readers, reading stories that are canonically juxtaposed, are unlikely to have read these two stories as opposing one another. Instead, apparent tensions or contradictions would surely have been smoothed over, somehow reconciled. Still, such readings will inevitably demand differences of emphasis or priority, that is, the reading of one of these two stories in light of the other. So, for example, the second, earth-bound story, might be viewed as a specification and elaboration of the first, God-directed story. But choices of emphasis are significant too, and the fact that living (and dying) Jewish culture, as portrayed by the rabbis, emphasized, in its death rituals, the second story instead of the first, is a matter of considerable note.

Imagine the alternative: If a Jewish society viewed as centrally important the belief that humans were created by God's word in God's image, then they might distance their dead from the earth—like Zoroastrians but for different reasons—or they might struggle to preserve the image of God, the human form, against deterioration—like ancient Egyptians but again for different reasons. The first version of the creation, like the second, could have been recapitulated in death ritual, and that ritual choice would have made an equally important point. The fact that this way was not taken, that the ritual draws our attentions to the primacy of the version of chapter two, shapes considerably our appreciation of the essential relationship between humans and the earth.

Moreover, the second creation story is not just about the creation of humans from the earth, as Ecclesiastes already appreciates. According to this same story, not only did God form humans out of the earth, but God also "formed out of the earth all the wild beasts and all the birds of the sky..." (2:19). All life emerges from the earth, all life (as Ecclesiastes teaches) must return to the earth—all life is one with the earth and with each other.

The essential relationship between humans and all life, therefore, is enacted in the rabbinic death rituals described above. This too, of course, was not necessary. Again, imagine the alternative: The first creation story describes animals and humans in a strictly hierarchical relationship—the former were created by way of preparation for the latter, the latter were created to "rule over" the former. There is no obvious or necessary relationship between the two (that is, in their essence). To symbolize this hierarchical division, humans might have been distanced from the earth upon death, because there, in the earth, is the final resting place of animals. If animals become one with the earth, humans might be imagined to flee terrestrial life to the heavens (by "mysteriously" disappearing from high mountains, for example). This is a way that might have been. It is a way not taken.

To reiterate, the death rituals teach a lesson. In their recapitulation of the second creation story, they declare that humans are one with the animal kingdom and with the earth—one with the natural world. This is a relationship not of subduing or conquest, but of natural partnership. An act of abuse against the natural world is an abuse against humanity, and vice versa. In fact, the dichotomy of "human" and "natural world" is undermined in the view of this ritual mythology, because humans and the natural world are one—originating in the same substance, temporarily taking different forms, but returning, in their end, to the same form.

What are the normative implications of this conclusion? If we understand, with Robert Cover, that law ("nomos") is the other side of narrative,[13] then the narrative and ritual telling of this story of the origins of humanity in-and-of-the-earth will have concrete ethical and normative consequences: The ancient Jewish ritual-narrative demands that we not view the natural world as "other," something to serve our needs, something to exploit. Instead, it requires us to relate to the natural world—that is, to ourselves and the non-human world around us—as parts of an organic whole. Moreover, the death ritual-narrative stands in tension with the basic premise of the (rabbinically construed) law of "*bal tashchit*" ("do not destroy")—that is, that any use of resources which serves human needs is not viewed as wasteful. Only if we recognize that no human need stands independent of the needs of the earth as a whole can we eliminate this tension. Indeed, though rabbinic teachings and practices might conflict with one another, in this case, the reconciliation of the apparent conflict might yield the simplest translation of rabbinic values: Our needs are part of, and must be harmonized with, the needs of the natural world.

Notes

1. Peter Metcalf and Richard Huntington, *Celebrations of Death: The Anthropology of Mortuary Ritual* (2nd edition; Cambridge: Cambridge University Press, 1991), pp. 106–7.
2. Henri Frankfort, *Ancient Egyptian Religion* (New York: Columbia U. Press, 1948; repr. New York: Harper, 1961), pp. 50–1.
3. Quoted in James Henry Breasted, *Development of Religion and Thought in Ancient Egypt* (New York: Scribner's, 1912), p. 57.
4. Frankfort, pp. 90 and 93.
5. *The Sacred Books of the East*, v. 3, *The Zend-Avesta*, trans. by James Darmesteter (New York: The Christian Literature Company, 1898), pp. 2–5.
6. Yasna 30:3–4, expresses the same belief in this language: "Truly there are two primal Spirits, twins renowned to be in conflict... And when these two Spirits first came together they created life and not-life, and how at the end Worst Existence shall be for the wicked, but (the House of) Best Purpose for the just man." Translation by Mary Boyce in *Textual Sources for the Study of Zoroastrianism* (Chicago: U. of Chicago, 1984), p. 35.
7. For this record of creation, see Mary Boyce, pp. 48–52. Though these traditions are included in a later record of the Zoroastrian Zand, Boyce's judgment is that they are earlier Zoroastrian beliefs; see p. 45.
8. See Boyce, p. 52.
9. Though the practices of non-rabbinized Jews, and even of the rabbis themselves, may often have diverged from the rabbinic record, as the evidence of Beth Shearim testifies.
10. The Mishnah is the first of the classical rabbinic compositions, completed in c. 200 CE. It is, by appearance, a law code, though some have argued for alternative interpretations of its intended or primary purpose.
11. See J.M.C. Toynbee, *Death and Burial in the Roman World* (Ithica, NY: Cornell University Press, 1971), p. 44.
12. Saul Lieberman, "Some Aspects of After Life in Early Rabbinic Literature," *Harry A. Wolfson Jubilee Volume* (Jerusalem: Journal of the American Academy of Religion, 1965), pp. 515–522.
13. See Robert M. Cover, "The Supreme Court, 1982 Term—Foreword: Nomos and Narrative," *Harvard Law Review* 97, 4 (1983).

Bibliography of Writings by David Kraemer

(Items are arranged chronologically in categories. Items marked with a * appear in this volume.)

BOOKS

The Meanings of Death in Rabbinic Judaism. London: Routledge, 1999.

Reading the Rabbis: The Talmud as Literature. New York: Oxford U. Press, 1996.

Responses to Suffering in Classical Rabbinic Literature. New York: Oxford University Press, 1995.

The Mind of the Talmud: An Intellectual History of the Bavli. New York: Oxford University Press, 1990. (Named an "Outstanding Academic Book of 1991" by *Choice*, May 1992.)

editor, *The Jewish Family: Metaphor and Memory.* New York: Oxford University Press, (New York and Oxford, 1989).

ARTICLES

"Kosher," "Midrash," "Talmud," and "Torah." In *Contemporary American Religion.* Ed. Wade Clark Roof. New York: Macmillan, forthcoming.

*"Evil and Suffering, Judaic Doctrines of." In *The Millennial Encyclopaedia of Judaism, The Religion.* Ed. W.S. Green et. al. Forthcoming.

*"Rabbinic Sources for Historical Study," in *Judaism in Late Antiquity*, part. 3, v. 1, *Where We Stand: Issues and Debates in Ancient Judaism.* Ed. J. Neusner and Alan J. Avery-Peck. Leiden: E.J. Brill, 1998, pp. 201-212.

*"Disputes that Unite." *Sh'ma* v. 28, n. 543 (December 12, 1997): 1-3.

*"The Spirit of the Rabbinic Sabbath." *Conservative Judaism*, (Summer, 1997): 42-9.

*"Child and Family Life in Judaism." In *Religious Dimensions of Child and Family Life.* Ed. Harold Coward and Philip Cook. Victoria: University of Victoria, 1996, pp. 113-121.

*"Local Conditions for a Developing Rabbinic Tradition" and *"Scriptural Interpretation in the Mishnah" In *Hebrew Bible/Old Testament: The History of its Interpretation*, v. 1. Ed. Magne Sæbø. Gottingen: Vandenhoeck and Ruprecht, 1996, pp. 270-284.

*"When God is Wrong." *Sh'ma: A Journal of Jewish Responsibility* (26/499, October 13, 1995): 1-3.

*"Dramatizing the Torah." *Sh'ma: A Journal of Jewish Responsibility* (24/463, December 10, 1993): 1-3.

"The Ideal Reader as a Key to Interpreting the Bavli." *Prooftexts* 13 (1993): 1-17.

*"On the Relationship of the Books of Ezra and Nehemiah." *Journal for the Study of the Old Testament*, 59 (1993): 73-92. Reprinted in *The Historical Books: A Sheffield Reader*. Ed. J. Cheryl Exum. Sheffield: Sheffield Academic Press, 1997, pp. 303-321.

*"Jewish Ethics and Abortion." *Tikkun* 8, n. 1 (Jan.-Feb. 1993): 55-8.

"Baraita" and "Tanna/Tannaim." *The Anchor Bible Dictionary* (Doubleday and Co.), v. 1, p. 608 and v. 6, p. 319.

guest editor, Shofar: *An Interdisciplinary Journal of Jewish Studies* 10, n. 2 (Winter 1992).

*"Rhetoric of Failed Refutation in the Bavli." *Shofar* 10, n. 2 (Winter 1992): 73-85.

"The Mind of the Talmud: Hubris, Piety and Divine Truth." *Proceedings of the Rabbinical Assembly* (1991): 89-99.

*"*Prozbul* and Rabbinic Power." *S'vara: A Journal of Philosophy, Law, and Judaism* 2, n. 2 (1991): 66-70.

*"The Formation of Rabbinic Canon: Authority and Boundaries." *Journal of Biblical Literature* 110, n. 4 (Winter 1991): 613-630.

"The Talmud According to Rabbi Adin Steinsaltz." *Congress Monthly* 57, n. 5 (July/August 1990): 17-9.

*"Critical Readings and Religious Insight: New Readings in the Bavli." *Conservative Judaism* 42, n. 3 (Spring, 1990): 48-53.

*"Scripture Commentary in the Babylonian Talmud: A Primary or Secondary Phenomenon?" *AJS Review*, v. XIV, n. 1 (Spring, 1989): 1-15.

*"On the Reliability of Attributions in the Bavli." *Hebrew Union College Annual*, v. 60 (1989): 175-190. Reprinted in *Essential Papers on The Talmud*. Ed. Michael Chernick. New York: NYU Press, 1994, pp. 276-292.

*"The Beginnings of the Preservation of Argumentation in Amoraic Babylonia." In *New Perspectives on Ancient Judaism*, v. 4, *The Literature of Early Rabbinic Judaism: Issues in Talmudic Redaction and Interpretation*. Ed. A. Avery-Peck. Lanham: University Press of America, 1989, pp. 37-46.

*"Images of Childhood and Adolescence in Talmudic Literature." In *The Jewish Family: Metaphor and Memory*. Ed. David Kraemer. New York: Oxford U. Press, 1989, pp. 65-80.

*"Composition and Meaning in the Bavli." *Prooftexts* 8, n. 3 (Sept. 1988): 271-291.

"New Meaning in Ancient Talmudic Texts: A Rhetorical Reading and the Case for Pluralism." *Proceedings of the Rabbinical Assembly* (1987): 201-214.

*"New Meaning in Ancient Talmudic Texts: A Time Poem." *Proceedings of the Rabbinical Assembly* (1987): 215-225.

*"The Scientific Study of Talmud." *Judaism*, v. 36, n. 4 (Fall 1987): 471-478.

"The Scholars Dilemma: In Tribute to Professor Louis Ginzberg." *Proceedings of the Rabbinical Assembly*, v. XLVIII (1986): 153-166.

"Tanna." In *The Encyclopedia of Religion*. New York: Macmillan Publishing Co., 1987.

"Gamliel of Yavneh." In *The Encyclopedia of Religion*.

"Eleazar ben Azariah." In *The Encyclopedia of Religion*.

"Eliezer ben Hyrcanus." In *The Encyclopedia of Religion*.

*"A Developmental Perspective on the Laws of Niddah." *Conservative Judaism*, vol. XXXVIII, n. 3 (Spring 1986): 26-33.

"The Origins of the Sugya as a Literary Unit." *Proceedings of the Ninth World Congress of Jewish Studies*, vol. 3, (August 1985) (publication date: 1986): 23-30.

"Critical Aids to Teaching Talmud." *Jewish Education* (Spring 1981).

REVIEWS

Review of Jack N. Lightstone, *The Rhetoric of the Babylonian Talmud, Its Social Meaning and Context*. In *The Toronto Journal of Theology*.

Review of *Talmudic Thinking: Language, Logic, Law*, by J. Neusner (Columbia, S. Carolina: U. of S. Carolina Press, 1992). *AJS Review*, 20, n. 1 (1995): 188-191.

Review of *Writing with Scripture: The Authority and Uses of the Hebrew Bible in the Torah of Formative Judaism*, by Jacob Neusner with William Scott Green. *The Journal of Religion* 71, n. 4 (Oct. 1991): 569-571.

Note on *Judaisms and their Messiahs*, J. Neusner, W.S. Green, and E. Frerichs, eds. *Religious Studies Review* 15, n. 2 (April, 1989): 175.

Note on *The Talmud of Babylonia, An American Translation* VIII: Tractate Besah, translated and explained by Alan J. Avery-Peck. *Religious Studies Review* 15, n. 1 (Jan. 1989): 82.

Note on *Jewish Marriage in Palestine, A Cairo Geniza Study*, by Mordechai Akiva Friedman. *Religious Studies Review* 14, n. 1 (Jan. 1988): 80.

Note on *At the End of the Second Temple and in the Period of the Mishnah* (Hebrew), by Shmuel Safrai. *Religious Studies Review* 13, n. 2 (April 1987): 172.

Review of *The Talmud as Law or Literature*, by Irwin H. Haut. *Conservative Judaism* 37, n. 1 (Fall 1983).

South Florida Studies in the History of Judaism

240001	Lectures on Judaism in the Academy and in the Humanities	Neusner
240002	Lectures on Judaism in the History of Religion	Neusner
240003	Self-Fulfilling Prophecy: Exile and Return in the History of Judaism	Neusner
240004	The Canonical History of Ideas: The Place of the So-called Tannaite Midrashim, Mekhilta Attributed to R. Ishmael, Sifra, Sifré to Numbers, and Sifré to Deuteronomy	Neusner
240005	Ancient Judaism: Debates and Disputes, Second Series	Neusner
240006	The Hasmoneans and Their Supporters: From Mattathias to the Death of John Hyrcanus I	Sievers
240007	Approaches to Ancient Judaism: New Series, Volume One	Neusner
240008	Judaism in the Matrix of Christianity	Neusner
240009	Tradition as Selectivity: Scripture, Mishnah, Tosefta, and Midrash in the Talmud of Babylonia	Neusner
240010	The Tosefta: Translated from the Hebrew: Sixth Division Tohorot	Neusner
240011	In the Margins of the Midrash: Sifre Ha'azinu Texts, Commentaries and Reflections	Basser
240012	Language as Taxonomy: The Rules for Using Hebrew and Aramaic in the Babylonia Talmud	Neusner
240013	The Rules of Composition of the Talmud of Babylonia: The Cogency of the Bavli's Composite	Neusner
240014	Understanding the Rabbinic Mind: Essays on the Hermeneutic of Max Kadushin	Ochs
240015	Essays in Jewish Historiography	Rapoport-Albert
240016	The Golden Calf and the Origins of the Jewish Controversy	Bori/Ward
240017	Approaches to Ancient Judaism: New Series, Volume Two	Neusner
240018	The Bavli That Might Have Been: The Tosefta's Theory of Mishnah Commentary Compared With the Bavli's	Neusner
240019	The Formation of Judaism: In Retrospect and Prospect	Neusner
240020	Judaism in Society: The Evidence of the Yerushalmi, Toward the Natural History of a Religion	Neusner
240021	The Enchantments of Judaism: Rites of Transformation from Birth Through Death	Neusner
240022	Åbo Addresses	Neusner
240023	The City of God in Judaism and Other Comparative and Methodological Studies	Neusner
240024	The Bavli's One Voice: Types and Forms of Analytical Discourse and their Fixed Order of Appearance	Neusner
240025	The Dura-Europos Synagogue: A Re-evaluation (1932-1992)	Gutmann
240026	Precedent and Judicial Discretion: The Case of Joseph ibn Lev	Morell
240027	Max Weinreich *Geschichte der jiddischen Sprachforschung*	Frakes
240028	Israel: Its Life and Culture, Volume I	Pedersen
240029	Israel: Its Life and Culture, Volume II	Pedersen
240030	The Bavli's One Statement: The Metapropositional Program of Babylonian Talmud Tractate Zebahim Chapters One and Five	Neusner

240031	The Oral Torah: The Sacred Books of Judaism: An Introduction: Second Printing	Neusner
240032	The Twentieth Century Construction of "Judaism:" Essays on the Religion of Torah in the History of Religion	Neusner
240033	How the Talmud Shaped Rabbinic Discourse	Neusner
240034	The Discourse of the Bavli: Language, Literature, and Symbolism: Five Recent Findings	Neusner
240035	The Law Behind the Laws: The Bavli's Essential Discourse	Neusner
240036	Sources and Traditions: Types of Compositions in the Talmud of Babylonia	Neusner
240037	How to Study the Bavli: The Languages, Literatures, and Lessons of the Talmud of Babylonia	Neusner
240038	The Bavli's Primary Discourse: Mishnah Commentary: Its Rhetorical Paradigms and their Theological Implications	Neusner
240039	Midrash Aleph Beth	Sawyer
240040	Jewish Thought in the 20th Century: An Introduction in the Talmud of Babylonia Tractate Moed Qatan	Schweid
240041	Diaspora Jews and Judaism: Essays in Honor of, and in Dialogue with, A. Thomas Kraabel	Overman/MacLennan
240042	The Bavli: An Introduction	Neusner
240043	The Bavli's Massive Miscellanies: The Problem of Agglutinative Discourse in the Talmud of Babylonia	Neusner
240044	The Foundations of the Theology of Judaism: An Anthology Part II: Torah	Neusner
240045	Form-Analytical Comparison in Rabbinic Judaism: Structure and Form in *The Fathers* and *The Fathers According to Rabbi Nathan*	Neusner
240046	Essays on Hebrew	Weinberg
240047	The Tosefta: An Introduction	Neusner
240048	The Foundations of the Theology of Judaism: An Anthology Part III: Israel	Neusner
240049	The Study of Ancient Judaism, Volume I: Mishnah, Midrash, Siddur	Neusner
240050	The Study of Ancient Judaism, Volume II: The Palestinian and Babylonian Talmuds	Neusner
240051	Take Judaism, for Example: Studies toward the Comparison of Religions	Neusner
240052	From Eden to Golgotha: Essays in Biblical Theology	Moberly
240053	The Principal Parts of the Bavli's Discourse: A Preliminary Taxonomy: Mishnah Commentary, Sources, Traditions and Agglutinative Miscellanies	Neusner
240054	Barabbas and Esther and Other Studies in the Judaic Illumination of Earliest Christianity	Aus
240055	Targum Studies, Volume I: Textual and Contextual Studies in the Pentateuchal Targums	Flesher
240056	Approaches to Ancient Judaism: New Series, Volume Three, Historical and Literary Studies	Neusner
240057	The Motherhood of God and Other Studies	Gruber
240058	The Analytic Movement: Hayyim Soloveitchik and his Circle	Solomon
240059	Recovering the Role of Women: Power and Authority in Rabbinic Jewish Society	Haas

240060	The Relation between Herodotus' *History* and Primary History	Mandell/Freedman
240061	The First Seven Days: A Philosophical Commentary on the Creation of Genesis	Samuelson
240062	The Bavli's Intellectual Character: The Generative Problematic: In Bavli Baba Qamma Chapter One And Bavli Shabbat Chapter One	Neusner
240063	The Incarnation of God: The Character of Divinity in Formative Judaism: Second Printing	Neusner
240064	Moses Kimhi: Commentary on the Book of Job	Basser/Walfish
240066	Death and Birth of Judaism: Second Printing	Neusner
240067	Decoding the Talmud's Exegetical Program	Neusner
240068	Sources of the Transformation of Judaism	Neusner
240069	The Torah in the Talmud: A Taxonomy of the Uses of Scripture in the Talmud, Volume I	Neusner
240070	The Torah in the Talmud: A Taxonomy of the Uses of Scripture in the Talmud, Volume II	Neusner
240071	The Bavli's Unique Voice: A Systematic Comparison of the Talmud of Babylonia and the Talmud of the Land of Israel, Volume One	Neusner
240072	The Bavli's Unique Voice: A Systematic Comparison of the Talmud of Babylonia and the Talmud of the Land of Israel, Volume Two	Neusner
240073	The Bavli's Unique Voice: A Systematic Comparison of the Talmud of Babylonia and the Talmud of the Land of Israel, Volume Three	Neusner
240074	Bits of Honey: Essays for Samson H. Levey	Chyet/Ellenson
240075	The Mystical Study of Ruth: *Midrash HaNe'elam* of the Zohar to the Book of Ruth	Englander
240076	The Bavli's Unique Voice: A Systematic Comparison of the Talmud of Babylonia and the Talmud of the Land of Israel, Volume Four	Neusner
240077	The Bavli's Unique Voice: A Systematic Comparison of the Talmud of Babylonia and the Talmud of the Land of Israel, Volume Five	Neusner
240078	The Bavli's Unique Voice: A Systematic Comparison of the Talmud of Babylonia and the Talmud of the Land of Israel, Volume Six	Neusner
240079	The Bavli's Unique Voice: A Systematic Comparison of the Talmud of Babylonia and the Talmud of the Land of Israel, Volume Seven	Neusner
240080	Are There Really Tannaitic Parallels to the Gospels?	Neusner
240081	Approaches to Ancient Judaism: New Series, Volume Four, Religious and Theological Studies	Neusner
240082	Approaches to Ancient Judaism: New Series, Volume Five, Historical, Literary, and Religious Studies	Basser/Fishbane
240083	Ancient Judaism: Debates and Disputes, Third Series	Neusner
240084	Judaic Law from Jesus to the Mishnah	Neusner
240085	Writing with Scripture: Second Printing	Neusner/Green
240086	Foundations of Judaism: Second Printing	Neusner

240087	Judaism and Zoroastrianism at the Dusk of Late Antiquity	Neusner
240088	Judaism States Its Theology	Neusner
240089	The Judaism behind the Texts I.A	Neusner
240090	The Judaism behind the Texts I.B	Neusner
240091	Stranger at Home	Neusner
240092	Pseudo-Rabad: Commentary to Sifre Deuteronomy	Basser
240093	FromText to Historical Context in Rabbinic Judaism	Neusner
240094	Formative Judaism	Neusner
240095	Purity in Rabbinic Judaism	Neusner
240096	Was Jesus of Nazareth the Messiah?	McMichael
240097	The Judaism behind the Texts I.C	Neusner
240098	The Judaism behind the Texts II	Neusner
240099	The Judaism behind the Texts III	Neusner
240100	The Judaism behind the Texts IV	Neusner
240101	The Judaism behind the Texts V	Neusner
240102	The Judaism the Rabbis Take for Granted	Neusner
240103	From Text to Historical Context in Rabbinic Judaism V. II	Neusner
240104	From Text to Historical Context in Rabbinic Judaism V. III	Neusner
240105	Samuel, Saul, and Jesus: Three Early Palestinian Jewish Christian Gospel Haggadoth	Aus
240106	What is Midrash? And a Midrash Reader	Neusner
240107	Rabbinic Judaism: Disputes and Debates	Neusner
240108	Why There Never Was a "Talmud of Caesarea"	Neusner
240109	Judaism after the Death of "The Death of God"	Neusner
240110	Approaches to Ancient Judaism	Neusner
240112	The Judaic Law of Baptism	Neusner
240113	The Documentary Foundation of Rabbinic Culture	Neusner
240114	Understanding Seeking Faith, Volume Four	Neusner
240115	Paul and Judaism: An Anthropological Approach	Laato
240116	Approaches to Ancient Judaism, New Series, Volume Eight	Neusner
240119	Theme and Context in Biblical Lists	Scolnic
240120	Where the Talmud Comes From	Neusner
240121	The Initial Phases of the Talmud, Volume Three: Social Ethics	Neusner
240122	Are the Talmuds Interchangeable? Christine Hayes's Blunder	Neusner
240123	The Initial Phases of the Talmud, Volume One: Exegesis of Scripture	Neusner
240124	The Initial Phases of the Talmud, Volume Two: Exemplary Virtue	Neusner
240125	The Initial Phases of the Talmud, Volume Four: Theology	Neusner
240126	From Agnon to Oz	Bargad
240127	Talmudic Dialectics, Volume I: Tractate Berakhot and the Divisions of Appointed Times and Women	Neusner
240128	Talmudic Dialectics, Volume II: The Divisions of Damages and Holy Things and Tractate Niddah	Neusner
240129	The Talmud: Introduction and Reader	Neusner
240130	*Gesher Vakesher:* Bridges and Bonds The Life of Leon Kronish	Green
240131	Beyond Catastrophe	Neusner

240132	Ancient Judaism, Fourth Series	Neusner
240133	Formative Judaism, New Series: Current Issues and Arguments Volume One	Neusner
240134	Sects and Scrolls	Davies
240135	Religion and Law	Neusner
240136	Approaches to Ancient Judaism, New Series, Volume Nine	Neusner
240137	Uppsala Addresses	Neusner
240138	Jews and Christians in the Life and Thought of Hugh of St. Victor	Moore
240140	Jews, Pagans, and Christians in the Golan Heights	Gregg/Urman
240141	Rosenzweig on Profane/Secular History	Vogel
240142	Approaches to Ancient Judaism, New Series, Volume Ten	Neusner
240143	Archaeology and the Galilee	Edwards/McCullough
240144	Rationality and Structure	Neusner
240145	Formative Judaism, New Series: Current Issues and Arguments Volume Two	Neusner
240146	Ancient Judaism, Religious and Theological Perspectives First Series	Neusner
240147	The Good Creator	Gelander
240148	The Mind of Classical Judaism, Volume IV, The Philosophy and Political Economy of Formative Judaism: The Mishnah's System of the Social Order	Neusner
240149	The Mind of Classical Judaism, Volume I, Modes of Thought:: Making Connections and Drawing Conclusions	Neusner
240150	The Mind of Classical Judaism, Volume II, From Philosophy to Religion	Neusner
241051	The Mind of Classical Judaism, Volume III, What is "Israel"? Social Thought in the Formative Age	Neusner
240152	The Tosefta, Translated from the Hebrew: Fifth Division, Qodoshim, The Order of Holy Things	Neusner
240153	The Theology of Rabbinic Judaism: A Prolegomenon	Neusner
240154	Approaches to Ancient Judaism, New Series, Volume Eleven	Neusner
240155	Pesiqta Rabbati: A Synoptic Edition of Pesiqta Rabbati Based upon all Extant Manuscripts and the Editio Princeps, V. I	Ulmer
240156	The Place of the Tosefta in the Halakhah of Formative Judaism: What Alberdina Houtman Didn't Notice	Neusner
240157	"Caught in the Act," Walking on the Sea, and The Release of Barabbas Revisited	Aus
240158	Approaches to Ancient Judaism, New Series, Volume Twelve	Neusner
240159	The Halakhah of the Oral Torah, A Religious Commentary, Introduction and Volume I, Part One, Between Israel and God	Neusner
240160	Claudian Policymaking and the Early Imperial Repression of Judaism at Rome	Slingerland
240161	Rashi's Commentary on Psalms 1–89 with English Translation, Introducion and Notes	Gruber
240162	Peace, In Deed	Garber/Libowitz
240163	Mediators of the Divine	Berchman
240164	Approaches to Ancient Judaism, New Series, Volume Thirteen	Neusner
240165	Targum Studies, Volume Two: Targum and Peshitta	Flesher
240166	The Text and I: Writings of Samson H. Levey	Chyet

240167	The Documentary Form-History of Rabbinic Literature, I. The Documentary Forms of Mishnah	Neusner
240168	Louis Finkelstein and the Conservative Movement	Greenbaum
240169	Invitation to the Talmud: A Teaching Book	Neusner
240170	Invitation to Midrash: The Workings of Rabbinic Bible Interpretation, A Teaching Book	Neusner
240171	The Documentary Form-History of Rabbinic Literature, II. The Aggadic Sector:Tractate Abot, Abot deRabbi Natan, Sifra, Sifré to Numbers and Sifré to Deuteronomy	Neusner
240172	The Documentary Form-History of Rabbinic Literature, III. The Aggadic Sector: Mekhilta Attributed to R. Ishmael and Genesis Rabbah	Neusner
240173	The Documentary Form-History of Rabbinic Literature, IV. The Aggadic Sector: Leviticus Rabbah and Pesiqta deRab Kahana	Neusner
240174	The Documentary Form-History of Rabbinic Literature, V. The Aggadic Sector: Song of Songs Rabbah, Ruth Rabbah, Lamentations Rabbati, and Esther Rabbah I	Neusner
240175	The Documentary Form-History of Rabbinic Literature, VI. The Halakhic Sector: The Talmud of the Land of Israel A. Tractates Berakhot and Shabbat through Taanit	Neusner
240176	The Documentary Form-History of Rabbinic Literature, VI. The Halakhic Sector: The Talmud of the Land of Israel B. Tractates Megillah through Qiddushin	Neusner
240177	The Documentary Form-History of Rabbinic Literature, VI. The Halakhic Sector: The Talmud of the Land of Israel C. Tractates Sotah through Horayot and Niddah	Neusner
240178	The Documentary Form-History of Rabbinic Literature, VII. The Halakhic Sector: The Talmud of the Land of Israel A. Tractates Berakhot and Shabbat through Pesahim	Neusner
240179	The Documentary Form-History of Rabbinic Literature, VII. The Halakhic Sector: The Talmud of Babylonia B. Tractates Yoma through Ketubot	Neusner
240180	The Documentary Form-History of Rabbinic Literature, VII. The Halakhic Sector: The Talmud of Babylonia C. Tractates Nedarim through Baba Mesia	Neusner
240181	The Documentary Form-History of Rabbinic Literature, VII. The Halakhic Sector: The Talmud of Babylonia D. Tractates Baba Batra through Horayot	Neusner
240182	The Documentary Form-History of Rabbinic Literature, VII. The Halakhic Sector: The Talmud of Babylonia E. Tractates Zebahim through Bekhorot	Neusner
240183	The Documentary Form-History of Rabbinic Literature, VII. The Halakhic Sector: The Talmud of Babylonia F. Tractates Arakhin through Niddah and Conclusions	Neusner
240184	Messages to Moscow: And Other Current Lectures on Learning and Community in Judaism	Neusner
240185	The Economics of the Mishnah	Neusner
240186	Approaches to Ancient Judaism, New Series, Volume Fourteen	Neusner
240187	Jewish Law from Moses to the Mishnah	Neusner

240188	The Language and the Law of God	Calabi
240189	Pseudo-Rabad: Commentary to Sifre Numbers	Basser
240190	How Adin Steinstalz Misrepresents the Talmud	Neusner
240191	How the Rabbis Liberated Women	Neusner
240192	From Scripture to 70	Neusner
240193	The Levites: Their Emergence as a Second-Class Priesthood	Nurmela
240194	Sifra	Ginsberg
240195	Approaches to Ancient Judaism, New Series, Volume Fifteen	Neusner
240196	What, Exactly, Did the Rabbinic Sages Mean by the "Oral Torah"?	Neusner
240197	The Book of Job with Commentary	Sacks
240198	Symbol and Theology in Early Judaism	Neusner
240199	The Ecological Message of the Torah: Knowledge, Concepts, and Laws which Made Survival in a Land of "Milk and Honey" Possible	Hütteman
240200	Pesiqta Rabbati: A Synoptic Edition of Pesiqta Rabbati Based upon All Extant Manuscripts and the Editio Princeps, Volume II	Ulmer
240201	Concepts of Class in Ancient Israel	Sneed
240202	The Rabbinic Traditions about the Pharisees before 70, Part I, The Masters	Neusner
240203	The Rabbinic Traditions about the Pharisees before 70, Part II, The Houses	Neusner
240204	The Rabbinic Traditions about the Pharisees before 70, Part III, Conclusions	Neusner
240205	Aphrahat and Judaism: The Christian-Jewish Argument in Fourth-Century Iran	Neusner
240206	Chronology and Papponymy: A List of the Judean High Priests of the Persian Period	Scolnic
240209	Approaches to Ancient Judaism, New Series, Volume Sixteen	Neusner
240210	Exploring Judaism: The Collected Essays of David Kraemer	Kraemer
240211	Rabbinic Judaism: Structure and System	Neusner
240214	The Tosefta: Translated from the Hebrew, Second Division, Moed, The Order of Appointed Times	Neusner
240215	The Tosefta: Translated from the Hebrew, Third Division, Nashim, The Order of Women	Neusner
240216	The Tosefta: Translated from the Hebrew, Fourth Division, Neziqin, The Order of Damages	Neusner
240217	A History of the Jews in Babylonia: I. The Parthian Period	Neusner
240218	A History of the Jews in Babylonia: II. The Early Sasanian Period	Neusner
240219	A History of the Jews in Babylonia: III. From Shapur I to Shapur II	Neusner
240220	A History of the Jews in Babylonia: IV. The Age of Shapur II	Neusner
240221	A History of the Jews in Babylonia: V. Later Sasanian Times	Neusner

South Florida Academic Commentary Series

243001	The Talmud of Babylonia, An Academic Commentary, Volume XI, Bavli Tractate Moed Qatan	Neusner
243002	The Talmud of Babylonia, An Academic Commentary, Volume XXXIV, Bavli Tractate Keritot	Neusner
243003	The Talmud of Babylonia, An Academic Commentary, Volume XVII, Bavli Tractate Sotah	Neusner
243004	The Talmud of Babylonia, An Academic Commentary, Volume XXIV, Bavli Tractate Makkot	Neusner
243005	The Talmud of Babylonia, An Academic Commentary, Volume XXXII, Bavli Tractate Arakhin	Neusner
243006	The Talmud of Babylonia, An Academic Commentary, Volume VI, Bavli Tractate Sukkah	Neusner
243007	The Talmud of Babylonia, An Academic Commentary, Volume XII, Bavli Tractate Hagigah	Neusner
243008	The Talmud of Babylonia, An Academic Commentary, Volume XXVI, Bavli Tractate Horayot	Neusner
243009	The Talmud of Babylonia, An Academic Commentary, Volume XXVII, Bavli Tractate Shebuot	Neusner
243010	The Talmud of Babylonia, An Academic Commentary, Volume XXXIII, Bavli Tractate Temurah	Neusner
243011	The Talmud of Babylonia, An Academic Commentary, Volume XXXV, Bavli Tractates Meilah and Tamid	Neusner
243012	The Talmud of Babylonia, An Academic Commentary, Volume VIII, Bavli Tractate Rosh Hashanah	Neusner
243013	The Talmud of Babylonia, An Academic Commentary, Volume V, Bavli Tractate Yoma	Neusner
243014	The Talmud of Babylonia, An Academic Commentary, Volume XXXVI, Bavli Tractate Niddah	Neusner
243015	The Talmud of Babylonia, An Academic Commentary, Volume XX, Bavli Tractate Baba Qamma	Neusner
243016	The Talmud of Babylonia, An Academic Commentary, Volume XXXI, Bavli Tractate Bekhorot	Neusner
243017	The Talmud of Babylonia, An Academic Commentary, Volume XXX, Bavli Tractate Hullin	Neusner
243018	The Talmud of Babylonia, An Academic Commentary, Volume VII, Bavli Tractate Besah	Neusner
243019	The Talmud of Babylonia, An Academic Commentary, Volume X, Bavli Tractate Megillah	Neusner
243020	The Talmud of Babylonia, An Academic Commentary, Volume XXVIII, Bavli Tractate Zebahim A. Chapters I through VII	Neusner
243021	The Talmud of Babylonia, An Academic Commentary, Volume XXI, Bavli Tractate Baba Mesia, A. Chapters I through VI	Neusner
243022	The Talmud of Babylonia, An Academic Commentary, Volume XXII, Bavli Tractate Baba Batra, A. Chapters I through VI	Neusner

243023	The Talmud of Babylonia, An Academic Commentary, Volume XXIX, Bavli Tractate Menahot, A. Chapters I through VI	Neusner
243024	The Talmud of Babylonia, An Academic Commentary, Volume I, Bavli Tractate Berakhot	Neusner
243025	The Talmud of Babylonia, An Academic Commentary, Volume XXV, Bavli Tractate Abodah Zarah	Neusner
243026	The Talmud of Babylonia, An Academic Commentary, Volume XXIII, Bavli Tractate Sanhedrin, A. Chapters I through VII	Neusner
243027	The Talmud of Babylonia, A Complete Outline, Part IV, The Division of Holy Things; A: From Tractate Zabahim through Tractate Hullin	Neusner
243028	The Talmud of Babylonia, An Academic Commentary, Volume XIV, Bavli Tractate Ketubot, A. Chapters I through VI	Neusner
243029	The Talmud of Babylonia, An Academic Commentary, Volume IV, Bavli Tractate Pesahim, A. Chapters I through VII	Neusner
243030	The Talmud of Babylonia, An Academic Commentary, Volume III, Bavli Tractate Erubin, A. ChaptersI through V	Neusner
243031	The Talmud of Babylonia, A Complete Outline, Part III, The Division of Damages; A: From Tractate Baba Qamma through Tractate Baba Batra	Neusner
243032	The Talmud of Babylonia, An Academic Commentary, Volume II, Bavli Tractate Shabbat, Volume A, Chapters One through Twelve	Neusner
243033	The Talmud of Babylonia, An Academic Commentary, Volume II, Bavli Tractate Shabbat, Volume B, Chapters Thirteen through Twenty-four	Neusner
243034	The Talmud of Babylonia, An Academic Commentary, Volume XV, Bavli Tractate Nedarim	Neusner
243035	The Talmud of Babylonia, An Academic Commentary, Volume XVIII, Bavli Tractate Gittin	Neusner
243036	The Talmud of Babylonia, An Academic Commentary, Volume XIX, Bavli Tractate Qiddushin	Neusner
243037	The Talmud of Babylonia, A Complete Outline, Part IV, The Division of Holy Things; B: From Tractate Berakot through Tractate Niddah	Neusner
243038	The Talmud of Babylonia, A Complete Outline, Part III, The Division of Damages; B: From Tractate Sanhedrin through Tractate Shebuot	Neusner
243039	The Talmud of Babylonia, A Complete Outline, Part I, Tractate Berakhot and the Division of Appointed Times A: From Tractate Berakhot through Tractate Pesahim	Neusner
243040	The Talmud of Babylonia, A Complete Outline, Part I, Tractate Berakhot and the Division of Appointed Times B: From Tractate Yoma through Tractate Hagigah	Neusner

243041	The Talmud of Babylonia, A Complete Outline, Part II, The Division of Women; A: From Tractate Yebamot through Tractate Ketubot	Neusner
243042	The Talmud of Babylonia, A Complete Outline, Part II, The Division of Women; B: From Tractate Nedarim through Tractate Qiddushin	Neusner
243043	The Talmud of Babylonia, An Academic Commentary, Volume XIII, Bavli Tractate Yebamot, A. Chapters One through Eight	Neusner
243044	The Talmud of Babylonia, An Academic Commentary, XIII, Bavli Tractate Yebamot, B. Chapters Nine through Seventeen	Neusner
243045	The Talmud of the Land of Israel, A Complete Outline of the Second, Third and Fourth Divisions, Part II, The Division of Women, A. Yebamot to Nedarim	Neusner
243046	The Talmud of the Land of Israel, A Complete Outline of the Second, Third and Fourth Divisions, Part II, The Division of Women, B. Nazir to Sotah	Neusner
243047	The Talmud of the Land of Israel, A Complete Outline of the Second, Third and Fourth Divisions, Part I, The Division of Appointed Times, C. Pesahim and Sukkah	Neusner
243048	The Talmud of the Land of Israel, A Complete Outline of the Second, Third and Fourth Divisions, Part I, The Division of Appointed Times, A. Berakhot, Shabbat	Neusner
243049	The Talmud of the Land of Israel, A Complete Outline of the Second, Third and Fourth Divisions, Part I, The Division of Appointed Times, B. Erubin, Yoma and Besah	Neusner
243050	The Talmud of the Land of Israel, A Complete Outline of the Second, Third and Fourth Divisions, Part I, The Division of Appointed Times, D. Taanit, Megillah, Rosh Hashannah, Hagigah and Moed Qatan	Neusner
243051	The Talmud of the Land of Israel, A Complete Outline of the Second, Third and Fourth Divisions, Part III, The Division of Damages, A. Baba Qamma, Baba Mesia, Baba Batra, Horayot and Niddah	Neusner
243052	The Talmud of the Land of Israel, A Complete Outline of the Second, Third and Fourth Divisions, Part III, The Division of Damages, B. Sanhedrin, Makkot, Shebuot and Abldah Zarah	Neusner
243053	The Two Talmuds Compared, II. The Division of Women in the Talmud of the Land of Israel and the Talmud of Babylonia, Volume A, Tractates Yebamot and Ketubot	Neusner
243054	The Two Talmuds Compared, II. The Division of Women in the Talmud of the Land of Israel and the Talmud of Babylonia, Volume B, Tractates Nedarim, Nazir and Sotah	Neusner
243055	The Two Talmuds Compared, II. The Division of Women in the Talmud of the Land of Israel and the Talmud of Babylonia, Volume C, Tractates Qiddushin and Gittin	Neusner
243056	The Two Talmuds Compared, III. The Division of Damages in the Talmud of the Land of Israel and the Talmud of Babylonia, Volume A, Tractates Baba Qamma and Baba Mesia	Neusner

243057	The Two Talmuds Compared, III. The Division of Damages in the Talmud of the Land of Israel and the Talmud of Babylonia, Volume B, Tractates Baba Batra and Niddah	Neusner
243058	The Two Talmuds Compared, III. The Division of Damages in the Talmud of the Land of Israel and the Talmud of Babylonia, Volume C, Tractates Sanhedrin and Makkot	Neusner
243059	The Two Talmuds Compared, I. Tractate Berakhot and the Division of Appointed Times in the Talmud of the Land of Israel and the Talmud of Babylonia, Volume B, Tractate Shabbat	Neusner
243060	The Two Talmuds Compared, I. Tractate Berakhot and the Division of Appointed Times in the Talmud of the Land of Israel and the Talmud of Babylonia, Volume A, Tractate Berakhot	Neusner
243061	The Two Talmuds Compared, III. The Division of Damages in the Talmud of the Land of Israel and the Talmud of Babylonia, Volume D, Tractates Shebuot, Abodah Zarah and Horayot	Neusner
243062	The Two Talmuds Compared, I. Tractate Berakhot and the Division of Appointed Times in the Talmud of the Land of Israel and the Talmud of Babylonia, Volume C, Tractate Erubin	Neusner
243063	The Two Talmuds Compared, I. Tractate Berakhot and the Division of Appointed Times in the Talmud of the Land of Israel and the Talmud of Babylonia, Volume D, Tractates Yoma and Sukkah	Neusner
243064	The Two Talmuds Compared, I. Tractate Berakhot and the Division of Appointed Times in the Talmud of the Land of Israel and the Talmud of Babylonia, Volume E, Tractate Pesahim	Neusner
243065	The Two Talmuds Compared, I. Tractate Berakhot and the Division of Appointed Times in the Talmud of the Land of Israel and the Talmud of Babylonia, Volume F, Tractates Besah, Taanit and Megillah	Neusner
243066	The Two Talmuds Compared, I. Tractate Berakhot and the Division of Appointed Times in the Talmud of the Land of Israel and the Talmud of Babylonia, Volume G, Tractates Rosh Hashanah and Moed Qatan	Neusner
243067	The Talmud of Babylonia, An Academic Commentary, Volume XXII, Bavli Tractate Baba Batra, B. Chapters VII through XI	Neusner
243068	The Talmud of Babylonia, An Academic Commentary, Volume XXIII, Bavli Tractate Sanhedrin, B. Chapters VIII through XII	Neusner
243069	The Talmud of Babylonia, An Academic Commentary, Volume XIV, Bavli Tractate Ketubot, B. ChaptersVII through XIV	Neusner
243070	The Talmud of Babylonia, An Academic Commentary, Volume IV, Bavli Tractate Pesahim, B. Chapters VIII through XI	Neusner
243071	The Talmud of Babylonia, An Academic Commentary, Volume XXIX, Bavli Tractate Menahot, B. Chapters VII through XIV	Neusner
243072	The Talmud of Babylonia, An Academic Commentary, Volume XXVIII, Bavli Tractate Zebahim B. Chapters VIII through XV	Neusner

243073	The Talmud of Babylonia, An Academic Commentary, Volume XXI, Bavli Tractate Baba Mesia, B. Chapters VIII through XI	Neusner
243074	The Talmud of Babylonia, An Academic Commentary, Volume III, Bavli Tractate Erubin, A. ChaptersVI through XI	Neusner
243075	The Components of the Rabbinic Documents: From the Whole to the Parts, I. Sifra, Part One	Neusner
243076	The Components of the Rabbinic Documents: From the Whole to the Parts, I. Sifra, Part Two	Neusner
243077	The Components of the Rabbinic Documents: From the Whole to the Parts, I. Sifra, Part Three	Neusner
243078	The Components of the Rabbinic Documents: From the Whole to the Parts, I. Sifra, Part Four	Neusner
243079	The Components of the Rabbinic Documents: From the Whole to the Parts, II. Esther Rabbah I	Neusner
243080	The Components of the Rabbinic Documents: From the Whole to the Parts, III. Ruth Rabbah	Neusner
243081	The Components of the Rabbinic Documents: From the Whole to the Parts, IV. Lamemtations Rabbah	Neusner
243082	The Components of the Rabbinic Documents: From the Whole to the Parts, V. Song of Songs Rabbah, Part One	Neusner
243083	The Components of the Rabbinic Documents: From the Whole to the Parts, V. Song of Songs Rabbah, Part Two	Neusner
243084	The Components of the Rabbinic Documents: From the Whole to the Parts, VI. The Fathers According to Rabbi Nathan	Neusner
243085	The Components of the Rabbinic Documents: From the Whole to the Parts, VII. Sifré to Deuteronomy, Part One	Neusner
243086	The Components of the Rabbinic Documents: From the Whole to the Parts, VII. Sifré to Deuteronomy, Part Two	Neusner
243087	The Components of the Rabbinic Documents: From the Whole to the Parts, VII. Sifré to Deuteronomy, Part Three	Neusner
243088	The Components of the Rabbinic Documents: From the Whole to the Parts, VIII. Mekhilta Attributed to Rabbi Ishmael, Part One	Neusner
243089	The Components of the Rabbinic Documents: From the Whole to the Parts, VIII. Mekhilta Attributed to Rabbi Ishmael, Part Two	Neusner
243090	The Components of the Rabbinic Documents: From the Whole to the Parts, VIII. Mekhilta Attributed to Rabbi Ishmael, Part Three	Neusner
243092	The Components of the Rabbinic Documents: From the Whole to the Parts, IX. Genesis Rabbah, Part One, Introduction and Chapters One through Twenty-two	Neusner
243093	The Components of the Rabbinic Documents: From the Whole to the Parts, IX. Genesis Rabbah, Part Two, Chapters Twenty-three through Fifty	Neusner
243094	The Components of the Rabbinic Documents: From the Whole to the Parts, IX. Genesis Rabbah, Part Three, Chapters Fifty-one through Seventy-five	Neusner
243095	The Components of the Rabbinic Documents: From the Whole to the Parts, X. Leviticus Rabbah, Part One , Introduction and Parashiyyot One through Seventeen	Neusner

243096	The Components of the Rabbinic Documents: From the Whole to the Parts, X. Leviticus Rabbah, Part Two, Parashiyyot Eighteen through Thirty-seven	Neusner
243097	The Components of the Rabbinic Documents: From the Whole to the Parts, X. Leviticus Rabbah, Part Three, Topical and Methodical Outline	Neusner
243098	The Components of the Rabbinic Documents: From the Whole to the Parts, XI. Pesiqta deRab Kahana, Part One, Introduction and Pisqaot One through Eleven	Neusner
243099	The Components of the Rabbinic Documents: From the Whole to the Parts, XI. Pesiqta deRab Kahana, Part Two, Pisqaot Twelve through Twenty-eight	Neusner
243100	The Components of the Rabbinic Documents: From the Whole to the Parts, XI. Pesiqta deRab Kahana, Part Three, A Topical and Methodical Outline	Neusner
243101	The Components of the Rabbinic Documents: From the Whole to the Parts, IX. Genesis Rabbah, Part Four, Chapters Seventy-six through One Hundred	Neusner
243102	The Components of the Rabbinic Documents: From the Whole to the Parts, IX. Genesis Rabbah, Part Five, A Methodical and Topical Outline; Bereshit through Vaere, Chapters One through Fifty-seven	Neusner
243103	The Components of the Rabbinic Documents: From the Whole to the Parts, IX. Genesis Rabbah, Part Six, A Methodical and Topical Outline; Hayye Sarah through Miqqes, Chapters Fifty-eight through One Hundred	Neusner
243104	The Components of the Rabbinic Documents: From the Whole to the Parts, XII., Sifré to Numbers, Part One, Introduction and Pisqaot One through Seventy-one	Neusner
243105	The Components of the Rabbinic Documents: From the Whole to the Parts, XII., Sifré to Numbers, Part Two, Pisqaot Seventy-two through One Hundred Twenty-two	Neusner
243106	The Components of the Rabbinic Documents: From the Whole to the Parts, XII., Sifré to Numbers, Part Three, Pisqaot One Hundred Twenty-three through One Hundred Sixty-one	Neusner
243107	The Components of the Rabbinic Documents: From the Whole to the Parts, XII., Sifré to Numbers, Part Four, A Topical and Methodical Outline	Neusner
243108	The Talmud of the Land of Israel: An Academic Commentary of the Second, Third, and Fourth Divisions, I. Yerushalmi Tractate Berakhot (Based on the Translation by Tzvee Zahavy)	Neusner
243109	The Talmud of the Land of Israel: An Academic Commentary of the Second, Third, and Fourth Divisions, II. Yerushalmi Tractate Shabbat. A. Chapters One through Ten	Neusner
243110	The Talmud of the Land of Israel: An Academic Commentary of the Second, Third, and Fourth Divisions, II. Yerushalmi Tractate Shabbat. B. Chapters Eleven through Twenty-Four and The Structure of Yerushalmi Shabbat	Neusner
243111	The Talmud of the Land of Israel: An Academic Commentary of the Second, Third, and Fourth Divisions, ÎII. Yerushalmi Tractate Erubin	Neusner

243112	The Talmud of the Land of Israel: An Academic Commentary of the Second, Third, and Fourth Divisions, IV. Yerushalmi Tractate Yoma	Neusner
243113	The Talmud of the Land of Israel: An Academic Commentary of the Second, Third, and Fourth Divisions, V. Yerushalmi Tractate Pesahim A. Chapters One through Six, Based on the English Translation of Baruch M. Bokser with Lawrence Schiffman	Neusner
243114	The Talmud of the Land of Israel: An Academic Commentary of the Second, Third, and Fourth Divisions, V. Yerushalmi Tractate Pesahim B. Chapters Seven through Ten and The Structure of Yerushalmi Pesahim, Based on the English Translation of Baruch M. Bokser with Lawrence Schiffman	Neusner
243115	The Talmud of the Land of Israel: An Academic Commentary of the Second, Third, and Fourth Divisions, VI. Yerushalmi Tractate Sukkah	Neusner
243116	The Talmud of the Land of Israel: An Academic Commentary of the Second, Third, and Fourth Divisions, VII. Yerushalmi Tractate Besah	Neusner
243117	The Talmud of the Land of Israel: An Academic Commentary of the Second, Third, and Fourth Divisions, VIII. Yerushalmi Tractate Taanit	Neusner
243118	The Talmud of the Land of Israel: An Academic Commentary of the Second, Third, and Fourth Divisions, IX. Yerushalmi Tractate Megillah	Neusner
243119	The Talmud of the Land of Israel: An Academic Commentary of the Second, Third, and Fourth Divisions, X. Yerushalmi Tractate Rosh Hashanah	Neusner
243120	The Talmud of the Land of Israel: An Academic Commentary of the Second, Third, and Fourth Divisions, XI. Yerushalmi Tractate Hagigah	Neusner
243121	The Talmud of the Land of Israel: An Academic Commentary of the Second, Third, and Fourth Divisions, XII. Yerushalmi Tractate Moed Qatan	Neusner
243122	The Talmud of the Land of Israel: An Academic Commentary of the Second, Third, and Fourth Divisions, XIII. Yerushalmi Tractate Yebamot, A. Chapters One through Ten	Neusner
243123	The Talmud of the Land of Israel: An Academic Commentary of the Second, Third, and Fourth Divisions, XIII. Yerushalmi Tractate Yebamot, B. Chapters Eleven through Seventeen	Neusner
243124	The Talmud of the Land of Israel: An Academic Commentary of the Second, Third, and Fourth Divisions, XIV. Yerushalmi Tractate Ketubot	Neusner
243125	The Talmud of the Land of Israel: An Academic Commentary of the Second, Third, and Fourth Divisions, XV. Yerushalmi Tractate Nedarim	Neusner
243126	The Talmud of the Land of Israel: An Academic Commentary of the Second, Third, and Fourth Divisions, XVI. Yerushalmi Tractate Nazir	Neusner
243127	The Talmud of the Land of Israel: An Academic Commentary of the Second, Third, and Fourth Divisions, XVII. Yerushalmi Tractate Gittin	Neusner

243128	The Talmud of the Land of Israel: An Academic Commentary of the Second, Third, and Fourth Divisions, XVIII. Yerushalmi Tractate Qiddushin	Neusner
243129	The Talmud of the Land of Israel: An Academic Commentary of the Second, Third, and Fourth Divisions, XIX. Yerushalmi Tractate Sotah	Neusner
243130	The Talmud of the Land of Israel: An Academic Commentary of the Second, Third, and Fourth Divisions, XX. Yerushalmi Tractate Baba Qamma	Neusner
243131	The Talmud of the Land of Israel: An Academic Commentary of the Second, Third, and Fourth Divisions, XXI. Yerushalmi Tractate Baba Mesia	Neusner
243132	The Talmud of the Land of Israel: An Academic Commentary of the Second, Third, and Fourth Divisions, XXII. Yerushalmi Tractate Baba Batra	Neusner
243133	The Talmud of the Land of Israel: An Academic Commentary of the Second, Third, and Fourth Divisions, XXIII. Yerushalmi Tractate Sanhedrin	Neusner
243134	The Talmud of the Land of Israel: An Academic Commentary of the Second, Third, and Fourth Divisions, XXIV. Yerushalmi Tractate Makkot	Neusner
243135	The Talmud of the Land of Israel: An Academic Commentary of the Second, Third, and Fourth Divisions, XXV. Yerushalmi Tractate Shebuot	Neusner
243136	The Talmud of the Land of Israel: An Academic Commentary of the Second, Third, and Fourth Divisions, XXVI. Yerushalmi Tractate Abodah Zarah	Neusner
243137	The Talmud of the Land of Israel: An Academic Commentary of the Second, Third, and Fourth Divisions, XXVII. Yerushalmi Tractate Horayot	Neusner
243138	The Talmud of the Land of Israel: An Academic Commentary of the Second, Third, and Fourth Divisions, XXVIII. Yerushalmi Tractate Niddah	Neusner
243139	The Talmud of Babylonia, An Academic Commentary, IX, Bavli Tractate Taanit	Neusner
243140	The Talmud of Babylonia, An Academic Commentary, XIV, Bavli Tractate Nazir	Neusner

South Florida International Studies in Formative Christianity and Judaism

242501	The Earliest Christian Mission to 'All Nations'	La Grand
242502	Judaic Approaches to the Gospels	Chilton
242503	The "Essence of Christianity"	Forni Rosa
242504	The Wicked Tenants and Gethsemane	Aus
242505	A Star Is Rising	Laato
242506	Romans 9–11: A Reader-Response Analysis	Lodge
242507	The Good News of Peter's Denial	Borrell
242508	ΛΟΓΟΙ ΙΗΣΟΥ, Studies in Q	Vassiliadis
242509	Romans 8:18–30: "Suffering Does Not Thwart the Future Glory"	Gieniusz

South Florida-Rochester-Saint Louis Studies on Religion and the Social Order

245001	Faith and Context, Volume 1	Ong
245002	Faith and Context, Volume 2	Ong
245003	Judaism and Civil Religion	Breslauer
245004	The Sociology of Andrew M. Greeley	Greeley
245005	Faith and Context, Volume 3	Ong
245006	The Christ of Michelangelo	Dixon
245007	From Hermeneutics to Ethical Consensus Among Cultures	Bori
245008	Mordecai Kaplan's Thought in a Postmodern Age	Breslauer
245009	No Longer Aliens, No Longer Strangers	Eckardt
245010	Between Tradition and Culture	Ellenson
245011	Religion and the Social Order	Neusner
245012	Christianity and the Stranger	Nichols
245013	The Polish Challenge	Czosnyka
245014	Islam and the Question of Minorities	Sonn
245015	Religion and the Political Order	Neusner
245016	The Ecology of Religion	Neusner
245017	The Shaping of an American Islamic Discourse	Waugh/Denny
245018	The Muslim Brotherhood and the Kings of Jordan, 1945–1993	Boulby
245019	Muslims on the Americanization Path	Esposito/Haddad
245020	Protean Prejudice: Anti-semitism in England's Age of Reason	Glassman
245021	The Study of Religion: In Retrospect and Prospect	Green
245024	Jacques Ellul on Religion, Technology and Politics: Conversations with Patrick Troude-Chastenet	France
245025	Religious Belief and Economic Behavior	Neusner
245026	Trying Times: Essays on Catholic Higher Education in the 20th Century	Shea

BM
500.2
.K75
1999